Reconstructing Nature

Reconstructing Nature

*The Engagement
of Science and Religion*

GLASGOW GIFFORD LECTURES

John Brooke and Geoffrey Cantor

OXFORD UNIVERSITY PRESS
New York   Oxford

OXFORD UNIVERSITY PRESS

OXFORD   NEW YORK

ATHENS AUCKLAND BANGKOK BOGOTÁ BUENOS AIRES CALCUTTA
CAPE TOWN CHENNAI DAR ES SALAAM DELHI FLORENCE HONG KONG ISTANBUL
KARACHI KUALA LUMPUR MADRID MELBOURNE MEXICO CITY MUMBAI
NAIROBI PARIS SÃO PAULO SINGAPORE TAIPEI TOKYO TORONTO WARSAW

and associated companies in
BERLIN   IBADAN

Published in Great Britain by T&T Clark Ltd
59 George Street, Edinburgh EH2 2LQ, Scotland

This edition published under license from T&T Clark Ltd by
Oxford University Press
198 Madison Avenue
New York, NY 10016

First issued as an Oxford University Press paperback, 2000

Oxford is a registered trademark of Oxford University Press, Inc.

First published 1998

Library of Congress Cataloging-in-Publication Data
Brooke, John Hedley.
    Reconstructing nature : the engagement of science and religion / John Brooke and
Geoffrey Cantor.
        p. cm. – (Glasgow Gifford Lectures)
    Originally published: Edinburgh: T&T Clark Ltd, 1998.
    Includes bibliographical references and indexes.
    ISBN 0–19–513706–X (pbk.)
        1. Religion and science – History. I. Cantor, G. N., 1943– II. Title. III. Series.
BL245.B765 2000
291.1'75 – dc21

                                                                99–059053

1 3 5 7 9 8 6 4 2
Printed in Great Britain

Contents

List of Illustrations   vii
Preface   ix
Introduction   1

Section I: *Science and Religion*
  1   Is There Value in the Historical Approach?   15
  2   Whose Science? Whose Religion?   43

Section II: *Reconstructing History*
  3   Against the Self-Images of the New Age   75
  4   The Contemporary Relevance of the Galileo
       Affair   106

Section III: *Having Designs on Nature*
  5   Natural Theology and the History of Science   141
  6   The Language of Natural Theology   176
  7   From Aesthetics to Theology   207

Section IV: *Structuring Experience*
  8   Biographical Narratives   247
  9   'A Taste for Philosophical Pursuits' – Quakers
       in the Royal Society of London   282
 10   Improving on Nature?   314

Index of Names   347
Index of Subjects   359

List of Illustrations

Introduction
1	Hooke's flea	2
2	Martin's monsters	3
3	Galileo's moon	3
4	Descartes's vortices	4
5	Newton's elliptical orbits	5

Chapter 1
6	Pigeons	29
7	Huxley and Wilberforce	35

Chapter 2
8	Auguste Comte's Madonna and child	51
9	Comte's calendar	53
10	Detail from Comte's calendar	54

Chapter 3
11	Kepler's celestial magnetism	90
12	Descartes's mechanistic account of magnetism	91

Chapter 4
13	Tychonic system	112
14	Phases of Venus	116
15	Leaning Tower of Pisa	125

Chapter 5
16	Eye of fly	146
17	Magnified needle	146
18	Owen's archetype	160

Chapter 6
19	Buckland's geological section	185
20	Megatherium	189

Chapter 7

Colour plate: Penicillin under electron microscope   208
21   Retrograde motion   211
22   Fish scales   218
23   Layout of the heavens   222
24   Ammonite   225
25   Conical fossil   225

Chapter 8

26   Cartoon of John Tyndall   250
27   St Chad's Cathedral   256
28   Portrait of St George Jackson Mivart   260
29   Portrait of William B. Carpenter   263
30   Portrait of Adam Sedgwick   271

Chapter 9

31   Block graph: Quakers in Royal Society   284
32   Graph: Quakers in Royal Society   285

Chapter 10

33   Alchemist following nature   317
34   Khunrath's oratorium   318
35   Kircher's subterranean chemistry   320

Preface

When Adam, Lord Gifford, penned the will that would soon bring the Gifford Lectures into existence, he carefully considered the scope of his bequests to the four Scottish universities. The lecturers appointed by his Trustees were, he instructed, to address 'Natural Theology, in the widest sense of that term'. This extended sense was to include 'The Knowledge of God, the Infinite, the All, the First and Only Cause ... and the Knowledge of His Nature and Attributes, the Knowledge of the Relations which men and the whole universe bear to Him, the Knowledge of the Nature and Foundation of Ethics or Morals, and of all Obligations and Duties hence arising'.[1]

This impressive range of subjects not only reflects Gifford's breadth of scholarship but also the areas that he considered in need of further investigation and continuing debate. In the decades following the advent of German higher criticism and the publication of Darwin's *Origin of Species* there was no shortage of questions to be confronted about how to conceptualise God, how to understand 'His' relation to the universe, and how to frame a theologically-based ethics. Writing his will in 1885 Gifford conceived Natural Theology as the appropriate umbrella to cover these important and diverse topics. He also instructed that in their investigations prospective lecturers were to deploy reason, not revelation. Indeed, he explicitly stated his intention that they should 'treat their subject as a strictly natural science, the greatest of all possible sciences, indeed, in one sense, the only science, that of Infinite Being, without reference to or reliance upon any supposed special, exceptional or so-called miraculous revelation'. If the reader of Gifford's will is left in any doubt about his conception of *Natural Theology*, his very next sentence is impressively concise: 'I wish it considered just as astronomy or chemistry is.'[2]

As Neil Spurway comments in his introduction to the Glasgow centenary series, professional scientists – even many among Gifford's contemporaries – might smile at this outdated conception of science and at the apparent implication that studies of 'the Infinite, the All, the First and Only Cause' should be conducted as a science, deploying the methods of experimental investigation.[3] Yet, as

Spurway notes, the term *Natural Theology* possesses a long and honourable history. Many earlier writers – particularly in the seventeenth and eighteenth centuries – committed themselves to the project of illuminating theology by the 'light of nature' or, what we might call, the power of reason. Gifford's notion of Natural Theology appears somewhat anachronistic today, but that is itself a reminder that both science and theology (and also the interaction between them) change with time and have changed considerably over the intervening period. The document responsible for the Gifford Lectures was the product of a Scottish lawyer born into a highly religious Edinburgh household in 1820. Moreover, the subjects that Gifford directed lecturers to address have not been static but possess rich histories. Consequently many of the published Gifford Lectures have themselves become key texts in the histories of theology, philosophy, ethics and science.

In 1885 the 'History of Science' did not exist as an academic subject and, not surprisingly, it did not feature in Lord Gifford's will. Yet he was probably aware that Adam Smith, William Whewell, Auguste Comte, among others, had written books about the way science had developed over the centuries. However, only in the twentieth century, in the years between the First and Second World War – and, increasingly, during the post-war period – did the History of Science become an academic subject. One of the many topics that have continually exercised historians of science is the 'interrelation of science and religion' as it has been understood by different individuals and communities in different periods. Gifford himself called for consideration of 'the Knowledge of the Relations which men and [particularly] the whole universe bear to Him'. Such phrases sound rather clumsy today, but they indicate a domain of enquiry that deserves serious historical analysis and that we intend in some measure to address. Although previous Gifford Lecturers, including Ian Barbour, Reijer Hooykaas and Stanley Jaki, have made impressive use of historical examples, the emphasis in the present volume is rather different. We are not seeking to support any particular theological position but rather to show how recent developments in the History of Science can contribute to the analysis and understanding of science–religion relationships and how they have been constructed. For those unfamiliar with the History of Science it should be emphasised that the field, already mediating between what C. P. Snow called the two cultures,[4] has been undergoing exciting developments largely due to further inter-disciplinary cross-fertilisation. Increasingly it has been enriched by insights developed in philosophy, sociology, linguistics, anthropology and in other branches of history. In this series of Gifford Lectures our primary aim has been to show how new ways of understanding past science can be used to suggest fresh approaches to the science–religion domain.

This is not a history in a conventional sense; still less a chronological account of some notional 'science–religion relationship'.[5] We shall not be starting with conceptions of the Creation as expressed in Genesis and ending with the implications for theology of evidence, widely reported in the summer of 1996, for life having once existed on Mars. The scope of this volume is much more limited and its aims more modest. In each of the ensuing chapters a particular form of analysis will be developed and applied to historical material. Each chapter – which is an extended and revised version of the corresponding lecture delivered in Glasgow – thus provides an historical commentary on a specific area of debate within the science–religion domain. Although the chapters can be read separately, there are many recurrent themes, the most important being the rejection of any 'master-narrative'. We use this term to refer to the widely-accepted assumption that there is a definitive historical account of how science and religion have been (and are) interrelated. Rejection of this assumption – which is explicitly challenged in chapters 2 and 3 – also justifies the diversity of approaches we develop throughout this volume. It should also be stressed that we have not applied these forms of analysis directly to the history of 'sacred texts' and their composition within particular religious traditions. We defer to others better acquainted with the respective bodies of scholarship.

The authors feel greatly honoured at having been invited to deliver the 1995–6 series of Gifford Lectures at the University of Glasgow. We would like to express our appreciation to the Principal, Professor Graeme Davies, the Administrator, Mrs E. E. Reynolds, and to members of the Gifford Lectureship Committee who warmly received us and generously entertained us during our time in Glasgow. We are particularly appreciative of the generosity and congeniality of Dr Neil Spurway (the Committee's Convenor) who added greatly to the intellectual vitality of the proceedings. All those who attended the lectures are thanked, particularly for their comments and criticism.

For helpful discussions relating to several of the topics encountered in the ensuing chapters we would like to express our sincere thanks to Janice Brooke, Barbara Cantor, Moti Feingold, Lynette Hunter, Chris Kenny, Edward Milligan, Jacqui Stewart, Jonathan Topham, Tomas Vanheste, and members of the Science/Theology Consultation held at the Center for Theological Inquiry, Princeton

(1993–6). We gratefully acknowledge the Master and Fellows of Trinity College, Cambridge, and the President and Council of the Royal Society of London for granting us permission to quote from manuscript material. Many of the illustrations were kindly supplied by the 'Special Collections' staff, Leeds University Library. For help in preparing illustrations we gratefully acknowledge the photographic units at the Universities of Lancaster and Leeds. Finally, we would like to express our appreciation to the staff of T & T Clark, for their help and support.

NOTES

1 S. L. Jaki, *Lord Gifford and his Lectures. A Centenary Retrospect*, Edinburgh and Macon, GA, 1986, 72–3.
2 *Ibid.*, 74.
3 N. Spurway, 'Introduction: 100 years (and more) of natural theology' in *Humanity, Environment and God. Glasgow Centenary Gifford Lectures* (ed. N. Spurway), Oxford, 1993, 10.
4 C. P. Snow, *The Two Cultures: and a Second Look*, New York, 1963.
5 As will become clear later, to speak of 'the relationship between science and religion' presupposes boundaries between them, which have in fact changed with time. Moreover, for many writers in earlier centuries there was not the separation between two domains that we tend to take for granted. See J. H. Brooke, *Science and Religion: Some Historical Perspectives*, Cambridge, 1991, 52–81; J. R. Moore, 'Speaking of "Science and Religion" – then and now', *History of Science*, 30 (1992), 311–23.

Introduction

A few years before London was scourged by plague and fire, a young Cambridge scholar privately recorded the sins of his youth. This penitent soul had, it seems, made a mousetrap on the sabbath, had swum in a tub on the Lord's Day and lied about a louse. More disturbingly perhaps, he confessed to 'unclean thoughts words actions and dreams'. His less than happy relations with his mother and stepfather were reflected in another wicked thought: that he might 'burn them and the house over them'.[1]

Twenty-five years later something rather more public appeared in Cambridge: a magisterial book on mechanics. According to the astronomer Edmond Halley, its author had penetrated the mansions of the gods and scaled the heights of heaven.[2] Reconstructing nature in mathematical terms, he had solved a great mystery: what kept moons and planets in their orbits? For some it may come as a surprise to learn that the penitent sinner of 1662, who had threatened to destroy his family home, was the same Isaac Newton who professed to rebuild the world with his gravitational forces and his laws of motion. But why juxtapose the confession with the profession? What has searching the soul to do with searching the cosmos?

In the case of Newton the answer is a great deal. His religious commitment profoundly affected the way he thought about nature – how it had been set up and how it worked.[3] Although historians have often spoken of a 'scientific revolution' in the seventeenth century, the term 'natural philosophy' remained in use for the study of motion and other physical problems. What we may think of as a natural science was then regarded as a branch of philosophy, which would often be discussed in relation to broader philosophical issues. In the second edition of his *Principia* Newton wrote that 'to discourse of [God] from the appearances of things does certainly belong to natural philosophy'. It would, however, be a mistake to imagine that his religious sensibilities were prompted only by feelings of guilt. God was to be feared but also to be celebrated – in love, thanks and praise.[4] There could be such a celebration because, in Newton's own words, 'this most beautiful system of the sun, planets, and comets could only proceed from the counsel and dominion of an intelligent and powerful being'.[5]

Newton is one among many creative thinkers who have reconstructed nature and seen beauty in their construction. But what does it mean to speak of reconstructing nature? Surely nature is nature? And yet it is not so simple. When we think of 'nature' we may be thinking of many things. It might be of a beautiful Scottish landscape or, dreaming of an exotic holiday, an unspoilt tropical beach. The word 'nature' might equally conjure up things one would hope not to meet in paradise: a mosquito perhaps or a flea. For an artist, the image might be quite different: of nature captured in a still life painting – 'nature morte', as the French would say. A work of art might show other facets of nature, conveying a sense of the sublime as in a Turner landscape, or a sense of violence as when John Martin depicted the writhing monsters of prehistoric times. Scientists as much as artists have their images of nature. For Galileo, a pictorial representation of the moon's surface was vital as he reported the results of his telescopic observations.[6] In the sciences, nature may be conceived in more abstract terms, as when Descartes depicted the heavens replete with swirling vortices of subtle matter – a far cry from

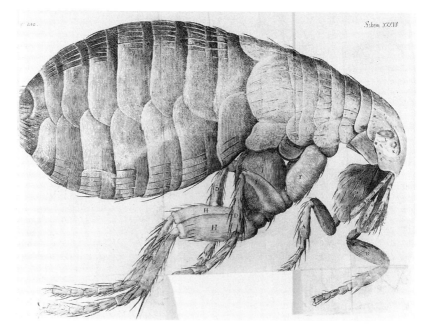

Figure 1: A magnified flea from Robert Hooke's *Micrographia*, first published in 1665.

Figure 2: John Martin's 'country of the iguanodon' from the Frontispiece to Gideon Mantell's *Wonders of Geology* (1839 edition). Reproduced by courtesy of the Science Museum Library, London.

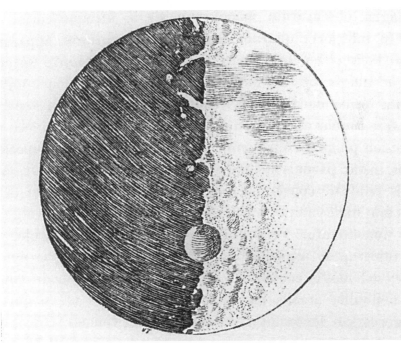

Figure 3: The depiction of a blemished moon in Galileo's *Sidereus Nuncius*, first published in 1610.

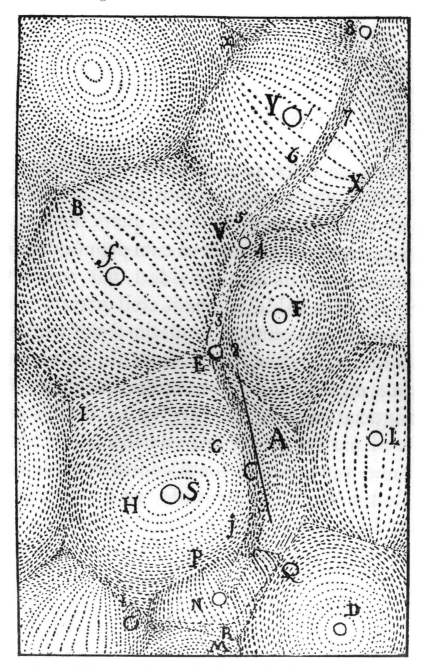

Figure 4: The mechanisation of the heavens from Descartes's *Principia Philosophiae,* first published in 1644.

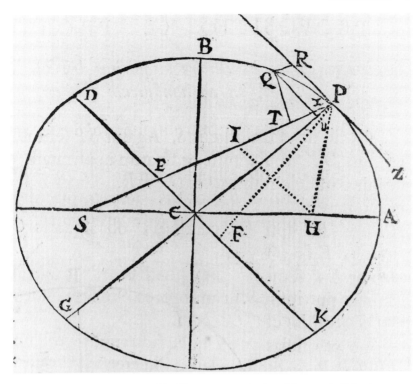

Figure 5: The diagram used by Newton to articulate his proof of the inverse square law governing planetary orbits. From the Geneva, 1739–42 edition of Newton's *Philosophiae Naturalis Principia Mathematica* (ed. T. Le Seur and F. Jacquier) in which errors that occurred in earlier editions were corrected.

the blue sky of the travel brochures. Descartes actually thought of nature as a huge piece of clockwork with the great clock of Strasbourg serving as a model. An even more abstract conception can be illustrated from Newton's *Principia*, where 'nature' was to be grasped in geometrical terms and where Newton gave his proof of an inverse square law of gravity governing the elliptical orbits of planets. An example from the twentieth century would be the double helix model for DNA, which encapsulated one of the most remarkable features of organic 'nature' – the coding of the reproductive process.

Each of these pictures could claim to represent nature. But the point is not just that 'nature' can be endowed with many different meanings. In every picture there is the hidden human hand. How carefully the photographer positions the camera to capture perfect reflections in the Scottish loch. We might even say that in every case nature is being idealised. This is perfectly explicit in the case of the tropical beach. In the purple prose of one tour operator's brochure, we see 'an oriental Eden where creature comforts leave nature undisturbed'.[7] The magnified flea in Robert Hooke's *Micrographia* reminds us that in this case two processes at least intervene to determine what we actually see: the magnification produced by a scientific instrument and the human hand in the drawing.[8] In works of art an emotional response can be evoked by exaggerating mountain grandeur, arcadian vistas or clashing tormented beasts. We are dealing in short with constructions of nature. John Martin even entitled his picture: 'The Country of the Iguanodon Restored'. The restoration was his and it was to illustrate a geological text.[9]

In the world of science, as in art, nature is apprehended through idealisation. It is not encountered, as it were, in the raw. Indeed, one meaning of the word 'nature' is that which is untouched by human hand. Where scientific enquiry involves interference with phenomena there can even be a sense in which the scientist denatures nature. An element of idealisation is visible in Galileo's picture of a magnified moon, which was no perfect replica of what he had seen: it was designed to spotlight the craters and mountains that would persuade his readers of its surface imperfections. Thus he allowed his engraver to exaggerate the crater lying on the lower portion of the picture.[10] In Descartes's model of the heavens there were vortices of subtle matter that no-one could see, not even Descartes. When nature was modelled on the great clock of Strasbourg, it was a construction based on a construction. More recently the path that led Francis Crick and James Watson to their double helix for DNA was a path strewn with models they had constructed, dismantled and reconstructed.[11] This may help to explain why we have chosen 'Reconstructing Nature' for our title. It is what scientists do and always have done. It is what Newton was doing with his mathematical models to explain the planetary orbits.

The mathematical analysis of nature had, for Newton, transcendental implications. The skill with which God had calculated the tangential component of each planet's velocity, to ensure that it went into a closed orbit, implied a deity no less brilliant than Newton himself, one 'very well skilled in mechanics and geometry'.[12] It is striking that in one of the great lights of the 'scientific revolution' there was such an *engagement* of science and religion. In Newton's case we seem to have an 'engagement' almost in the sense in which one might speak of two people engaged to be married. There is the promise of intimacy, commitment to the good of each, of mutual support and the prospect of union. Indeed one historian has claimed that in seventeenth-century natural philosophy, and in

Newton *par excellence*, we see not the separation of science from religion but an unprecedented fusion.[13]

We chose for the sub-title of our lecture series 'the engagement of science and religion' because the richness and ambiguity of the word *engagement* helps to capture the many different ways in which the relationship between the two has been presented. If we turn from a great British scientist of the seventeenth century to one of the most familiar of the nineteenth, another sense of engagement may seem more apposite. Charles Darwin once wrote that he could not see how anyone could wish Christianity to be true. Its doctrine of eternal damnation for those outside the fold was itself a damnable doctrine.[14] When champions of his theory of evolution found themselves berated by bishops, the engagement was surely an engagement in battle? We must all have heard of that celebrated occasion in 1860 when the British Assocation for the Advancement of Science met in Oxford. The local bishop, Samuel Wilberforce, tried to score a point against the Darwinian T. H. Huxley by asking whether he preferred to think of himself as descended from an ape on his grandmother's or grandfather's side. Huxley, so the legend goes, emerged triumphant with a devastating riposte, effectively implying that he would rather have an ape for an ancestor than a bishop – certainly than a person who used his high position to pronounce on matters of which he was ignorant.[15] It is not so long since that occasion in Edinburgh when Richard Dawkins and the then Archbishop of York, John Habgood, had their action replay. It led to a memorable headline in the press: 'Apes have souls too, says primate'.[16] When Dawkins compares religious belief to a self-perpetuating computer virus, the engagement of science and religion becomes – well, engaging!

Which leads to a third sense of engagement. We may speak of an engaging personality or of an idea that engages our attention. The sense here is of a fascination with an idea or person. The mutual bearings of science and theology have often been of this kind. Innovations in one domain make an impression in the other. A modern example might be the manner in which new models of scientific rationality have been adopted to explore the rationality or otherwise of discourse about God.[17] But the links can be stronger than this. When referring to a mechanical system it is not unusual to speak of one part engaging another. The connection, here, will be so tight that movement in the one part induces movement in the other. Such an interlocking of science and theology has occurred in the past. The interleaving of Aristotelian philosophy and Christian theology in the early modern period is an obvious example. The interlocking was sometimes so strong that threats to the authority of Aristotle would be read as threats to the Catholic Church.[18]

It is not our intention to resuscitate every meaning of *engagement* listed in dictionaries. But it would be a pity to overlook one archaic usage. Here, to engage meant to 'win over, as an adherent or helper'. This may remind us that scientific knowledge has often been a resource for religious apologists, as it was for Newton's correspondent Richard Bentley. Conversely to gain the approval of religious authorities was once a necessity for scientific thinkers, even if it has become less so today. One of our aims is to show that engagement in each of these senses has featured in debates about 'science and religion'. We should certainly not think only of marriage, of divorce or of war. Examples of contact are legion and they are remarkably diverse.

In chapter 1 we shall explore something of this diversity, drawing attention to the inadequacy of popular accounts that have routinely constrained discussion by imposing master-narratives on historical data. We shall argue that there are many stories to be told and that they cannot correctly be reduced to over-arching schemata, such as those based on conflict or harmony. Arguments for the value of an historical approach will be presented, with particular reference to the insights made possible by different styles and methods of historical scholarship. One consequence of such an analysis is that it becomes extremely difficult, if not impossible, for the historian to sympathise with projects designed to uncover the essence of 'science', the essence of 'religion' and therefore of some timeless, inherent 'relationship' between them.[19] In chapter 2 this point is developed by showing just how problematic the terms 'science' and 'religion' really are. The 'scriptural geologists' of the early nineteenth century will be introduced to show the difficulties that may arise in circumscribing 'science'; Auguste Comte's highly influential positivist philosophy, with its attendant Religion of Humanity, will serve a similar purpose for the discussion of 'religion'.

A critique of the master-narratives is developed further in chapters 3 and 4. In recent years a version of the history of science favoured by prophets of 'New Age' persuasion has achieved a certain popularity. Our purpose in chapter 3 is to see how well it stands up to serious examination. The older, but still enduring, narratives of an essential 'conflict between religion and science' would always feast off those well-known episodes in which the freedom of scientific enquiry was stifled by ecclesiastical authorities.[20] In chapter 4 we therefore examine perhaps the most famous case of all: the trial and condemnation of Galileo by the Roman Catholic Church. We shall try to show that the best historical scholarship presents a very different picture from that of popular mythology. The value of an historical approach is also underlined by showing how each generation has reinterpreted the affair in the light of its own interests and perceptions.

At the heart of the book are chapters 5–7, which discuss the erstwhile theme of the Gifford Lectures – natural theology – from different but largely complementary points of view. In chapter 5 we provide some general perspectives on the engagement of natural theology and the natural sciences. In accord with recent practice in the history of science, chapter 6 is devoted to the rhetorical strategies deployed by scientists and theologians. Here we show how, in Britain, the design argument was elaborated in order to convince the waverer and thus provide a bulwark against the enemies of Christianity. These two chapters are intended to enrich an understanding of natural theology by exposing the contexts in which, and the purposes for which, it was used. This is in contrast to standard philosophical approaches which tend to focus on the logical structure of the classic arguments for God's existence. In chapter 7, however, we adopt a more philosophical approach in order to comment on a feature of natural theology that might be said still to survive. This is the appeal to elegance and beauty in descriptions both of nature and of scientific theory. Historically, statements concerning the hidden beauties disclosed by scientific effort have often graduated in theistic discourse. In some constituencies they still do. In providing a commentary on this phenomenon, we also suggest that, in the history of natural theology, there is support for what has been called the 'religious ambiguity' of the universe.[21]

In chapters 8 and 9 two very different historical techniques are brought to bear on the engagement of science and religion, those of the biographer and the social historian. An advantage of the biographical approach is that it can expose the issues as they were perceived and worked out in the life of an individual. Instead of concentrating on abstract relations between ideas, there is value in seeing how lives were affected by religious experience and the experience of sometimes threatening scientific innovation. By contrast with a focus on the individual, historians have sometimes asked whether particular religious communities might have had distinctive attitudes towards the value of the sciences. In a celebrated and much criticised thesis, Robert Merton argued that the Puritan movement in seventeeth-century England made a distinctive contribution to the expansion of the practical sciences.[22] Because we believe there is value in studying social groups with distinctive practices, the reader will find in chapter 9 a case-study based on the Quakers and their involvement in science – particularly those elected to the Royal Society.

In chapter 10 we adopt a different method again, examining the changing relations between just one science and the religious sensibilities it could arouse. Of all the sciences, chemistry has had perhaps the lowest profile in the history of natural theology. With ambitions to imitate (even to improve upon) nature, chemists have been in the forefront of blurring distinctions between the 'natural' and the 'artificial'. In this way they have made their distinctive contribution to a problematising of the 'natural' which has, in turn, had implications for the survival of natural theology. Nevertheless, chemico-theologies *have* existed and their character as process-theologies invites some concluding reflections on what a future historian might make of our bio-technology and the public anxieties it has occasioned.

NOTES

1 I. Newton, Notebook, Fitzwilliam Museum Cambridge. See J. H. Brooke, 'The God of Isaac Newton', in *Let Newton Be!* (ed. J. Fauvel, R. Flood, M. Shortland and R. Wilson), Oxford, 1988, 169–83.
2 From the Ode dedicated to Newton by Halley and prefixed to Newton's *Philosophiae Naturalis Principia Mathematica*, London, 1687.
3 For detailed discussion of Newton's religious beliefs, see F. Manuel, *The Religion of Isaac Newton*, Oxford, 1974; R. S. Westfall, *Never at Rest*, Cambridge, 1984; B. J. T. Dobbs, *The Janus Faces of Genius*, Cambridge, 1991.
4 *Newton's Philosophy of Nature: Selections from His Writings* (ed. H. S. Thayer), New York, 1953, 66.
5 *Ibid.*, 42.
6 Galileo, *Sidereus Nuncius*, Venice, 1610, transl. by S. Drake in *Discoveries and Opinions of Galileo*, New York, 1957, 27–58.
7 *Thomas Cook Holidays: Worldwide Faraway Collection*, December 1995 – November 1996, 26.
8 J. T. Harwood, 'Rhetoric and graphics in *Micrographia*', in *Robert Hooke: New Studies* (ed. M. Hunter and S. Schaffer), Woodbridge, 1989, 119–47.
9 G. Mantell, *Wonders of Geology*, London, 1839, Frontispiece. For a detailed study of the visual rhetoric of geological texts, see M. J. S. Rudwick, *Scenes From Deep Time: Early Pictorial Representations of the Prehistoric World*, Chicago, 1992.
10 S. Y. Edgerton, 'Galileo, Florentine "Disegno" and the "strange spotted-nesse" of the moon', *Art Journal*, Fall 1984, 225–31, especially 229. See also M. G. Winkler and A. Van Helden, 'Representing the heavens: Galileo and visual astronomy', *Isis*, 83 (1992), 195–217.

11 J. D. Watson and F. H. C. Crick, 'Molecular structure of nucleic acids: a structure for deoxyribonucleic acid', *Nature*, 171 (1953), 737–8; J. D. Watson, *The Double Helix*, New York, 1968; R. C. Olby, *The Path to the Double Helix*, London, 1974.

12 Thayer, op. cit. (4), 49.

13 A. Funkenstein, *Theology and the Scientific Imagination from the Middle Ages to the Seventeenth Century*, Princeton, 1986, 89–97.

14 N. Barlow (ed.), *The Autobiography of Charles Darwin*, London, 1958, 85–7.

15 This is one of those episodes that begins to look rather different when critical historical scholarship comes into play. See J. R. Lucas, 'Wilberforce and Huxley: a legendary encounter', *The Historical Journal*, 22 (1979), 313–30; S. Gilley, 'The Huxley–Wilberforce debate: a reconstruction', in *Religion and Humanism* (ed. K. Robbins), Oxford, 1981, 325–40; J. V. Jensen, 'Return to the Wilberforce–Huxley debate', *British Journal for the History of Science*, 21 (1988), 161–79; F. J. L. James, 'The Huxley–Wilberforce debate revisited', paper presented at the Birmingham meeting of the British Association for the Advancement of Science, 10 September 1996.

16 *The Daily Telegraph*, 9 September 1994.

17 See for example M. C. Banner, *The Justification of Science and the Rationality of Religious Belief*, Oxford, 1990; N. Murphy, *Theology in the Age of Scientific Reasoning*, Ithaca, 1990; P. Clayton and S. Knapp, 'Rationality and Christian self-conceptions', in *Religion and Science: History, Method, Dialogue* (ed. W. M. Richardson and W. J. Wildman), New York, 1996, 131–42.

18 For a recent discussion of this familiar theme, see R. Feldhay, *Galileo and the Church: Political Inquisition or Critical Dialogue?*, Cambridge, 1995.

19 A critique of this essentialist project also featured prominently in J. H. Brooke, *Science and Religion: Some Historical Perspectives*, Cambridge, 1991.

20 *Ibid.*, 33–42.

21 J. Hick, *An Interpretation of Religion*, London, 1989, 85–6, 94, 123–4.

22 R. K. Merton, *Science, Technology and Society in Seventeenth Century England*, New York, 1970, first published in *Osiris*, 4 (1938), part 2, 360–632.

Section I: *Science and Religion*

1

Is there Value in the Historical Approach?

We might begin by marking an anniversary. One hundred and fifty years before we delivered the lecture series on which this book is based, William Thomson presented his first introductory lecture as Glasgow's new Professor of natural philosophy. Not that the lecture itself was a resounding success. Thomson confided to his friend George Stokes that it had been 'rather a failure as I had it all written, and I read it very fast'.[1] In order to expand his laboratory space this great enthusiast for precision measurement commandeered an unused wine-cellar in an old professor's house, the noise of the alterations producing predictable complaints from those preferring old bottles to new. It is doubly appropriate to refer to Thomson, or Lord Kelvin as he has become better known, because it is possible to detect in his thinking certain ways of relating science to theology that do not fit present-day preconceptions.

In a recent biography the connections between Thomson's research laboratory and industry are explored. The engineering career of his brother James encouraged William to examine technical concepts such as 'work' and 'waste'.[2] But connections of another kind are also underlined. These were theological and may have been reinforced by William's friendship with the great evangelical preacher Thomas Chalmers, whose services he attended. Chalmers himself had made connections between science and theology. His immensely popular *Astronomical Discourses* had been designed to rebut the allegation that the expansion of the universe and a concomitant plurality of worlds rendered Christianity incredible.[3] In the case of William Thomson, the impress of a Scottish voluntarist theology can be seen in his thermodynamics. The principle of energy *conservation* was a reminder that only God could create and destroy the energy inherent in the universe, whilst the principle of energy *dissipation* was a potent reminder that the present form of the world was as transitory as Chalmers had deduced it to be from his reading of 2 Corinthians 4:18.[4] In a preliminary draft of his 'dynamical theory of heat' Thomson wrote of a 'tendency in the material world for motion to become diffused'.[5] There was a 'reverse of concentration ... gradually going on'. In his own mind there was resonance with Psalm 102: 'Of old hast thou laid the foundation of the earth: and the heavens are the work of thy hands. They shall perish, but thou shalt endure: yea, all of them shall wax old like a garment.'[6]

The point is not that Thomson's 'science' was at bottom a form of theology; nor that his theology was rooted in nothing but 'science'. The example rather shows that key words, such as 'conservation' and 'dissipation' could mediate between scientific and religious beliefs. Statements about the technical workings of nature and statements within biblical texts could function as commentaries on each other, sometimes reinforcing deeply held convictions about human destiny. It is an example that could also be used to show that there may be separation of scientific and religious discourse on some levels but integration or overlap on others.

This last point deserves special attention. The most renowned diplomat for experimental science in the seventeenth century, Francis Bacon, warned about the dangers of mixing biblical exegesis with scientific practice. But to regard this as a complete detachment of 'science' from 'religion' would be simplistic because in Bacon's view there were profound religious sanctions for improving the natural sciences. Not only did their cultivation encourage the Christian virtue of humility, their practical application could help restore a dominion over nature that the human race had lost at the Fall.[7] The need to talk about different levels in this way is crucially important. In his mechanisation of nature, Robert Boyle insisted on a clear separation of nature and God.[8] Natural phenomena were to be explained in terms of the architecture and motion of particles. But on other levels, this very mechanisation reinforced an integration of natural philosophy and theology. The more mechanical the world, the more transparent that it had been the product of design. Machines simply do not spring into existence by themselves.

For the historian, Thomson, Bacon and Boyle are just three of an enormous gallery of thinkers whose science and theology were interrelated in interesting, unpredictable and extraordinarily diverse ways. To reduce religious beliefs to primitive forms of science, as Richard Dawkins among others has encouraged us to do, is to be unprepared for the richness and diversity in the engagement of science and religion. It would be to miss the moral sanction for altruistic science that in Bacon stemmed, at least in part, from his Protestant theology. It would miss the sense of awe at the beauty of nature voiced both by Boyle and Newton even when they *could* provide scientific explanations for the phenomena in question. It would even be to miss Charles Darwin's willingness, certainly for a while, to entertain the belief that the Creator creates through laws.[9] It certainly misses the subtlety of a Thomas Chalmers or a William Thomson whose reconstructions of nature were informed by physical *and* intrinsically theological considerations. The many different levels on which theology has impinged on the scientific enterprise, and vice versa, should make us suspicious of reductionist claims and of the master-narratives that reflect them.

How Many Stories?

History is frequently used to defend polemical positions. Richard Dawkins states that he sees God as a 'competing explanation for facts about the universe and life'[10] – competing that is with scientific theories. No sooner has he made that declaration than he adds in justification: 'This is certainly how God has been seen by most theologians of past centuries and by most ordinary religious people today.' By implication one could write a history to prove the point. The subservience of history to partisan interests is of course a familiar theme. We have all met those narratives in which the interpretation of historical events is controlled by a master-narrative that may reflect national or political interests. A typical example might be that curiously English view of Scotland which sees the Act of Union as a necessary step in subduing a troublesome and unruly people. Or it might be that curiously Scottish view of England which in looking down on the size of her mountains, also looks down on the quality of her educational system, on the lack of fortitude in matters spiritual and on the relative incompetence of the English to run their Empire.[11] As the Scots mayor of the Australian colony of Victoria put it in 1885: 'We want more Scots. Give us Scots. Give us the whole population of Glasgow.'[12] One of the two nationalist views could, of course, be right; but we also smile because we recognise the mythological element in these master-narratives.

This subservience of history to partisan interests is just as conspicuous in the contested domain of 'science-and-religion'. A century has now elapsed since Andrew Dickson White published the best known of the conflict narratives. His *History of the Warfare of Science with Theology in Christendom* was in part a response to the clerical battering he had personally received after proposing a non-sectarian charter for Cornell University. There had been widespread indignation that a university should be founded without the purpose of protecting the Christian faith. The prominence White gave to the sciences and his forthright view that 'it shall not be the purpose of the Faculty to stretch or cut Science exactly to fit "Revealed Religion" ' had exposed him to censure as the architect of a Godless institution.[13] He had been forced to conclude that there was 'antagonism between the theological and scientific view of the universe and of education in relation to it'.[14] Here was a thesis that could be turned into a riveting story – a tragi-comedy in which science had triumphed over obscurantism. White would count the number of bell ringers killed across Europe when their belfries were struck by lightning – and all because of a reluctance on the part of the clergy to interfere with providence by erecting lightning rods when the technology had become available. White's strictures against theological dogmatism have repeatedly struck a popular chord. It takes a little more discernment to see that much of the perceived conflict was not between science and theology but between competing forms of science in which theologians might have an interest or between competing forms of theology in which appeal might be made to the authority of science. White himself claimed that there need be no opposition between the spirit of scientific enquiry and the spirit of true religion.[15] His enemy was dogmatic theology of the kind preached against him by the slighted Christian Colleges. His *History*, as he told Ezra Cornell, would teach them a lesson they would remember.[16]

One of the features of this kind of master-narrative is that it will ignore issues that might break the predetermined mould, or it will find ways of assimilating them within the single narrative. When Georges Cuvier, the eminent and powerful French zoologist of the early nineteenth century, opposed the evolutionary theory of his contemporary Jean-Baptiste Lamarck, he might be said to create problems for White's categories. Evolutionary theory in the later hands of Darwin was to mark for White the final triumph of science over dogmatic theology. But what is to be done when forward looking science is contested by one of the great scientific minds of the age? Cuvier, after all, did more than Lamarck to establish the fact that some species had become extinct.[17] Wedded to the unilinear march of truth, White needed his controversies to be between science and theology, not between science and science. Hence the device: Cuvier, he claimed, was fighting in the name of science, but unconsciously for theology.

The single master-narrative has not always been structured around the theme of conflict. Science has sometimes been given a high profile in the secularisation of society not through a series of confrontations with religious authority but through the gradual displacement of spiritual sensibilities – much as Charles Darwin lost his resolve to become a clergyman during his long and enthralling voyage on *HMS Beagle.* Less flamboyant, less pervasive histories have also been written in the name of harmony and peace. Particularly in the physical sciences, belief in a world of order, of a pattern behind the appearances, had been clearly expressed by European natural philosophers. For example, there is no doubt that both Copernicus and Kepler based their reconstructions of astronomy on the premise that a greater harmony could be conferred on the heavenly motions if only a different vantage point could be found.[18] To have the earth move created the sort of harmony one would expect from an intelligent Creator who, in Kepler's view, had equipped the human mind with the power to uncover the hidden mathematical patterns. In the mind of Kepler was a sense not of conflict between astronomy and religion but of union. When he articulated what we know as his third law of planetary motion (that which correlates the time it takes for a planet to complete its orbit with its mean distance from the sun) he reported that he felt carried away by unutterable rapture at the divine spectacle of heavenly harmony.[19]

We should note those words: rapture, divine, spectacle, heavenly, harmony. Each has a continuum of meaning which enables the scientific 'discovery' to be at the same time a religious experience. It was the view of A. N. Whitehead that modern science was an unconscious derivative of medieval theology in that the latter provided the crucial presupposition of an ordered and intelligible Creation.[20] This basic idea has been developed in different ways. The Marxist historian of science Edgar Zilsel even insisted that the concept of physical law had religious origins.[21] The founders of modern science had reconstructed nature by analogy with a human society. A divine legislator had impressed his Will on the world much as an absolute monarch might try to do for human subjects. The late Joseph Needham, in comparing the preconditions of science in Europe with cultural norms in China, noted the absence of a legislating God as one of a constellation of circumstances that conferred a different character on Chinese science.[22]

It has been possible, therefore, to construct a narrative very different in flavour from those preoccupied with conflict. For the Cambridge philosopher Michael Foster, writing in the 1930s, a Christian doctrine of creation had not only made the quest for laws of nature a rational pursuit. It had helped to purge classical theologies of nature of pantheistic elements that had obstructed the conceptual separation of the Creation from its Creator. Ingeniously

Foster even suggested that a Trinitarian theology had played its part. His argument was that Plato had conflated two images of God's relation to the world – that of parent to offspring and artificer to artifact. Christian theology had then effected a conceptual clarification by transferring a father/son relation to the domain of Christology. This left the natural world as a created artifact, the artistry of which could be elucidated and appreciated.[23]

The story which makes modern science in some sense the offspring of a doctrine of Creation has gone through many variants and refinements. Foster, and later Francis Oakley, suggested that it was specifically a *voluntarist* theology of creation that produced the most auspicious presuppositions for the natural sciences.[24] The point here is that a theology that emphasises the freedom of the divine will to make one world rather than another is a theology that makes it inappropriate to reason *a priori* about how the world must be. Empirical methods are necessary to discover which of the many possible worlds the deity might have made has in fact been made.[25] There are indeed echoes of such reasoning in seventeenth-century natural philosophy. Marin Mersenne, who was at the nerve-centre of one of the first scientific correspondence networks, objected to Aristotle's claim that the earth must be at the centre of the cosmos. For Mersenne there was no 'must' about it. It was wrong to say that the centre was the earth's *natural* place. God had been free to put it where He liked. It was incumbent on us to find where this was.[26]

Mersenne was a Catholic, a member of the order of Minims; a minor embarrassment perhaps to another variant of the single narrative which would locate the preconditions of the scientific movement in the Protestant Reformation, in the freedom of thought which it supposedly unleashed, in the mercantile economies of those societies in which it gained most ground and in a new emphasis on the Bible. A distinguished historian of science and Gifford Lecturer, the late Reijer Hooykaas, argued that the Bible itself allowed a reconstruction of nature in which the residues of pantheism were swept away. He spoke of a de-deification of nature, visible in Calvinist theology and propitious for the sciences. Nature could be studied as a created system having its own integrity, dependent for its continued existence on an external Sovereign Will.[27]

At first sight it is difficult to believe that two such incompatible narratives could co-exist. In the one we have Christian theology and ecclesiastical institutions acting as a persistent obstruction to scientific progress. In the other – and it is often expressed this way – without a Christian doctrine of Creation there would have been no modern science. Both theses are vulnerable because they are selective in their use of evidence. They gloss over the diversity and the complexity of positions taken in the past. Each tends to assume that 'science' and 'religion' can be given timeless definitions and that there is some inherent, some essential, relationship between them.[28] This last assumption is often on display when scientists and theologians meet for dialogue. High on conference agendas one finds papers with titles such as: 'What is the best account of the relations between science and religion?' Such a quest for the Holy Grail is worrying to the historian, because it assumes that a single account can be given of relations that have patently changed over time, that have been different in different societies and which continue to change. Many such attempts have been made in the past to construct an ideal model. The study of history is humbling because it shows how ephemeral most have been. This is a lesson that ought to be troubling to those who sometimes speak as if they have achieved the definitive account.

There may also be value in an historical approach if it alerts us to the way in which prior interests, political, metaphysical and religious, have shaped the models that have been sought. For an example we might take a truly fundamental issue: the epistemological status of scientific theories. Should we regard our physical models as candidates for a true description of the 'real world' external to ourselves? Or should we see them simply as sophisticated attempts to impose order and coherence on experimental data? On this second view a theory could be valued as an instrument of prediction, or an exemplar of coherence, without the question of truth or falsehood arising. In seeking some general model of the relations between science and religion, a question of this kind would have to be faced. Yet religious apologists have been drawn to both these positions.

The attraction of a realist view is that, with due caution, it allows the sciences to uncover the 'real' structure of God's creation.[29] But the second, more instrumentalist, view has also appealed to vested religious interests. And it is not difficult to see why. It enables one to say of a theory that might look threatening to belief that it poses no problem because it is merely a hypothesis, merely a calculating device. The point is that there is no single story one can tell about this. Precisely because religious apologists have sometimes opted for the realist position, their opponents may surface among the instrumentalists, or among those positivists who may have rejected the use of theoretical entities altogether. One of the most vociferous secular scientists of the Third Republic in France was the chemist Marcellin Berthelot. One of his reasons for rejecting the concept of atoms is particularly intriguing: 'I do not want chemistry to degenerate into a religion; I do not want the chemist to believe in the existence of atoms as the Christian believes in the existence of Christ in the communion wafer.'[30] A single tenseless model of *the* relations between science and religion would be unlikely to capture such niceties – in this case a misplaced scepticism towards a transcendent entity *within* science.

Henceforward we shall be avoiding master-narratives. We have many stories to tell and we hope that some at least will be instructive. There really are cogent reasons for not hoisting the big screen. Suppose one were to enquire about the impact of a particular scientific innovation, Newton's gravitational theory for example, on religious thought. It would be straightforward for the historian if there had been a consensus reached by religious thinkers about its implications. But reactions to Newton's theory were so diverse that to speak coherently of a unified impact becomes impossible. In Cambridge the gravitational force was welcomed by Richard Bentley and William Whiston precisely because it was non-mechanical. There was a sense in which it rendered visible the invisible hand of God. But for the philosopher Leibniz, a non-mechanical agency was either unintelligible or a perpetual miracle, and on either count to be dismissed. It may be tempting to speak of *the* implications of the new 'mechanical philosophy' of the seventeenth century when matter and motion became the primary variables for the explanation of natural phenomena. But for no two thinkers were they the same. To regard nature as machinery could constitute a programme for eliminating miracles. For some Catholic philosophers, notably Mersenne, it was a means of preserving them – by clarifying the boundaries between the natural and the supernatural.[31] The absorbing question is why different individuals and social groups should be drawn to different interpretations and how far we may account for their predispositions.

How Should the Stories be Told?

We have been suggesting reasons why some definitive account of *the* relations between science and religion should not be expected. There are practical reasons for making the point. Those who enjoy discussing contemporary issues in this domain, whether scientists, philosophers, theologians or members of the public, often feel the need for historical perspective. Understandably they turn to a reputable source. The danger is that if only one historical account is consulted, it may acquire an authority for them that it probably should not have. In all historical writing there is so much by way of inference and reconstruction that to imagine the history of science, of religion, or of the relations between them as in some way 'given' would be an unfortunate mistake. Moreover, there is progress in historical research as in scientific research. As we shall see in chapter 4, a far richer understanding of the Galileo affair is possible now than a few years ago. Not only are there many stories that might be told. There are many ways of telling them. But how *should* they be told? In the remainder of this chapter we shall outline several different approaches that have been adopted in recent historical studies. We shall then be in a position to assess what value they may have.

The Contextual Approach

Before the discipline of the history of science became profession-alised it was not uncommon to find histories in which there was little or no reference to the social and cultural context in which particular forms of scientific enquiry had been conducted. The history of science was simply the history of scientific ideas, of progress in the acquisition of truth. There was an inner logic to scientific development in that each generation inherited a set of problems; hypotheses would be designed to solve them, and in the process of testing these hypotheses, new theoretical knowledge would be forged and accumulate. This is, however, an inadequate picture, not least because it leaves out the manner in which scientific practice may depend upon the social or economic reasons why one project may take priority over another. It excludes matters of intellectual taste and fashion that may regulate the kind of theories that are acceptable. It certainly leaves out the political aspects of making a career in science – how scientists, for example, have had to cultivate a sometimes wary public. For these and other reasons there has been a shift away from the image of scientific knowledge as completely autonomous, gradu-ally accumulating and floating above the sites in which it took shape.

One effect of this shift of sensibility has been to create a greater interest in religious parameters, because they, after all, have been constitutive elements in many of the contexts in which science has been pursued. A contextual approach turns out not to be a luxury but a necessity. This can be illustrated with a brief reference to that famous episode in the engagement of science and religion – the condemnation of Galileo by the Roman Catholic Church. This is such a celebrated case that it will be more fully examined in chapter 4.

For the moment let us consider statements made by two of the actors. The first goes like this:

> I say that if there were a true demonstration that the sun is at the centre of the world and the earth in the third heaven, and that the sun does not circle the earth but the earth circles the sun, then one would have to proceed with great care in explaining the Scriptures that appear contrary, and say rather that we do not understand them than that what is demonstrated is false.

The second actor, by contrast, has this to say:

> In the learned books of worldly authors are contained some propositions about nature which are truly demonstrated, and others which are simply taught; in regard to the former, the task of wise theologians is to show that they are not contrary to Holy Scripture; as for the latter (which are taught but not demonstrated with necessity), if they contain anything contrary to the Holy Writ, then they must be considered indubitably false and must be demonstrated such by every possible means.

Despite the reference to *contrast*, the two statements are very similar. Both seem to say that if there were a demonstration that the Copernican system were correct, then it would be necessary to reconsider the exegesis of certain biblical texts. In fact it makes a nice game to ask which is Galileo and which Cardinal Bellarmine, who had the task in 1616 of admonishing him. In some respects it is the second statement that looks the more reactionary. Our second speaker is prepared to say that an undemonstrated proposition must be deemed false if it goes against the grain of Scripture. The first seems perfectly liberal in allowing that if there were a proof of the Copernican system, it would be no great shakes – just a bit of biblical reinterpretation and all would be well. But the author of that seemingly liberal statement was Bellarmine;[32] the person who gave the Bible jurisdiction over dubious science was actually Galileo.[33]

The point of this game is simply to show that when texts are lifted from their contexts one's understanding is immediately impoverished. Inspecting these statements alone one would find it difficult to see why Galileo should have come into conflict with his Church. Place them in the political context of the time, however, and they take on a different complexion. Galileo behaved as if he had got decisive proof of the earth's motion. Neither Bellarmine nor Pope Urban VIII could bring themselves to believe that such a proof would be possible.

As a corollary of the contextual approach, historians of science have come to appreciate the importance of local circumstances in encouraging a scientific career or in shaping intellectual attitudes.[34] Biographies of scientific or religious leaders have to be rooted in place as well as time. As recent research has shown, representatives of one and the same doctrinal tradition have evinced different attitudes towards the same scientific theory according to where they happen to be. Geographical co-ordinates therefore assume a greater importance than one might imagine.

The research we have in mind concerns the reception of Darwinism in Belfast and Princeton. In both places there were Calvinists who opposed Darwin's theory; but the resistance in Belfast was to prove the more enduring. The reason has to do with local circumstances. There was nothing at Princeton to compare with the notorious Belfast Address of the physicist John Tyndall. When Tyndall delivered his Presidential Address at the 1874 meeting of the British Association he had gone on the offensive in more ways than one. His return to Ireland concentrated his mind on the refusal of local Catholic institutions to allow the sciences a place in their curricula – a refusal he deplored. In retaliation he offered a more completely naturalistic account of Darwinism than Darwin himself, pledging that science would wrest from theology the entire domain of cosmological theory. This coupled with a rebuke meted out by the Association to the theologian Robert Watts so soured feelings within the Presbyterian camp that Darwinism would henceforward be associated with intolerant materialism. Watts had prepared a paper for the meeting in which he urged conciliation between Christianity and science. The rebuke had consisted in a refusal to give it a place in the programme. The point, as David Livingstone has stressed, is that in exploring the historical relations between Calvinism and Darwinism it is not enough to focus on doctrinal issues. Local circumstances must be considered. His comparative study yields a telling contrast. Whereas in Belfast traditional Calvinism was used to refute both the science and metaphysics of evolution, at Princeton, under the leadership of James McCosh, just the opposite was occurring. While Watts in Belfast was campaigning against evolution as subversive of the Westminster Confession of Faith, Princeton's Benjamin Warfield would evolutionise human origins and claim Calvin as the intellectual precursor of Darwin.[35]

It is not the purpose of this book to dissolve the great issues that have been debated under the banner of 'science and religion' into fragments of local history; but there surely is value in reflecting on the extent to which our own attitudes to the big questions have been shaped by exigencies of both time and place.

A Functional Approach

In the scientific and theological literature of the past there has often been an interpenetration of ideas about nature and ideas about God. We have already seen examples of this in Kepler and Newton. In the literature of natural theology, the interpenetration was often so complete that one and the same book could be read as a work of scientific popularisation or of contemporary theology.[36] As long as the natural sciences could supply evidence of design, the prospect of some kind of union remained. An approach that historians have found useful here is to ask what *function* the theology may be playing within the science and vice versa. In either case attention must also be paid to historical context.

It is not always appreciated, for example, that religious beliefs can function as presuppositions of science. Beliefs about the uniformity of nature have been grounded in the constancy and fidelity of God. Thomas Chalmers certainly thought in those terms. On another level, religious belief could be presented as a sanction for science as it was by Francis Bacon: the altruistic application of scientific knowledge would be for the glory of God and the relief of man's estate. Religious convictions could even provide motivation for science if one happened to believe, with Boyle or Newton, that the more one uncovered of the intricacies of nature the greater the evidence of divine intelligence. There might be the motivation too to accept one theory rather than another if by so doing one could score a point or two against a theological opponent! On yet another level religious beliefs have materialised in the discussion of scientific methodology. In evangelical circles there has often been a moratorium on the speculative hypothesis, a favourite text being Newton's famous 'hypotheses non fingo': I frame no hypotheses. In selecting between rival theories religious beliefs have intruded both consciously and unconsciously. Enthusiasm among religious leaders for evolutionary theories was in pretty short supply until the case for them became difficult to resist. Religious beliefs have also been invoked to reinforce aesthetic criteria in theory selection. Why do scientists opt for the most elegant equations? Why does nature seem to respond to them? Religious meaning has often been accorded to the ideas of simplicity, elegance and harmony that have so often regulated theory choice.[37] Werner Heisenberg could say of his equations that it was as if he had been lucky enough to 'look over the good Lord's shoulder while He was at work'.[38]

A functional approach need not be confined to the internal content of natural theology. One may also ask what wider purposes texts on natural theology fulfilled both for those who wrote them and for their audiences, both real and presumed.[39] The contrast here might be with a more conventional philosophical approach, which seeks to expose the logical structure of the design argument. The aim of a functional analysis would be to uncover the uses to which natural theology was put. For example it would help to unify what might otherwise be disparate scientific and religious interests.

Appeals to design in nature might assist in the promotion of the sciences themselves, pre-empting criticism that might be born of theological suspicion. Design arguments might assist the religious apologist in attacking the atheist. They might even help to establish common ground in the context of missionary encounters with other cultures. They might gain a high profile, too, in contexts where it was diplomatic to play down doctrinal differences within the same confessional tradition. The design argument could be used as a means of corroborating a pre-existing faith or even of assuaging religious doubts that might be occasioned by disturbing scientific disclosures. The Cambridge geologist Adam Sedgwick once reassured a friend that he had nothing to fear from geology: ten thousand creative acts were recorded in stony tablets.[40] Similarly, an essay of William Whewell casting doubt on a plurality of worlds was addressed to the perplexed believer.[41]

It is instructive, too, to consider the political functions of natural theology. When, in 1838, Adam Sedgwick addressed some three or four thousand colliers on Tynemouth beach he explained how the existing social order was also a natural order. According to John Herschel, Sedgwick had 'led them on from the scene around them to the wonders of the coal-country below them, thence to the economy of a coal-field, then to their relations to the coal-owners and capitalists, then to the great principles of morality and happiness, and last to their relation to God, and their own future prospects'.[42] To make sense of Sedgwick's moralising we need both a contextual and a functional analysis. He was speaking during a meeting of the British Association for the Advancement of Science at Newcastle, where coal-mining was vital to the local economy. In weaving science, industry and Christian morality into a seamless web, he was at the same time inculcating both resignation and deference to authority in those whom he addressed. There was clearly more to natural theology on this occasion than the bare bones of the design argument.

A Linguistic Approach

A contextual and functional analysis can be enriched by a third approach. This involves a closer study of the language in which claims about the relations between science and religion are expressed. Recent scholarship has shown that scientific texts perform rhetorical functions and that these can be fruitfully analysed.[43] It must be emphasised that the word 'rhetorical' here is not being used in the disparaging sense of *merely* rhetorical. The question 'Who is the author trying to persuade?' and the question 'What techniques of persuasion are being used?' are both of central importance. What one is prepared to say may depend rather crucially on one's audience. As a defendant on trial Galileo, initially at least, claimed that he had not privileged the Copernican system in his discussion of the 'two chief world systems'.[44] But to a trusted correspondent he confessed that his book was 'a most ample confirmation' of the Copernican doctrine.[45] Even the most technical scientific report is an exercise in communication and persuasion. But a report written for one's peers is very different from an exercise in popularisation.

The kind of rhetoric employed in statements that link nature to God may also depend on the particular role adopted by scientist or theologian. Scientists, for example, have written as investigators of nature, as reporters of their findings, as popularisers of science, as philosophers and as preachers. A theologian may write as an exegete, as an evangelist, as an apologist, pastor or preacher. These roles can of course overlap, but the language in which the arguments are couched is likely to be differently nuanced according to audience and occasion. Simply to lift statements linking nature and God, or science and religion, from the texts in which they were embedded can be a flat, two-dimensional exercise. To study the tropes, the metaphors, the linguistic structures employed by authors in winning over their audiences can bring the issues to life.

As an example let us take the famous case of Charles Darwin. References to a Creator do appear in the privacy of his transmutation notebooks. In the late 1830s he had as yet no reason to reject the belief that the Creator might create through laws.[46] But one is immediately aware of a problem because in these same notebooks Darwin is deliberately calculating on how best to present his insights. In his metaphysical notebook, explicitly marked 'private', he issued instructions to himself: 'to avoid stating how far, I believe, in materialism, say only that emotions, instincts, degrees of talent, which are hereditary are so because [the] brain of [a] child resembles [the]

Figure 6: Artificial selection at work in the breeding of fancy pigeons. Human intervention had produced forms of such diversity that, according to Darwin, they would strike the observer as separate species even though they were all descendants of the rock pigeon. From G. J. Romanes, *Darwin, and after Darwin*, 2nd edn. (1893), vol. i.

parent stock'.[47] Given that self-conscious calculation, is it surprising that Darwin scholars should stress the ambiguity of his God-talk?[48]

In studying Darwin's project and its presentation, it is impossible to avoid the study of metaphor. At the heart of his theory was the concept of 'natural selection'. In the struggle for existence was a filtering process, the better adapted variants within a species having the better chance of survival and of leaving progeny at the expense of their competitors. But where did the metaphor of 'selection' come from? Darwin was thinking of the familiar processes of artificial selection – the breeding of more productive cattle or fancier pigeons. In order to develop the desired characteristic the breeder would select the most promising individuals for mating. For Darwin it was a helpful analogy in reaching his audience. But as with all metaphors and analogies it also created ambiguities. In the case of artificial selection human intelligence intervened to accumulate the favoured characteristics. Did this mean there was a divine intelligence working through nature? The metaphor at the heart of Darwin's theory was also at the heart of the ensuing theological debate.[49] One of the reasons why Darwin's use of language has remained an absorbing subject for study is that he was apt to ignore or forget the metaphorical basis of his model. When he wrote in the *Origin of Species* that 'natural selection is daily and hourly scrutinising, throughout the world, every variation, even the slightest; rejecting that which is bad, preserving and adding up all that is good', he was moving beyond analogy, attributing to natural selection the characteristics of an active *being*.[50] In many of the classic texts on natural theology the admission of design had been supposed to rest on reason. As we show in chapter 6, an historical approach to those texts can be especially valuable if it is sensitive to the linguistic techniques employed by their authors to persuade their readers.

Underlying any discussion of the engagement of science and religion is the question of authority: how it is constituted and exercised. The linguistic approach can be particularly helpful here because it helps us to see how techniques employed in sermons, for example, would enable the clergy to exercise power and influence over their congregations, enlisting support for their message. Scientists have had to establish and sustain their authority in similar ways. It is no coincidence that when T. H. Huxley set out to boost the authority of the scientific expert he treated his audiences to what he called 'lay sermons'.[51] There was deliberate irony in the label, but the point remains. Scientists can and do behave as preachers. As one Frenchman observed of Humphry Davy: 'You may foresee by a certain tuning or pitching of the organ of speech to a graver key, thrusting his chin into his neck, and even pulling out his cravat, when Mr. Davy is going to be eloquent.'[52]

A Biographical Approach

If the investigation of linguistic techniques sounds rather impersonal, there is another approach that is emphatically not. This is to shift the site of enquiry to the biography of particular individuals. A good biography will show us how its subject coped with the hopes and fears, the anxieties that are part of what it is to be human. If the subject happens to be a scientist who thought deeply about religion, the biographer may be able to bring alive the issues as they were played out, not merely in philosophical texts, but socially and, more intimately, in the inner life of an individual.[53] An innovative biography of Darwin has helped us to appreciate how the illness of which he incessantly complained may have been primarily psychosomatic. We are shown what it meant to live through the consequences of harbouring in secret a theory that, if published, was likely to bring social stigma.[54] Biographies can also be enthralling because they show us a life in flux. In the case of Darwin we now have poignant accounts of how the last vestiges of his faith were destroyed – not by some new scientific insight but by the shattering experience of bereavement. The death of his father in February 1849 was followed by the loss of his favourite daughter Annie early in 1851. In different but profound ways they tested beyond endurance his will to believe in the God he associated with Christianity. His heterodox father did not deserve eternal damnation; his angelic daughter had not deserved to die.[55]

The spiritual odyssey of Darwin's contemporary John Ruskin would also illustrate the value of a biographical approach. In his intellectual formation a love of the observational sciences as well as Romantic poetry contributed to his identity as an artist. His interest in geology is reflected in his membership of the London Geological Society. His intellectual biography is one in which, initially at least, there was a harmonious union of his artistic, scientific and religious interests. Operating with the concept of God's two books he saw himself supplying the spiritual dimension lacking in neutral, scientific descriptions of nature. Yet the more he learned of biblical criticism, the more he read the latest geology, the greater his hidden doubts became. His private frustration was confessed to Henry Acland in a letter that has often been quoted: 'You speak of the flimsiness of your own faith. Mine, which was never strong, is being beaten into mere gold leaf, and flutters in weak rags from the letter of its old forms; but the only letters it can hold by at all are the old Evangelical formulae. If only the geologists would let me alone, I could do very well, but those dreadful hammers! I hear the clink of them at the end of every cadence of the Bible verse.'[56] By focussing on ever-changing perceptions, a biographical approach can reveal more of the subtlety in the way that scientific and religious considerations may combine. The historical sciences clearly corroded Ruskin's convictions. Nevertheless when he spoke of his *de-conversion* the final straw had more to do with art than science. In one of his own accounts he could pin-point the exact moment:

> I was still in the bonds of my old Evangelical faith; and, in 1858, it was with me, Protestantism or nothing: the crisis of the whole turn of my thoughts being one Sunday morning, at Turin, when, from before Veronese's Queen of Sheba, and under quite overwhelmed sense of his God-given power, I went away to a Waldensian chapel, where a little squeaking idiot was preaching to an audience of seventeen old women and three louts, that they were the only children of God in Turin; and that all the people in the world out of the sight of Monte Viso, would be damned. I came out of the chapel, in sum of twenty years of thought, a conclusively *un-*converted man.[57]

The examples of both Darwin and Ruskin suggest that to focus only on the proverbial 'relations between science and religion' may not be the best way of understanding how an individual thinker came to construct them. A biographical approach may show that, in some cases at least, piety and a commitment to the investigation of nature could co-exist in one and the same person. It may reveal anxiety, even torment, as new ideas were assimilated. It may reveal a whole range of strategies worked out by a particular individual to preserve a living faith and a scientific integrity. Or again, it may reveal impiety and hostility towards established religions. It may reveal fluctuations in the strength of one's convictions, of the kind that Darwin recorded: 'As you ask,' he replied to one correspondent, 'I may state that my judgment often fluctuates....I think that generally (and more and more as I grow older), but not always, ... an Agnostic would be the more correct description of my state of mind.'[58]

A Practical Approach

An exclusive preoccupation with the relations between scientific and religious *ideas* can be attacked from another angle. It is surely important to examine practice as well as theory. With the history of science specifically in mind, it has been said that 'knowledge is the product of human actions'.[59] What kinds of action are involved in the practice of science? How do they compare with religious practices? As soon as the questions are transposed in this way, the methods of the social scientists assume an immediate importance.[60] There can be anthropological studies of how scientists behave in their laboratories,[61] sociological studies of how scientific communities control knowledge claims,[62] and social histories of science in which changes in the status of the practitioner are explored.[63]

To dwell on practice rather than theory may well intensify our sense of two different language games and of a chasm between them. It is not immediately obvious, for example, how the experimental methods of laboratory life have any parallel in the practice of prayer, meditation, or worship. Indeed, when science and religion are sharply distinguished it is often through contrasting statements about practice. For example, it is sometimes said that scientists make predictions that can be rigorously tested whereas the forms of religious prophecy seem to belong to another world, sometimes in more senses than one. Nevertheless, there have been bridges in the past and the social historian may see some that would otherwise be missed.

Today we take the value of an experimental methodology more or less for granted, despite problems that can arise in the replication of results.[64] In the seventeenth century what became known as the 'experimental philosophy' had to establish its credentials. The problem in a nutshell was why the report of an experimental result should be believed in preference to statements about nature derived from authoritative texts such as Aristotle and the Bible. Studies of Robert Boyle, one of the most ardent defenders of experimental enquiry, have disclosed the various techniques used to gain the trust of his audience. Experiments were described in ways that drew the audience in, as 'virtual witnesses'. Or there might be reference to some unimpeachable dignatory – a clergyman, for example – present when the experiment was performed, who could testify to the veracity of the report. Above all, in conferring authority on an experimental result it helped if the reporter, and in this Boyle had his advantage, was an honourable, and Christian, gentleman. Questions of social standing and religious respectability could be relevant to substantiating claims for scientific truth.[65]

The study of religious, as well as scientific, practices can be equally revealing. The case of Michael Faraday provides a striking example because one can ask how Faraday's commitment to a biblical

Christianity was manifest in his daily life. What did it mean in practice to be a member of a minority sect, the Sandemanians, whose
beliefs implied a withdrawal from the rewards of this world? It clearly
meant a life of moral discipline, of regular attendance at the meeting
house – on Wednesday evenings as well as most of Sunday. The
Sunday service involved hours of prayer, Bible study and exhorta-
tion. Following a simple meal, known as the 'love-feast', the service
would resume, culminating in a celebration of the Lord's Supper.
Faraday became an elder in the Church and certainly delivered
exhortations. In these, biblical texts were in the foreground,
minimising the distortion of God's word that might come from the
human voice.

Living by the Bible also meant pastoral duties, ministering to the
sick and dying. Faraday was conspicuous in supporting other
Sandemanian fellowships outside London. He would visit elders in
Glasgow, Edinburgh and Dundee. When schism threatened he
would be active as a diplomat. His religion made stern practical
demands, a life of discipline within a framework of moral law. It is
possible to see a parallel with his role as a disciplined scientist, inves-
tigating the God-created, lawlike universe.[66] There was even a sense
in which Faraday 'transferred the Sandemanian social philosophy to
science'.[67] His vision of the scientific community was one in which
there should be no avarice, partisan interests or personal disputes. In
the practice of science, as in the practice of religion, he mistrusted
earthly rewards. He mistrusted the entrepreneurial spirit and interventionist forms of patronage that would detract from the purity of
scientific investigation. The scientist was a moral agent whose knowledge was for sharing and for edification.[68]

The Value of the Historical Approach

Central to this chapter is the question whether the historical
approach is of value. It has been important to raise this issue
because, as a resource, history is infinitely fickle. If one believes in
some inherent conflict between criteria of truth in the domains of
science and religion, histories can be constructed that will reinforce
that belief. If one prefers to assert the theistic roots of modern
science there is no shortage of histories to oblige. Isaac Newton, with
whom we began, was arguing some three hundred years ago, that
science had only flourished in monotheistic cultures.[69] So often
when historical case-studies are made subservient to a philosophical
thesis, the history is selectively reconstructed to do the necessary

work. The value, however, may consist precisely in the fact that there is multiplicity – both in the stories to be told and in the manner of their telling. And this can be of practical value if it induces a little humility in those who habitually pronounce as if the issues are cut and dried.

If the study of philosophy can be justified because it helps us to recognise bad philosophy, the same is true of history. Once on a visit to Belfast one of the authors was asked if he would take part in a radio interview. He agreed on the condition that he would not be asked any loaded questions of a partisan nature. The condition was readily granted. Then the first question came. Did he believe that Catholics or Protestants had made the greater contibution to science? But the real point of this anecdote is that, in his introduction, the presenter, broadcasting loud and clear, announced that 'we

Figure 7: Caricatures of Thomas Henry Huxley and Bishop Samuel Wilberforce from *Vanity Fair.*

all know' that Galileo got into trouble for believing the earth was round! It may be the most rudimentary service history can perform but popular understandings clearly remain in need of correction.

'We all know' that Huxley defeated Wilberforce. Yet it is far from clear that, on the day, Huxley enjoyed the victory that posterity has awarded him. Joseph Hooker reported that Huxley's voice had not carried and that he had not carried the audience with him. One convert to Darwin in the audience, Henry Baker Tristram, was apparently de-converted on witnessing the exchange.[70] Instead of seeing this event as a typical confrontation in some timeless battle between 'science' and 'religion', it may more usefully be seen as reflecting an ulterior social transformation taking place in Britain at the time. The clergy were losing their power as cultural leaders and arbiters of knowledge.[71] Huxley and others of his generation urged the claims of a scientific meritocracy, whose high professional standards demanded respect. In Huxley's view they were standards that a clerical amateur could no longer meet. This is not the whole story but this social transformation, associated with the increasing professionalisation of science, has to be taken into account when examining the fate of natural theology.

How might the case for the value of historical work be extended? Principally, it helps us to break out of the tired moulds in which treatments of science and religion are routinely cast.[72] If we are used to thinking only in terms of harmony, it can deliver uncomfortable shocks. If we are used to thinking in terms of polarity between extreme positions, it can be liberating to discover other options through the many thinkers who have occupied middle ground and sought conciliation. Anecdotes about apes and bishops can give the impression that in 1860 one had to be either a committed Christian or a committed Darwinian. One might never suspect that during the Oxford meeting of the British Association another Anglican clergyman spoke out and expressed opinions very different from those of Bishop Wilberforce. This was Frederick Temple, headmaster of Rugby School and future Archbishop of Canterbury. In a sermon preached on the first of July he argued that the finger of God could be seen at work in the laws of nature. Too often, he explained, religious apologists had tried to make capital out of scientific ignorance. There was no need to oppose the extension of natural law into new territory. In saying this he was tacitly creating the space for Darwin's science. He did so confidently because he believed that proof of the existence of natural laws served to reinforce belief in the existence of moral laws.[73]

There is value, too, in the realisation that we should not talk about either 'science' or 'religion' as if they are things in themselves. The word 'scientific' is often used indiscriminately to describe bodies of knowledge, methods of enquiry, forms of reasoning and even institutions. Historians and philosophers of science cannot help but see scientific activity in dynamic terms as a multi-faceted and ongoing process. But in that process, and in the different branches of science, many different – even conflicting – methods have been practised. And they have been practised by men and women not by that phantom presence who enables it to be said that the test tube was heated. The scaffolding by which our modern knowledge has been produced bears the marks of the cultures in which it was erected. And the scaffolding itself, as in the case of Newton's science, sometimes left an enduring mark on the edifice. The instability of the solar system was associated by Newton with the belief that occasional 'reformations' were required, under the guiding arm of Providence. In the later science of Laplace, the inherent stability of the system with its self-correcting powers tied in perfectly with the more secular culture of the Revolutionary era in France.[74] It is instructive to see that scientific knowledge has both shaped and been shaped by religious belief. There has been two-way traffic and, in some contexts, there still is.

We cannot, in the last analysis, keep history at arm's length. It is ultimately inescapable because we are all part of the same stream, albeit tossed by different currents. Because the present depends on the past, there will always be a symbiotic relationship between our understanding of the one and of the other. Despite, or rather because of, the complexities that they bring to light, the historical approaches we have identified in this chapter should be pursued with redoubled vigour. Those who follow them find so much that is enriching in the process of exploration. No-one should doubt that it is possible to gain inspiration from the great minds of the past, many of whom (Immanuel Kant for example) wrote with greater sophistication than one frequently finds today. This is not the same as saying that we should scour the history of philosophy for that 'best account of the relations between science and religion'. If we are asked to provide *that*, we can only ask in return, 'whose science and whose religion?'

NOTES

1 C. Smith and M. N. Wise, *Energy and Empire: A Biographical Study of Lord Kelvin*, Cambridge, 1989, 120.

2 *Ibid.*, 130.

3 D. Cairns, 'Thomas Chalmers's Astronomical Discourses: a study in natural theology', *Scottish Journal of Theology*, 9 (1956), 410–21.

4   'The things which are seen are temporal; but the things which are not seen are eternal.' C. Smith, 'From design to dissolution: Thomas Chalmers' debt to John Robison', *British Journal for the History of Science*, 12 (1979), 59–70; B. Hilton, *The Age of Atonement: The Influence of Evangelicalism on Social and Economic Thought 1785–1865*, Oxford, 1988, 361–2.

5   Smith and Wise, op. cit. (1), 330.

6   *Ibid.*, 317, 330–1.

7   C. Webster, *The Great Instauration: Science, Medicine and Reform 1626–1660*, London, 1975, 21–5.

8   E. M. Klaaren, *Religious Origins of Modern Science*, Grand Rapids, 1977; R. Hooykaas, *Religion and the Rise of Modern Science*, Edinburgh, 1972, 13–19. For an introduction to more recent scholarship on Boyle, see M. Hunter (ed.), *Robert Boyle Reconsidered*, Cambridge, 1994.

9   J. H. Brooke, 'The relations between Darwin's science and his religion', in *Darwinism and Divinity* (ed. J. Durant), Oxford, 1985, 40–75, especially 46–7.

10   R. Dawkins, 'A reply to Poole', *Science and Christian Belief*, 7 (1995), 45–50, on 46.

11   Most of these motifs can be found, for example, in Hugh Miller's *First Impressions of England and its People*, London, 1847. See also R. A. Houston, *Scottish Literacy and the Scottish Identity: Illiteracy and Society in Scotland and Northern England, 1600–1800*, Cambridge, 1988.

12   J. M. MacKenzie, 'Scotland and the Empire', Inaugural Lecture, Lancaster University, 13 May 1992, 9.

13   J. R. Moore, *The Post-Darwinian Controversies: A Study of the Protestant Struggle to Come to Terms with Darwin in Great Britain and America 1870–1900*, Cambridge, 1979, 34–5.

14   A. D. White, *A History of the Warfare of Science with Theology in Christendom*, 2 vols., London, 1896, i, Preface.

15   In his *Autobiography*, White recalled how the Darwinian hypothesis had affected him, revealing a 'whole new orb of thought' fatally at variance with the claims of churches, sects, and sacred books to be custodians of the final word of God to man. But he also insisted that a greater influence had been 'Stanley's life of Arnold [which] showed that a man might cast aside much which churches regard as essential, and might strive for breadth and comprehension in Christianity, while yet remaining in healthful relations with the church'. *Autobiography of Andrew Dickson White*, 2 vols., New York, 1905, ii, 559–62.

16   Moore, op. cit. (13), 35.

17   W. Coleman, *Georges Cuvier: Zoologist*, Cambridge, Mass., 1964; R. W. Burckhardt, *The Spirit of System: Lamarck and Evolutionary Biology*, Cambridge, MA, 1977; P. Corsi, *The Age of Lamarck: Evolutionary Theories in France 1790–1830*, Berkeley, 1988.

18   F. Hallyn, *The Poetic Structure of the World: Copernicus and Kepler*, New York, 1993.

19   M. Caspar, *Kepler*, London, 1959, 267.

20   A. N. Whitehead, *Science and the Modern World*, New York, 1925, 9–25.

21 E. Zilsel, 'The genesis of the concept of the physical law', *Philosophical Review*, 51 (1942), 245–79. Zilsel's collected writings are to be republished under the editorship of D. Raven.

22 J. Needham, *The Grand Titration: Science and Society in East and West*, London, 1969, 299–330.

23 Foster's articles, which appeared in *Mind*, 43 (1934), 446–68, 44 (1935), 439–66 and 45 (1936), 1–27, have been republished, together with interpretative essays, in C. Wybrow, *Creation, Nature, and Political Order in the Philosophy of Michael Foster (1903–1959)*, Lampeter, 1992.

24 F. Oakley, 'Christian theology and Newtonian science: the rise of the concept of laws of nature', *Church History*, 30 (1961), 433–57.

25 J. R. Milton, 'The origin and development of the concept of the "laws of nature"', *European Journal of Sociology*, 22 (1981), 173–95.

26 Mersenne's voluntarist theology is discussed by R. Lenoble, *Mersenne ou la Naissance du Mécanisme*, 2nd edn., Paris, 1971, and by P. Dear, *Mersenne and the Learning of the Schools*, Ithaca, 1988.

27 Hooykaas, op. cit. (8). For a sympathetic treatment of Hooykaas' thesis, in the context of evaluating the most prominent general explanations for the rise of European science, see H. F. Cohen, *The Scientific Revolution – A Historiographical Inquiry*, Chicago, 1994.

28 Even among accomplished critics of the revisionist thesis that modern science was crucially dependent on a Christian doctrine of Creation, there is a residual tendency to frame their critique in essentialist terms. See, for example, R. Gruner, 'Science, nature and Christianity', *Journal of Theological Studies*, 26 (1975), 55–81. A more comprehensive historical survey is given by C. Kaiser, *Creation and the History of Science*, Grand Rapids, 1991.

29 Among contemporary writers on science and theology, critical realist positions are represented by Arthur Peacocke, John Polkinghorne, William Stoeger and many others. A. R. Peacocke, *Intimations of Reality: Critical Realism in Science and Religion*, Notre Dame, 1984; J. Polkinghorne, 'The metaphysics of divine action', in *Chaos and Complexity: Scientific Perspectives on Divine Action* (ed. R. J. Russell, N. Murphy, and A. R. Peacocke), Vatican, 1995, 147-56; W. R. Stoeger, 'Describing God's action in the world in light of scientific knowledge of reality', in *ibid.*, 239–61.

30 Cited by H. W. Paul, *The Edge of Contingency*, Gainesville, Fla., 1979, 10–12.

31 J. H. Brooke, *Science and Religion: Some Historical Perspectives*, Cambridge, 1991, 117–51; P. Dear, 'Miracles, experiments and the ordinary course of nature', *Isis*, 81 (1990), 663–83.

32 Cardinal R. Bellarmine to P. Foscarini, 12 April 1615: M. Finocchiaro (ed.), *The Galileo Affair: A Documentary History*, Berkeley, 1989, 67–9, on 68.

33 Galileo, 'Letter to the Grand Duchess Christina' (1615), in *ibid.*, 87–118, on 101–2.

34 An excellent example is provided by C. A. Russell, *Lancastrian Chemist: The Early Years of Sir Edward Frankland*, Milton Keynes, 1986.

35 D. N. Livingstone, 'Darwinism and Calvinism: The Belfast–Princeton Connection', *Isis*, 83 (1992), 408–28.

36 J. R. Topham, 'Science and popular education in the 1830s: the role of the *Bridgewater Treatises*', *British Journal for the History of Science*, 25 (1992), 397–430.

37 The taxonomy of functions summarised in this paragraph is based on that suggested in Brooke, op. cit. (31), 19–33.

38 Cited by S. Chandrasekhar, *Truth and Beauty: Aesthetics and Motivations in Science*, Chicago, 1987, 22.

39 For a fuller introduction to the functions identified in this paragraph, see Brooke, op. cit. (31), 192–225.

40 J. W. Clark and T. Hughes, *The Life and Letters of the Reverend Adam Sedgwick*, 2 vols., Cambridge, 1890, ii, 79–80.

41 W. Whewell, *Of the Plurality of Worlds – An Essay*, London, 1853.

42 Clark and Hughes, op. cit. (40), i, 515–16.

43 For access to this recent literature see P. Dear (ed.), *The Literary Structure of Scientific Argument: Historical Studies*, Philadelphia, 1991.

44 A. Fantoli, *Galileo: For Copernicanism and For the Church*, Vatican Observatory, 1994, 405–8.

45 S. Drake, *Galileo at Work: His Scientific Biography*, Chicago, 1978, 310.

46 Brooke, op. cit. (9), 46–7.

47 C. Darwin, Notebook M 57, in *Charles Darwin's Notebooks, 1836–1844* (ed. P. H. Barrett, P. J. Gautrey, S. Herbert, D. Kohn and S. Smith), Ithaca, 1987.

48 D. Kohn, 'Darwin's ambiguity: the secularization of biological meaning', *British Journal for the History of Science*, 22 (1989), 215–39, especially 224.

49 R. M. Young, *Darwin's Metaphor: Nature's Place in Victorian Culture*, Cambridge, 1985.

50 D. N. Livingstone, *Darwin's Forgotten Defenders: The Encounter Between Evangelical Theology and Evolutionary Thought*, Grand Rapids, 1987, 45–7.

51 T. H. Huxley, *Lay Sermons, Addresses and Reviews*, London, 1870; D. M. Knight, 'Getting science across', *British Journal for the History of Science*, 29 (1996), 129–38; A. Desmond, *Huxley: The Devil's Disciple*, London, 1994.

52 Cited by J. V. Golinski, *Science as Public Culture: Chemistry and Enlightenment in Britain, 1760–1820*, Cambridge, 1992, 195.

53 *Telling Lives in Science. Essays on Scientific Biography* (ed. M. Shortland and R. Yeo), Cambridge, 1996.

54 A. Desmond and J. Moore, *Darwin*, London, 1991.

55 There is a particularly poignant account of the death of Annie in *ibid.*, 375–87.

56 Cited by T. Hilton, *John Ruskin: The Early Years, 1819–1859*, New Haven, 1985, 167.

57 *Ibid.*, 254.

58 *The Life and Letters of Charles Darwin* (ed. F. Darwin), 3 vols., London, 1887, i, 304.

59 S. Shapin and S. Schaffer, *Leviathan and the Air-Pump: Hobbes, Boyle and the Experimental Life*, Princeton, 1985, 344.

60 For a review of the conceptual resources that the sociologists have provided, see J. V. Golinski, 'The theory of practice and the practice of theory: sociological approaches in the history of science', *Isis*, 81 (1990), 492–505.

61 B. Latour and S. Woolgar, *Laboratory Life: The Social Construction of Scientific Facts*, London, 1979.

62 B. Barnes, *Scientific Knowledge and Sociological Theory*, London, 1974; M. Mulkay, *Science and the Sociology of Knowledge*, London, 1979.

63 An instructive example is provided by Golinski, op. cit. (52), where the efforts of chemists to create an audience for their science is explored with sensitivity.

64 H. M. Collins, *Changing Order: Replication and Induction in Scientific Practice*, London, 1985.

65 S. Shapin, *A Social History of Truth: Civility and Science in Seventeenth-Century England*, Chicago, 1994.

66 G. N. Cantor, *Michael Faraday: Sandemanian and Scientist*, London, 1991, 201–5.

67 *Ibid.*, 295.

68 *Ibid.*

69 F. E. Manuel, *The Religion of Isaac Newton*, Oxford, 1974, 42.

70 I. B. Cohen, 'Three notes on the reception of Darwin's ideas on natural selection (Henry Baker Tristram, Alfred Newton, Samuel Wilberforce)', in *The Darwinian Heritage* (ed. D. Kohn), Princeton, 1985, 589–607.

71 F. M. Turner, 'The Victorian conflict between science and religion: a professional dimension', *Isis*, 69 (1978), 356–76; T. W. Heyck, *The Transformation of Intellectual Life in Victorian England*, London, 1982.

72 This point is forcefully made by C. A. Russell, 'Without a memory', *Science and Christian Belief*, 5 (1993), 2–4.

73 F. Temple, *The Present Relations of Science to Religion: a Sermon Preached on July 1, 1860 before the University of Oxford*, Oxford, 1860.

74 R. Hahn, 'Laplace and the mechanistic universe', in *God and Nature: Historical Essays on the Encounter between Christianity and Science* (ed. D. C. Lindberg and R. L. Numbers), Berkeley, 1986, 256–76.

2

Whose Science? Whose Religion?

The John Templeton Foundation's Science & Religion Program: Up to 100 Awards of $10,000 each to be granted for New or Improved Courses Joining Science & Religion

In these troubled times, when academics spend sleepless nights worrying about cost centres and 'units of resource', prizes of $10,000 are a veritable godsend. As the above advertisement indicates, the Templeton Foundation has offered substantial prizes for courses on science and religion. Winners of these prizes must be the envy of colleagues in other areas, since undergraduate courses on the eighteenth-century novel or on quantum mechanics do not qualify for such large cash bonanzas. Although the Templeton Foundation's munificence is to be welcomed as a way of directing scholarly attention to issues in the science and religion domain, it is clear from the advertisement that the Foundation is not prepared to fund *any* such course. The small print that follows the above caption specifies certain limitations: The course must be academically respectable; a 'balance [must be struck] in the treatment of science and religion' and 'intellectual humility [must be achieved] – stressing optimistic, progressive, exploratory, and non-pejorative attitudes towards both science and religion'. These latter specifications are informed by the views on 'humility theology' previously published by Sir John Templeton.[1]

Some readers will be horrified and others delighted to hear that students at a number of universities, especially in Christian colleges in America, are struggling with such deep problems as the theological implications of modern cosmological theory and the bearing of both science and religion on the question of free will; problems that necessarily require knowledge of a range of disciplines and that also engage the students' personal religious beliefs. With our far more secular and aloof tradition in British universities some of the material offered by previous winners of Templeton awards may seem rather biased in favour of a theistic perspective. Yet one senior British academic has publicly applauded Templeton's initiative, adding, 'Thus an increasing number of scientists and theologians will be taught that there is no conflict between science and religion, when both are properly understood.'[2]

Should outside bodies clearly committed to a theistic perspective (however broad-based) offer such hefty carrots to academics? Is this an unwarranted intrusion of religion into secular academe? Should universities teach courses that (according to the academic quoted above) so manifestly support 'religion'? While not wishing to ignore these important value-laden questions we intend instead to focus on a closely related problem that we regularly encounter as historians teaching in British universities. What should we include in our own undergraduate courses on the history of science and religion? At an early stage in planning such courses a decision has to be made about how broadly to define both science and religion. This decision will, in turn, affect the scope of the science–religion domain. The assertion – quoted above – that 'there is no conflict between science and religion' is unhelpful since it imposes a simple and anachronistic rule on the past. Indeed, as a general claim it is as indefensible as the conflict thesis which we argued, in chapter 1, is an untenable master-narrative. The rider, 'when both [science and religion] are rightly understood', does not resolve the issue but merely raises further problems: Whose understanding of religion? Should we accept the views of foot soldiers attending a recent Christian Coalition meeting in Washington who cheered every speaker who lambasted evolutionary theory?[3] Should we listen instead to the ministers of the Church – and if so, which ministers? (for they don't all speak with one voice). Or should we attend to the Dalai Lama? The situation in science may seem more straightforward, but although there is much that seems settled, it is worth remembering that many areas of profound but honest disagreement exist. The interpretation of quantum theory remains a live issue, with Bohm's hidden-variable version attracting renewed attention. Likewise, at the time of writing, scientists are far from unanimous on the pressing question whether BSE can be transmitted to humans in the form of CJD. Again, Daniel Dennett's recent attempt to 'swat' Steven Jay Gould and all liberal Darwinians reminds us of ongoing controversies over the specific processes responsible for evolutionary change.[4] Indeed, contrary to the conventional emphasis on consensus in science, for some commentators the essence of the scientific lies in its challenge to the received wisdom, so that science becomes, in the late Karl Popper's apt phrase, an 'unended quest'. Although science is, from Popper's standpoint, the most critically tested form of knowledge, it is also always tentative and open to revision.[5]

If we move from the present to times past, the problem of deciding what counts as a proper understanding of science becomes all the more complex. Science offered a very different understanding of the world in 1695, compared with 1795, let alone 1995. Even if we acknowledge what is accepted as science today, we are bound to distort the past if we interpret it through a presentist lens. The past needs to be accorded its own integrity. In this sense, Templeton's requirements of balance and intellectual humility have much to commend them. However, these very values raise some challenging problems for the historian; problems that we shall engage in the present chapter which aims to show that the perceived relation between science and religion depends on how both of these terms are defined, when and by whom.

It is important to stress that the historian is a Jekyll-and-Hyde character, leading a double life. With one foot in the present and one in the past, historians can – and usually do – study movements and views which they do not personally endorse. For example, one does not have to accept the truth of alchemy in order to study its history. Equally, a devout Protestant can make important contributions to the history of Catholicism; an example in our own field being the late Richard S. Westfall who contributed greatly to the study of Galileo and his clerical contemporaries. Indeed, historians must tread carefully when dealing with the history of their own religious denomination. While we cannot suspend our own religious beliefs and our present-day scientific understanding, they may inform but should not confine what we study in the past and how we study it. Hence, to the question Whose science?, one answer is 'not necessarily ours'. The very same response should be given to the question Whose religion?

We shall return to these questions later after examining two specific examples that pose these questions in extreme forms, since they exemplify positions that almost all readers will reject outright. The first case study addresses Auguste Comte's attempt to create a religion based on science; the other is scriptural geology, which sought to create a science based on religion. These two examples make us confront the problems of interpreting both science and religion.

Scientism

Before proceeding we must introduce the term *scientism* which has often been used to describe the extension of science beyond its usual disciplinary boundaries. Scientistic imperialists argue that there is no limit to science and that all aspects of life can, and indeed should, be encompassed. One recurrent claim is that there is no room for Christianity, Judaism, Islam or any other traditional religion that is not based on scientific knowledge. In this sense scientism is profoundly opposed to our conventional understanding of religion. Yet paradoxically scientism also demands the replacement of traditional forms of religion by a science-based philosophy that in effect takes over many of the functions of religion and thus itself becomes a religion, or what the late nineteenth-century chemist Wilhelm Ostwald called an *Ersatzreligion* – a substitute religion. Why then did Ostwald develop his Ersatzreligion? Enthused by the scientifically-successful new field of thermodynamics, he sought to construct a complete world-view using its principles. Having earlier jettisoned the Christianity of his childhood, Ostwald loudly proclaimed that energetics would provide the key to understanding all aspects of life including the laws of sociology, the psychology of the individual and, of course, religion. Interestingly, some vestigial aspects of Christianity remained, although they were attributed with new and, in his opinion, proper scientific significance. Thus he advocated a form of meditative prayer which he considered psychologically efficacious since it enabled individuals to relax and recharge their batteries. He even preached Sunday sermons and retained Christmas as the festival of light. However the lights on the Christmas tree were stripped of their specifically Christian connotations and were instead interpreted physically as an energy source and as a reminder of the winter solstice.[6]

Viewed historically the roots of scientism can be traced to the Enlightenment with its ideology of progress and perfectibility.[7] Yet many versions of scientism have emerged over the last three centuries. Like other anti-religious scientists of our day, Richard Dawkins has adopted a strong form of scientism based on the theory of evolution. Another familiar version assumes that there is a distinctive scientific method which is, moreover, the only legitimate means of gaining knowledge in all domains. For example, dialectical materialism, which Marx proposed as the basic process operating in history, has often been touted as the method governing both science and society, but also a method that undermines traditional religions. It is important to recognise that all forms of scientism demand a realignment of authority; science being accorded absolute authority.

Comte's Religion of Humanity

Although now widely rejected by professional philosophers of science, positivism has a long and honourable history. Put simply, positivism requires that all knowledge is empirical; that is, founded on observation, experience or experiment. While many positivists have deployed their philosophical creed to confute religion, the French Catholic Pierre Duhem can be cited as an important counter-example. Writing at the turn of the century Duhem insisted that science can only deal with constant conjunctions between observed events; the scientist is therefore restricted to mapping correlations but cannot offer a causal account of nature. This limited prescription for science enabled Duhem to retain a separate domain for religious truths, which are not empirical. Science and Catholicism could thus co-exist unhindered.[8] While Duhem deployed a positivist philosophy of science to maintain the integrity of his religion, many other positivists – perhaps the majority – have advocated scientistic imperialism and rejected religious claims as non-empirical and therefore metaphysical and even meaningless. For example, one of the explicit aims of the highly influential Vienna Circle, whose members propounded logical positivism in the 1920s, was the repudiation of 'metaphysics and theology'. Indeed, according to their demarcation criterion, all statements about God have to be rejected as meaningless.[9]

One of the best-known nineteenth-century positivists to adopt an anti-religious stance was the French social philosopher who coined the term *positivism*, Auguste Comte (1798–1857). According to his later reflections on his childhood, he grew up in an 'eminently Catholic and monarchical' bourgeois family that had managed to survive the Revolutionary period with its religious and social values intact. By his mid-teens he had rebelled against this traditional upbringing and had encompassed the Republican cause. He had also repudiated any belief in God and any adherence to Catholicism.[10] In 1817 he began working for the Comte de Saint-Simon whose views on social and religious reform influenced him deeply. However, by the time Comte came to write about the Religion of Humanity in the 1850s he had rejected most of his earlier radical ideas and had aligned himself with a conservative backlash, even publishing in 1855 a work entitled *Appel aux Conservateurs*.

Despite the vicissitudes of his political views the adult Comte was consistent in his opposition to Catholicism, one of his crucial statements on theology being published in the first volume of his *Cours de Philosophie Positive* (1830). This work opens with his famous characterisation of the three historical stages through which each branch of human knowledge must pass: 'the theological, or fictitious; the metaphysical, or abstract; and the scientific, or positive'.[11] He briefly – and arrogantly – characterised the theological stage as the search for essences and for first and final causes. During this stage, phenomena in the natural world are ascribed to the actions of super-natural beings; thus thunder and lightning are due to the activities of the gods, while the attraction of material bodies (*pace* Newton[12]) result from the immediate imposition of God's will. For Comte, theology represented an immature stage through which civilisation had passed on the progressive road to the metaphysical stage and ultimately to positive knowledge.

Although in his earlier *Cours de Philosophie Positive* Comte appears to reject religion as an outmoded world-view, his writings of the 1850s, especially his *Système de Politique Positive*, were centred on constructing what he called the 'Religion of Humanity'. As the name suggests this religion was an Ersatzreligion; a religion to replace traditional religions, especially the Catholicism of Comte's child-hood that he rejected so vehemently. Considered politically, this project appears to have been a conservative reaction to the revol-utionary movements that had inflicted so much disruption across Europe in the late 1840s and which were, in Comte's opinion, responsible for the breakdown of society and for undermining all stabilising institutions. He contended that a return to religion was required in order to bring an end to anarchy in the Western world.[13] Yet he was not advocating Christianity in any form, but rather a new religion. As he frequently emphasised, the main function of religion is to enable people to live together in unity and harmony. This was the ultimate aim of his Religion of Humanity, which would presage the final triumph of science and positivism.

A major root of Comte's programme for a new social order was his positivist philosophy of science with its search for order – the laws of nature – and the rejection of an intervening, capricious God. The Religion of Humanity was Comte's practical prescription for the human condition in a world dominated by science. Through science we can discover the laws governing nature, man and society. As one of his most enthusiastic British disciples explained, he had been attracted to the Religion of Humanity because Comte was 'the one thinker of the modern world professing to offer men a religion – a religion of love, poetry and service – *founded on science*'.[14] It reaf-firmed the Enlightenment ideal of extending rationality and science to encompass the human sciences and thus to create a social environ-ment that united all people and also provided unity between humankind and nature.

One of the key documents for studying Comte's Ersatzreligion is his *Catéchisme Positiviste, ou Sommaire Exposition de la Religion Universelle* (1852; English translation, 1858). This remarkable text contains thirteen instructive conversations between a priest from the Church of Humanity and a woman – as we shall see, gender roles were of great importance for Comte. Through their dialogue the priest introduces the woman to the Positivist Church's beliefs, doctrines and practices and responds sympathetically to her questions. Based on the dialogue format of a traditional Catholic catechism, in which a priest satisfactorily answers the doubts of an aspiring (male) communicant, Comte's dialogue also provides an effective narrative for conveying the basic tenets of his Religion of Humanity and for answering standard objections.

In this and other later writings Comte adopted a sociological perspective. Acknowledging that human nature was not entirely fixed, he insisted that progressive social organisations must take full cognisance of the social and psychological laws governing human action. He particularly emphasised the role of the individual within three types of social organisation – (1) the family, (2) the state and (3) *Humanity*. Describing the function of state government as a 'cohesive force ... at once to combine and to direct',[15] he readily acknowledged that individuals are not all equal. He therefore envisaged the more powerful citizens and families directing the state apparatus for the public good. Each person would have to fulfil his or her own role – no matter how humble or how elevated – within society. Yet he considered that individuals could only live peaceably with one another if they acknowledged their relation to the collective Humanity. By considering the role of the individual within these social groups Comte produced a blueprint for a stable but manifestly hierarchical society.

Comte considered that morality was not only necessary for the smooth-functioning of social organisations but was essential for providing the individual with the psychological comfort necessary to live in a physical universe that science has shown to be impersonal and ultimately meaningless. Because religion had traditionally endowed people's lives with meaning and value, Comte conceived his Religion of Humanity as providing a similar support for citizens of his scientifically-organised society. He therefore prescribed an elaborate set of doctrines and rituals that, he claimed, would psychologically satisfy the individual and unite citizens into a stable society.[16]

In Comte's writings we find many examples of religious language, although necessarily redefined for his own purposes. Thus he stated that the soul is a 'valuable term [to be used] to stand for the whole of our intellectual and moral functions, without involving any allusion to some supposed entity answering to the [same] name'. Likewise when he referred to the 'Great Being' or 'Supreme Being' he was not evoking the God of the Bible but *Humanity*, which he described as 'the prime mover of ... [our] existence, ... [and] the centre of our affections'. Comte's definition of Humanity is surprisingly vague: within this term he included not only everyone alive today but also all past and future generations. Thus the 'Great Being' possesses the attributes of immensity and eternity that are traditionally accorded to God.[17] He could even write in quasi-religious vein: 'We adore her [Humanity], ... in order to serve her better by bettering ourselves.' In short, he substituted his *goddess* Humanity for the Christian God.[18]

Turning to ritual, the Positivist is expected to pray three times each day for a total of approximately two hours. Comte argued that the aim of prayer is 'to give expression to [our] best affections ... [our] fervent wish [being] to become more tender, more reverential, more courageous even'. Through prayer individuals rise above their introverted and selfish states in order to identify themselves with Humanity and its transcendental values. The highest good is necessarily social good. Poetry plays a particularly important role in private prayer: 'Poetry', wrote Comte, 'is the soul of our worship.'[19] While private prayer is of crucial importance for strengthening the moral powers, the intellect is also enhanced through acts of contemplation during prayer sessions. In this scheme prayer is essential for both moral and intellectual improvement.[20]

But worship also possesses a public dimension and here we find Comte adopting and adapting the Catholic sacraments. While some of his nine sacraments possess purely secular and social significance – such as maturity (men aged 42) and retirement (for men aged 63) – others bear a marked resemblance to the Catholic sacraments, but with the traditional meanings interestingly subverted. For example, at 'transformation' – that is, death – the life of the departed is celebrated as 'a just appreciation of the life that is ending'. The priest's role is to visit the remaining members of the family in order to express the sorrow of the whole community; in this way the family and society are united in grief.[21]

Clearly-defined gender roles are much in evidence. For example, in response to the woman's enquiry about her specific office, the priest answers: 'The most important duty of woman is to form and perfect man.'[22] Women, he asserted, should not pursue work outside the home but should devote themselves to serving the family.

Marriage is portrayed as an altruistic ideal with the husband providing financial support and the wife, who possesses no wealth of her own, complementing the husband by taking responsibility for the moral sustenance of the family. It is clear that Comte held women in awe. He considered that women are endowed with naturally superior moral qualities and they therefore personify the noblest endowments of Humanity. Comte even claimed that women would fare far better in the Religion of Humanity than they did under either Catholicism or socialism! Ironically the priest drew on traditional Catholic iconography when he explained that the

L'HUMANITÉ

Personnifiée par CLOTILDE de VAUX
L'enfant adore naïvement l'image d'AUGUSTE
COMTE sur le *Don du cœur*.

(Dernière ébauche du peintre brésilien
Decio Villares)

Figure 8: The traditional image of the Madonna and child as reinterpreted in a late edition of Comte's *Catéchisme Positiviste ou Sommaire Exposition de la Religion Universelle* (Rio de Janeiro, 1957).

'symbol of our Divinity will always be a woman of the age of thirty, with her son in her arms'.[23] In Comte's scheme Humanity was female.

This exemplary role for women is in sharp contrast to Comte's own brief and disastrous marriage to a self-willed prostitute named Caroline Massin, who refused to behave like his ideal woman.[24] Equally important to Comte's biography was his infatuation with the attractive Clotilde de Vaux whom he transformed into his super-woman after her death in 1846 at the early age of thirty. Unlike Caroline, but like his idealisation of Clotilde, women in his exemplary society are loyal to their husbands and preserve social morality and stability. Women, then, become the moral guardians of the family and the three principal female relationships – mother, wife and daughter – are associated respectively with the qualities of veneration, attachment and kindness.[25] In many respects Comte evoked a highly conservative vision of women and of their social roles. However, one aspect of his earlier more liberal views remained when he proposed that women should receive a similar education to men – that is, a scientific education.

One of the most remarkable aspects of the Religion of Humanity was its calendar which was based on the Catholic almanac, but rewritten from a positivist perspective. In rejecting the solar and lunar calendars Comte, like Napoleon, sought to rationalise and impose order on time. He therefore divided the year into thirteen equal months of twenty-eight days. The traditional names for days of the week were retained and Comte insisted that his calendar was more rational than the Gregorian calendar since any date always fell on the same day of the week. One extra day had to be added every year – which was to commemorate the Festival of the Dead, 'happily introduced by Catholicism'.[26] On leap years an additional day was included on which the Festival of Holy Women was celebrated. Each month possessed its proper educational theme – marriage in the second month, women in the tenth month, the priesthood in the eleventh. There were to be festivals of science, art and inventors; of animals, fire, iron and the sun.

The days of the year were also occasions for implementing another part of Comte's grand design. Since the Religion of Humanity required the worshipper to contemplate the lives of those worthy paragons of Humanity who had lived in the past, a notable man (or occasionally woman) was celebrated on each day of the year. Thus the history of Humanity was recapitulated each year starting with the theocratic period – symbolised by Moses – and ending with the modern scientific era represented by the French histologist and

TABLE D.

POSITIVIST CALENDAR,

ADAPTED TO ALL YEARS EQUALLY, OR,

CONCRETE VIEW OF THE PREPARATORY PERIOD OF MAN'S HISTORY,

ESPECIALLY INTENDED FOR THE FINAL PERIOD OF TRANSITION THROUGH WHICH THE WESTERN REPUBLIC HAS TO PASS; THE REPUBLIC WHICH, SINCE CHARLEMAGNE, HAS BEEN FORMED BY THE FREE CORESPO... OF THE FIVE LEADING POPULATIONS, THE FRENCH, ITALIAN, SPANISH, BRITISH, AND GERMAN.

Day	FIRST MONTH — MOSES (The Initial Theocracy)	SECOND MONTH — HOMER (Ancient Poetry)	THIRD MONTH — ARISTOTLE (Ancient Philosophy)	FOURTH MONTH — ARCHIMEDES (Ancient Science)	FIFTH MONTH — CÆSAR (Military Civilisation)	SIXTH MONTH — ST. PAUL (Catholicism)	SEVENTH MONTH — CHARLEMAGNE (Feudal Civilisation)
Mon. 1	Prometheus	Hesiod	Anaximander	Theophrastus	Miltiades	St. Luke	Theodoric the Great
Tue. 2	Hercules	Tyrtæus	Anaximenes	Herophilus	Leonidas	St. Cyprian	Pelayo
Wed. 3	Orpheus	Anacreon	Heraclitus	Erasistratus	Aristides	St. Athanasius	Otho the Great
Thu. 4	Ulysses	Pindar	Anaxagoras	Celsus	Cimon	St. Jerome	St. Henry
Fri. 5	Lycurgus	Sophocles	Democritus	Galen	Xenophon	St. Ambrose	Villars
Sat. 6	Romulus	Theocritus	Herodotus	Avicenna	Phocion	St. Monica	Don John of Austria
Sun. 7	NUMA	ÆSCHYLUS	THALES	HIPPOCRATES	THEMISTOCLES	ST. AUGUSTIN	ALFRED
Mon. 8	Belus	Scopas	Solon	Euclid	Pericles	Constantine	Charles Martel
Tue. 9	Sesostris	Zeuxis	Xenophanes	Aristæus	Philip	Theodosius	The Cid
Wed. 10	Menu	Ictinus	Empedocles	Theodosius of Bithynia	Demosthenes	St. Chrysostom	Richard I
Thu. 11	Cyrus	Praxiteles	Thucydides	Hero	Ptolemy Lagus	St. Pulcheria	Joan of Arc
Fri. 12	Zoroaster	Lysippus	Archytas	Pappus	Philopoemen	St. Genevieve of Paris	Albuquerque
Sat. 13	The Druids	Apelles	Apollonius of Tyana	Diophantus	Polybius	St. Gregory the Great	Bayard
Sun. 14	BOUDDHA	PHIDIAS	PYTHAGORAS	APOLLONIUS	ALEXANDER	HILDEBRAND	GODFREY
Mon. 15	Fo-hi	Æsop	Aristippus	Eudoxus	Junius Brutus	St. Benedict	St. Leo the Great
Tue. 16	Lao-Tseu	Plautus	Antisthenes	Pytheas	Camillus	St. Boniface	Gerbert
Wed. 17	Meng-Tseu	Terence	Zeno	Aristarchus	Fabricius	St. Isidore of Seville	Peter the Hermit
Thu. 18	The Theocrats of Thibet	Phædrus	Cicero	Eratosthenes	Hannibal	Lanfranc	Suger
Fri. 19	The Theocrats of Japan	Juvenal	Pliny the Younger	Ptolemy	Marius	St. Bruno	Alexander III
Sat. 20	Manco-Capac	Lucian	Epictetus	Albategnius	Æmilius Paulus	St. Francis of Assisi	St. Francis of Assisi
Sun. 21	CONFUCIUS	ARISTOPHANES	SOCRATES	HIPPARCHUS	SCIPIO	ST. BERNARD	INNOCENT III.
Mon. 22	Abraham	Ennius	Xenocrates	Varro	Augustus	St. Francis Xavier	St. Clotilde
Tue. 23	Samuel	Lucretius	Philo of Alexandria	Columella	Vespasian	St. Charles Borromeo	St. Bathilde
Wed. 24	Solomon	Horace	St. John the Evangelist	Vitruvius	Hadrian	St. Theresa	St. Stephen of Hungary
Thu. 25	Isaiah	Tibullus	St. Justin	Strabo	Antoninus	St. Vincent de Paul	St. Elisabeth of Hungary
Fri. 26	St. John the Baptist	Ovid	St. Clement of Alexandria	Frontinus	Papinian	Bourdaloue	Blanche of Castille
Sat. 27	Mahomet...	Lucan	Origen	Plutarch	Alexander Severus	William Penn	St. Ferdinand III.
Sun. 28	MAHOMET	VIRGIL	PLATO	PLINY THE ELDER	TRAJAN	BOSSUET	ST. LOUIS

Day	EIGHTH MONTH — DANTE (Modern Epic Poetry)	NINTH MONTH — GUTENBERG (Modern Industry)	TENTH MONTH — SHAKESPEARE (The Modern Drama)	ELEVENTH MONTH — DESCARTES (Modern Philosophy)	TWELFTH MONTH — FREDERIC II (Modern Policy)	THIRTEENTH MONTH — BICHAT (Modern Science)
Mon. 1	The Troubadours	Marco Polo	Lope de Vega	Albertus Magnus	Marie de Molina	Copernicus
Tue. 2	Boccaccio	Jacques Coeur	Moreto	Roger Bacon	Cosmo de Medici the Elder	Kepler
Wed. 3	Rabelais	Vasco da Gama	Rojas	St. Bonaventura	Philippe de Comines	Huyghens
Thu. 4	Cervantes	Napier	Otway	Ramus	Isabella of Castile	James Bernoulli
Fri. 5	La Fontaine	Lacaille	Lessing	Montaigne	Charles V.	Bradley
Sat. 6	De Foe	Cook	Goethe	Campanella	Henry IV.	Volta
Sun. 7	ARIOSTO	COLUMBUS	CALDERON	ST. THOMAS AQUINAS	LOUIS XI.	GALILEO
Mon. 8	Leonardo da Vinci	Benvenuto Cellini	Tirso	Hobbes	Ximenes	Vieta
Tue. 9	Michael Angelo	Amontons	Vondel	Pascal	Barneveldt	Wallis
Wed. 10	Holbein	Harrison	Racine	Locke	Gustavus Adolphus	Clairaut
Thu. 11	Poussin	Dollond	Voltaire	Vauvenargues	De Witt	D'Alembert
Fri. 12	Velasquez	Arkwright	Metastasio	Diderot	Ruyter	Lagrange
Sat. 13	Teniers	Conté	Schiller	Cabanis	William III.	Euler
Sun. 14	RAPHAEL	VAUCANSON	CORNEILLE	LORD BACON	WILLIAM THE SILENT	NEWTON
Mon. 15	Froissart	Stevin	Alarcon	Grotius	Sully	Bergmann
Tue. 16	Camoens	Mariotte	Mme. de Motteville	Fontenelle	Colbert	Priestley
Wed. 17	The Spanish Romancers	Papin	Mme. de Sévigné	Vico	Walpole	Cavendish
Thu. 18	Chateaubriand	Black	Mme. de Staël	Fréret	D'Aranda	Guyton Morveau
Fri. 19	Walter Scott	Jouffroy	Mme. Kirkpatrick	Montesquieu	Turgot	Berthollet
Sat. 20	Manzoni	Dalton	Fielding	Buffon	Campomanes	Berzelius
Sun. 21	TASSO	WATT	MOLIÈRE	LEIBNITZ	RICHELIEU	LAVOISIER
Mon. 22	Petrarch	Bernard de Palissy	Pergolesi	Robertson	Sidney	Harvey
Tue. 23	Thomas à Kempis	Guglielmini	Sacchini	Adam Smith	Franklin	Boerhaave
Wed. 24	Mme. de Lafayette	Duhamel (du Monceau)	Gluck	Kant	Washington	Linnæus
Thu. 25	Mme. de Staël	Saussure	Beethoven	Condorcet	Jefferson	Haller
Fri. 26	Klopstock	Coulomb	Rossini	Joseph de Maistre	Bolivar	Lamarck
Sat. 27	Byron	Carnot	Bellini	Hegel	Francia	Broussais
Sun. 28	MILTON	MONTGOLFIER	MOZART	HUME	CROMWELL	GALL

Complementary Day .... Festival of all THE DEAD.

Additional Day in Leap-years .... Festival of HOLY WOMEN.

The names in italics are those of the men who, in Leap-years, take the place of their principals.

Seventh Edition, Aug. 1855, in Appel aux Conservateurs, p. 118, Paris, Monday, 22 Charlemagne 67 (9 July, 1855).

Figure 9: Auguste Comte's positivist calendar. From Comte, *The Catechism of Positive Religion* (1858).

physician Marie François Xavier Bichat (1771–1802). Comte's calendar is dated 'Paris, Monday, 22 Charlemagne 67 (9 July, 1855)' – that is, the twenty-second day of the seventh month of the 67th year since the fall of the Bastille, which he considered the provisional

THIRTEENTH MONTH.

BICHAT.

MODERN SCIENCE.

Copernicus	*Tycho Brahé.*
Kepler	*Halley.*
Huyghens	*Varignon.*
James Bernouilli	*John Bernouilli.*
Bradley	*Reaumur.*
Volta	*Sauveur.*
GALILEO.	

Vieta	*Harriott.*
Wallis	*Fermat.*
Clairaut	*Poinsot.*
Euler	*Monge.*
D'Alembert	*Daniel Bernouilli.*
Lagrange	*Joseph Fourier.*
NEWTON.	

Bergmann	*Scheele.*
Priestley	*Davy.*
Cavendish.	
Guyton Morveau	*Geoffroy.*
Berthollet.	
Berzelius	*Ritter.*
LAVOISIER.	

Harvey	*Ch. Bell.*
Boërhaave	*Stahl.*
Linnæus	*Bernard de Jussieu.*
Haller	*Vicq-d'Azyr.*
Lamarck	*Blainville.*
Broussais	*Morgagni.*
GALL.	

Figure 10: Detail from Comte's calendar. From Comte, *The Catechism of Positive Religion* (1858).

start of the Positivist era. However, he also claimed that dates should properly be calculated from 1855, which he decreed was the formal start of the Positivist epoch.[27]

Every month is divided into four weeks, each associated with a sub-division of the month and with a leading personage who is commemorated especially on the Sunday of that week. Thus the month of modern science is divided between Galileo and other physical scientists, especially astronomers; Newton and fellow mathe-maticians; Lavoisier and other chemists; Gall and fellow physiologists. Each day of the year is devoted to the commemoration of the noble thoughts and deeds of a particular illustrious person (often with a substitute name for leap-years), while children born on that day would take the pertinent name. Although a few British men and women are memorialised, the list is dominated by the French. Also, perhaps surprisingly, several biblical characters and other reli-gious leaders – including Abraham, Isaiah, Mohammed, and a bevy of saints – found niches in the Positivist calendar, although Jesus is noticeably absent.

Despite his Religion of Humanity being conceived in stark opposi-tion to Catholicism, it is ironic how closely it parallels Catholic practices. As T. H. Huxley perceptively commented in one of his own *Lay Sermons*, 'Comte's ideal … is Catholic organization without Catholic doctrine, or, in other words, Catholicism *minus* Christianity'. Huxley also dismissed Comte's views about scientific method as 'a complete failure'.[28] Many of the other leading scientists of the day likewise remained unimpressed.

However, Comte's writings attracted much attention in both Britain and France. Several of his works were translated into English and made a considerable impact on the intellectual life of the mid-Victorian period. Harriet Martineau, John Stuart Mill, George Eliot, Thomas Hardy and George Henry Lewes were among the leading philosophical and literary figures who took him and his philosophy seriously. Martineau even issued a two-volume highly-edited version of the *Cours* under the title *The Positive Philosophy of Auguste Comte* (1853). Moreover, a relatively small group of his followers openly espoused the Religion of Humanity. The stormy history of this cohort sheds remarkable light on the attraction of Comte's Ersatzreligion and some of the difficulties in implementing it.[29]

Like several of the other main figures in English Positivism its first leader, Richard Congreve, hailed from a strong evangelical back-ground. Having attended Rugby School and Wadham College, Oxford, Congreve took holy orders in 1843 and, after a period teaching at Rugby, returned to Wadham in 1849 as a Fellow and tutor. By then he was already familiar with Positivism and came progressively under Comte's influence. Resigning his Fellowship in 1854 in order to marry, he moved to London and three years later – the year of Comte's death – renounced his orders. By this time he had dedicated himself to the Positivist cause, delivering regular lectures and publishing an English edition of the *Catéchisme Positiviste* in 1858. Nine years later he was one of the co-founders of the London Positivist Society. However, Congreve was not a charismatic leader and his lectures drew few auditors. He was also moody and difficult to work with. One of the ironies of the history of his Church is that far from achieving its ideal of uniting humanity it became a microcosm of schism and dissent.

A major source of disunity was the extent to which the Church should look to Comte and his writings as its final authority. Congreve exhibited this extreme position, asserting that the Church of Humanity must follow Comte's scriptures to the letter and requiring passive obedience from his followers. A hymn, written to commemorate the twenty-fifth anniversary of Comte's death, indicates this orientation:

> We praise thee, Humanity, as for all thy great servants, so more especially on this day devoted to his memory, for thy greatest servant, Auguste Comte, through whose teaching Thou standest revealed to all future generations as the source to man of all good which through long ages of effort and suffering he has attained, and as the power by which throughout the rest of his existence on earth he may increase that good; and we pray that in proof of our gratitude we may become thy more willing and complete servants; that, guided by his teaching and influenced by his example, we may consecrate our lives more wholly to the carrying forward the work for which he lived – the attainment by man of that unity which has been the aspiration of all thy noblest saints, but which he alone has taught us how to reach. In his name, and through him, we praise and magnify thee as the Queen of our devotion, the Lady of our loving service, the one centre of all our being, the one bond of all the ages, the one shelter for all the families of mankind, the one foundation of a truly Catholic Church. To thee be all honour and glory. Amen.[30]

By contrast with Congreve's deification of Comte, his opponents considered that Comte had merely provided the basis for a religion so that individuals were free to develop their own insights in whatever way they chose. Moreover these dissidents eschewed a fixed liturgy and rituals, instead devoting their Sunday services to talk, readings, hymns, music and poetry, all of which were frowned on by Congreve and his followers.

The Positivist movement was not confined to London; branches were established in Birmingham, Leicester and Manchester while Churches of Humanity flourished in Liverpool and Newcastle.[31] Never a large movement in Britain, the Religion of Humanity was in sharp decline by the opening decades of the twentieth century. Yet it provides a particularly instructive example of scientism; for Comte and his followers the Religion of Humanity was scientifically-based and replaced existing forms of religious life.

Scriptural Geology

Our second case-study is of scriptural geology, which has received a harsh press. Like its antagonists in the early nineteenth century and the opponents of Creationism in our own time, some historians have rounded on scriptural geologists as simplistic fundamentalists who defended an untenable and anti-scientific world-view. For example, in his 1951 book entitled *Genesis and Geology* the American historian of science Charles Gillispie chastised these 'men of the lunatic fringe, like Granville Penn, John Faber, Andrew Ure, and George Fairholme, [who] got out their fantastic geologies and natural histories, a literature which enjoyed a surprising vogue, but which is too absurd to disinter'. Despite readily acknowledging the popularity of the genre, Gillispie made no attempt to explain why these books were written and why they commanded a not inconsiderable audience.[32]

To take another, more recent and less biased example, scriptural geologists enter Martin Rudwick's impressive study of the Great Devonian Controversy only as dogmatic irritants opposed to the gentlemanly geologists who were trying to win public support for a secular, scientific geology. Yet in his more recent book on geological illustrations Rudwick has adopted a different approach. Concentrating on the illustrations in Johann Scheuchzer's *Physica Sacra* of 1731 he recognises two important continuities between the much maligned scriptural geologists and the scientific geologists to whom they have so often been opposed. Firstly, they were both concerned with time and sequence: however foreshortened the chronology of the Bible, it postulated a successive series of changes in the world's animal and plant populations, concluding with the creation of man. Much the same sequence was adopted by secular scientists during the nineteenth century to show the progressive changes in flora and fauna. Secondly, many of the pictorial conventions deployed by Scheuchzer and other scriptural geologists were carried over to later illustrations of the geological and organic changes, now seen as natural – rather than supernatural – developments.[33] Thus, in contrast to Gillispie's demonisation of scriptural geology, Rudwick's more recent work indicates a possible means of accommodating it within geological history while (in his earlier book) accepting that rival programmes for pursuing geology remained opposed to one another.

Our principal concern here will be to show that by embracing a non-judgemental attitude we can appreciate scriptural geology as a legitimate subject for historical analysis and as one strategy for unifying science and religion that was widely adopted in the eighteenth and early nineteenth centuries. We shall concentrate on a scriptural geologist named George Fairholme, who published *A General View of the Geology of Scripture* in 1833.[34] The date is significant since the book appeared just when a vocal generation of geologists was striving to make their subject secular and to control the meaning of their science. In one sense his book represents the very antithesis of scientism, since rather than building a world-view on contemporary scientific 'truths' Fairholme was seeking to understand the physical world by using the truths contained in the Bible. Yet such a characterisation of Fairholme's book oversimplifies his argument and does not do justice to its complex mixture of history, biblical exegesis, empirical observation and appeals to the laws of nature.

We are apt to misunderstand Fairholme unless we interpret him primarily as an historian or antiquary. Thus he pursued his enquiry not only into the history of the earth but also devoted his final chapter to the origin of languages and sought to determine the history of the different tribes and races by drawing on Josephus's writings. Moreover, using a familiar biblical chronology he pronounced dates for both the Creation and the Deluge. In pursuing this programme he explicitly adopted 'Mosaical History for my guiding star, to be kept constantly in view throughout my course'.[35] As Nicolaas Rupke noted, scriptural geologists had grown up in the tradition of classical scholarship that prized written texts. Thus, '[q]uestions about the history of the world, its chronology, its periodization, even its major vicissitudes ... were to be answered first and foremost from a study of ... written documents, the most reliable of which was believed to be the Bible'.[36] In a particularly illuminating passage Fairholme described his geology as 'grounded on the Inspired History, and so strongly supported by the evidence of physical facts ... [that] the current of the narrative runs smoothly along, and our minds feel satisfied, and at rest'. Thus he conceived his geology as providing a coherent account of the past that would satisfy the mind and leave it in a state of repose. On this account the truths contained in the Bible meshed smoothly with empirical information from a number of different sources, creating no dissonance to disturb the reader. By contrast, secular geological theories created a confused historical narrative that engendered feelings of 'doubt and uncertainty', leaving the mind in 'a bewildered and uncertain state' because, he claimed, they are 'so repulsive to reason and common sense'.[37]

Throughout his book Fairholme was alert to the threat posed to religion by modern geological theories. Drawing on a long tradition of anti-speculative thought he – like present-day Creationists – charged many of his contemporary geologists with indulging in 'the very excesses of hypothesis'. In place of the geologists' extravagant hypotheses he appealed to authenticated facts as the basis of both history and geology, since only a science founded on facts – including the facts contained in the Bible – would lead to truth and be proof against error. But his opposition to modern geological theories stemmed not only from their shaky foundations but also from their untenable moral implications. Thus he argued that the 'great end of the study of geology ought to be a *moral*, rather than a *scientific* one' and he conceived that the proper 'coalition ... between *science* and *religion*, will bid defiance to the utmost efforts of Infidelity and Scepticism'.[38] Fairholme felt particularly obliged to respond to Charles Lyell's recently-published *Principles of Geology* and particularly Lyell's rejection of the Deluge as a major agent in the earth's history.[39] The unlimited time-scale demanded by Lyell was not only preposterous but was based on a mistakenly low estimate for the quantity of mud eroded each day by the Ganges. If the empirically correct figures were adopted, claimed Fairholme, then a much shorter time-scale would suffice and Lyell's theory would be rendered false. This move legitimated a geological time-scale of a few thousand years which cohered with his understanding of Mosaic narrative.[40]

Creationists have disagreed over whether the 'days' of Creation should be interpreted literally or as extended epochs – thus lengthening the pre-Adamic period considerably.[41] Fairholme adopted the former position and insisted that God had created the world in six days, each of twenty-four hours duration. Indeed, the Creation was a specific divine act that had occurred in the past and to which a precise date could be assigned – 4004 BC, in accordance with the biblical chronology devised by Archbishop Ussher in the seventeenth century. Likewise the Deluge was a real, well-authenticated historical event; its commencement being dated to 2348 BC. Moreover, the Deluge, which wrought havoc across the whole earth, occupied a definite timespan – one year and ten days according to Fairholme. Thus the key events in the history of the world could be uniquely located on a chronological chart, just like the annals of Noah's family or the descendants of the House of Stuart.

Despite his historical and antiquarian orientation, Fairholme shared a surprising amount with contemporary secular geologists, for although the Creation and the Deluge were manifestly miraculous events that transcend science, he insisted that throughout the remainder of its history the earth was shaped by natural causes. While he was careful to stress that such causes were, by themselves, inadequate to account for all geological evidence, he allowed the same laws of nature to operate in both the ante-diluvial and post-diluvial periods. Like most contemporaries – even those geologists he most opposed – he readily acknowledged the law-likeness of nature. However, he gave this familiar dictum a theological twist by claiming that 'by the laws to which all things have been submitted by the Almighty, (to which we generally give the unmeaning name of the *laws of nature*), matter is constantly assuming a different form'. He also insisted that the term 'laws of nature' was a malapropism since these laws are really the laws of God; that is, laws that God framed and imposed on matter.[42]

Turning to geology, he claimed that the primary rocks were forged at the Creation, whereas the secondary formations were the result of law-like changes subsequently affecting the material comprising these primary rocks. One implication of this distinction was that only secondary rocks can contain fossil remains; indeed, he used the presence of fossils to help identify secondary formations. Most plants were likewise to be found growing on secondary formations. Yet to explain the existence of plants growing in regions comprising primary rocks, Fairholme was forced to postulate that primitive soil had been deposited at the Creation. Throughout its history the earth had been subject to the law of gravity and the laws affecting both the air and the seas. It is clear from this discussion that he was familiar with some of Newton's views, even citing extensive passages from David Brewster's *Life of Newton* on the shape of the earth and the action of tides.[43] In accepting the operation of physical and chemical laws Fairholme incorporated into his Mosaic geology one of the basic principles of contemporary science.

But the common ground does not end there. Fairholme emphasised the role of facts – because facts firmly grounded science on the bedrock of truth. The facts, as he constituted them, included information gleaned from the Bible but also empirical evidence. Much of his book is filled with descriptions of observations made by himself and by others. For example, he described in some detail the stratig-raphy displayed by a ridge in the Jura mountains, the geology of St Michael's cave in Gibraltar (quoting from a seaman who visited the Island in 1823–4), the plains of South America (published by Humboldt), the fossilised human bones from Kostritz in Germany (as described by Schlotheim in 1820), and the bones of hyenas discovered at Kirkdale in Yorkshire by the Oxford geologist William Buckland. The book also contains two plates – a geological cross-section of the chalk basin at Sandwich in Kent and a fossil tree discovered at Craigleith quarry near Edinburgh. Add to this his claim to have undertaken extensive geological fieldwork and we begin to appreciate that, like his opponents, Fairholme insisted on the importance of empirical observations in geology.

One interesting facet of Fairholme's (admittedly restricted) empiricism concerns his positioning of the reader. In contrast to the impersonal style adopted by many of his opponents, he sought to make his narrative coherent and psychologically acceptable by inviting the reader to witness events in the past. For example, when discussing the Deluge he wrote: 'Let us imagine to ourselves, the whole vegetable kingdom of the earth deposited at various depths'. Again, 'What a scene now presents itself to the mind's eye! for no human eye could look upon it.'[44] In these and similar passages Fairholme sought to present to the mind's eye scenes derived from his biblically-based history of the earth. Although such scenes could not have been witnessed by any human observer he portrayed them as real and solid. Thus Fairholme offered not only authenticated facts from the Bible and from human observation but also a series of historical tableaux – as if the reader were a visitor to a museum displaying models of the earth and its inhabitants at different times. By contrast, he claimed that his opponents dealt in hypotheses that were both fanciful and erroneous.

In reacting against Gillispie and others who have simply dismissed scriptural geology as ludicrously unscientific, we have emphasised that like the gentlemanly geologists who controlled the Geological Society, Fairholme incorporated natural laws into his science and accepted empirical evidence as crucially important. Yet we must also appreciate the differences. Most importantly, the new-style geologists would not accept all of Fairholme's sources; they dispensed not only with the Mosaic account but also with citations from ancient histo-rians such as Pliny and Josephus. They would not countenance a geology anchored in passages from the Bible, nor would they have endorsed his textual analysis of a passage from the gospels, which forms part of his chapter entitled 'On the situation of paradise'. His chapter 'On the origin of language' also fell far outside their new programme for geology.

As historians have often noted, the 1830s was a decade of radical change not only in society but also in conceptions of science. Fairholme's topics and sources were no longer deemed legitimate by a new breed of geologist that had colonised positions of power and came to control the history of geology – thus further marginalising most scriptural geologists. Adam Sedgwick was doubtless speaking for an influential constituency when, in his Presidential Address before the Geological Society in 1830, he lashed at Andrew Ure's scriptural geology as confused and worthless: Ure's book, he insisted, was neither a contribution to geology nor a legitimate use of Scripture.[45] Despite the numerous works on scriptural geology that were published in the 1830s and ensuing decades, the tradition was becoming increasingly marginal to mainstream science. This is apparent from the list of 534 subscribers prefacing Samuel Kinns's *Moses and Geology* (1882). Of these, 79 (15%) were in holy orders, of whom only two were listed as members of a national scientific society. But perhaps the most telling statistic is that only three Fellows of the Royal Society of London appeared on Kinns's list. By the time Kinns's book appeared, scriptural geology had become marginalised by the scientific community, although it still had a substantial following among religious non-scientists. Queen Victoria graciously accepted a copy from Lord Shaftesbury. Unfortunately her views on the book are not recorded.[46]

Whose Science?

With these case-studies under our belts let us return to the question, Whose science? Defining science is a notoriously difficult exercise. Some have tried to characterise it in terms of its theories, others by its methods, others still by its social organisation. Yet these attempts to define the essence of science are rarely of much assistance when we discuss the past. Moreover, the map of science has changed considerably. For example, Biology (as a discipline) originated early in the nineteenth century, Psychology dates from late in that century, and Physics has been variously dated from the early seventeenth to the late nineteenth centuries. The historian must also be prepared to depart from currently-accepted notions of science and engage those sciences and theories that do not feature in the modern pantheon, such as alchemy, scriptural geology, phlogistic chemistry and phrenology. One of the challenges facing the historian is to study such subjects in a non-anachronistic manner, combining understanding and distance in appropriate measures.

The historical study of science and religion must encompass positions and views that would be entertained by few respectable scientists today – such as scriptural geology and Comte's Religion of Humanity. A further reason why such cases deserve study is because their questionable scientific status has been the subject of long-running controversies that shed light on changing conceptions of science. Thus we would argue that scriptural geology deserves inclusion in the historical study of science and religion since it represents a significant (if ultimately unsuccessful) attempt to construct a synthesis of science and religion (although both selectively defined). Even Charles Gillispie recognised the contemporary popularity of scriptural geology texts, but – owing to his deep aversion to their project – he did not pursue this topic.

Whose Religion?

Many of the issues encountered in defining science recur when we try to define religion. While some writers have emphasised its intellectual content by concentrating on theology, others have sought to interpret it socially and culturally. An example of the latter is Durkheim's claim that a religion is 'a unified system of beliefs and practices relative to sacred things'. However, in contrast to most attempts to characterise science, religion is often conceived as possessing substantial individualistic, spiritual and transcendental dimensions. Thus in his celebrated analysis of personal religious experience an earlier Gifford Lecturer, William James, emphasised 'the feelings, acts and experiences of individual men in their solitude, so far as they apprehend themselves to stand in relation to whatever they may consider the divine'.[47] There is no consensus over the definition of religion. Moreover, as historians of religion have repeatedly stressed, definitions of religion have changed considerably over time. Thus what passes as religion depends on the historical context: for example, under the Roman Empire Christians were denominated 'atheists' since they did not accept the dominant belief system. The situation is further complicated if we move outside the Judeo-Christian tradition and confront non-Western cultures which often lack a word to describe what we understand by religion. That there is no universally-accepted definition of religion is all too apparent.[48]

One way of moving beyond this impasse is to try to specify the nature of religion by characterising its recurring elements. For example, Eric Sharpe has postulated four 'modes' of religion:

1. The existential mode which emphasises the experience and faith of the individual;
2. The intellectual, being principally the belief system or theology;
3. The institutional; and
4. The ethical, which is concerned with conduct.[49]

Such a functionalist approach is helpful in providing a check-list of parameters that the historian needs to address. Moreover, it is clear that the prominence given to each of these four 'modes' differs considerably from one case to the next. Thus, to draw on the preceding examples, the institutional dimension of Christianity was largely irrelevant for Fairholme while it was crucially important in Comte's Religion of Humanity (some would say too important). We should also be sensitive to the diversity of religions and not be too hasty to exclude or belittle unusual or problematic cases. This is particularly important when moving outside the Judeo-Christian tradition. Indeed, one of the great challenges facing not only historians but also scientists and religious scholars is to extend the study of science and religion to include the many non-Western religions, especially Islam.

Cultural Relativism

Our problem of specifying the nature of both science and religion takes on a further level of complexity when viewed through a cultural lens. Some years ago the social anthropologist Robin Horton sought to capture both the similarities and the differences between two ways of understanding the world – first, the Western scientific approach and, second, the world-view accepted by traditional African communities.[50] He argued that we fail to make much headway if we dismiss African belief systems as mystical or non-empirical (in contrast with the assumption that science is manifestly rational and empirical). Instead he stressed that, as with modern science, African cosmologies seek to bring order to the world: 'Like atoms, molecules, and waves ... the[ir] gods serve to introduce unity into diversity, simplicity into complexity, order into disorder, regularity into anomaly'. In this respect, at least, Western science and African cosmology are similar.

Despite finding such impressive functional similarities, Horton emphasised one fundamental difference. African belief systems are 'closed', in the sense that their theories are unable to change in response to empirical anomalies. Thus if the remedy prescribed by a diviner fails to work, the patient will conclude that the diviner is incompetent but will not cast doubt on the dominant medical theory. Although some philosophers and sociologists have attributed similar protective strategies to Western science, Horton views science as far more open to revision in the light of disconfirming empirical evidence than its African counterpart.

But Horton also emphasised another crucial issue. If we in the West usually experience no difficulty in drawing a sharp divide between science and religion, this is not so for the African. Our terminology breaks down if we try to decide whether an African diviner diagnosing a patient and offering a medical cure falls on the 'science' or the 'religion' side of the divide. Indeed, for Horton, this difficulty results from viewing their 'closed' system from the perspective of our 'open' one. At the outset we must acknowledge that the diviner's activity is not adequately captured by our conventional terminology. Thus the diviner would surely look at us uncomprehendingly if we were to ask him whether his science is in harmony or in conflict with his religion. From this other-cultural perspective both Western science and Western religion appear strangely parochial. Yet, it may be objected, this line of argument possesses limited applicability in our own culture because of the way we conventionally contrast science with religion. But, if we look closely, and particularly at the past, we shall also find many instances where religion and science cannot be so easily distinguished from one another – scriptural geology being one such case. Indeed, one of the enduring legacies of the conflict thesis is that we have continually to remind ourselves and our students that this is not the natural or necessarily valid way of conceptualising the relation between science and religion. Moreover, the very term 'the relation between' implicitly demarcates science from religion. Linguistic conventions seem to impose unreasonable restrictions on what we say, write and, perhaps, think.[51]

In introducing this anthropological perspective we also wish to emphasise that Western and Judeo-Christian notions of both science and religion become highly problematic when applied outside familiar territory. Recognising the cultural scope of our subject should make us appreciate this further problem in entering the science–religion domain, not least because the past often needs to be treated like another country, if not another culture.

Positioning the Historian

That both science and religion are susceptible to a wide range of definitions has direct implications for the historian. Firstly, in the light of this diversity there is unlikely to be any canonical thesis – any master-narrative – interrelating science and religion. The widely discussed theses of conflict, harmony, independence, dialogue and integration possess a high degree of relativism depending on how an individual conceives both science and religion. Thus for Fairholme – as for the senior academic cited earlier – science and religion have to be wedded into a unity; whereas in the 1830s the gentlemanly geologists in London sought to dissociate geology from the Genesis narrative. While one sought harmony, his opponents sought independence.

Secondly, the historian must decide which religion or religions to include in undergraduate courses on the history of science and religion. There is likely to be little disagreement over the inclusion of the main confessional traditions within Christianity, but what about the minority evangelical sects often regarded with suspicion by outsiders? What about Judaism and Islam? (In many Islamic countries the current engagement with science and technology is a matter of pressing concern and a source of political and religious controversy.) Should our courses include anti-religions or substitute religions like Comte's Religion of Humanity? Of the Templeton prizewinning courses to date, few appear to have stepped outside Christianity or included the many individuals and movements that have made extensive and often effective use of science to challenge traditional religious authority. Yet a rounded understanding of the subject surely demands the inclusion of these topics.

Whatever their intrinsic fascination to the historian, there are other, broader reasons why both scriptural geology and Comte's Religion of Humanity have legitimate places in the historical study of science and religion. Both of these cases exemplify more general and recurrent forms of engagement between science and religion. As indicated in chapter 1, one of the values of the historical approach is to pursue perspectives through which to understand contemporary positions and controversies in the science–religion domain. Thus Comte's Religion of Humanity is not *sui generis* but provides an instance of scientism, which is a major and recurrent theme connecting Comte with Marxism, certain forms of humanism and Richard Dawkins' polemics. To appreciate the full richness of the past, the historian should be prepared to engage such topics and not be constricted by whatever passes today as mainstream theology. One of the obvious yet crucial features of history is that it engages people who are not ourselves and periods that are not our own.

Finally, we return to the problems raised earlier concerning the positions that historians of science and religion can adopt towards their material – the historian's position being particularly relevant to planning courses for students. Two familiar stances are outlined below and then an alternative is sketched.

History has often been used to bolster partisan religious positions and many of the scholars working in the science–religion area have written histories that promote their own religious beliefs and affiliations. Thus much recent scholarship – some of which achieves a very high standard – has been written by committed Christians who have sought to show that there is no essential conflict between science and religion. They find no shortage of scientists in the past who maintained harmony between their scientific and their religious views: the cases of Newton, Priestley and Faraday have proved particularly serviceable. But, one might object, there is surely a danger of bias in accentuating examples of manifest harmony while ignoring cases that don't fit this scenario.

A more specific example is the impressive scholarship of the late Reijer Hooykaas who argued that biblical theology, especially Reformed theology, was the crucial factor in transforming Greek science into modern science. In one of his books he put the matter rather more metaphorically: 'whereas the bodily ingredients of science may have been Greek, its vitamins and hormones were biblical'. In identifying as pro-science such Calvinist themes as the glorification of God and His works, Hooykaas sought not only to rebut the conflict thesis but also to explain the relatively poor showing of Catholics in early modern science when compared with Protestants. Reading his work one is left in no doubt where his sympathies lay; indeed, there was no shortage of hormones or vitamins in his life since he was, he confessed, 'an old-fashioned Calvinist'.[52] Yet Hooykaas's thesis for the superiority of Protestantism over Catholicism in the promotion of the sciences is neither manifestly true nor so readily substantiated by the evidence.[53]

Turning to the other extreme, we find Adrian Desmond's recently-published biography of T. H. Huxley with the sub-title *The Devil's Disciple*. That Desmond chose to write on Huxley and that two of his previous books likewise centred on scientists' opposition to Christian authority doubtless reflects his personal views. Desmond clearly sides with the agnostic Huxley in such passages as the following:

> [Huxley] was undercutting the spiritual sanction of a rival profession, reforming God's rotten-borough. *Religion* was not the problem: 'My screed was meant as a protest against Theology & Parsondom ... both of which are in my mind the natural & irreconcilable enemies of Science. Few see it but I believe we are on the Eve of a new Reformation and if I have a wish to live thirty years, it is that I may see the foot of Science on the necks of her [ecclesiastical] Enemies.'

Here we have not only an arresting statement by Huxley of the conflict between science and 'Theology & Parsondom' but also its deployment in an historical narrative that reiterates and supports Huxley's position.[54]

These examples indicate that while some historians use their history to accentuate harmony others revel in earlier conflicts between science and religion. Although both approaches are manifestly partisan, we must be clear that to label history as partisan does not necessarily condemn it as bad history. Indeed, much excellent scholarship has been written from sectarian positions. However, partisan history from whichever camp tends to downplay or distort opposing positions. Thus although Desmond's book has many strengths, appreciation of the arguments of Huxley's critics – such as Bishop Samuel Wilberforce or the Catholic St George Mivart – is not one of them. Yet as historians we do not have to align ourselves either with Desmond's atheism or with Hooykaas's Calvinism. There are many other positions that can be occupied in science–religion space.

A third possibility is to 'stand far enough back' so that one may appreciate the arguments of the protagonists and the contexts in which they operated. To help characterise this third position we shall evoke the writings of the lad from Kirkcaldy who became both a student and a professor at Glasgow University. Adam Smith postulated the 'impartial observer' – the voice that dwells within every breast, the inner person who continually judges our conduct. For Smith those people who heed this 'impartial observer' live a wise, just and balanced existence, while those who do not are tossed by the storms of life.[55] We wish to borrow (and somewhat modify) Smith's 'impartial observer' in order to develop this third position. Our impartial observer would insist that historians should use the following methodological rule: they should strive not to be partisan but instead should seek to understand all the protagonists and the historical nexus in which they operated. This does not strip us of our own personal views on either science or religion; indeed such a demand would be impossible. Historians are certainly not objective

– for to be objective would, as it were, remove them altogether from the historical plane. Yet, like well-trained mediators or marriage guidance counsellors, they can achieve a degree of impartiality by consciously refusing to be aligned with any one party or protagonist. By not taking sides historians are better placed to appreciate the range of historical protagonists – to understand not only Galileo but also Bellarmine; not only Huxley but also Wilberforce. It might be argued that in this sense the third position possesses some advantage over the other two. Moreover, from this standpoint historians should be able to appreciate such 'monsters' as the scriptural geologists and those who advocated the Religion of Humanity.

But there is a price to be paid for adopting this liberal, irenic position. While many who adopt the other two positions espouse master-narratives that specify the nature of both science and religion as well as their interaction, the third option remains highly suspicious of such simplistic solutions. Instead, from this third perspective history becomes more complex and unruly; but, we would insist, also more exciting! Instead of imposing on the past the conflict thesis or any of its alternatives the historian will attempt to capture the richness and diversity of science–religion relations throughout history. The position we have been advocating leads to an open and challenging view of history that can – and should – inform contemporary debates on science and religion.

NOTES

1 J. M. Templeton, *The Humble Approach: Scientists Discover God*, revised edn., New York, 1995.

2 C. Humphreys, 'The science–faith debate: Important new developments', *Science and Christian Belief*, 7 (1995), 2. Emphasis added.

3 *Independent on Sunday*, 15 October 1995, 5.

4 D. Dennett, *Darwin's Dangerous Idea: Evolution and the Meanings of Life*, London, 1995.

5 K. Popper, *Conjectures and Refutations. The Growth of Scientific Knowledge*, London, 1963.

6 C. Hakfoort, 'Science deified: Wilhelm Ostwald's energeticist world-view and the history of scientism', *Annals of Science*, 49 (1992), 525–44.

7 J. Passmore, *The Perfectibility of Man*, London, 1970.

8 R. N. D. Martin, *Pierre Duhem: Philosophy and History in the Work of a Believing Physicist*, La Salle, 1991.

9 H. Hahn, O. Neurath and R. Carnap, *Wissenschaftliche Weltauffassung: Der Wiener Kreis*, Vienna, 1929.

10 M. Pickering, *Auguste Comte. An Intellectual Biography, Volume 1*, Cambridge, 1993, 16.

11 *Auguste Comte and Positivism: The Essential Writings* (ed. G. Lenzer), Chicago, 1983, 71.

12 The claim that gravity is the direct result of God's will has often been attributed to Newton. Although he certainly entertained this view on a number of occasions, the issue turns out to be far more complex. In the 'General Scholium' added to the 1713 edition of the *Principia* he speculated that gravity might instead be produced by 'a certain most subtle spirit'. His contemporary comments on electrical phenomena indicate that he envisaged a highly-active 'electric spirit' fulfilling this role. However, in later editions of the *Opticks* he sought to explain gravity by the action of an ubiquitous ether composed of very small particles that repel both matter particles and other ether particles. In hypothesising both the 'electric spirit' and the ubiquitous ether Newton sought causes of gravity that did not posit God's immediate action. See R. S. Westfall, *Force in Newton's Physics*, London and New York, 1971; E. McMullin, *Newton on Matter and Activity*, Notre Dame, 1978.

13 A. Comte, *The Catechism of Positive Religion*, London, 1858, 71.

14 M. Quin, *Memoirs of a Positivist*, London, 1924, 41; Quoted in S. Budd, *Varieties of Unbelief: Atheists and Agnostics in English Society 1850–1960*, London, 1977, 194. Emphasis added.

15 Lenzer, op. cit. (11), 430; from *Système de Politique Positive* (1851–4).

16 T. R. Wright, *The Religion of Humanity: the Impact of Comtean Positivism on Victorian Britain*, Cambridge, 1986.

17 Comte, op. cit. (13), 63–4.

18 *Ibid.*, 87 and 315.

19 *Ibid.*, 110.

20 *Ibid.*, 106.

21 *Ibid.*, 135.

22 *Ibid.*, 137.

23 *Ibid.*, 142.

24 Pickering, op. cit. (10), 315–26.

25 Comte, op. cit. (13), 121.

26 *Ibid.*, 158.

27 Lenzer, op. cit. (11), 467–8.

28 T. H. Huxley, 'The scientific aspects of positivism' in *Lay Sermons, Addresses, and Reviews*, London, 1870, 133.

29 Wright, op. cit. (16).

30 R. Congreve, *Essays Political, Social, and Religious*, 3 vols., London, 1874–1900, ii, 721.

31 Wright, op. cit. (16), 253.

32 C. C. Gillispie, *Genesis and Geology: the Impact of Scientific Discoveries upon Religious Beliefs in the Decades before Darwin*, New York, 1959, 152. Despite a degree of ambiguity in the book's main title, Gillispie charts the rise and impact of uniformitarian geology, concentrating on the views of Charles Lyell. Cf. response (to 1951 edition) by M. Millhauser, 'The scriptural geologists: An episode in the history of opinion', *Osiris*, 11 (1954), 65–86. Also relevant is K. B. Collier, *Cosmogonies of our Fathers: Some Theories of the*

Seventeenth and Eighteenth Centuries, New York, 1934. Nineteenth-century scriptural geologists are not cited in W. Sarjeant's massively detailed *Geologists and the History of Geology: An International Bibliography from the Origins to 1978*, 5 vols., London and Basingstoke, 1980.

33 M. J. S. Rudwick, *The Great Devonian Controversy: The Shaping of Scientific Knowledge among Gentlemanly Specialists*, Chicago, 1985, 43; *Idem.*, *Scenes from Deep Time: Early Pictorial Representations of the Prehistoric World*, Chicago, 1992.

34 G. Fairholme, *A General View of the Geology of Scripture, in which the Unerring Truth of the Inspired Narrative of the Early Events in the World is Exhibited, and Distinctly Proved, by the Corroborative Testimony of Physical Facts, on every Part of the Earth's Surface*, London, 1833. This work also went through two American editions. Fairholme also published a *New and Conclusive Physical Demonstration both of the Fact and the Period of the Mosaic Deluge*, London, 1837.

35 *Ibid.*, 470 and xii.

36 N. A. Rupke, *The Great Chain of History: William Buckland and the English School of Geology (1814–1849)*, Oxford, 1983, 42–50.

37 Fairholme, op. cit. (34), 324 and 2.

38 *Ibid.*, 28–9.

39 C. Lyell, *Principles of Geology, being an Attempt to Explain the former Changes of the Earth's Surface, by Reference to Causes now in Operation*, 3 vols., London, 1830–3.

40 Fairholme, op. cit. (34), 30–4 and 107–8.

41 Ronald L. Numbers, *The Creationists. The Evolution of Scientific Creationism*, Berkeley and Los Angeles, 1992.

42 Fairholme, op. cit. (34), 81–2 and 53.

43 *Ibid.*, 45–9 and 94–6.

44 *Ibid.*, 160 and 157. See also 118, 232, 259 and 285.

45 A. Sedgwick, 'Presidential address to the Geological Society [1830]', *Proceedings of the Geological Society of London*, 1 (1826–33), 187–212. The book criticised by Sedgwick was Andrew Ure's *A New System of Geology, in which the Great Revolutions of the Earth and Animated Nature are reconciled at once to Modern Science and Sacred History*, London, 1829. Unlike Fairholme, Ure's status in the scientific community did not depend solely on his writings on scriptural geology. He had lectured extensively to artisans at the Andersonian Institution in Glasgow and written on the application of science to industry. He later became a consulting chemist in London.

46 S. Kinns, *Moses and Geology, or the Harmony of the Bible with Science*, London, 1882, vii–xiii. James Moore also uses Kinns's book as a resource – see 'Geologists and interpreters of Genesis in the Nineteenth Century' in *God and Nature. Historical Essays on the Encounter between Christianity and Science* (ed. D. C. Lindberg and R. L. Numbers), Berkeley and Los Angeles, 1986, 322–50.

47 W. James, *The Varieties of Religious Experience* [1902], Harmondsworth, 1985, 31. Italicised in original.

48 E. J. Sharpe, *Understanding Religion*, London, 1983, 33–48. We should also not ignore the problems of contrasting religion with irreligion – see C. Campbell, *Towards a Sociology of Irreligion*, London, 1971.

49 Sharpe, op. cit. (48), 91–107.

50 R. Horton, 'African traditional thought and western science', *Africa*, 37 (1967), 50–71 and 155–87.

51 J. Moore, 'Speaking of "Science and Religion"—then and now', *History of Science*, 30 (1992), 311–23.

52 R. Hooykaas, *Religion and the Rise of Modern Science*, Edinburgh, 1972, esp. 162; O. R. Barclay, 'Obituary: Professor Reijer Hooykaas', *Science and Christian Belief*, 6 (1994), 129–32.

53 J. H. Brooke, *Science and Religion: Some Historical Perspectives*, Cambridge, 1991, 82–116.

54 A. Desmond, *Huxley: the Devil's Disciple*, London, 1994, 253. The passage in quotation marks is from a letter by Huxley to Frederick Dyster, 30 January 1859. See also Desmond, *The Politics of Evolution: Morphology, Medicine and Reform in Radical London*, Chicago, 1989; A. Desmond and J. Moore, *Darwin*, London, 1991. In the preface to his *Huxley* (xv, also 385) Desmond complains that in his earlier book (*The Post-Darwinian Controversies: A Study of the Protestant Struggle to Come to Terms with Darwin in Great Britain and America 1870–1900*, Cambridge, 1979) Moore sought to harmonise science and religion. Dismissing this book as a product of the Anti-Vietnam War Movement, Desmond championed one of Moore's later articles ('Theodicy and Society: The Crisis of the Intelligentsia' in *Victorian Faith in Crisis. Essays on Continuity and Change in Nineteenth-Century Religious Belief* (ed. R. J. Helmstadter and B. Lightman), Basingstoke, 1990, 153–86) in which he adopted 'a gutsier political analysis' of the Victorian crisis of faith.

55 A. Smith, *Theory of Moral Sentiments* [1759], Indianapolis, 1976, 71, 161–2, 211, 228, 147–9, 352, 371 and 422.

Section II: *Reconstructing History*

3
Against the Self-Images of the New Age

History, it is often claimed, enables us to understand the present. In constructing our position in society, in religion, in the family, as well as our manners and social norms, we turn to history, real or imagined. Likewise, every politician knows how to mobilise the past for political ends; how to appeal to the collective consciousness of a group by evoking its glorious history and the ignominious deeds of its enemies. Although it is customary to emphasise the dissimilarities between science and politics, they both make extensive, although different, use of history. In contrast to politics and many other domains, science is usually portrayed as progressive and the past is therefore often treated as irrelevant – or, at best, subservient – to the present. Yet history does play a major (although often implicit) role in science precisely because the all-important notion of progress is predicated on a posited relation between past, present and future. Thus when scientists celebrate a hero – such as Newton or Darwin – they utilise historical narratives to describe how the 'great man' dispelled the clouds of error and superstition. Despite some noteworthy exceptions, such as Stephen Jay Gould, most scientists who construct these progressivist narratives ignore the work of historians of science who, over the last thirty years, have laboured to show the inadequacy of these accounts and have developed alternative historiographical perspectives that grant greater integrity to the past.

Although possessing privileged access to the past, the historian must also acknowledge a deep sense of humility since the past is elusive and its quest more often ends in questions and uncertainties than in triumph. By contrast there are no questions and uncertainties in the writings of those scientists who look upon the history of science as an unproblematic record of the success and progress of science. Consider, for example, the physicist Paul Davies who has written several best-selling panegyrics on science. In some of his earlier books Davies portrays the period prior to the seventeenth century as dominated by hopelessly primitive and animistic beliefs about the physical world. The (supposed) intellectual and social bankruptcy of religion looms large in these books since Davies considers that progress was inhibited by the intervention of corrupt religious authorities that controlled people's lives. However, with the rise of the new science in the seventeenth century salvation was at hand. Science liberated humanity from its naive, degenerate state. Moreover, the beacon of science, and particularly modern theories in physics and cosmology, provided a fresh understanding of the mysterious forces in the universe. Yet Davies displays some ambivalence towards the new science of the seventeenth century; not only does he champion the rise of classical physics as responsible for the new-found rationality and progress but he also criticises it for imposing a sterile, mechanistic view of the universe. Finally, in his account of the twentieth century, Davies identifies a second scientific revolution with the emergence of a beautiful new paradigm that not only transcends the old mechanistic picture but also provides humankind with an understanding of the reality that must replace traditional religions.[1] Although Davies postulates two revolutions he still adheres to the traditional mythology in which rational science displaces dogma – especially religious dogma – and error. Thus science comes to play an apocalyptic role, finally revealing the truth after many centuries of ignorance and superstition. However, to the historian, Davies's account smacks of crude pro-science propaganda and of a marked disinclination to reflect on the past.

Paradoxically, many critics of science, such as the journalist Bryan Appleyard, adopt strikingly similar historical accounts by emphasising that a major cultural shift occurred with the rise of science in the seventeenth century. Yet, unlike Davies, they often portray the earlier period as idyllic and, instead of extolling the virtues of science, they view science as alienating, spiritually corrosive and as responsible for undermining the previously-existing happy certainties. In his *Science and the Soul of Modern Man* (1993) Appleyard argues that from its inception in the seventeenth century science has grown ever more powerful and has increasingly dominated every aspect of life. It has repeatedly challenged and destroyed traditional religious beliefs and has recently spawned a degenerate and scientised mutant, which he labels 'liberal theology'.[2] The very aspects of science that Davies champions are deplored by Appleyard. One writer sees progress where the other sees regress.

The preceding examples illustrate how master-narratives have been employed for apologetic purposes. Both writers tell simple, straightforward and strikingly similar stories about how science arose and challenged the prevailing cultural norms. Although outwardly they offer contrasting visions of science, they are principally concerned with values, the imperialism of science, and the relation between past and present. They are also very persuasive stories deploying easily-recognisable images of science and (in the case of Davies's book) introducing the reader to the fascinating world of modern physics.

Are these accounts acceptable as history? Do the narratives offered to the wider public by Davies and Appleyard accord with recent work in the History of Science? Historians of science have a duty to analyse such accounts of the past and to identify any defects, since misunderstanding the past is likely to result in misconstruing the present. Moreover, any prescriptions for the future are thereby compromised. In the next section we shall therefore examine in detail one construction of the history of science that claims to offer a vision of the past, present and future. This construction appeared in a book that has achieved cult status among a significant sector of the reading public, and even on occasions informs essays written by our students. Because it has achieved such popularity we are devoting this chapter to analysing the view of history that it propagates. In bringing the insights of academic history to criticise a very condensed but popular account we are not wishing to score easy points against an author who is mainly concerned with the relationship between science and human values. Rather, our aim is to show that an informed view of the history of science is required if we are to make adequate judgements concerning the ways in which science and religion have been related.

An Historical Romance

The story opens with the ancient Greeks who laid the foundations of physics. In particular, the

> Greek atomists [who] drew a clear [dividing] line between spirit and matter, picturing matter as being made of several 'basic building blocks' [which] were purely passive and intrinsically dead particles moving in a void. In subsequent centuries, this image became an essential element of Western thought, of the dualism between mind and matter, between body and soul.

The story then shifts to the late sixteenth century when 'the study of nature was approached, for the first time, in a truly scientific spirit'. The two most important developments during that period were, firstly, the introduction of experiments, and, secondly, the mathematisation of nature. Because he was the first to combine mathematics with empirical investigations, Galileo became 'the father of modern science'.[3]

By contrast, Descartes and Newton emerge as heirs to Greek atomism and therefore as the villains of the piece. To Descartes is attributed the ultimate sin of steadfastly separating mind from matter, which 'allowed scientists to treat matter as dead and completely separate from themselves'. Blame for the death of nature is laid firmly at Descartes's feet; he was responsible for producing a major shift in Western thought with his mind–matter dualism. This move was ultimately responsible for producing fragmentation and conflict both within ourselves and between individuals. The author of the narrative continues,

> The natural environment is [also] treated as if it consisted of separate parts to be exploited by different interest groups. The fragmented view is further extended into society, which is split into different nations, races, religious and political groups. The belief that all these fragments – in ourselves, in our environment, and in our society – are really separate can be seen as *the essential reason* for the present series of social, ecological and cultural crises. It has alienated us from nature and from our fellow human beings. . . .[4]

This is stirring stuff! If we understand this account correctly the author is claiming that Cartesian dualism is the cause of virtually all problems in the modern world. Descartes's soul (if he had one) must surely be undergoing the most excruciating torment as he repents the sin of having uttered 'I think, therefore I am'.

In the next stage in the narrative Descartes' mechanistic programme was extended by Isaac Newton. For Newton both space and time are absolute and within this manifold move small, indestructible particles that are acted on by forces, such as the force of gravity. Newton also framed new mathematical techniques that could analyse the movement of these 'mass points' under the influence of forces and in accordance with the laws of motion. Although Newton believed that God had set the particles in motion, his rigorous account of mechanics implied that the physical universe 'had continued to run ever since, like a machine, governed by immutable laws'. Thus the world is a 'giant cosmic machine' that is completely subservient to deterministic causal laws. As the following quotation is intended to show, Newtonian mechanics had an immense impact:

> Such a mechanistic world view was held by Isaac Newton, who constructed his mechanics on its basis and made it the foundation of classical physics. From the second half of the seventeenth century to the end of the

nineteenth century, the mechanistic Newtonian model of the universe dominated all scientific thought.[5]

That the post-Newtonian universe was causal and deterministic is illustrated in this account by a well-known passage by the Marquis de Laplace in which he hypothesised an intellect that knows both the laws of motion and the present state of the universe. From this knowledge the intellect can predict with certainty the dispositions of all particles at some future time. This provides a 'rigorously deterministic' picture of the universe which our author refers to as the 'Newtonian paradigm' or the 'Newtonian world-view'. Laplace is also introduced to show that even the Creator had been edged out of this mechanistic universe. When interviewed by Napoleon, Laplace is supposed to have replied that he did not require the 'hypothesis' of a Creator.[6] The author whose argument we are quoting also states that since the start of the Enlightenment we have been enslaved and our universe despiritualised by Newton's science and its attendant philosophy.

The next act in this drama takes us to the nineteenth century when the first cracks in the mechanistic world-view became apparent. The key developments were Faraday's and Maxwell's electromagnetic investigations which resulted in the introduction of spatially-extended fields of electric and magnetic force. Hence by the beginning of the twentieth century, 'the Newtonian model had ceased to be the basis of all physics'.[7]

In the final chapter of the story, physics underwent a radical transformation in the three opening decades of the twentieth century.

> At the beginning of modern physics stands the extraordinary intellectual feat of one man: Albert Einstein. In two articles, both published in 1905, Einstein initiated two revolutionary trends of thought. One was his special theory of relativity; the other was a new way of looking at electromagnetic radiation which was to become characteristic of quantum theory, the theory of atomic phenomena.[8]

Einstein's innovations resulted in the demise of the Newtonian conceptions of space and time. Likewise Newton's picture of hard, impenetrable particles was rejected in favour of a plethora of sub-atomic particles. Newtonian mechanics was superseded by quantum mechanics. In sum, Newton's world-view was replaced by one that was totally different. Historically, the rise of this new world-view marks the transition from one scientific paradigm to another, while in conceptual terms it constitutes a totally new and different philosophy of nature. According to the author of this account, the new physics (unlike the old) portrays the universe 'as a dynamic, inseparable whole which always includes the observer in an essential way'. The two main features of the new physics were, firstly, the recognition that the world constitutes a dynamic unity. Secondly, 'the classical ideal of an objective description of nature is no longer valid'; rather, 'we can never speak about nature without, at the same time, speaking about ourselves'.[9] These two aspects of modern physics herald the negation of Cartesianism which set man apart from nature three centuries earlier. Now, at last, nature has become re-spiritualised and we are again part of nature.

The story sketched above constitutes a master-narrative: a synoptic overview of how science has developed across the centuries. It contains condensed descriptions of what occurred at various periods – the rise of the 'Cartesian–Newtonian paradigm' in the seventeenth century and its replacement by the new physics in the early twentieth. The account is also highly evaluative – it has its villains and its heroes. Greek atomism, but more emphatically, Cartesian dualism and Newtonian mechanism are viewed as responsible for destroying our environment and our civilisation. By contrast, modern physics, as exemplified in the work of Einstein, Bohr and Heisenberg, is applauded as unifying and therefore as irenic and humane.

Unless readers have already guessed the author's name or looked at the accompanying notes they will doubtless want to know the source of the preceding account. All the material we have cited is from Fritjof Capra's *The Tao of Physics*, which first appeared in 1976. Since then it has become one of the best-selling books on science. This, and similar, historical narratives have achieved great popularity and we find them reappearing in books and magazine articles. That Capra's narrative has achieved such popularity necessitates a close examination of his historical account of the development of science.

Capra's book is not only an exposition of science and its history but also one of the canonical texts of the New Age movement. The term 'New Age movement' is difficult to define either doctrinally or institutionally but it provides a convenient label encompassing a wide range of positions. Most New Agers express deep disillusionment with modern Western society – its rank materialism, its science, its politics and often its traditional religious beliefs and institutions. Instead they advocate a pantheistic spirituality and also emphasise the urgent need to transform both the individual and the world. These latter features justify its inclusion in this book. While there are many New Agers who view all aspects of science as part of the malaise of Western society, there is also a significant group that looks to specific aspects of modern science as providing crucial elements in the new understanding of the world.

Like many other New Age writers Capra claims that there exist close parallels between modern physics and the doctrines of Eastern religious philosophies. Holism and, by implication, the negation of Cartesian dualism are, he insists, to be found in many Eastern philosophies. Herein lies the *Tao of Physics*. Another well-known work in this genre is Gary Zukav's *The Dancing Wu-li Masters* (1979).[10] Both books first appeared in the late 1970s and are very much products of both time and place. They offer a green, spiritual and decidedly Californian analysis of the ills of the West – and you can't get much further west than California! It should be emphasised that the New Age movement has not stood still and while the preceding account continues to be retailed as the route to our present malaise, there are some more sophisticated historical accounts by such recent writers as Rupert Sheldrake, Morris Berman, Ken Wilber and Arthur Zajonc.[11] Nevertheless, Capra's first book remains the most widely-cited example of this genre, and has generally been adopted as providing the standard account not only by New Agers but also by some who reject the New Age philosophy. Hence we are dealing with a much broader phenomenon than either Capra or the New Age Movement since similar historical narratives have been propounded by people of various religious persuasions or none. For example, in his *Holy Ground: The Spirituality of Matter* (1990), Ross Thompson, an Anglican cleric, protests against the despiritualisation of the universe by Descartes and others. His chapter heading – 'Dualism and disenchantment' – says it all. Likewise in his recent book Bryan Appleyard shares many of Capra's criticisms of seventeenth-century science and its supposed legacies, although he does not follow Capra in encompassing modern physics. Instead, like many conservatives, he seeks salvation in traditional social and religious values.[12]

Concern with the history of science may, at first sight, appear irrelevant when analysing a book aimed principally at elucidating the relation between physics and Eastern philosophy. However, central to Capra's account and to much New Age thinking is a construction of the past that criticises classical physics and legitimates modern physics. Moreover, New Agers are not only committed to the view that paradigm shifts have occurred in the past but also that we live in an age of sharp transition – the Age of Aquarius heralding a new world-order that will replace the old. As one adept has written,

> This [present] transformation ... is reflected in what is being recognised as
> a general paradigm shift away from a predictable Newtonian billiard-ball

> model of life to a more open-ended and intuitively understood model ...
> [This transformation] is perhaps at its most intellectually respectable and
> acceptable when it speaks purely of the paradigm shift and reflects on the
> new insights from sub-atomic physics, from the new biology, [and] from
> humanistic and transpersonal psychology.[13]

As this quotation indicates, radical, even discontinuous, changes in
the sciences seem both to presage the Aquarian Age and also to help
legitimate the movement's message before the wider public. Thus
history in general and the history of science in particular are integral
to the New Age movement's understanding of science and form an
intrinsic part of its self-image.

As historians of science working in academic institutions we should
welcome any books that popularise our subject. However, without
wishing to appear ungenerous we must express some reservations
about the stories regaled by Capra and the many authors who have
published similar narratives. Invariably such accounts are delivered
with nonchalant authority. These writers tell their readers how it
really happened – how the West was won – or lost. Yet, have Davies,
Capra or Appleyard ever pursued historical research? Have they
taken account of recent work in the History of Science? Judging
from his bibliography Capra's reading in the history of physics was
minimal; he cites only Maurice Crosland's collection of articles on
matter theory, Bertrand Russell's passé *History of Western Philosophy*
(1945) and two books on Greek philosophy. Milic Capek's *The
Philosophical Impact of Contemporary Physics* (1961) is the single serious
work on the philosophy of science cited, but it is a profoundly ahis-
torical piece that is now outdated. Interestingly, the physicist Werner
Heisenberg appears to have been Capra's main source of information on the background to modern physics – two sets of
Heisenberg's essays being frequently cited by Capra. If Heisenberg
was indeed Capra's intellectual mentor then we should approach
Capra's account with a healthy dose of scepticism. After all,
Heisenberg was not an historian. We might also expect his view of
the history of physics to be highly coloured since he was one of the
chief architects of the new physics.[14]

Writers who deliver these master-narratives with so much aplomb
fail to appreciate that history is a critical discipline and it is incumbent on the historian not to rest satisfied with any particular story.
We intend in the remainder of this chapter to identify some of the
areas in which Capra's master-narrative is to be found wanting.

General Critiques

Let us begin by making a few general points about Capra's account. Firstly, he has not written a critical history; instead he used the history of science to support his evaluations of the Newtonian mechanistic paradigm, which he denigrates, and the holistic paradigm of modern physics, which he champions. Moreover, he deployed history to legitimate the sharp contrast he insists on drawing between these two paradigms. These are the only two ways of doing science that he allows. He then constructs history by projecting this contrast back onto the past, thereby imposing a radical discontinuity on the historical record. History is thus made to recapitulate what he sees as the necessary conflict between these two world-views.

While historians of science would not deny that there were significant differences between physics pre-1900 and post-1930, they would also insist that the contrasts cannot be drawn as simplistically or starkly as Capra's story requires. Highly relevant to his discussion is the theory developed by Thomas Kuhn in the early 1960s to describe the development of scientific disciplines. Appealing to the term 'paradigm' – the consensual form of science practised by a scientific community – Kuhn postulated that revolutions occur when one paradigm replaces its predecessor. For example, a revolution occurred when the wave theory of light replaced the particle theory *c.*1830; the new wave optics being incommensurable with its predecessor. Viewing this change through a Kuhnian lens imposes discontinuity on the historical record.[15] However, closer historical study of the 'optical revolution' shows up problems with Kuhn's theory of paradigm change. For example, instead of two stark alternatives, a geat variety of optical theories abounded during the eighteenth and early nineteenth centuries. These cannot be reduced simply to wave versus particle paradigms. Moreover, Jed Buchwald has argued that in the early nineteenth century the opposition between waves and particles was not the crucial issue; instead, he emphasises the importance of the different mathematical constructions used to explain complex polarisation phenomena.[16] More generally, historians have found Kuhn's master-narrative inadequate.

Although Kuhn applied his theory of revolutions specifically to science, he did not take out patent rights on the term 'paradigm' which has been extended by New Age writers, among others, in ways that bear little relationship to its use by historians, philosophers and sociologists of science. In entering popular culture the term has become a shorthand for any package of ideas. Thus, according to Zukav, a 'paradigm is an established thought process, a framework'.

Another New Age writer has characterised a paradigm as 'a framework of thought ... a scheme for understanding and explaining certain aspects of reality'. Hence a 'paradigm shift is a distinctly new way of thinking about old problems'.[17] In line with this redefinition, traditional ways of thinking (about ourselves, about society or about the cat next door) constitute a paradigm, as does the New Age mentality. By drawing on this notion of competing paradigms Capra encompassed a theory of historical discontinuity. This appeal to abrupt changes in science through shifts in paradigm imposes discontinuities on the historical record. Indeed, the second section of *The Turning Point*, in which Capra delineates the contrasting world-views of classical and modern physics, is entitled 'The two paradigms'.[18]

We also wish to question some of the general assumptions underlying Capra's description of Galileo as the 'father of modern science'; his justification being that Galileo was the first to combine mathematics and empirical investigation. This is however factually incorrect. There were many earlier examples, such as the astronomers of ancient Greece who were not only competent observers of the heavens but also made extensive use of mathematical models to describe the motions of the stars and planets. But there is a further and more fundamental problem with Capra's assertion. Historians have questioned whether Galileo was the thoroughgoing empiricist that Capra portrays. Instead his attitude to experiment now seems far more complex, even ambivalent.

As we shall have occasion to note in the next chapter, there is little evidence that Galileo ever performed the most famous 'experiment' usually attributed to him; by dropping two balls of different weight from the Leaning Tower of Pisa he is said to have refuted Aristotle's theory of motion. Moreover, some of the experiments he reported are now recognised as thought experiments rather than practical investigations of the physical world. This is not a criticism of Galileo but a recognition that in the early seventeenth century the notion of experiment was both new and controversial.[19] Some historians have also emphasised that if Galileo's considerable debt to Platonism is adequately recognised, then we should interpret him as an opponent of empiricism, at least in its popular and unsophisticated forms.[20] In ignoring these more subtle interpretations Capra creates a straw man in order to make Galileo fit a conventional and rather unsatisfactory image of scientific endeavour. It is surely ironic that while Capra offers a vision of science based on holistic metaphysics, his historical account draws on a tired positivistic philosophy of science. If the New Age perspective is to contribute to writing the history of science – and we believe it can offer important insights – then it should not draw uncritically on such stale clichés derived from positivism.

It should also be noted that although Capra is primarily concerned with the development of physics, he often switches unannounced to broader claims about how science, in general, developed. As a physicist he may consider that physics is the queen of the sciences, but it is not unreasonable to insist that such subjects as natural history, chemistry and geology should also be included in any account of science. Yet none of these subjects followed the simple transition from mechanism in the seventeenth century to holism in the twentieth.

Specific Criticisms

Turning to specifics, it is appropriate to question the relation Capra posits between the Greek atomists and Descartes. Since he readily acknowledges that the Greek atomists dissociated matter and spirit, it might appear that Descartes was simply following a programme stretching back some two millennia. Why, then, does he single out Descartes for such harsh criticism if he was not the originator of atomism? Also, if atomism has proved such a destructive doctrine, as Capra claims, then we need to be clear why Descartes's 'formulation of the spirit/matter dualism' was 'extreme'. In what ways did his views go beyond the Greek atomists? Capra's account also fails to recognise that in the mid seventeenth century Descartes was not alone in courting Greek theories of matter; indeed, many of his contemporaries identified Pierre Gassendi as the writer primarily responsible for the revival of Greek atomism.[21]

Another relevant issue is raised by the work of Emilios Bouratinos who claims that the breakdown of holism can be traced to developments in Egyptian and ancient Greek cultures. In these cultures science first became possible through drawing a distinction between the perceiving subject and the perceived object. Yet this distinction also destroyed a previously-existing dynamic, holistic mode of understanding.[22] If we adopt this perspective, then atomism was not solely responsible for fragmenting the universe; indeed, atomism was an effect rather than the cause of the breakdown of holism. Descartes's central position in Capra's story is also further compromised by Bouratinos's analysis.

It should also be remembered that in Descartes's day Aristotelianism was the dominant natural philosophy taught in universities. Although Aristotle allowed a crucial role for teleology, much of his physics was concerned with efficient causation. For example, he posed the problem of determining how many men were required to move a boat on a sandy beach. This involved the relationship between what we might call 'force' and 'speed'. Again, in order to account for the flight of an arrow through the air he postulated flow currents in a plenum. In these and many other examples Aristotle focused on material causation. Although Aristotle insisted on the importance of teleology – every natural phenomenon having a purpose – his universe was certainly not holistic in the sense required by Capra. In contrast to Bouratinos's argument, some New Age writers consider Greek philosophy to have portrayed the universe as holistic and dynamically interdependent. One severe New Age critic of Descartes, Danah Zohar, has even contrasted his 'sterile' view of the physical world with 'the living cosmos' of the Greeks, 'filled with purpose and intelligence'.[23] This characterisation of Greek natural philosophy is clearly inaccurate and does not apply either to the atomists or to Aristotle (except in respect to purpose). From these widely differing accounts it is clear that Capra and other New Age writers are faced with a number of problems in characterising Greek natural philosophies and Descartes's relationship to his Greek sources.

There are also numerous problems with Capra's central contention that in the 'mechanical world-view' mind and matter were fragmented, whereas in modern physics mind and matter constitute a unity. Here Capra implicitly assumes that the meanings of both terms have remained sufficiently constant across three and a half centuries. However, Descartes's deployment of the word 'mind' bears but a tenuous relation to modern concept(s) of mind. For the term that is conventionally translated as 'mind' he used the words *mens*, *l'esprit* and *l'âme* (which should probably be translated as 'soul').[24] Even for the person in the street Freud's notions of the libido and the unconscious form part of our late-twentieth-century concept of mind. Yet these notions are alien to Descartes's understanding of mind (or should it be soul?). Likewise views about the nature of matter have not remained static for the past three and a half centuries, but have been affected by shifts in technology, science and philosophy. In the light of such significant changes in the meanings of terms historians of philosophy have warned that we misread Descartes if we uncritically attribute to him notions of mind and matter that carry so much twentieth-century baggage.

Again, we are concerned about the glib references to reductionism versus holism found in Capra's book and in many other works in this genre. There are practical and definitional difficulties with both terms and particularly with the widespread notion that they stand in stark and manifest opposition. Even the much-maligned Descartes can be read as a holist. In the fifth part of his *Discourse on Method* he rejected the following analogy as inadequate. Consider a pilot who is able to steer the ship. At first sight this situation may seem analogous to the way the soul moves the body. However Descartes decisively rejected this analogy: his reason for rejecting it is instructive. He stated that in contrast to the case of the pilot in a ship,

> it is necessary that the soul be joined and united more closely to the body, in order to have, in addition to this power of movement, feelings and appetites similar to ours, and thus compose a true man.[25]

This is a telling comment, for far from fragmenting the 'true man' into two irreconcilable parts, Descartes here emphasised the integration of soul and body in the constitution of the complete human being. Certainly matter and soul are very different substances according to his theory, one being material and extended, the other immaterial and non-extended. Although commentators remain divided over whether his (all too brief) resolution is philosophically sound, Descartes addressed the problem of interactionism – how the body affects the mind and the mind affects the body – and, in specifying the human condition, he clearly asserted the necessary unity of mind and matter.[26] They are indivisible in the 'true man'. Had Capra concentrated on this text he might have championed Descartes as a card-carrying holist. We shall return to this point in chapter 7.

Our next criticism is that, contrary to Capra's thesis, there was no single world-view shared by 'scientists', let alone 'physicists', from the early seventeenth to the late nineteenth century. Instead, there was considerable diversity throughout this period, with a significant proportion of scientists rejecting any all-encompassing mechanistic programme as the basis for their science. Indeed one significant problem with Capra's account is that the sciences – especially the more experimental sciences – were rarely driven by such a grand metaphysical engine. This is not to deny that metaphysics has played an important role in the development of science, but its role has often been oversimplified and overstated. Contrary to the thesis that metaphysics is the engine of science, much recent work by historians and sociologists has emphasised the pragmatic and piecemeal development of science. For example, ever the opportunist, Galileo embraced corpuscularianism in his 1623 polemic entitled *The*

Assayer. Here he assumed that matter consisted of corpuscles in order to account for the densities of different materials. It was also a handy stick to beat the Aristotelians. Yet atomism rarely plays an explanatory role in the remainder of Galileo's works.[27]

Although seventeenth-century 'scientists' often viewed Descartes as a mechanist, his theories were widely discussed but frequently rejected in favour of alternative natural philosophies. For example, in seventeenth-century Britain mechanistic views were often perceived as both physically inadequate and conducive to atheism. Thus Henry More, the Cambridge Platonist, who had initially been excited by Cartesian natural philosophy, criticised Descartes for restricting the role of God in the physical universe to the act of creation and for precluding God's subsequent interaction with it. As More complained in a letter to Robert Boyle, 'the phaenomena of the world cannot be solved merely mechanically, but ... there is the necessity of the assistance of a substance distinct from matter, that is, of a spirit, or a being incorporeal'. Only by admitting a major role for spirit could More frame an adequate, Christian natural philosophy.[28]

More's response to 'the Cartesian dream' was not unique among British natural philosophers. Most importantly, it coloured the views of Isaac Newton whose intellectual debt to Descartes was both complex and ambivalent – he did not simply adopt and expand on Descartes's views, as Capra's account implies. Although Newton read Descartes closely, key passages in his *Principia* (1687) indicate the extent of his criticisms of Descartes's *Principia Philosophiae* (1644). Indeed, not only did Newton devote the second book of the *Principia* to refuting Descartes's theory of motion, but the preface opens with an argument against the Cartesian account of the solar system. Newton asserted that the Cartesian theory of vortices cannot provide a satisfactory explanation of the planetary orbits. Even more pertinent is Newton's rejection of the Cartesian doctrine of contact action. On the Cartesian account matter is considered to be particulate and inert. The only way in which two moving particles of matter can interact is through contact. By contrast, Newton introduced the notion of force allowing particles to act at a distance. Newton considered that forces, such as the force of gravitation, are immaterial. Although associated with matter, they are not necessary properties of matter. Moreover, forces suffuse space and constitute what he variously called 'powers' or 'active principles'.

These notions of force or activity were of central importance to Newton and in many passages he emphasised that passive mechanical principles are inadequate in accounting for many natural phenomena, which instead manifest intrinsic activity. He thereby highlighted his rejection of the Cartesian theory of matter. As a paradigmatic instance of activity he cited the way we move our limbs by the power of the human will. In one manuscript he even claimed, with typical circumspection, that 'We cannot say that all nature is not alive.' Such passages have led historians to speculate on the extent to which he was indebted to Neoplatonism and to the alchemical tradition.[29] His theory of activity also played a significant role in his physico-theology since, in some of his writings, Newton advanced the view that God operates in the universe through the agency of immaterial forces extending across space. Indeed, in her study of Newton's alchemy the late Betty Jo Dobbs emphasised the extent to which he conceived many classes of natural phenomena as manifesting sources of activity, such as the growth of vegetables. Nature was therefore definitely not mechanistic in the Cartesian sense. Moreover, he considered that this activity is ultimately – if not directly – derived from God.[30] From Newton's repeated emphasis on the sources of activity of nature it is clear that he did not endorse the view of nature which Capra disparages as the 'Newtonian world-machine'. We thoroughly misconstrue Newton's science if we portray him as a naive mechanist who reduced the universe to inert lumps of matter which attract or repel one another.

A further caveat needs to be entered against the paramount position attributed to Descartes in Capra's story. It should be remembered that Descartes was but one of many early-seventeenth-century natural philosophers. His vision of explaining physical phenomena in purely physical terms – that is, by matter and motion – remained partly a fantasy since he could offer only a limited range of examples to illustrate how particular physical phenomena could be explained by these principles. Although some of his near contemporaries pursued similar programmes, others – such as Johannes Kepler, William Harvey and Simon Stevin – made substantial contributions to science while pursuing philosophies of science opposed to that of Descartes. The problem of magnetism, which proved particularly contentious, provides an instructive example showing the diversity of approaches and the sterility of the Cartesian solution. A number of earlier scientists, including William Gilbert and Kepler, had discussed magnetic attraction as the non-material sympathetic interaction between a magnet and a piece of iron. Gilbert even envisaged the earth and planets as possessing souls and considered magnetism to be a manifestation of these souls. Likewise Kepler viewed the sun as a large magnet responsible for moving the attendant planets in their orbits. Rejecting these Neoplatonic ideas

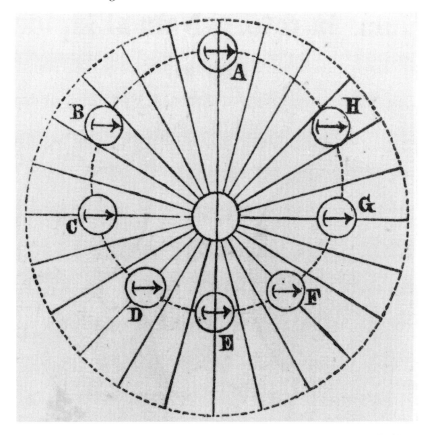

Figure 11: In his *Epitome Astronomiae Copernicanae* (first published 1618–21) Johannes Kepler envisaged the planets carried round on a magnetic field emanating from the sun. From Kepler's *Opera Omnia* (1858–71).

Descartes sketched a mechanical explanation that postulated screw-threaded particles travelling along bevelled tubes linking the magnet's poles. Even his explanation of such basic phenomena as magnetic attraction and repulsion was open to major objections. Not surprisingly this cumbersome theory attracted few adherents. It is therefore simplistic either to single out Descartes as the only important scientist in the early seventeenth century or to portray the mechanistic world-view (as characterised by Capra) as the key to early modern science.

More generally, while there were certainly some self-proclaimed followers of Descartes (mostly in France), we can make little sense of the science developed over the next three centuries if we read it

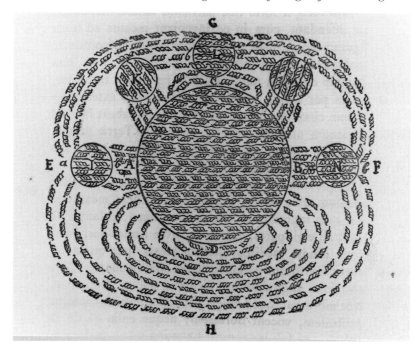

Figure 12: In contrast to Kepler's account of magnetism René Descartes
sought to explain magnetism mechanically. From Descartes's *Principia
Philosophiae*, first published in 1644.

simply as the implementation of Descartes's programme. Capra's
portrayal of the influence of Descartes – via Newton – over the
ensuing three centuries therefore needs to be severely qualified
since his vision remained controversial and was not the only key
available to unlock the secrets of nature. We shall outline one of
several alternative approaches.

There has been a long-running dispute in the life sciences over
whether matter and its properties suffice in explaining a wide range
of biological phenomena. While some phenomena – such as
muscular contraction producing movement of the arms – seem
readily explicable by physical processes, others have proved more
intractable. In contrast to mechanistic accounts 'vitalist' explanations were offered by many physiologists, including Robert Whytt
the eighteenth-century Scottish physician who addressed the question of 'spontaneous motion' (such as breathing or the use of the
muscles when we walk). He dismissed any explanation 'purely by

virtue of [the body's] mechanical construction' since such 'a notion of the animal frame [is] too low and absurd to be embraced by any but the most minute philosophers!'[31] Here Whytt rejected the Cartesian programme as incapable of offering an adequate explanation of the phenomena. Instead he argued the need for a non-rational and immaterial 'sentient principle', residing primarily in the brain, to account for physical effects – like spontaneous motions – that were not produced by physical causes. This appeal to an immaterial principle indicates that although Whytt responded to Cartesianism he firmly rejected the view that physiological explanation should appeal only to matter and motion.

Whytt's vitalist orientation was shared by many subsequent physiologists.[32] The history of embryology also indicates the limitations of Cartesianism. The central question was how to account for the growth and development of a perfectly-formed child from a small quantity of semen (later embryologists also attributing a role to the female's egg). To many embryologists inert matter seemed hopelessly inadequate at explaining the phenomenon. Even the addition of Newtonian forces of attraction and repulsion was of little assistance. Instead, they insisted, powerful, vital, organic principles must be responsible for organising material particles according to a pre-ordained plan. Observations of spermatozoa under the microscope supported this argument since they were often seen as minute creatures displaying internal organisation. Although scientists disagreed over the exact nature of this vital principle and how it operated, it was widely accepted as the distinguishing feature of living organisms.[33] In postulating an active non-material entity some scientists were motivated by religious considerations, yet the diversity of positions cannot be reduced simply to religious orientations. The examples of physiology and embryology indicate that even if mechanism had proved successful in physics we should not follow Capra and assume that it could readily be applied with equal success to other sciences.

Having portrayed the Newtonian view of the world as a causal, deterministic machine, Capra then represents Laplace as the arch mechanist and exemplar of the 'Cartesian–Newtonian paradigm'. Yet this characterisation is also problematic. According to Capra Laplace considered that if the state of a physical system were known at a particular time, 'the future of any part of the system could – in principle – be predicted with absolute certainty'. The qualification 'in principle' is soon overlooked and Capra proceeded to cite the following passage by Laplace as the 'clearest expression' of 'rigorous determinism':

An intellect [*une intelligence*] which at a given instant knew all the forces
acting in nature, and the position of all things of which the world consists
... nothing would be uncertain for it, and the future, like the past, would
be present to its eyes.

Not only does this quotation illustrate strict determinism for Capra,
but also 'the fundamental division between the I and the [mechan-
ical] world [as] introduced by Descartes'. By appearing to identify
'the intellect' cited in the quotation with the observer, Capra conveys
to the reader the impression that in a mechanical universe the mechanism is transparent to the human intellect.[34]

The first point to note is that in the above passage Laplace, unlike
Capra, does not attribute this knowledge to humans, either now or
in the future. Indeed, the 'intellect' in the preceding quotation bears
a closer relation to the infinite intelligence traditionally attributed to
God than to the finite intelligence of any mundane scientist.

To identify the leading problem with Capra's interpretation we
must restore the passage to its proper historical context. It was
published in Laplace's *Essai Philosophique sur les Probabilités* (1814) but
was based on a similar but much earlier discussion of the doctrine of
chances that appeared in a memoir first published in 1776. It is
important to notice that both of these evocations of a superhuman
intelligence appeared in works discussing probability. Laplace
argued that only in physical astronomy can reasonably accurate
predictions be made from the present to the future state of a system.
However, in fields other than astronomy we can be less sure of the
causal factors involved. Moreover, in such fields the phenomena are
far more complex. For these reasons we are prevented from
achieving the same certainty about phenomena. Instead 'we seek to
compensate for the impossibility of knowing' these causes by turning
to the calculus of *probabilities*. In other words, in direct contradiction
to Capra's interpretation, it is clear that for Laplace we do *not* share
this superhuman intelligence's knowledge of the universe. Except
possibly in the realm of positional astronomy we do not have access
to the complex causal laws governing the universe. In line with
Laplace's insistence that science provides us with limited knowledge
of the natural world, he considered that the theory of probabilities
must be developed to cope with such apparent complexity.[35] Thus,
far from dealing with rigid determinism, Laplace acknowledges that
we must often rest satisfied with a limited, statistical understanding
of the world. In this sense Laplace was not Capra's rigorous deter-
minist. Indeed, in the light of the foregoing discussion we might
fantasise that he might have accepted the statistical interpretation of

quantum mechanics that Capra champions as the harbinger of the new anti-mechanistic physics!

Déjà Vu

As historians we find many of the ingredients of New Age thought all too familiar, having encountered them in the writings of previous generations. Certainly, some of the crises that mark the end of the second millennium seem without parallel in former epochs, but there have been many earlier periods when the condition of the world has appeared dire. Particularly in such situations people tend to look back to a Golden Age or forward to the dawn of a bright new era. Millenarians were thick on the ground in the seventeenth century, and as the eighteenth drew to a close, with great convulsions in France, 'new ages' were proclaimed in both religious and secular colours. Fascinating comparisons can be drawn between these earlier movements and the New Age movement of our own day. It is also important to notice that like many of its apocalyptic predecessors the current New Age movement attributes a significant role to science.

While the science of previous centuries could not deploy the insights of quantum theory, chaos theory or sub-atomic physics, there was no shortage of scientific concepts that served similar purposes. The themes of idealism, holism and anti-mechanism are not recent innovations but have appeared on many occasions in the history of both science and general culture. Indeed, one historian of physics, Stephen Brush, has argued, perhaps somewhat tongue-in-cheek, that like other aspects of our culture, science oscillates between the two contrasting styles of Realism and Romanticism, the period of oscillation being about seventy years.[36] According to Brush, the Copenhagen Interpretation of quantum theory was framed during the inter-War years and reflected the dominant Romanticism of the period. Some seven decades later we are again in the midst of a Romantic revival in which Capra finds much affinity with the founders of the Copenhagen Interpretation (who were likewise steeped in Eastern philosophy). Whatever the strengths and weaknesses of Brush's thesis, it can usefully remind us that styles of science fluctuate and that patterns often recur. Echoes of holism and anti-mechanism are to be found in many earlier writers, perhaps none more forcefully than in the German Romantic movement of the late eighteenth and early nineteenth centuries.

Like its counterparts in the arts, Romanticism in science defies any single definition, yet it is usually associated with the following characteristics: a breadth of vision (as opposed to specialisation); the unity of man and nature; the essential unity of nature; the view that nature is mysterious (not transparent to reason), organic (as opposed to mechanistic) and holistic; the scientist is accorded imagination and empathy (rather than possessing rational faculties). Although the term has been applied to scientists of other periods, Romanticism reached its peak in science (as in other subjects) in the late eighteenth century and the first half of the nineteenth, particularly in Germany where *Naturphilosophie* flourished. Blumenbach, Coleridge, Davy, Fichte, Goethe, Oersted, Humboldt, Oken, Ritter, Schelling, Steffens and Tyndall are some of the names often cited in discussions of scientific Romanticism.[37] Most noticeably, New Age writers share with these Romantically-inclined scientists a strong aversion to mechanism and an insistence on holism and organicism. Although the historical context is different, James Lovelock's evocation of Gaia does not look out of place when set beside the works of Goethe or Oken.

To illustrate the high Romantic view of science we might introduce *The Novices of Sais* by Friedrich von Hardenberg who wrote under the pseudonym Novalis during the closing years of the eighteenth century. The *dramatis personae* include the master who is the true prophet of nature, several novices – including the narrator – who are seeking the path to the Golden Age, and four travellers who are seeking to understand how man and nature are interrelated. Although different positions are adopted by the interlocutors, conventional science receives short shrift and is portrayed as responsible for mechanising, and thereby killing, nature. In the words of one of the novices, scientists have 'debased nature to the level of a uniform machine, without past and future'.[38] Running through the dialogue is a sharp contrast between scientists and poets: 'Scientists [Naturforscher] have cut into the inner structure [of nature] and sought after the relations between its members. Under their hands friendly nature died, leaving behind only dead, quivering remnants, while the poet inspired her like a heady wine.' This theme received its most trenchant statement in the speech by the fourth traveller, a youth with sparkling eyes, who asserts:

> How strange that precisely the most sacred and charming manifestations of nature should be in the hands of such dead men as scientists tend to be. These phenomena whose potency calls forth nature's creation, phenomena which should be a secret of lovers, a mystery of higher mankind, are shamelessly and senselessly evoked by unfeeling minds, which will never know what miracles their retorts contain. Only poets should deal in the fluid element and be empowered to speak of it to ardent youth; then laboratories would be temples....[39]

This is not the language of wave-particle dualism nor the physics of non-locality, but the image of a unified integrated world was central to Novalis's vision.

Unlike Novalis and his contemporaries, few New Agers would think of contrasting the scientist with the poet. Nevertheless, despite such significant differences, Romanticism remains an apposite category in which to understand the New Age movement and its attitudes to science. Yet this tentative association between the two movements raises an important historical question: Why did the earlier manifestation fail to overturn the then-prevailing patterns of science? There is no simple answer, but some historians have pointed to the failure of the Romantics, with their highly individualistic prescriptions for science, to gain influence within the walls of the leading scientific institutions. Again, the mid-nineteenth-century opponents of *Naturphilosophie* – such as Hermann von Helmholtz and Emil du Bois-Reymond – were very effective in convincing contemporaries that it was an empty, fantastic and useless enterprise. Reinforcement of this view was doubtless aided by the scientific successes of these opponents, many of whom promulgated an extreme vision of the world as a mechanism.[40] Whatever the reasons, the fate of this earlier movement suggests that the New Age movement will face an up-hill battle to change attitudes within the scientific community. However, public concern about environmental issues may strengthen their hand.

The New Physics

There is a host of problems in depicting the relation between the old and the new physics as a radical break. Some of these problems are historical. For example, Kuhn has argued that the quantum theory of radiation did not appear overnight as a blinding revelation of the truth. Instead, it was the sum of a number of small innovations that occupied many scientists over a period of some twenty years. By examining this period closely, Kuhn portrays the transition as a continuous development, not as a sharp discontinuity.[41] Moreover, individual scientists of the period were divided over how to respond to quantum theory and did not simply abandon classical physics even in (what became) the quantal domain. For example, Max Planck, who first imposed the restriction that the energy of an oscillator is an integral multiple of $h\nu$, remained wedded to the ideals of classical physics. Again, Niels Bohr did not simply abandon classical physics but sought strenuously to retain the language of classical physics – the language of 'waves' and 'particles' – in the description of the quantum realm.[42] This diversity has continued down to the present, with numerous critics of the Copenhagen Interpretation and, over the last few years, an increasing interest in Bohm's hidden variable theory.[43]

In Capra's account the position of Einstein is considerably inflated and provides an example of outmoded 'great man' history. While not belittling Einstein, historians have been at pains to emphasise that he was not a lone genius but was responding in his 1905 papers (which Capra locates as the key documents for both quantum theory and relativity) to the work of Paschen, Lummer, Pringsheim, Rayleigh, Planck, Maxwell, Larmor, Fitzgerald, Lorentz, Mach and many others. More importantly, the portrayal of Einstein as the guru of the new physics overlooks many nuances in his work. For example, in contrast to Capra's claim that he was 'bold enough to postulate that light ... can appear not only as electromagnetic waves, but also in the form of ... quanta',[44] Einstein insisted in 1911 'on the provisional character of this concept [light-quanta] which does not seem reconcilable with the experimentally verified consequences of the wave theory'.[45] As is well known, Einstein also expressed severe reservations about the Copenhagen Interpretation of quantum theory which Capra champions unquestioningly.[46] Moreover, the example of Einstein undermines Capra's portrayal of modern physics as internally consistent, since Einstein sought (unsuccessfully) to reconcile quantum theory and the theory of relativity.

The relation between Newtonian mechanics and the new physics raises numerous historical and philosophical problems. For example, as Hasok Chang has pointed out, one such problem arises from the continuing use of formulae derived from classical physics in descriptions of experiments basic to quantum mechanics. Thus in describing the trajectory of particles through a mass spectrograph physicists deploy the formulae of classical mechanics and electromagnetism. Far from quantum theory having displaced classical physics, there are many such sites where the old and new theories coexist, however uncomfortably. Moreover, their continued intimate interconnection provides further evidence against the sharp historical discontinuity that Kuhn's theory appears to postulate.[47] Yet throughout most of his book Capra sharply contrasted classical and modern physics as if they inhabited separate domains, with the former having been displaced by the latter. Only in his 'Epilogue' did he concede that the two theories can coexist since both provide useful descriptions of the world.[48] While accepting their coexistence he still implicitly maintained that the two 'paradigms' were completely separate and non-interacting.

Perhaps we are reading too much into Capra's account, but it seems to imply that scientists working in the Newtonian mould are spiritual cripples while those adhering to quantum theory are spiritually aware. This is surely a contentious thesis that is unlikely to be true. Moreover, without an adequate definition of spirituality it is also difficult to test. However, we are not alone in expressing this concern. Confused by the repeated and sweeping claims that modern physics lends impressive support to transcendental religion and mysticism, Ken Wilber, a leading New Age writer, took the trouble to collect and examine the writings of several key scientists – including Heisenberg, Schrödinger, Einstein and Eddington – who forged the new physics. He also rightly noted that all these physicists were steeped in religious or spiritual traditions. From this evidence Wilber argues that they were unanimous in denying any symbiotic relationship between their physics and their spiritual meditations. Instead he claims that their concern with spirituality and mysticism arose from their recognition that the domain of physics is limited to abstract, mathematical forms of representation. Thus physics cannot engage 'reality', which is accessible only through mystical experience.

In support of this thesis Wilber quotes from the Quaker Arthur Eddington: Science provides only 'a shadow world of symbols, beneath which those methods are unadapted for penetrating'. Instead, 'that mental and spiritual nature of ourselves, known in our minds by an intimate contact transcending the methods of physics, supplies just that ... which science is admittedly unable to give'.[49] Here Eddington seems to be postulating, not a parallel between physics and spirituality, but a disjunction such that the spiritual puts us in touch with the reality that physics cannot reach. Although Wilber did not attempt to engage the historical contexts in which Eddington and his other physicists were writing, he offers a welcome and critical counter-blast to the all-too-familiar scenario of modern physics paralleling spiritual self-awareness. If Wilber is correct then we should be looking for a very different relationship between science and spirituality than the one Capra suggests. Moreover, Wilber's thesis implies that classical and modern physics equally offer a 'shadow world of symbols', to which spiritual reality is opposed, and that modern physics has no special affinity to that reality. It should be noted that the theses of Capra and Wilber are variants of the more general claims about the science–religion relationship discussed in our opening chapter: Capra adopts what Ian Barbour calls an 'integrationist strategy', while Wilber asserts an 'independence' thesis.[50]

While some in the New Age movement are enamoured with the new physics, many others remain highly critical of the whole scientific enterprise. This latter position is well illustrated by the following passage written by a doyen of the New Age movement a few years before the *Tao of Physics* achieved cult status. In *Where the Wasteland Ends* (1972) Theodore Roszak pointed to 'the psychological continuities that bind the old and new physics together':

> To be sure, over a certain range of phenomena in atomic physics and astronomy, the old machine metaphor has lost its serviceability ... But the psychology of the enterprise has not changed; this is the string that holds all the scientific heads together from Galileo and Newton to the present day ...
>
> The basic effect of Newtonian mechanism was to produce a nature that was felt to be dead, alien, and purely functional. This estranged relationship of scientist to nature has remained unchanged [in the new physics ... T]he tunes have been altered but the mode of the music is the same always. We are still performing in the key of objective consciousness.[51]

For Roszak the new physics fails to provide an adequate basis for a thoroughgoing anti-mechanist view of the world commensurate with his conception of our inner consciousness. Indeed, Roszak seems to question whether relatively recent innovations in scientific *theory* can offer any real alternative to its traditional modes of thought. We share his scepticism – not for reasons of psychology – but because there are many respects in which the new physics is contiguous with the old. Some might even argue that the distinguishing feature of modern science is that so much of it is dominated by industry and by the military. From this standpoint the niceties of interpreting quantum mechanics seem pretty irrelevant. While it is certainly true that some scientists find spiritual solace in the rarefied realm of quantum mechanics, this is not the face of science that most people perceive. Moreover, these scientists' response may have more to do with traditional aesthetic criteria (which will be discussed in chapter 7) than with any putative connection between 'man and nature'.

Capra also claims that modern physicists speak holistically about 'man and nature' and they thereby acknowledge that we are part of nature. We have some difficulty making sense of this assertion. There is, surely, a sense in which we can appreciate being part of nature when we hike in the Cairngorms or feel the spray of the Atlantic Ocean beating against our faces. Viewing the magnificence of the night sky may also persuade us that we are part – but a very small part – of this immense universe. Physics doubtless produces similar 'highs' in its aficionados but it seems doubtful whether quantum theory leads necessarily to such unmitigated holism. Does the modern physicist struggling to solve Schrödinger's equation or fumbling with an electronic detector attached to the synchrocyclotron hidden deep in the ground beneath Geneva appreciate that there must be an essential unity between mind and matter? We doubt it. Does a 'Newtonian' physicist trying to solve Newton's equations or fighting to persuade Atwood's machine to work feel any different from his 'quantum' sibling? The answer is far from clear, but we would need a lot of persuading that they experience the world so differently. Recent work on the philosophy of experiment has also shed considerable light on the intimate, symbiotic interaction between experiment and experimenter. This work also suggests that even in classical physics the experimental situation cannot be characterised as the observer standing apart from nature.[52] We therefore remain highly sceptical about the claim – so often touted in New Age circles – that the new physics makes us more part of nature than the old.

This brings us to one of our main criticisms. Even if the story we recounted earlier in this chapter is accepted by the historian of scientific ideas, there remains Capra's insistent Hegelian claim that ideas in science and philosophy determine all aspects of life. Capra condemned Cartesian dualism because it 'can be seen as *the essential reason* for the present series of social, ecological and cultural crises. It has alienated us from nature and from our fellow human beings.'[53] The model is of downward influence. Metaphysical ideas about the world shape all aspects of our lives. The ideas of Descartes and Newton have led inexorably to ecological crisis. Historians of philosophy should feel flattered that Capra has prioritised philosophical ideas and has attributed such dramatic impact to them. Yet such claims are highly problematic and most historians would not attribute such a powerful role to metaphysics.

There is also the problem of why the holistic, irenic message Capra locates in modern physics has not already delivered the green, beautiful world he seeks. After all, quantum theory has been with us for two-thirds of a century. Over this period we have not witnessed the impact of the new physics in changing the world for universal good; instead, wars, human strife and the degradation of nature have continued, even accelerated, during these past seventy years. There is clearly a major problem concerning the downwards-influence model. We might put it more strongly: that model is disastrously wrong. While metaphysics has certainly been influential in science so have the social, political, religious and technological forces that shape so many aspects of our lives, science included. For example, while Capra is commendably cautious in claiming that Laplace's response to Napoleon about God being a redundant hypothesis is only a story, the context of post-Revolutionary France is also highly pertinent. While championing a picture of the universe which was law-like Laplace also insisted that the scientist should not concern himself with philosophical and religious questions that fell outside the domain of science. Moreover, although Laplace had been trained in theology at the University of Caen, he was a reticent man who was careful not to discuss his religious beliefs in public. The position he adopted was, moreover, particularly serviceable in the anti-clerical atmosphere of the post-Revolutionary period. It is also highly relevant that Napoleon became a patron of Laplace, showering him with honours and appointing him minister of the interior – until he found how useless Laplace was at administrative duties![54] Put more generally, the downwards influence model is profoundly a-historical and fails to recognise the degree to which science is shaped by practice, by society, by technology, by politics and by religion.

Does the metaphysics of holism lead inevitably to the beautiful, green world that we would all welcome? It is worth remembering that the word 'holism' was coined in 1926 by Jan Christian Smuts, whose holistic views about evolution were used to legitimate the separation between the races and thus to justify apartheid in South Africa. Likewise, in Nazi Germany holism was held in high esteem and was used to sanction the racial superiority of Aryans and the persecution of non-Aryans.[55] There may be nothing intrinsically dangerous about holism, but it is always encountered in specific social situations. That it has appeared in the contexts of apartheid and racism should give us pause. Moreover, there may be dangers inherent in the widely-held belief that through its force as a pure idea holism can provide a new social order and even a new religion.

These comments take us far from the start of this chapter. We must stress that we did not set out to attack the New Age movement, but only a version of history that has often been peddled not only by New Agers but also by writers opposed to that movement. From the preceding criticisms it is abundantly clear that Capra's master-narrative is unacceptable as history. Indeed, as historical research progresses the complexity of the relationship between science and religion becomes increasingly apparent and irreducible to any master-narrative.[56] As historical research has progressed, the spotlight has turned increasingly to smaller pictures that clarify specific science–religion interactions. Yet, as the ensuing chapters indicate, such pictures can be satisfying, exciting and informative.

NOTES

1   P. Davies, *God and the New Physics*, Harmondsworth, 1984; *Idem., Other Worlds. Space, Superspace and the Quantum Universe*, Harmondsworth, 1990.

2   B. Appleyard, *Understanding the Present: Science and the Soul of Modern Man*, London, 1993, 83–100.

3   F. Capra, *The Tao of Physics: An Exploration of the Parallels between Modern Physics and Eastern Mysticism*, 2nd edn., New York, 1984, 7–8. Capra dates the rise of modern science to the late fifteenth century (*ibid.*, 8), but may have intended the sixteenth century.

4   *Ibid.*, 9. Emphasis added.

5   *Ibid.*, 43–4.

6   *Ibid.*, 45–6. See also F. Capra, *The Turning Point*, London, 1982, 54; D. Zohar, *The Quantum Self*, 1991, 4.

7   Capra, op. cit. (3), 48.

8   *Ibid.*, 50.

9   *Ibid.*, 70 and 57.

10   G. Zukav, *The Dancing Wu Li Masters. An Overview of the New Physics*, Toronto, 1980.

11   R. Sheldrake, *The Presence of the Past*, London, 1988; M. Berman, *Coming to our Senses. Body and Spirit in the Hidden History of the West*, New York, 1990; K. Wilber, *Eye to Eye. The Quest for a New Paradigm*, Garden City, 1973; *Quantum Questions. Mystical Writings of the World's Great Physicists* (ed. K. Wilber), Boston & London, 1985; A. Zajonc, *Catching the Light. The Entwined History of Light and Mind*, London, 1993. Our thanks to Tomas Vanheste in drawing our attention to Wilber's work. Judging by a talk Sheldrake delivered in Leeds in December 1994 he now endorses the main lines of the story recounted in this section.

12   R. Thompson, *Science and the Soul of Modern Man*, London, 1993; Appleyard, op. cit. (2).

13   W. Bloom, quoted by M. Perry, *Gods within. A Critical Guide to the New Age*, London, 1992, 35.

14   *The Science of Matter* (ed. M. P. Crosland), Harmondsworth, 1971; B. Russell, *History of Western Philosophy*, London, 1945; M. Capek, *The Philosophical Impact of Contemporary Physics*, Princeton, 1961; W. Heisenberg, *Physics and Philosophy*, New York, 1962; *Idem., Physics and Beyond*, New York, 1971. Heisenberg is the most cited author in the *Tao of Physics*.

15   T. S. Kuhn, *The Structure of Scientific Revolutions*, Chicago, 1962.

16   G. Cantor, *Optics after Newton. Theories of Light in Britain and Ireland, 1704–1840*, Manchester, 1983; J. Z. Buchwald, *The Rise of the Wave Theory of Light: Optical Theory and Experiment in the Early Nineteenth Century*, Chicago, 1989.

17   Zukav, op. cit. (10), 257; M. Ferguson, *The Aquarian Conspiracy. Personal and Social Transformation in the 1980s*, Los Angeles, 1981, 26. In these examples we see that some facets of Kuhn's use of 'paradigm' have been lost. Thus, for example, neither Zukav nor Ferguson retain its problem-solving function. Also, by emphasising the paradigm as a framework for ideas, they fail

to recognise that for Kuhn the paradigm not only encompassed ideas about the world but also directed scientific practice.

18 Capra, op. cit. (6), 35.

19 S. Shapin, *A Social History of Truth*, Chicago, 1994.

20 For example, A. Koyré, 'Galileo and Plato', *Journal of the History of Ideas*, 4 (1943), 400–28; *Galileo, Man of Science* (ed. E. McMullin), New York, 1967.

21 For example, W. Charleton, *Physiologia Epicuro-Gassendo-Charltoniana*, London, 1654. See also R. H. Kargon, 'Walter Charleton, Robert Boyle, and the acceptance of Epicurean atomism in England', *Isis*, 55 (1964), 184–92; *Idem.*, *Atomism in England from Hariot to Newton*, Oxford, 1966.

22 E. Bouratinos, paper delivered at the Third International Symposium on Science and Consciousness, Olympia, January 1993.

23 Zohar, op. cit. (6), 2.

24 G. P. Baker and K. J. Morris, 'Descartes unlocked', *British Journal for the History of Philosophy*, 1 (1993), 5–27.

25 R. Descartes, *Discourse on Method, Optics, Geometry, and Meteorology*, Indianapolis, 1965, 47. Gilson comments: 'C'est-à-dire: une substance complète, formée de l'union réelle d'un corps et d'une âme, et non une âme que ne ferait que se servir d'un corps' – *Discours de la Methode* (ed. E. Gilson), Paris, 1930, 435. See also Meditation 6 of Descartes' *Meditations*.

26 See, for example, D. Radner, 'Descartes' notion of the union of the mind and body', *Journal of the History of Philosophy*, 9 (1971), 159–70; R. C. Richardson, 'The "scandal" of Cartesian interactionism', *Mind*, 91 (1982), 20–37.

27 G. Galileo, *The Assayer*, in *The Controversy on the Comets of 1618* (ed. S. Drake), Philadelphia, 1960, 151–336; P. Redondi, *Galileo: Heretic*, Harmondsworth, 1988.

28 *The Cambridge Platonists* (ed. C. A. Patrides), Cambridge, 1980, 30.

29 J. E. McGuire, 'Force, active principles, and Newton's invisible realm', *Ambix*, 15 (1968), 154–208, on 171; *Idem.*, 'Neoplatonism and active principles: Newton and the *Corpus Hermeticum*' in *Hermeticism and the Scientific Revolution* (ed. R. S. Westman and J. E. McGuire), Los Angeles, 1977, 93–142; E. McMullin, *Newton on Matter and Activity*, Notre Dame, 1978; B. J. T. Dobbs, *The Foundations of Newton's Alchemy, or 'The Hunting of the Greene Lyon'*, Cambridge, 1975.

30 B. J. T. Dobbs, *The Janus Faces of Genius: The Role of Alchemy in Newton's Thought*, Cambridge, 1991.

31 R. Whytt, *An Essay on the Vital and other Involuntary Motions in Animals*, Edinburgh, 1751, 291. See T. S. Hall, *Ideas of Life and Matter. Studies in the History of General Physiology, 600BC–1900AD*, 2 vols., Chicago, 1969.

32 Closer inspection shows that there was not a straight shoot-out between vitalists and mechanistic reductionists. For a sophisticated discussion see T. Lenoir, *The Strategy of Life. Teleology and Mechanics in Nineteenth-Century German Biology*, Dordrecht, 1982.

33 J. Roger, *Les Sciences de la Vie dans la Pensée Française du XVIIIe Siècle. La Génération des Animaux de Descartes à l'Encyclopédie*, Paris, 1963; S. A. Roe, *Matter, Life, and Generation: Eighteenth-Century Embryology and the Haller–Wolff Debate*, Cambridge, 1981.

34 Capra, op. cit. (3), 45. The middle part of the quotation has been omitted. Capra's source was Capek, op. cit. (14), 122.

35 *Oeuvres Complètes de Laplace, Publiées sous les Auspices de l'Académie des Sciences, par MM. les Secrétaires Perpétuels*, 14 vols., Paris, 1878–1912, vii, vi–vii; viii, 144–5.

36 S. G. Brush, 'The chimerical cat: Philosophy of quantum mechanics in historical perspective', *Social Studies of Science*, 10 (1980), 393–447.

37 See, for example, contributions to *Romanticism and the Sciences* (ed. A. Cunningham and N. Jardine), Cambridge, 1990.

38 Novalis [F. von Hardenberg], *The Novices of Sais*, New York, 1949, 83–5 and 41.

39 *Ibid.*, 107.

40 Cunningham and Jardine, op. cit (37), 7–8. While the extreme critics of *Naturphilosophie* were highly vocal there were also many others, such as Justus von Liebig, who were more moderate in their criticisms and may even have accepted some aspects of Romanticism. It should also be noted that despite the apparent eclipse of scientific Romanticism, many historians now recognise that it exerted a long-term influence on science. See Lenoir, op. cit. (32) and papers contributed in *Osiris*, 5 (1989).

41 T. S. Kuhn, *Black-Body Theory and Quantum Discontinuity, 1894–1912*, Oxford, 1978; B. Wheaton, *The Tiger and the Shark. Empirical Roots of Wave–Particle Dualism*, Cambridge, 1983.

42 D. Murdoch, *Niels Bohr's Philosophy of Physics*, Cambridge, 1987.

43 D. Bohm, 'A suggested interpretation of the quantum theory in terms of "hidden" variables, I and II', *Physical Review*, 85 (1952), 166–93; J. T. Cushing, *Quantum Mechanics: Historical Contingency and the 'Copenhagen' Hegemony*, Chicago, 1994.

44 Capra, op. cit. (3), 56.

45 A. Pais, *'Subtle is the Lord . . .': The Science and the Life of Albert Einstein*, Oxford, 1982, 383.

46 Only in the 'Afterword' added to the second edition does Capra acknowledge Einstein's opposition, and then only to dismiss it. Capra, op. cit. (3), 301. It is interesting to note that Zukav, a non-scientist, provides a much more balanced account in op. cit. (10).

47 H. Chang, 'The quantum counter-revolution: Internal conflicts in scientific change', *Studies in History and Philosophy of Modern Physics*, 26B (1995), 121–36.

48 Capra, op. cit. (3), 294–5. The applicability of quantum mechanics to bridge building does seem rather limited!

49 Cited in Wilber, ed., op. cit. (11), 10.

50 I. G. Barbour, *Religion in an Age of Science*, London, 1990, 3–30. See also E. N. Hiebert, 'Modern physics and Christian faith' in *God and Nature: Historical Essays on the Encounter between Christianity and Science* (ed. D. C. Lindberg and R. L. Numbers), Berkeley, 1986, 424–47.

51 T. Roszak, *Where the Wasteland Ends. Politics and Transcendence in Postindustrial Society*, Berkeley, 1989, 182–4. We are grateful to Jonathan Coope for bringing this passage to our attention. Roszak has subsequently moved closer to Capra's position.

52 I. Hacking, *Representing and Intervening. Introductory Topics in the Philosophy of Natural Science*, Cambridge, 1983; D. Gooding, *Experiment and the Making of Meaning. Human Agency in Scientific Observation and Experiment*, Dordrecht, 1990.

53 Capra, op. cit (3), 9. Emphasis added.

54 C. C. Gillispie et al., 'Pierre-Simon, Marquis de Laplace', in *Dictionary of Scientific Biography* (ed. C. C. Gillispie), 16 vols., New York, 1970–80, xv, 273–403; M. Crosland, *The Society of Arcueil. A View of French Science at the Time of Napoleon I*, London, 1967; R. Hahn, 'Laplace and the vanishing role of God in the physical universe', in *The Analytical Spirit. Essays in the History of Science in Honor of Henry Guerlac* (ed. H. Woolf), Ithaca & London, 1981, 85–95, esp. 86.

55 J. C. Smuts, *Holism and Evolution*, London, 1926.

56 A number of issues relating to master-narratives are discussed by the contributors to the *British Journal for the History of Science*, 26 (1993), 387–483.

4

The Contemporary Relevance of the Galileo Affair

The scene is a piazza in Florence. Two drunks enter and confront the statue of a great scientist. In their inebriated state they find it impossible to articulate a name as testing as Galileo Galilei. 'What's he famous for?' asks the one. 'Wasn't it he who proved the earth spins?' comes the reply. 'Hic ... a colleague then' splutters the first.

Another monument, this time in Rome, stands as a reminder that a spinning earth was a terribly sober matter. The inscription on a column adjacent to the Villa Medici reads: 'It was here that Galileo was kept prisoner by the Holy Office, being guilty of having seen that the earth moves around the sun.'[1] Now it is true that Galileo, through his telescope, had seen many new things in the heavens, the moons of Jupiter for example and the phases of Venus; but one thing he had not seen – in the common meaning of 'see' – was the earth moving around the sun. He saw what everybody saw: the sun moving across the sky. In another sense of 'see', that of grasping or under-standing, the inscription may be less misleading; but it still carries a barbed message. The implication seems to be that Galileo was condemned for having seen the truth.

This simple message lies at the centre of what one might call the popular mythology of the Galileo affair. His forced recantation in June 1633 has been a potent, perhaps the most potent, symbol of the suppression of truth in the name of religion. When the actor Richard Griffiths, who had been playing the part of Galileo in Brecht's play, was asked to review a recent biography, he delivered the lines that have become all too familiar: 'By stifling the truth, which was there for anyone to see, the Church destroyed its credibility with science.'[2] Note the investment again in that powerful verb to 'see'. By contrast with the modern actor, the historian is obliged to ask whether the 'truth' was so transparent, whether Galileo's problems did not arise in part because he was trying to demonstrate motions of the earth that were *invisible.*[3] In this chapter we take a fresh look at the events surrounding Galileo's trial. Every generation re-examines the issues, placing its own construction on events and signalling the lessons that can be learned from them. Our own age is no exception. In recent years the Vatican itself has given the newspapers a field day. One has read headlines to the effect that 'Vatican admits Galileo was right all along', as if it is only in the 1990s that the Catholic Church has woken up to the fact that the earth is a planet.

Under such circumstances, arguments for the value of historical enquiry are not difficult to find. For example, we might ask how the Catholic Church sought to exonerate itself in the past and how far the admission of error is a recent phenomenon. Without a knowledge of the issues as they were perceived at the time, how can we begin to evaluate the rather bland remark of Pope John Paul[4] that 'in this affair the agreements between religion and science are more numerous and above all more important than the incomprehensions'? Such a remark may raise the deeper and more disturbing question: who controls the histories that have been constructed and reconstructed, whether in the service of the Catholic Church or in the interests of scientific humanism? Can an impartial history be written, or a consensus achieved, when the issues may still carry an emotional charge?

Inherent Conflict between Science and Religion – An A-historical Mould

There is a way of writing about the Galileo affair that has popular appeal but which has the effect of removing the need for serious historical enquiry. It could be described as fitting the history into an a-historical mould. The mould is shaped by the assumption that there is an inherent conflict between 'science' and 'religion', arising from competing sources of authority, competing methodologies, or competing criteria for truth. This view, that there is something essential to science and something essential to religion that keeps them perpetually at war, provides a ready-made interpretation of Galileo's misfortune. His trial is simply seen as the kind of event one would expect when a persecuting Church encountered a troublesome scientific innovator. It is a seductive interpretation because, scanning the events that led to the trial, it is easy enough to pick out those features which at first sight fit the picture.

There were, for example, genuine difficulties raised by the Copernican system, which the Church authorities could not disregard.[5] It violated the Aristotelian dichotomy between the corrupt sublunar and the perfect superlunary regions of the cosmos. It posed a dilemma concerning the status of humanity in the universe. There was a sense in which it elevated humankind by placing us in the heavenly region among the planets. But there was also a sense in which we were downgraded, wrenched from the centre of the cosmos. The telescopic observations for which Galileo became famous challenged the perfection of the heavens: there were mountains on the moon and spots on the sun.[6] There was also a formidable epistemological issue: whether through the practice of mathematical astronomy one could presume to construct a physical model that revealed the true geography of the cosmos. When the Lutheran Andreas Osiander had composed his anonymous *Preface* to Copernicus's great book of 1543, he had advised his readers not to be perturbed by the heliostatic proposal, for it was nothing more than a mathematical model.[7] Galileo believed otherwise.

If we are looking for sources of conflict they are not difficult to find. The authority of Scripture was undoubtedly an issue. Joshua's command to the sun to stand still was not a little curious if the sun were already at rest.[8] That the earth had become a planet opened up other possibilities. Perhaps other planets were inhabited? Perhaps, as Giordano Bruno had argued, there was an infinite plurality of worlds?[9] Where would we be then, bereft of our cosmic identity?[10] When Galileo compared the appearance of the moon's surface to that of Bohemia, he was quickly warned by his friend Giovanni Ciampoli to withdraw the comparison. Otherwise trouble-makers would soon be asking how descendants of Adam and Eve could possibly have got up there.[11]

The temptation to speak of warfare between religion and science may become even greater when we look at the behaviour of Galileo and his adversaries. There *were* ignorant priests among his detractors. One Niccolo Lorini vouchsafed to Galileo that 'the opinion of *Ipernicus* ... appears to be against Holy Scripture'.[12] Another Dominican, Tommaso Caccini, declared from his pulpit that all mathematicians were magicians and enemies of the faith. 'You can see how and by whom poor philosophy suffers', wrote Galileo to Prince Cesi, the founder of the scientific academy to which he belonged.[13] Galileo's own belligerent language is also too good to miss. He complained that his opponents were incapable of following the simplest argument and he wrote as if he had a patent on any discovery made in the heavens. In his slanging match with the Jesuit mathematician Horatio Grassi he pushed the display of satire to its limits. In a challenge to Galileo's ideas on the nature of heat, Grassi had observed that the Babylonians had cooked their eggs by whirling them in slings. Galileo's riposte was enough to make a Pope laugh:

> If Sarsi wants me to believe ... that the Babylonians cooked eggs by whirling them rapidly in slings, I shall do so; but I must say that the cause of this effect is very far from that which he attributes to it. To discover the truth I shall reason thus: 'If we do not achieve an effect which others formerly achieved, it must be that in our operations we lack something which was the cause of this effect succeeding, and if we lack but one single thing, then this alone can be the cause. Now we do not lack eggs, or slings, or sturdy fellows to whirl them; and still they do not cook, but rather they cool down faster if hot. And since nothing is lacking to us except being Babylonians, then being Babylonians is the cause of the eggs hardening'. And this is what I wished to determine.[14]

By a selective reading of the evidence the model of inherent 'conflict between science and religion' can begin to look plausible as an account of what lay behind the trial. But this is to squeeze events into a preconceived mould.[15] With the intervention of the historian the story does not simply become fuller. It takes on twists and turns that are sometimes surprising. And as they may break the mould of our expectations, so they may have a contemporary relevance. There are complications that are both fascinating and instructive.

Breaking the Mould: Some Historical Complications

One of the most enthralling aspects of the Galileo story concerns his relationship with Pope Urban VIII, which initially had been one of friendship. Even during the difficult year 1616 when the motion of the earth was prohibited, Maffeo Barberini, as he then was, did his best to reassure Galileo that as long as he spoke as a mathematician and avoided theological matters he would have nothing to fear. Although the consultants used by Cardinal Bellarmine reported that a central immobile sun was formally heretical, the official pronouncement by the Congregation of the Index did not employ the word 'heresy'.[16] There is evidence from a letter to Campanella, written many years later in 1630, that Barberini's presence may have been behind that deletion. In the letter Barberini implied that he had not even approved the weaker terms of the prohibition: 'It was never our intention [to prohibit Copernicus]; and if [it] had been left to us, that decree ... would not have been made'.[17] Galileo and his friends were elated when the cultured cardinal became Pope.

Mario Biagioli has recently written that 'Urban was a sophisticated courtier, humanist, and poet, not a scholastic theologian. He was a courtier-pope (and that it is why he appreciated Galileo so much).'[18]

Our earlier quip that Galileo's dismissal of the Jesuit Grassi was enough to make a Pope laugh was not a throwaway line. Galileo's *Assayer* (1623) had been dedicated to Barberini and it is known that parts of it were read aloud to him. Not only did he chortle while he dined; he was particularly impressed by a fable, told by Galileo, about a man who tried to discover the origin of a certain sound. Each time the man thought he had found the cause he heard the same sound again produced in some other way. In a crucial experiment on a cicada to solve the riddle once and for all, the man had pierced the poor creature's ligaments so severely that he had accidentally silenced *it*. It has been suggested that one reason why Barberini loved the story was that it resonated with his own conviction that the fun of scientific debate consisted in the cut and thrust of the duel, not in reaching closure and a definitive answer.[19]

The crucial point is that we are not dealing with a straightforward case of 'religion versus science'. Barberini had even written an adulatory poem in which the pursuit of astronomy was a moral and glorious enterprise.[20] Consequently the historian's question becomes, 'What went wrong with this relationship of mutual respect?' No general model of '*the* relations between science and religion' can possibly capture the nuances of such a change. Part of the explanation would seem to be that in his *Dialogue Concerning the Two Chief World Systems* (1632) Galileo mishandled an official instruction. He had been instructed to include the Pope's argument that definitive conclusions could not be reached in the natural sciences. God in his omnipotence could produce a natural phenomenon in any number of ways and it was therefore presumptuous for any philosopher to claim that he had determined a unique solution.[21] It was surely possible that the tides were produced by some mechanism quite other than by the earth's compound motions. Galileo did include the argument but he placed it in the mouth of Simplicio, often the dullard in the *Dialogue*.[22] As a defender of Aristotelian common sense Simplicio had been corrected time and again. Urban was not amused.[23] It would be easy to claim that a friendship had been betrayed, though it is difficult to believe this was Galileo's intention.[24]

A second complication concerns the origins of animosity towards Galileo. On the basis of the simple conflict model, one would expect his enemies to be powerful figures in the Church. Galileo, however, did not see it that way – at least initially. His *Letter to the Grand Duchess*

Christina, which dates from 1615, began with a quite different complaint. It was that academic professors were stirring up trouble for him and were trying to inveigle the Church authorities into denouncing him.[25] Here the crucial point is that Galileo made academic enemies because his scientific innovations were a threat to Aristotelian principles. On such matters as floating bodies, falling bodies, and imperfection in the heavens he was contravening an established science of nature. Because the Catholic Church had a heavy investment in Aristotelian philosophy, the conflict was not a simple one between 'science' and 'religion'. It was rather between new science and the science sanctified by previous generations. Such complications in fact make it extremely difficult to use words such as 'science' and 'religion' when reconstructing the issues. It has been said, for example, that Galileo perceived the Aristotelian professors as if they were members of a religious order.[26] The point could perhaps be made this way. Whereas those who revered the authority of Aristotle in natural philosophy were bound to oppose Galileo's innovations, the question for churchmen who took an interest in nature was how far their Church was bound to protect Aristotelian principles. When Galileo asked whether the affirmation of change in the heavens was admissible, Cardinal Carlo Conti replied that the Bible did not support Aristotle. The common opinion of the Fathers, contrary to Aristotle, had been that the heavens are corruptible.[27]

Between 1610 and 1620 there was even movement among the Jesuits away from Aristotelian dogma. Cardinal Bellarmine, who had to break the news to Galileo in 1616 that he was no longer free to promote the Copernican system, nevertheless accepted the argument that Scripture did not favour the immutability of the heavens.[28] In conceding that fresh consideration might have to be given to certain biblical texts, were the motion of the earth to be demonstrated, Bellarmine also diverged from what has been seen as the standard Dominican position – that astronomical hypotheses were mathematical models only and in principle untranslatable into physical truths.[29] The Jesuit Grassi, with whom Galileo quarrelled, was prepared to abandon Aristotle's notion that comets were sublunar phenomena.[30] There was even a willingness among Jesuit astronomers to embrace the system of the Protestant Tycho Brahe. This was an ingenious model, conservative in that the earth remained stationary at the centre, but also radical in that all the planets were allowed to orbit the sun. Necessarily on this view, the sun orbited the earth, carrying the planets with it.[31] To Galileo this was a cumbersome compromise, but it was difficult to disprove. It is worth stressing again that we are dealing here not with competition

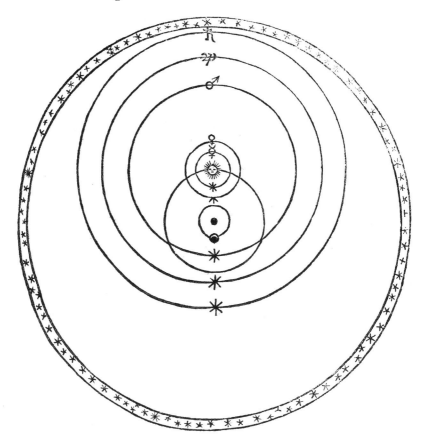

Figure 13: The earth-centred system of Tycho Brahe with the planets circling the sun. From *De Mundi Aetherei Recentioribus Phaenomenis*, in *Opera Omnia* (1648).

between 'science' and 'religion' , but with competing scientific models that can also be differentiated in terms of their respective theological appeal.

Divisions of opinion within the Catholic Church constitute a third complication. In popular writing on science and religion, 'the Church' is often presented as a monolithic institution with a non-negotiable set of beliefs. But when the Copernican system was placed under review in 1615–16, it was partly because Bellarmine was genuinely uncertain about the kind of response that was required. We have already seen that the future Pope, Maffeo Barberini, took a different view from those whom Bellarmine consulted. And whilst the discussion was underway, the Dominican Tommaso Campanella developed forceful arguments which, had they been accepted, would have left Galileo free to continue his Copernican rhetoric.[32] That there could be real divisions over strategy becomes perfectly clear from Campanella's warning about the consequences if his Church were to condemn the Copernican system. Rather like Galileo himself, he warned that if the new astronomy were vindicated it would 'bring upon our Roman faith no small mockery in the eyes of heretics, for all [Galileo's] doctrine and the telescope have found avid acceptance in Germany, France, England, Poland and Sweden'.[33] Doctrinal divisions and political jealousies between Dominicans and Jesuits were also part of the complex. Their interminable controversy over divine grace and free will combined with the Jesuits' commitment to an education in the physical sciences had produced a situation in which Galileo and the Jesuit astronomer Christopher Scheiner were to become enemies because they had so much in common.[34] In one of the most original recent studies, Galileo's downfall is ascribed to his pushing the Jesuits one step too far, asking them to accept too much without the requisite proof. According to Rivka Feldhay we have to recognise a 'triple struggle for cultural hegemony' within the Church, the science of Galileo upsetting a precarious balance and polarising existing forces.[35] It is the disparity of views among those who became embroiled in the Galileo affair that makes historical research so rewarding. A further illustration comes from the period leading up to the trial when Galileo's friend Benedetto Castelli reported an exchange with Vincenzo Maculano, the Commissary of the Holy Office. Castelli's report is particularly pertinent because Maculano was eventually to be Galileo's interrogator. According to Castelli, Maculano had said that he personally did not believe that the matter of the earth's motion could be decided by the authority of Scripture and that he wanted to write on the subject himself. Galileo's interrogator may have been more sympathetic to his plight than external formalities allowed.[36]

This brings us to our fourth complication: the authority of Scripture and how it should be constituted. The issue arises because, as Galileo himself had pointed out, a flat appeal to the Bible simply glossed over the fact that everything hinged on how it was to be interpreted. Only his crudest opponents, such as Lodovico delle Colombe, had adopted the principle that 'when Scripture can be understood literally, it ought never be interpreted differently'.[37] Colombe claimed that all theologians, without exception, adopted this view. Yet Galileo could retaliate that, on the contrary, it was the principle of biblical accommodation that was 'so commonplace and so definite among all theologians that it would be superfluous to present any testimony for it'.[38]

The crucial contrast, however, is not between Galileo and Colombe but between Galileo and Bellarmine. It was Bellarmine who had to clarify the official position in 1615 in response to the work of Paolo Foscarini who had published a text in which the earth's motion was shown to be compatible with Scripture. Bellarmine's reply to Foscarini is one of the most fascinating documents in the whole affair. As we indicated in chapter 1 there is one paragraph in his letter that almost suggests he was more liberal on biblical exegesis than Galileo himself. Bellarmine wrote, 'that if there were a true demonstration that the sun is at the centre of the world and the earth in the third heaven ... then one would have to proceed with great care in explaining the Scriptures that appear contrary, and say rather that we do not understand them than that what is demonstrated is false'.[39]

This seems a long way from the view that Galileo was condemned because he had seen the truth. Superficially at least, Bellarmine seems to be allowing room for manoeuvre. But there was also a reactionary note in Bellarmine's letter, illustrating a point that historians feel obliged to underline. When it comes to the defence of authority, several different argumentative strategies may be more attractive than one, even though they may not all cohere. If there is inconsistency between them, it may also indicate uncertainty about how to proceed.

Arguably, Galileo himself was inconsistent on the extent to which Scripture had jurisdiction over science. Invoking the authority of St Augustine, he had contrasted propositions that were rigorously demonstrated with those that were not. As to the former, the onus was on wise divines to show that they did not contradict the Bible, but the latter were to be rejected if they contravened Scripture.[40] We can see in retrospect that problems arose because the Copernican theory was still being developed and did not properly fit into either of Galileo's categories.[41] The inconsistency in his position concerns the implication that Scripture retains its jurisdiction over undemonstrated propositions whereas he had earlier said that biblical language had been 'accommodated' to the needs of simple folk and was not to be confused with the technical vocabulary of the natural philosopher.[42] If undemonstrated propositions that clashed with Scripture were to be held 'undoubtedly false', Galileo could be regarded as having undermined his own position.[43]

It was, however, an inconsistency in Bellarmine's position that was to prove the more dangerous. Although he appeared to leave the door open for reinterpretation in the event of a rigorous proof, that possibility was not seriously entertained. The door had, in effect, already been shut. Bellarmine had locked it by referring to the Council of Trent's ruling that where there was agreement among the Fathers on the exegesis of a particular text, that consensus had to be respected. And their consensus had in fact been in favour of a literal interpretation of the ostensibly geostatic verses.[44] Galileo had two counter arguments. One was that the Fathers could not have come to a deliberate conclusion because they had written long before it had become, with Copernicus, a real issue. The other was that physical propositions should be distinguished from matters of faith – a contention famously expressed in the aphorism that the Bible teaches how to go to heaven, not how heaven goes.[45] But he was in for a shock when Bellarmine gave a new twist to what might be meant by a matter of faith. In Bellarmine's letter to Foscarini there was a stern warning that the issue after all was a matter of faith. It might not be 'as regards the topic' but it was 'as regards the speaker'.[46] In the last analysis it was the Holy Spirit who had spoken and who could not be gainsaid. The tragedy is that, in placing his own gloss on the Tridentine decree, Bellarmine extended the domain of truths to be believed on the basis of faith. There was a sense in which the category of 'faith and morals' was now all-embracing.[47] In the long run the Catholic Church had to abandon that hard, undiscriminating line. The irony is that *Galileo*'s principles of exegesis are now declared by the Vatican to have been in the best traditions of his Church.[48]

If the theology is to be contextualised, so must the science be. Just how convincing were Galileo's proofs of the earth's motion? This is a difficult question and a further complication because what is convincing to one scholar may not be to another. What is clear is that the situation was far more complex than would be implied by the popular antithesis between truth and error. Galileo had powerful arguments against Aristotelian philosophy and against a traditional cosmography. Mountains on the moon and spots on the sun told against the perfection of the heavens. The observed phases of Venus were only possible if that planet at least were in orbit around the sun. Even on such straightforward matters, however, the case had not been without its problems. Suppose the dark spots were not on the sun's surface but the shadows cast by satellites in orbit around it? That suggestion was made by Christopher Scheiner, who buttressed his case by pointing out that to postulate satellites around the sun was perfectly in keeping with Galileo's own discovery of satellites around Jupiter![49] There was of course a logical problem too. To remove objections to the earth's motion is one thing, but it is not the

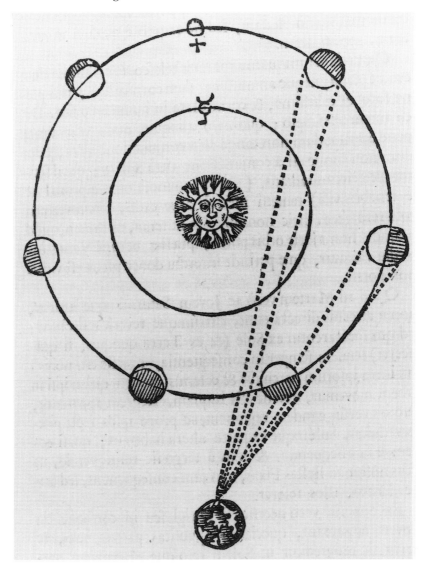

Figure 14: The phases of Venus become explicable if Venus orbits the sun.
From Pierre Gassendi, *Institutio Astronomica* (1653).

same as proving that it moves. Had there been only two chief world
systems, the Ptolemaic and the Copernican, to disprove the one
would have been to establish the other. Galileo himself saw all the
advantages of presenting the case that way. But there were other

options, notably the system of Tycho Brahe to which we have referred, in which all the planets but not the earth orbited the sun, and the sun continued to circle a stationary earth. Not a single one of the telescopic observations refuted it. How then were the earth's invisible motions to be demonstrated?

One of Galileo's tactics was to argue indirectly by analogy. From the changing pattern of the sunspots he inferred that the sun must be rotating, lending plausibility to the case for a rotating earth. Such arguments, however compelling, were not conclusive. He obviously needed a trump card. But in the game he was playing it was easy to over-reach himself. And brilliant philosopher though he was, he was not infallible.

His confidence was placed in an argument from the tides. His readers were to imagine a Venetian barge carrying water. When the barge hit the side of the quay, the sudden impact would set up an oscillation in the water. The phenomenon of the tides is one in which there is similar oscillation of the seas. It could therefore be produced if the earth were subject to a comparable jolt or regular series of jolts. And because the earth has both its axial and orbital revolutions, points on its surface will experience such an effect. Judged against an appropriate frame of reference there would be changes in their absolute speed, arising from a combination of motions that partially reinforced each other but which, for part of every day, did not. Thus were the tidal motions produced.

It is now generally agreed that Galileo over-reached himself scientifically because within the frames of reference defined by the earth's motions such an effect would not be experienced. By giving this argument prominence in the *Dialogue*, he also over-reached himself diplomatically. Urban VIII had not liked the argument because it unequivocally transposed the Copernican hypothesis into a physical and not merely a mathematical conception.[50] Moreover, a proper respect for the omnipotence of God required the concession that other mechanisms might have been created to produce the tides. The upshot of all this has been correctly conveyed by Maurice Finocchiaro when he writes:

> We are dealing with nonapodictic arguments which are not completely conclusive but rather susceptible of degrees of rational correctness, and so it is entirely conceivable that there should sometimes be equally good arguments in support of opposite sides, as well as that the arguments for one side should be better than those for the opposite, without the latter being worthless.[51]

Once this is acknowledged there can be no black and white treatment of the Galileo affair. There is, however, a residual irony. Galileo was not condemned in 1633 because he had failed to produce adequate proof. His crime was to have presented his proofs in such a way that they were made to appear strong and effective. It was this that convinced the team of investigators that he had overstepped the mark in positively promoting the Copernican system when he had been forbidden to do so.[52]

Historical Context

We have been suggesting that, for the historian, events no longer fall into the simple mould of 'science versus religion' or 'religion versus science'. Even among Galileo's detractors, such as Caccini, it was acknowledged that he was widely regarded as a loyal Catholic.[53] To place the Galileo affair in context means placing it in the context of Counter-Reformation culture. At its most theological, this meant a working out of the principle that authority was not to be vested in Scripture alone, as Protestant reformers demanded, but in tradition as well. As Melchior Cano, one of the founders of post-Tridentine theology, insisted, tradition had preceded the Scriptures in the early history of the Church and arguably contained the greater part of revelation.[54] In his influential work *De Locis Theologicis* (1563), Cano had recognised that 'when the authority of the saints ... pertains to the faculties contained within the natural light of reason, it does not provide certain arguments but only arguments as strong as reason itself when in agreement with nature'.[55] That could have provided just the space that Galileo required. But when speaking of the exposition of Scripture, Cano had declared that 'the common interpretation of all the old saints provides the theologian with a most certain argument for the corroboration of theological assertions; for indeed the meaning of the Holy Spirit is the same as the meaning of all of the saints'. As if that were not enough he had added that 'all the saints taken together cannot err on dogmas of the faith'.[56] This was the message Bellarmine preferred and which he delivered back to Foscarini. Why? It is difficult not to see the effect of a life-time's engagement with Protestant heretics – an engagement that had led to a creeping rigidity on both sides.[57] Bellarmine had also presided over the trial of Giordano Bruno whose extension of Copernican ideas to embrace an infinite plurality of worlds was only one heresy among many.[58] It had been rumoured at the time that Bruno had declared Christ a rogue who got what he deserved, that all monks were asses, and Catholic doctrines asinine. In the long struggle to control heresy both within and without his Church, Bellarmine was inexorably driven towards his reactionary stance. Galileo did not fight shy of interpreting Scripture for himself. He even suggested that the miracle of the long day of Joshua was more comprehensible on the Copernican than the Ptolemaic system.[59] It would not have been difficult to perceive Galileo as a crypto-Protestant, tarred with the same brush as his friend Paolo Sarpi who had led a Venetian revolt against the papacy.[60]

The impact of Protestant–Catholic dialectics on Galileo's fate may have been indirect but it was real enough.[61] Urban VIII had had his own concerns about protecting the faithful. The problem was the loss of authorial control. New ideas in cosmology, even if presented by loyal members of the Church, were liable to have more dangerous and dissident ideas read into them: 'One man amplifies, the next one alters, and what came from the author's own mouth becomes so transformed in spreading that he will no longer recognize it as his own.'[62] By contrast Galileo implied that one of his reasons for publishing his *Dialogue* was that it would prove a good Catholic could be at the forefront of astronomical thinking.

Despite his qualms, as late as 1630 Urban still believed that the ban of 1616 had been too severe.[63] Why then was he so severe on Galileo? He was evidently insulted by the *Dialogue*, but was he working under other pressures that might have provoked an over-reaction? As part of the context in which the dénouement occurred, at least two such pressures have been identified. One came from Spain through complaints that the Roman Inquisition was being too soft on dissidents.[64] The other, with which it was connected, arose from Urban VIII's foreign policy during the Thirty Years War.

Having sided with France to prevent a Hapsburg hegemony, he found himself in an exposed position when Louis XIII agreed to an alliance with the Protestant Gustavus Adolphus of Sweden. Gustavus was enjoying military success against the German Empire and so it appeared that Urban was betraying the Catholic cause.[65] This compounded the criticism from Spain, which was voiced in a dramatic manner on 8 March 1632. At a meeting of the consistory, Cardinal Borgia, who represented the Spanish interest, read out a harsh protest at Urban's failure to support the Spanish campaign against Protestants in Germany. There was even the insinuation that a Council was needed to assess the Pope's will to defend Christianity. Urban and his nephew tried to silence the man but unsuccessfully. Urban's brother was moved to grab him but was stopped in his tracks. Eventually the guards were called in to control the unrest. Cardinals, we are told, broke their glasses and tore their hats.[66]

Having failed to protect himself against charges of nepotism, Urban VIII clearly had enough worries without having to consider whether the earth was moving under his feet. His treatment of Galileo has been seen, not surprisingly, as part of a determination to reassert his authority. A nervous Pope, having his horoscope read and fearing poison, was not perhaps the most balanced judge of Galileo's machinations, or his loyalty.[67]

Galileo himself needed an explanation of the Pope's disaffection. He found it in the conjecture that Urban had been got at by the Jesuits.[68] Was he right? Or was this self-delusion? Either way his relations with the Jesuit Order become an aspect of the context that cannot be ignored. It is certainly tempting to implicate the Jesuits with whom Galileo had fallen out. Christopher Scheiner was in Rome at the time of the trial and still smarting from the controversy over sunspots in which Galileo, so he believed, had cheated him of priority. Scheiner's flattering description of his adversary was of an impudent usurper.[69] The evidence for estrangement is certainly there. One of the ironies is that the ban on the Copernican system issued in 1616 created a situation in which, even if Galileo had got a decisive proof of the earth's motion, he was not allowed to publish it. The Jesuits were aware of this and displayed the kind of anxiety that comes from wondering whether Galileo, after all, knew something they did not. The quarrel with Grassi over the nature of comets undoubtedly created an atmosphere in which Galileo and the Jesuits became locked in an intellectual trial of strength. Any vestige of friendship Grassi might have retained was to disappear when he saw a letter from Florence claiming that the Jesuits would be powerless to answer Galileo's arguments. Grassi's reported reaction was that if his Order could answer a hundred heretics a year, they would not be beaten by one Catholic.[70]

At this point we should remember that Urban VIII had not vetoed discussion of the Copernican system as a mathematical hypothesis, but he had precluded its presentation as a physical reality. A deeper exploration of the context becomes necessary here because an ambiguity in what might be meant by a scientific hypothesis arguably created scope for misunderstanding. The importance of the distinction has been brought out by saying that it could be a more radical position to interpret the Copernican system as a physical hypothesis and *reject* it, than to interpret it in the purely mathematical sense and to *accept* it. It could be accepted as an instrument facilitating the prediction of planetary positions without transgressing a traditional hierarchy of the sciences in which mathematical astronomy could not dictate terms to physics.[71] The conservative position on this matter had been expressed by the Dominican theologian Giovanni Tolosani when he had judged the Copernican system to be heretical. Revealingly he castigated Copernicus for mixing the disciplinary realms of physics and astronomy.[72]

It would be misleading to suggest that within the Catholic Church there had been no movement towards a *physical* astronomy. Before his death in 1612, the Jesuit astronomer Christopher Clavius had already rejected a purely instrumentalist approach to astronomical theory.[73] This means that even within the Church there was the possibility of misunderstanding when reference was made to astronomical hypotheses. There is evidence, too, that the very possibility of a shift towards a physical astronomy was dividing Jesuits and Dominicans around 1615–1616 when the Copernican hypothesis was subject to scrutiny.[74] Misunderstanding actually arose because Galileo was so often told that he should treat the Copernican system only as a supposition. To him this might have meant that he was allowed to discuss it as a provisional truth-claim, as long as the emphasis was on the provisional. But the instruction to confine himself to a hypothetical discussion might have been intended quite differently: that he should remain within the bounds of a mathematical model that had no pretensions to physical representation.

It was, therefore, possible for Galileo and Urban VIII to talk past each other and for each to be unpleasantly surprised by the eventual moves of the other.[75] Divergences of perception were accentuated because those who mediated between Galileo and Urban tended to be selective in what they communicated. In either direction the diplomacy could leave both men deceived. It was only parts of Galileo's *Assayer*, notably the 'fable of sound', that Urban had had read to him. Likewise with another of Galileo's productions, his *Letter to Ingoli*. This had been written in the summer of 1624 and was construed by Galileo's friends as an explicit defence of Copernicus. It was eventually read to Urban by Ciampoli who reported back to Galileo a favourable reaction. But as Fantoli shrewdly observes, 'it is probable that Ciampoli chose with dexterity those passages where there was no risk of offending the susceptibility of the Pope'.[76] We can therefore understand how it was possible for relations to remain cordial until the storm broke over the *Dialogue*.[77] According to the Tuscan ambassador, Niccolini, what really irked the Pope was that 'when asking Ciampoli many times what was happening with Galileo, His Holiness had never been told anything but good and had never been given the news that the book was being printed, even when he was beginning to smell something'.[78] Urban was incensed because he saw a mixture of deception and betrayal in the promotion of a physical doctrine already condemned.

The Uses of History

We have been suggesting that a richer understanding of the Galileo affair can be gained if we refrain from squeezing it into a preconceived mould. It is also instructive to see how the story has been used in subsequent historical contexts. As a deeply symbolic episode in the cultural history of Europe it has been endlessly reconstructed to satisfy new needs and to support new agendas. So many different images of Galileo have been constructed that one scholar has wryly referred to a 'trial of Galileos'.[79]

An obvious place to start would be with the early histories written by Roman Catholic scholars in the defence and exoneration of their Church. Their writing was all the more urgent because there was undoubtedly a current of opinion within Catholic Europe that Galileo had been unjustly treated.[80] It could always be argued that through his disobedience he had been responsible for his own downfall. One could point to his impetuosity, to the scorn he arrogantly poured on others. It was not difficult to paint a picture in which he had tried to foist the Copernican system on his Church before he had decisive proof. Within what we might call a conservative Catholic historiography, it would be taken for granted that the Church has a moral right to discipline its members. The immorality could always be imputed to Galileo who, at his trial in 1633, had denied what was manifestly true – that he had championed, in print, the moving earth.[81]

There were many variations on these themes. In attacks on the cogency of Galileo's science, it would sometimes be said that his proof from the tides was misconceived. With even more ingenuity, unfavourable contrasts would later be drawn between Galileo and Kepler. The trick here was to say that the Copernican theory, as defended by Galileo, was in fact false. Galileo had continued to regard a circular motion for the planets as natural, despite Kepler's proof that they moved in ellipses. Taking the system as a whole, Galileo was wrong. Because of this, the Church might be excused for stamping on inferior science! The arguments were not always that devious, but there would usually be reference to the inconclusiveness of the scientific evidence at the time.

It is striking that when the Church's position eventually changed in the early 1820s, the history of science gained a peculiar significance. Guiseppe Settele, a professor of astronomy at the University of Rome, was given permission by the Commissary of the Holy Office to present the Copernican system as fact rather than hypothesis, but only on the condition that he showed his readers that the scientific difficulties with which the system had once been beset were no longer cogent.[82] This shift had at least two consequences. By 1835, Copernican books, including Galileo's *Dialogue*, were removed from the Index. And henceforward Catholic scientists could cite the Galileo affair as a warning of what would happen again if a scientific doctrine that might ultimately prevail were outlawed. As we shall see in chapter 8, the Catholic evolutionist St George Mivart would present himself as a latter-day Galileo when his relations with Rome deteriorated in the closing decades of the nineteenth century.

New histories often reflect new historical circumstances. We can perhaps best appreciate this from recent events. Why did Pope John Paul II choose to encourage new historical initiatives? One answer that *he* gave was to help avoid similar mistakes in the future. It was recognised that the Church had burdened itself with an image of repression that elicits scorn from those who value the autonomy of the sciences. As others have observed, it can hardly be coincidence that a Polish pope should take so distinctive an interest in the treatment accorded the theory of a Polish astronomer. But if there has been a re-writing of history and a frank admission of error, it is not the end of the story. One recent biographer of Galileo, James Reston, remains disillusioned. Having asked why the latest official statements contain no specific criticism of Pope Urban VIII, he was told that this was because the Commission's study was about events not personalities. As the author of a lively study of the personalities involved, Reston found this reply lame. To be told that the errors had been made by Galileo's judges, not by Urban VIII, was a hard pill to swallow if one believed that Urban had been involved in the orchestration of events.[83] In the eyes of a Catholic biographer of Galileo there is still unfinished business.[84]

What of the alternative historiographical traditions in which Galileo has been the hero, the scientific genius, the brilliant empiricist who unequivocally had the truth on his side? From his trial and tribulation messages of contemporary relevance have been repeatedly drawn. His first biographer, Vincenzio Viviani, launched the heroic Galileo. Although Galileo's date of birth is usually given as 15 February 1564, Viviani wanted it to be 18 February because it would then be the same day on which Michelangelo had died. Florence could then boast its unbroken succession of genius. As Michelangelo had been made the patron-saint of the artists, so Galileo might become the same for the mathematical philosophers.[85] It had been the fashion in Renaissance biography to project an image of the artist as a child prodigy, gifted with an almost supernatural knowledge of nature. An artist's date of birth would assume the highest significance, as if a god were being born. To conform to literary taste a little 'image enhancement' was the order of the day.[86] Viviani, writing in Italian for a cultured audience, duly obliged. Galileo was the child prodigy who had been self-taught, had read his first Latin authors at a tender age, had learned Greek, mastered the lute and shown exceptional promise as a painter. For an audience that would appreciate the force of visual demonstration more than mathematics, Viviani gave them Galileo the shrewd observer, the acute experimenter. He was only nineteen, according to Viviani, when he inferred the principle of the pendulum from a swinging lamp in Pisa cathedral. And he was still a young man when he spectacularly refuted Aristotle on falling bodies. Did the rate of fall depend on the weight of the object, as Aristotle had taught? Such a view could not withstand the simple test of experiment. Ostentatiously dropping different weights from the leaning tower of Pisa, Galileo showed they hit the ground simultaneously. Viviani even spoke of 'repeated experiments in the presence of other lecturers and philosophers and all the student body'.[87]

There is only one problem with these towering images. They are almost certainly untrue. The swinging lamp that so transfixed Galileo was not itself fixed in the cathedral until four years after the date assigned by Viviani. As for the constant frequency of the pendulum swing, this was not mentioned by Galileo himself until some fifteen years later. The story of the leaning tower became so embellished in later accounts that some wit once calculated that if Galileo had really dropped the massive weights ascribed to him, they would have sunk so far into the foundations that he and the tower would have crumbled to the ground. The evidence suggests that at the time he was allegedly conducting his experiment Galileo still believed that objects made from different materials would fall at different rates. And what he actually reported was an even more curious result – that when balls of lead and wood were released simultaneously, the wood got off to a flying start, only to be overtaken by the lead in due course.[88] One of the most heroic images of Galileo is at the very least distorted.

Viviani was associated with the Tuscan court throughout his life. In Galileo's declining years, he had become his amanuensis. The brief life that he composed reflected the biographical style of his day and a desire to defend his master's reputation. Not everyone of his

GALILEO, 1590.

Figure 15: The depiction of a famous myth. From Baden Powell, *Essays on the Spirit of Inductive Philosophy, the Unity of Worlds, and the Philosophy of Creation* (1855).

generation would have accepted his portrayal of the discerning empiricist. There were practical men like the unfortunate gunner Giovanni Battista Renieri who aimed his artillery in accord with Galileo's theory of projectiles, only to complain that he kept missing his target. He had to be reminded by Galileo's pupil Torricelli that his master spoke the language of geometry and was not bound by any empirical result.[89] The methods of the real Galileo were certainly more subtle than Viviani implied. But his narrative provided the raw materials for many later accounts in which Galileo would be cast as the heroic founder of modern science. One could set the heroic interpreter of nature against the obscurantism of the Church and so create a parable for one's own time. Wherever anti-Catholic and anti-clerical feelings ran high, as they so often did in Europe during the eighteenth and nineteenth centuries, Galileo would become an emblem for the causes of secularity and freedom of enquiry.

During the nineteenth century a hagiographic line became so entrenched, especially in Italy, that to question it was to suffer ignominy. A serious, six-volume, reappraisal was made by Raffaello Caverni in the 1890s. One of his concerns was that Galileo had scooped the credit for many innovations that should be properly ascribed to his predecessors and contemporaries. But nobody wished to know. Since the unification of Italy, Galileo had been such a national hero that dissenting scholarship was marginalised.[90] In the English-speaking world, the 1870s saw John Draper returning to the Galileo affair when blasting new claims for papal infallibility. 'What a spectacle!', Draper exclaimed. 'This venerable man, the most illustrious of his age, forced by the threat of death to deny facts which his judges as well as himself knew to be true! He was then committed to prison, treated with remorseless severity during the remaining ten years of his life.'[91] Here is a classic statement of the mythology with which we began. Galileo's judges condemned him knowing that he was right.[92]

In the twentieth century the fate of Galileo was to have a profound contemporary relevance for Bertolt Brecht struggling against the oppression of Hitler and the Nazis in the late 1930s. In his play, *The Life of Galileo*, a drama unfolds in which the characters are all too human: we recognise vanity, passion, cunning, loyalty, betrayal and humiliation. For this reason, the play has a certain timeless quality: it has been described as a human tragedy of universal significance.[93] But it is also a play deeply rooted in its time. The pressing moral issue was how the responsible intellectual should behave in the face of an oppressive and terrifying regime. Through the life of Galileo, Brecht could explore the issue of intellectual liberty in the face of an absolute power. The issue was not now science versus religion. Brecht was using the Catholic Church in Galileo's day as an example, a symbol of autocratic power. We should not forget that there were frightening parallels in Nazi Germany. A Nobel Prize winner, the physicist Philipp Lenard had sought to banish Einstein from the community of scientists and was now busy on a substantial work of 'German Physics' designed to show that physics was an Aryan subject to which Jews had made no contribution.[94] It would be difficult to find a more telling example of the ideological uses of history. In his play Brecht tackled the question of how truth could be spread in the face of oppression. The answer had to be illegally, as Galileo had done when smuggling his last great work out of the house where it had been completed.

In writing his play Brecht was forced to think about the moral responsibility of scientists themselves. He disliked the view that they should accumulate knowledge in ivory towers, with never a thought for the welfare of humanity. Once again there were events in the late 1930s that gave this question a new urgency. Scientists themselves were speaking of a new age in which undreamed-of energy could be unleashed from the atom. But with war looming, Brecht immediately saw that the scientists' dreams could turn into nightmares. He would write the prophetic line that 'practically every new invention is greeted with a shout of triumph, which immediately turns into a cry of horror'.[95] On 6 August 1945 the bomb was dropped on Hiroshima.

We have been referring to the contemporary relevance of the Galileo affair in the sense that each generation has found its own meanings in those events of long ago. New perspectives can come into force with explosive suddenness. Brecht was working on an English version of his play when the bomb fell. 'Overnight', he wrote, 'the biography of the founder of modern physics had to be read differently. The infernal effect of the huge bomb projected the conflict between Galileo with the authorities of his day into a new, sharper light.'[96]

Philosophers as well as playwrights have seen contemporary relevance in Galileo's life. In 1975 Paul Feyerabend published a book with the provocative title *Against Method.* His opposition was directed against attempts to construct formal accounts of scientific methodology which had the effect of imposing a spurious uniformity on disparate scientific practices. Feyerabend's aim was to show that 'science is an essentially anarchistic enterprise'.[97] History was the perfect accomplice. With acknowledgement to Lenin, he set out his stall: history generally, and the history of revolutions in particular, is always richer in content, more varied, more many-sided, more lively and subtle than even the best historian and the best methodologist can imagine.[98] Streamlined histories of science that purported to show the success of a unique and privileged methodology were a form of 'brainwashing' that had to be resisted.[99] What the history of science really showed was that progress had been made by breaking every rule in the book.[100] The proliferation of theories was to be encouraged. In fact the only principle that does not inhibit progress is that *anything goes.*[101]

Galileo's attempt to prove that the *earth* goes was now enlisted in support of this more chaotic image of science. On Feyerabend's reading we must emphatically not begin from the premise that Galileo had the truth on his side. There is a sense in which the Copernican system could be said to have been refuted. Only with *ad hoc* assumptions, such as the expansion of the universe, could it be saved. Nor was it obvious that the images Galileo had seen through his telescope were to be trusted. In fact his own report of the lunar surface showed a crater so large that it ought to be visible to the naked eye. Since the circle did not square with what could be seen, Feyerabend spoke of another 'refuted view' – that is the view that telescopic phenomena are faithful images of the sky.[102] Speaking now as a historian, Feyerabend pressed his interpretation: 'while the pre-Copernican astronomy *was in trouble* ... the Copernican theory *was in even greater trouble*; but ... being in harmony *with still further inadequate theories* it gained strength, and was retained, the refutations being made ineffective by *ad hoc* hypotheses and clever techniques of persuasion'.[103] A long way indeed from the triumphalist rhetoric of scientific rationalism.

Feyerabend was speaking to a generation that, in his view, had come to revere too much the scientific experts with their stylised images of scientific rationality. Images of uniformity, whether of theory or practice, conveyed by the scientific community positively endangered 'the free development of the individual'.[104] Nor did he pull any punches. As the accepting and rejecting of ideologies should be left to the individual, it followed that 'the separation of state and *church* must be supplemented by the separation of state and *science*, that most recent, most aggressive, and most dogmatic religious institution'.[105] Tendentiously he wrote of science as a kind of superstition. And, horror of horrors to those on the inside, he even envisaged circumstances in which the State, political party *or the Church* might have to interfere in order to re-direct research priorities.[106] We seem to have come full circle. But times have changed again. In the 1990s we are more conscious of the need to restore public confidence in scientific expertise and to reverse that broader cultural trend towards the devaluation of scientific authority which has taken turns that even Feyerabend may not have envisaged in the 1970s.

Do we have a Galileo for today? Because fashions change within the practice of history, new images keep appearing. Galileo the courtier appeared in 1993. His advocate Mario Biagioli showed how at critical junctures in Galileo's career his fortunes were tied to his quest for patronage.[107] Thus his dedication of the moons of Jupiter to the Medici family was a calculated gift, part of the etiquette that he hoped would win him the patronage of the new Grand Duke Cosimo II whom he had earlier taught. It worked wonderfully well and in 1610 he was able to leave Padua for Florence. Here he enjoyed not merely more leisure for his work, but enhanced social status as court philosopher. Biagioli notes the earnest diplomacy through which he secured for himself that title: not merely mathematician but philosopher to the Grand Duke of Tuscany. The distinction was emblematic of the status Galileo wished to confer on the Copernican system: no mere mathematical device but a physical system worthy the attention and defence of the philosopher.[108] Later in his career Galileo courted his friend Barberini when he became Urban VIII. This time the dedication of his book *The Assayer* to the new Pope was the self-commending gift. Papal patronage, after all, would be the most glittering prize. From this courtly perspective many features of Galileo's behaviour can be seen in a new light.

For example, it was part of one's duty as a court philosopher to respond to the provocation of others because the honour of one's patron was at stake. One had no choice but to retaliate and the dispute had the character of a duel. This helps us to understand the vituperative, insulting style that Galileo would adopt in such disputes. It was all part of what was expected in a good duel.[109] Galileo's aggressive style has often been seen as a character trait that helps to explain his downfall. As Arthur Koestler once put it, with every argument that he won he was apt to make a new enemy.[110] But, as Biagioli observes, 'once it is contextualised within these patronage dynamics Galileo's well known aggressive and sarcastic style ceases to be just a character trait'.[111] Biagioli's line, that science was an admirable subject for a duel, makes it appropriate to talk about the patron's aesthetics of good sport.[112] This may seem a long way from heavy issues concerning scientific truth; but, on Biagioli's reading, it is not because one of the rules of the game was that one should not bring the debate to a definitive conclusion. The sport lay in the sparring, the rhetorical display, not in what the sociologists of science call closure. This may be the reason, Biagioli suggests, why Galileo was so insistently told that he should present the Copernican system only as a hypothesis. When it suited his purpose, he would play by the rules, as in his controversy with Grassi. On the nature of comets he did not commit himself to any one theory.[113] But, as Biagioli points out, he did not play by the rules in his *Dialogue*. There he thwarted the 'refined eclecticism' that conventionally protected the patron from having to take a stand.[114]

What light does this shed on the trial itself? Biagioli suggests that the rise and fall of Galileo conforms to a well documented pattern in the courtly life of the period: the rise and fall of a favourite, whose fall, once triggered, becomes absolute, swift and inexorable.[115] A characteristic of many such falls was the pretext spelled out by the patron: he had been betrayed.[116] And because he had been betrayed by a close friend there was no alternative but to take decisive action. The way Urban VIII spoke of Galileo was in precisely these terms. As we have already seen, it was not difficult for him to do so. His own wishes concerning the *Dialogue* had certainly not been respected.

We may also ask what bearing this may have on traditional accounts of the 'conflict between religion and science'. Biagioli is perfectly explicit on this point. The conflict between a Christianised Aristotelian and a Copernican cosmology was certainly a trigger that precipitated this most famous of trials. But his thesis is that 'the events of 1633 were as much the result of a clash between the dynamics and tensions of baroque court society and culture as they were caused by a clash between Thomistic theology and modern cosmology'.[117]

Historical Plausibility

Clearly the contemporary relevance of the Galileo affair has not only changed with time and context but has depended very largely on the presuppositions of the historian. This, however, raises an obvious and disturbing problem. Can we all have the history we want? Are there no controls? Are all histories historical novels? Can an innovative interpretation ever be refuted?

The reaction to another recent account suggests that a degree of consensus can be achieved if a historical argument ceases to look plausible. An exciting new slant on the Galileo affair was published by Pietro Redondi in 1983. In his book *Galileo Heretic*, he suggested that the principal heresy of which Galileo was guilty was not his Copernicanism but rather his commitment to a dangerous theory of matter.[118] This set a cat among the pigeons. It was well known that, in his *Assayer* of 1623, Galileo had included a short passage in which he argued that tastes, smells, colours, and sensations such as tickling, were precisely that – subjective sensations produced in us by an ulterior world of colourless, odourless, particles. It was also well known that Galileo correlated the sensation of heat with the motion of corpuscles. Redondi's message was that this departure from an Aristotelian theory of matter was theologically dangerous because it compromised an essential element in Catholic worship – the transubstantiation of bread and wine into the body and blood of Christ. The language of transubstantiation made sense in terms of a theory of matter that sharply distinguished between substance and form. There could be a miraculous change of substance without change in the external appearance of the bread or wine. On the corpuscular view, however, the external appearances depended on the ulterior structure and arrangement of particles. A miraculous change in the substance would have sensible consequences.[119]

The plot thickened when Redondi produced an anonymous document from the Vatican archives in which reservations about this aspect of Galileo's *Assayer* were expressed. Moreover, he argued that it was the work of none other than Galileo's Jesuit opponent Grassi, with whom he had quarrelled over comets. Into a brilliant account of the political complexities of the case, Redondi wove his startling thesis. The trial of 1633 was not about Copernicanism at all. It was a show-trial, a façade behind which Galileo's real crime could be concealed. Under political pressure the Pope had thrown Galileo to the wolves to appease his critics, and conveniently to protect himself. Urban VIII was willing to shield Galileo from the worse charge concerning the Eucharist because he simply could not afford that issue to be made public. The *Assayer* had after all been dedicated to him and it would look as if he had been soft on a central point of doctrine. Redondi certainly supplied a new Galileo and a quite different angle on the trial. A new Galileo because he was presented not primarily as an astronomer or student of mechanics but as prime mover in the revival of atomism. And a new angle on the trial because Urban's protective attitude towards Galileo was not required to undergo any profound change.

How plausible is this reconstruction? It is impossible to do it justice in a brief compass; but something like a consensus has emerged among Galileo scholars that it is not plausible enough.[120] After all, the Copernican theory had been a genuine issue in 1616, seven years before the *Assayer* appeared. It also continued to be so in the years before the trial. In April 1625, Galileo was warned by his friend Mario Guiducci that to keep the Copernican opinion alive was to risk persecution from those who could punish with impunity.[121] And after the trial, as late as 1638, when Galileo sought permission for medical treatment in Florence, it was only granted by the Pope on condition that the Copernican doctrine was not to be discussed.[122] In that same year Galileo's old friend Castelli was warned 'under pain of excommunication' that he must not discuss with Galileo the condemned opinion of the earth's motion. It is difficult to reconcile this intensity of papal concern over a private meeting with the claim that the trial had not been about Copernicanism.[123] Nor was Galileo ever able to persuade Urban VIII that he had not meant to mock him through the scepticism of Simplicio – a scepticism directed against a Copernican explanation for the tides. On Redondi's reading Urban almost becomes the hero who saved Galileo from a worse fate.[124] Yet this is difficult to square with the Pope's evident fury preceding the trial[125] and what has been described as an 'unremitting vindictiveness in private transactions'.[126]

Criticisms of another kind have surfaced. Few if any experts on Galileo have been persuaded that the document ascribed by Redondi to Grassi was composed by him. With a touch of irony one critic has added that Redondi's thesis would actually be stronger if Grassi was not the author because there would then be at least more than one person who allegedly saw a problem with Galileo's account of matter and its sensible properties.[127] This may be unduly severe because we know that corpuscular theories of matter developed later by Descartes did run into the sort of trouble on which Redondi's case rests. Nevertheless, the idea that Galileo's fate was determined by speculations on the nature of matter that he did not develop, rather than by the arguments for heliocentrism which he did, has proved difficult to sustain.

In conclusion it is hard to resist an aphorism acribed to Samuel Butler: though God cannot alter the past, historians can; it is perhaps because they can be useful to him in this respect that he tolerates their existence. History *is* invention, often brilliant invention; but it would not be appropriate to apply Feyerabend's aphorism that *anything goes*. Underlying all the complexities of the Galileo affair were ineradicable issues concerning the methods of gaining knowledge – both of nature and of God. One of the many respects in which Galileo chanced his arm was his claim that *as much* could be known of God through the study of nature as through the Scriptures.[128] In that claim he was raising the profile of natural theology, seemingly at the expense of revelation. The subsequent connections of natural science with natural theology will be the subject of the next chapter.

NOTES

1   M. A. Finocchiaro, *The Galileo Affair: A Documentary History*, Berkeley, 1989, 5.

2   Richard Griffiths, 'Very very frightening', *The Daily Telegraph*, 5 November 1994, 6.

3 For an apposite stress on the invisibility of the earth's motions and the diffi-culties this created for him, see R. Feldhay, *Galileo and the Church: Political Inquisition or Critical Dialogue*, Cambridge, 1995, 267–8.

4 John Paul II, 'Deep harmony which unites the truths of science with the truths of faith', *L'Osservatore Romano*, weekly English edn., 26 November 1979, in *Galileo Galilei: Toward a Resolution of 350 Years of Debate – 1633–1983* (ed. P. Poupard), Pittsburgh, 1987, 195–200.

5 For an introduction to the issues here, see T. S. Kuhn, *The Copernican Revolution*, Cambridge, MA, 1957; A. O. Lovejoy, *The Great Chain of Being* (1936), reprint edn., New York, 1960, 99–143; J. H. Brooke, *Science and Religion: Some Historical Perspectives*, Cambridge, 1991, 82–116; J. Dobrzycki (ed.), *The Reception of Copernicus's Heliocentric Theory*, Dordrecht, 1972; P. Rossi, 'Nobility of man and plurality of worlds', in *Science, Medicine and Society in the Renaissance* (ed. A. G. Debus), 2 vols., New York, 1972, ii, 131–62; R. S. Westman, 'The Copernicans and the Churches', in *God and Nature: Historical Essays on the Encounter between Christianity and Science* (ed. D. C. Lindberg and R. L. Numbers), Berkeley, 1986, 76–113.

6 S. Drake (ed.), *Discoveries and Opinions of Galileo*, New York, 1957, 27–58.

7 B. Wrightsman, 'Andreas Osiander's contribution to the Copernican achievement', in *The Copernican Achievement* (ed. R. S. Westman), Berkeley, 1975, 213–43.

8 The evidence that Martin Luther cited this verse against a heliostatic system was critically assessed by W. Norlind, 'Copernicus and Luther', *Isis*, 44 (1953), 273–6. That Galileo felt obliged to provide an exegesis of this text suggests that it had acquired a special significance in the debate, along with Psalm 93:1. Drake, op. cit. (6), 212–16.

9 S. J. Dick, *Plurality of Worlds: The Extraterrestrial Life Debate from Democritus to Kant*, Cambridge, 1982, 61–105.

10 It was clearly recognised by Tommaso Campanella that a plurality of worlds could be set up as an inference from, and therefore an argument against, Galileo's position. J. D. Moss, *Novelties in the Heavens: Rhetoric and Science in the Copernican Controversy*, Chicago, 1993, 153–4.

11 Drake, op. cit. (6), 158.

12 J. Reston, *Galileo: A Life*, New York, 1994, 147.

13 *Ibid.*

14 *The Controversy on the Comets of 1618* (ed. S. Drake and C. D. O'Malley), Philadelphia, 1960, 301.

15 The temptation to do this is still very strong even among informed commentators. At the end of his recent biography, James Reston refers to an interview he had had with Cardinal Poupard. He complains that he heard yet again the standard Church line – that Galileo had been condemned because he insisted on treating his Coperncian theory as truth rather than hypothesis when he had no proof. Reston's impatience finds expression in a single sentence: 'This position deflected attention from a simple fact: The Copernican theory *was* true, and the church had used extreme and rigorous methods to crush that truth and protect its false-hood.' Reston, op. cit. (12), 285. With this sharp polarity between truth

and falsehood Reston glides over the fact that, in theory construction, truth has to be negotiated. The status of scientific hypotheses and the nature of the 'truth' that mathematical astronomy could supply were two of the issues at stake in the affair.

16 A. Fantoli, *Galileo: For Copernicanism and For the Church*, Vatican, 1994, 198–209.

17 *Ibid.*, 239 and 299.

18 M. Biagioli, *Galileo Courtier: The Practice of Science in the Culture of Absolutism*, Chicago, 1993, 351.

19 *Ibid.*, 301–2.

20 Reston, op. cit. (12), 190.

21 Fantoli, op. cit. (16), 299–300.

22 The relevant closing pages are reproduced in Finocchiaro, op. cit. (1), 217–18.

23 See the letter from Francesco Niccolini to Lord Bali Cioli, 28 August 1632, in Finocchiaro, op. cit. (1), 229.

24 In this respect it should be noted that Simplicio did not have the last word in the *Dialogue*. Although it was he who introduced the argument for scepticism based on divine omnipotence, Galileo carefully allowed Salviati, the chief protagonist, to agree with it. In retrospect his literary device looks like a grievous miscalculation, but it must have seemed to him an attractive way of creating consensus on what Salviati calls a 'truly angelic doctrine'.

25 Galileo, 'Letter to the Grand Duchess Christina', in Drake, op. cit. (6), 173–216, especially 175; also accessible in Finocchiaro, op. cit. (1), 87–118.

26 Biagioli, op. cit. (18), 236–8.

27 On the important exchange between Galileo and Conti, see M. Sharratt, *Galileo: Decisive Innovator*, Oxford, 1994, 103. Conti even referred Galileo to a commentary on *Job* by Diego de Zuñiga, where the Copernican system had been incorporated. He also indicated that the principle of biblical accommodation would permit conciliation between the new astronomy and Scripture – the very principle that Galileo later adopted in his apologetics. It is true that Conti advised caution, but, as on so many occasions, Galileo was able to reassure himself that there were ways forward.

28 *Ibid.*, 103.

29 Feldhay, op. cit. (3), 34–44.

30 Drake and O'Malley, op. cit. (14), 17.

31 For commentary on Brahe's geoheliocentric system, see O. Gingerich and R. S. Westman, 'The Wittich connection: conflict and priority in late sixteenth-century cosmology', *Transactions of the American Philosophical Society*, 78, Part 7 (1988), 1–148; N. Jardine, *The Birth of History and Philosophy of Science: Kepler's A Defence of Tycho Against Ursus, With Essays on its Provenance and Significance*, Cambridge, 1984. For Scheiner's willingness to centre the orbits of Mercury and Venus on the sun, which has itself been called 'revolutionary', see Feldhay, op. cit. (3), 260–1. And for Tychonic cosmology at the Jesuit College in Rome: J. M. Lattis, *Between Copernicus and Galileo: Christopher Clavius and the Collapse of Ptolemaic Cosmology*, Chicago, 1994, 205–16.

32 Moss, op. cit. (10), 151–2.

33 *Ibid.*, 160–1.

34 Feldhay, op. cit. (3), 93–127, 171–98, 256–91.

35 *Ibid.*, 53–4.

36 Fantoli, op. cit. (16), 388.

37 *Ibid.*, 119.

38 Galileo, op. cit. (25), in Finocchiaro, op. cit. (1), 92.

39 Bellarmine to Foscarini, 12 April 1615, in Finocchiaro, op. cit. (1), 67–9, on 68.

40 Galileo, op. cit. (25), in Finocchiaro, op. cit. (1), 101–2.

41 Galileo's tactics were however transparent in that he was cleverly shifting the burden of proof: 'before condemning a physical proposition, one must show that it is not conclusively demonstrated'. *Ibid.*, 102. This was one of many facets of Galileo's behaviour that incited an unsympathetic response from Arthur Koestler in *The Sleepwalkers*, Harmondsworth, 1964, 439–45.

42 Galileo, op. cit. (25), in Finocchiaro, op. cit. (1), 92–3.

43 To our knowledge, one of the first to analyse the inconsistency was Ernan McMullin in an as yet unpublished paper. It is also exposed by Sharratt, op. cit. (27), 123.

44 O. Pedersen, 'Galileo and the Council of Trent', *Journal of the History of Astronomy*, 14 (1983), 1–29.

45 Galileo, op. cit. (25), in Finocchiaro, op. cit. (1), 96.

46 Bellarmine, op. cit. (39), 68. Bellarmine immediately clarified what he meant by this: 'it would be heretical to say that Abraham did not have two children and Jacob twelve, as well as to say that Christ was not born of a virgin, because both are said by the Holy Spirit through the mouth of the prophets and apostles'.

47 Fantoli, op. cit. (16), 178.

48 Sharratt, op. cit. (27), 131 and 212–22.

49 W. R. Shea, 'Galileo, Scheiner, and the interpretation of sunspots', *Isis*, 61 (1970), 498–519; Feldhay, op. cit. (3), 256–91.

50 There is a letter from the Vatican secretary to the Florentine Inquisitor, dated 24 May 1631, in which it is explicitly stated that 'Our Master thinks that the title and subject should not focus on the ebb and flow but absolutely on the mathematical examination of the Copernican position.' Finocchiaro, op. cit. (1), 212.

51 Finocchiaro, op. cit. (1), 9. See also *ibid.*, 20–24 for the new physics that was required in order that arguments for a moving earth could be sustained.

52 Thus a superficial reading of Galileo's abjuration, in which he confessed to having adduced 'very effective reasons' in favour of a condemned doctrine, might leave the erroneous impression that the prosecution had conceded the strength of his scientific defence. Finocchiaro, op. cit. (1), 292; Fantoli, op. cit. (16), 423–5.

53 Finocchiaro, op. cit. (1), 139.

54 R. J. Blackwell, *Galileo, Bellarmine and the Bible*, Notre Dame, 1991, 16.

55 *Ibid.*, 18.

56 *Ibid.*, 19.

57 J. Dillenberger, *Protestant Thought and Natural Science*, London, 1961, chs. 1–3.

58 F. Yates, *Giordano Bruno and the Hermetic Tradition*, Chicago, 1964, 348–59.

59 Galileo, op. cit. (25), in Finocchiaro, op. cit. (1), 114–18. Galileo argued that the miracle only required the sun to stop turning on its axis for a while and all the planetary motions would temporarily cease. The beauty was that this would not involve a violation of the entire cosmos, as would be the case if the sun had been stopped in its tracks on the old system.

60 When denouncing Galileo, Caccini drew attention to his friendship with Sarpi, 'famous for his impieties'. Finocchiaro, op. cit. (1), 139. On the Venetian revolt against Rome, see P. F. Grendler, *The Roman Inquisition and the Venetian Press, 1540–1605*, Princeton, 1977.

61 Brooke, op. cit. (5), 94–9.

62 Fantoli, op. cit. (16), 170–1.

63 *Ibid.*, 239 and 299.

64 G. de Santillana, *The Crime of Galileo*, Chicago, 1955; Reston, op. cit. (12), 239.

65 This political dimension has been given special prominence by P. Redondi, *Galileo Heretic*, Princeton, 1987.

66 Biagioli, op. cit. (18), 335.

67 *Ibid.*, 336.

68 In a letter to Elia Diodati, written by Galileo in January 1633, there is a forlorn prediction: 'From reliable sources I hear the Jesuit Fathers have managed to convince some very important persons that my book is execrable and more harmful to the Holy Church than the writings of Luther and Calvin. Thus I am sure it will be prohibited.' Finocchiaro, op. cit. (1), 225.

69 Fantoli, op. cit. (16), 459; Feldhay, op. cit. (3), 295–6.

70 S. Drake, *Galileo at Work: His Scientific Biography*, Chicago, 1978, 288. The extent to which the Jesuits could have helped Galileo, even if there had been a wish to do so, has been re-examined by Fantoli, op. cit. (16), 213–15, 243, 277, 428–30, 435 and 459–61. Fantoli stresses that within the Jesuit Roman College the mathematicians and astronomers were a small minority. For the philosophy teachers there was as yet no serious alternative to the comprehensive system of Aristotle. To compound the difficulty, the Father General of the Jesuit Order, Claudio Acquaviva, had been issuing instructions to maintain their unity through renewed allegiance to Aristotle. *Ibid.*, 126–7, 215.

71 R. S. Westman, 'The Melanchthon circle, Rheticus and the Wittenberg interpretation of the Copernican theory', *Isis*, 66 (1975), 165–93; *idem.*, 'The astronomer's role in the sixteenth century: a preliminary study', *History of Science*, 18 (1980), 105–74.

72 Moss, op. cit. (10), 156.

73 Sharratt, op. cit. (27), 41. The efforts of Clavius to raise the status of mathematics and astronomy and their linkage to questions of natural philosophy are most fully discussed in Lattis, op. cit. (31).

74 Feldhay, op. cit. (3), 44–69.

75 Sharratt, op. cit. (27), 145; Finocchiaro, op. cit. (1), 35.

76 Fantoli, op. cit. (16), 306.

77 For the honour and esteem ostensibly accorded to Galileo at the Papal Court as late as June 1630, see the letter from Francesco Niccolini, the Tuscan ambassador, cited by Fantoli, op. cit. (16), 316.

78 Finocchiaro, op. cit. (1), 239.

79 N. Jardine, 'A trial of Galileos', *Isis*, 85 (1994), 279–83.

80 The warmth of hospitality shown to Galileo by Ascanio Piccolomini, Archbishop of Siena, following the sentence of house-arrest, has been taken to epitomise the unease of the more open-minded. Reston, op. cit. (12), 268; Fantoli, op. cit. (16), 510.

81 Fantoli attaches particular weight to the perceived mendacity of Galileo in turning the more unyielding of his judges against him. *Ibid.*, 425 and 477.

82 *Ibid.*, 475.

83 Reston, op. cit. (12), 285. It would be extremely difficult to delete Urban's involvement. See, for example, Finocchiaro, op. cit. (1), 38.

84 Sharratt, op. cit. (27), 215–16.

85 M. Segre, *In the Wake of Galileo*, New Brunswick, 1991, 116–22; Biagioli, op. cit. (18), 87–8.

86 Segre, *ibid.*, 123.

87 *Ibid.*, 35.

88 Sharratt, op. cit. (27), 50.

89 Segre, op. cit. (86), 43–4.

90 *Ibid.*, 44–5.

91 J. W. Draper, *History of the Conflict between Religion and Science* (1875), 18th edn., London, 1883, 171–2.

92 A few pages later, Draper included a passage which, had he thought through its implications, might have checked his allegation. He noted that there had been arguments against the Copernican system, particularly that of Tycho Brahe concerning the absence of stellar parallax. In reply to Tycho it had been said that the stars must be so far from the earth that the predicted effect is imperceptible. Draper knew that 'this answer proved to be correct'. *Ibid.*, 176. It proved to be; but when? In 1633 this expansion of the universe could still look like an *ad hoc* hypothesis designed to save the Copernican theory. On Draper's own account, two hundred years were to elapse before the parallax of Alpha Centauri was observed. *Ibid.*, 176. But his sights had been set elsewhere.

93 Finocchiaro, op. cit. (1), 4.

94 F. Ewen, *Bertolt Brecht: His Life, His Art and His Times*, London, 1970, 333.

95 *Ibid.*, 339.

96 *Ibid.*, 342.

97 P. Feyerabend, *Against Method*, London, 1975, 17.

98 *Ibid.*

99 *Ibid.*, 19.

100 One such rule, called by Feyerabend the consistency condition, dictated that new hypotheses must be in accord with accepted theories. This he

considered an unreasonable prescription because it preserves the older, not necessarily the better, theory. *Ibid.*, 11. There was, he believed, a kind of chauvinism within scientific communities that militated against what was really beneficial: the proliferation of theories.

101 *Ibid.*, 10.
102 *Ibid.*, 130–5.
103 *Ibid.*, 143.
104 *Ibid.*, 11.
105 *Ibid.*, 15.
106 *Ibid.*, 52.
107 Biagioli, op. cit. (18).
108 *Ibid.*, 89, 106–10, 128–9.
109 *Ibid.*, 61.
110 Koestler, op. cit. (41), 458–9.
111 Biagioli, op. cit. (18), 66, 71, 277; Jardine, op. cit. (79), 281. This need not lead to a whitewash of Galileo. There was a determination in his manner that attracted adverse comment. At the moment of crisis in 1616 one observer noted the 'violence' with which he forced his views on others. Reston, op. cit. (12), 166.
112 Biagioli, op. cit. (18), 75.
113 *Ibid.*, 303–5.
114 *Ibid.*, 301–3, 310.
115 *Ibid.*, 333–52.
116 *Ibid.*, 333.
117 *Ibid.*, 10.
118 Redondi, op. cit. (65).
119 *Ibid.*, 203–26.
120 R. S. Westfall, '*Galileo Heretic*: Problems, as they appear to me, with Redondi's thesis', *History of Science*, 26 (1988), 399–415; Fantoli, op. cit. (16), 341–4; Sharratt, op. cit. (27), 149.
121 Reston, op. cit. (12), 201.
122 Sharratt, op. cit. (27), 186.
123 Westfall, op. cit. (121), 412.
124 *Ibid.*, 406.
125 Niccolini, op. cit. (23). For a colourful if somewhat overdramatised account of the Pope's wounded sensibilities, see Reston, op. cit. (12), 236–44.
126 Westfall, op. cit. (121), 408.
127 *Ibid.*, 411.
128 Galileo, op. cit. (25), in Finocchiaro, op. cit. (1), 93: 'God reveals Himself to us no less excellently in the effects of nature than in the sacred words of Scripture.'

Section III: *Having Designs on Nature*

5
Natural Theology and the History of Science

In December 1815 a precocious Cambridge student, writing home to a schoolmaster friend, confessed to 'certain yearnings after the whole circle of the sciences, certain ecstatic aspirations after universal knowledge, certain indefinite desires to approximate to something like omniscience'. To be fair, he recognised that 'not much good would be likely to come to me if I were to remain in such an all-reading, all-learning mood for ever'.[1] But he was wrong. Son of a Lancaster carpenter, William Whewell was to become Master of Trinity College, Cambridge. It was he who first coined the word 'scientist' in the 1830s and of whom it was famously quipped that science was his forte, omniscience his foible.[2] Omniscience and popularity are not the most natural of partners and when England's polymath underestimated Scottish pride, he had a rude awakening. Whewell's three large tomes on the history of science fell into the hands of David Brewster, *well known* for his work in optics. But to read Whewell's *History* one might not think so. As Brewster studied his review copy he searched in vain for his name and for those compliments that would have boosted his self-esteem. Worse was to follow. When he wrote his review he concluded that one successful generalisation, and one alone, had Whewell pursued: 'the gross neglect of the claims of the philosophers and authors of Scotland'.[3] Whewell was flabbergasted by Brewster's review. 'He says ... that I even hate Scotchwomen. I think this last charge is hard, but what can I say?'[4]

One of Whewell's more interesting claims was that each of the sciences had depended for its progress on a distinctive leading idea that had regulated thinking about nature. His fundamental idea was that there *are* 'fundamental ideas' peculiar to each science. In crystallography, for example, the idea of symmetry had played a crucial role. Or consider the case of chemistry. In Whewell's day the neutralisation of acids by bases to give a salt was a model being applied to all chemical reactions. The mechanism was thought to be electrical, as opposite charges were neutralised. Accordingly, Whewell identified the idea of polarity as the fundamental idea governing chemical progress. His thesis was that for science to be possible there had to be a constant interplay between the mind and experimental data. It was through these fundamental ideas, their unfolding and refinement, that scientific understanding was achieved.[5]

What has this to do with natural theology? For Whewell, everything – because the *way* the mind worked in gaining scientific knowledge was, in his view, evidence of Providential design. The very possibility of scientific progress implied the existence of a deity.[6] This association between natural science and natural theology was even more intimate. Whewell claimed that the great discoveries in biology had been made by asking questions about purpose. William Harvey had discovered the circulation of the blood by asking what purpose was served by valves in the veins. In living systems, the idea of function or purpose was so fundamental that it was inescapably involved in the analysis of organic structures.[7] Whewell pointed to a creature not that common in Cambridge: the kangaroo. When the baby first starts to take milk from its mother, it is so small that it cannot suck. Accordingly nature has provided a special muscle in the adult female that allows the milk to be injected into the baby's mouth. Whewell's point was that this muscle must be a special contrivance, designed for that purpose. And from there it was not a kangaroo jump to statements about the foresight shown by the Creator.[8] Natural science and natural theology were once again joined. The possibility of gaining knowledge through the mediation of fundamental ideas pointed to design. And a specific fundamental idea, that of final cause, pointed directly to a Designer. It was a case of wheels within wheels – one might almost say Whewells within Whewells.

The question we wish to raise in this chapter is whether historians have anything distinctive to say about this kind of natural theology in which scientific knowledge was turned into arguments for design. We have used the past tense because this habit of mind, as Whewell would have called it, had its heyday in the English-speaking world from the second half of the seventeenth century until the middle of the nineteenth. But the use of the latest physics to affirm some kind of intelligence behind the universe is a practice that still continues. We hear of a universe so finely tuned that if the forces unleashed during the first few seconds of the Big Bang had been even minutely different, human life could never have evolved. And we hear of a universe that chaos theory has shown to be so delicately balanced that future events have become less predictable than a mechanistic determinism might once have suggested.[9]

Because arguments for the existence of God have so often been the staple diet in courses on the philosophy of religion, there has been a preoccupation with the logical structure of the design argument and its imperfections. Our aim is not to cast doubt on the value of such analysis. But it has encouraged the ransacking of classic texts in order to furnish examples of philosophical argument that are then made grist to the mill. For the historian this is a constrictive approach to historical texts because there are so many more questions that need to be asked. There is a sense in which 'we murder to dissect' if we extract the bare bones of an argument from the intellectual project of which it formed a part. The historian will want to recapture the larger project in so far as it is possible. The absorbing question then becomes: why did a particular project become urgent at a particular time and place?

Projects of Time and Place

To illustrate what may be lost in extracting a theistic 'proof' from its context we might consider a distant example from another cultural tradition. Had we been a student of law in eleventh-century Baghdad, we might have been taught by a scholar who still attracts interest today as a mystic, saint and theologian. Al-Ghazali became professor of law in 1091 at an institution set up to neutralise the power of extremist and sectarian groups within Islam. In setting down the fundamentals of Muslim belief Ghazali had recourse to a theistic 'proof' that we recognise as a form of the cosmological argument. 'It is self-evident to human reason', he began, 'that there must be a cause for the origination of anything originated. Since the universe is originated, it follows that there was a cause for its origination.'[10] It may be tempting to treat this syllogism as a proof devised to convince sceptical philosophers that atheism is not a rational option. But that would be to misrepresent Ghazali, who clearly stated that a reasoned proof for the existence of God is superfluous. It was not needed because the testimony of the Qur'an and the wonders of creation were sufficient grounds in themselves. Within the Muslim culture of his time, he could take it for granted that one lived by a sacred text. What then was the purpose of his argument about origins? In the last analysis it had to do with how the sacred text was to be read. The threat came from within Islam itself, from Shi'ites who were gaining ground politically at the expense of Sunni 'orthodoxy'. According to a recent study, Ghazali had a very specific worry: 'the insinuation of Greek and Hellenistic ideas into Islam through the more speculative of the Shi'ites'.[11] These ideas included the Aristotelian notion of a world that had existed from eternity. To accept such a view required a non-literal interpretation of the sacred text. G̲h̲azali turned his face against these tendencies. What at first glance looks like a classic theistic proof was actually serving a quite different purpose. His argument was directed against Muslim philosophers, notably Ibn Sina, who in G̲h̲azali's view were guilty of erroneous belief. Their denial that the world was created *ex nihilo* was only one of several errors. Those who had favoured the immortality of the soul rather than the resurrection of the body were also censured. G̲h̲azali's project was not the construction of a natural theology independent of his cultural heritage. He argued about origins in order to protect that heritage from an enemy within. In a created universe one could speak of the Will of a personal God, as Islamic belief required. In an Aristotelian universe one could not.

There are many comparable examples from the history of Christendom, suggesting that to abstract what may look like 'proofs' of God's existence from their contexts misses the significance that such arguments had within specific religious communities. Thus the ontological argument of Anselm, commonly abstracted as a theistic proof, acquires a different meaning when relocated in its own place and time – the Benedictine community of Bec in the eleventh century. For Anselm, God was a being whose non-existence cannot be conceived. But this was not intended as a piece of natural theology, independent of faith. His intention was to guide other monks towards a fuller knowledge of God. This required the recognition that God was not only that-than-which-nothing-greater-can-be-thought, but something greater than that which can be thought.[12] This assertion of the radical otherness of God contrasts sharply with anthropomorphic images of the deity permeating much of later natural theology.

Shifting time and place, we might arrive in London in the 1660s, shortly after the restoration of the Stuart monarchy. For historians of science this is a significant time because the first two enduring scientific societies were established: the Royal Society of London, and the Académie Royale des Sciences in Paris. It was also a time when in England natural theology gained a higher profile. Robert Boyle was comparing the natural philosopher with a priest in the temple of nature and rebuking Descartes for his neglect of the design argument.[13] If G̲h̲azali had been worried by threats from within Islam, Boyle had been concerned by divisions within Christendom. The proliferation of puritan sects during the Interregnum had posed a particular threat because each had claimed some special illumination. The danger was that the Christian faith would lose all credibility. 'Let a man come to London', Boyle had written, 'and he shall come near to losing his faith.'[14] Consequently there had been pressures to reaffirm the rational foundations of faith in order to deactivate the many hot lines to God.

The threat to Christianity did not only come from within. In Restoration comedies Christian virtues and the sanctity of marriage were under attack, cuckolds abounded, and a pervasive air of frivolity smacked of practical atheism.[15] Bishops were not amused. John Wilkins, founder member of the Royal Society and a bishop, complained of living in a 'degenerate age ... miserably over-run with scepticism and infidelity'.[16] His project for that time and place was to 'establish the great principles of religion, the Being of God, and a future state; by showing how firm and solid a foundation they have in the nature and reason of mankind'.[17] In London in the 1660s a spectacular new resource had become available. Robert Hooke, curator of experiments at the Royal Society, had published his *Micrographia* (1665). This was an illustrated guide to a new world – the world under the microscope. The fact that life had been packed into the minutest mite was a stupendous marvel. Hooke himself drew attention to the exquisite forms visible under the new instrument. But the new resource was the contrast he drew between human artifacts and the works of nature.[18] The best that we could do looked like a botched job under the microscope. But look at the eye of a fly or even a snowflake and there was no trace of imperfection. The perfection of nature's art, and by implication the work of the Creator, was thrown into even sharper relief.

We shall return to this argument in chapter 7. Boyle, Wilkins, and the naturalist John Ray all used it in their defence of Christianity. During the eighteenth century, however, yet another project took shape – not the defence of Christianity, nor that of any revealed religion. There were moves in different parts of Europe to construct a 'natural religion' to which all rational persons could subscribe. For many this was an attractive project because it offered the prospect of transcending party lines. The doctrinal disputes that had led to bloody wars could be discarded. In their place would be a simpler creed, famously recited by Voltaire:

> When reason, freed from its chains, will teach the people that there is only one God, that this God is the universal father of all men, who are brothers; that these brothers must be good and just to one another, and that they must practise all the virtues; that God, being good and just, must reward virtue and punish crimes; surely, my brethren, men will be better for it, and less superstitious.[19]

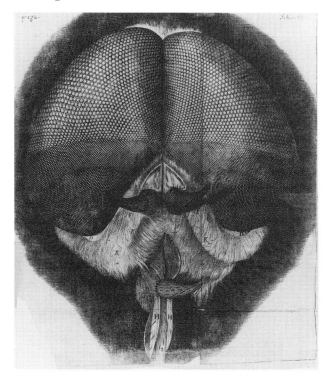

Figure 16: The compound eye of the fly from Robert Hooke's *Micrographia*, first published in 1665.

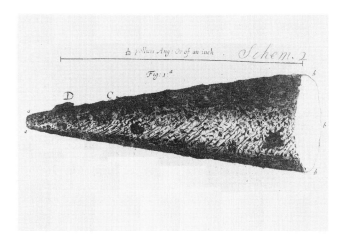

Figure 17: The rough appearance of a human artefact, in this case a needle, when viewed under the microscope. Also from Robert Hooke's *Micrographia* first published in 1665.

This was natural religion, grounded in human nature, in natural reason. It is well known that in his campaign against the Catholic Church, Voltaire found an ally in the God of Newton, or more correctly in what he took to be Newton's God. Natural religion and natural science came together in a new combination, and with tangible results. It was Voltaire who ensured that the elements of Newton's philosophy were available in French.[20]

The attempt to construct a consensual rational religion that would render all others obsolete was an Enlightenment project that ultimately failed. As failed projects go, it was nevertheless pretty successful. Apologists for a distinctively Christian religion, such as Joseph Butler in his *Analogy of Religion* (1736), found themselves conceding that 'natural religion' was the *foundation* and *principal* part of Christianity, even if it was not the whole.[21] One of the more enduring legacies of the quest for an independent natural religion, so it has been argued, has been the modern practice of isolating theistic proofs from their original contexts in order to offer independent rational evaluation.[22] But this is precisely the tendency that the historian seeks to avoid.

For a telling example we migrate again – to Scotland in the middle of the nineteenth century. It is particularly instructive because it shows how, in a context of faith, David Hume's critique of natural theology was not only indecisive but ingeniously contested. It is January 1852 and Hugh Miller is giving his Presidential address before the Royal Physical Society of Edinburgh. Miller was that remarkable 'stonemason of Cromarty' who became the populariser of geology without equal. He was editor of the Free Church newspaper, *The Witness*, to which he contributed a mere ten million words between 1840 and 1856.[23] He had become a household name in Scotland in part because of his political stand on the issue of Non-Intrusion that had led, in 1843, to the Disruption.[24] Miller was keenly aware that geology was often held in suspicion by religious writers and he sought to remove their scruples. As an evangelical he would attack the moderates with every means at his disposal, including condescension towards their science. Writing of the Disruption itself, when the 'fatal die' was cast, Miller reported: 'On the one side we saw *Moderate* science personified in Dr Anderson of Newburgh – a dabbler in geology, who found a fish in the Old Red Sandstone, and described it as a beetle, we saw science, not *moderate*, on the other side, represented by Sir David Brewster.'[25] Miller was embattled on other fronts. Popular sciences, like phrenology, had been woven into manifestos for secular education as in George Combe's *Essay on the Constitution of Man* (1828);[26] and perhaps worse still, it was from

Edinburgh that Robert Chambers had launched another best seller: his anonymous *Vestiges of the Natural History of Creation* (1844). Miller's verdict on the latter, which proposed a theory of species transformation, could not have been more succinct: 'one of the most insidious pieces of practical atheism that has appeared in Britain during the present century'.[27]

In response to all these pressures Miller produced an argument for his Edinburgh audience that was a masterpiece of ingenuity. It took the form of an explicit critique of Hume. Could anything be known about the cause of the universe? Hume had said not. He had also said that nothing could be known about the creation of worlds because no-one had experience of it. Nor could one argue for the infinite qualities of a deity based on a natural world whose qualities were finite. To do so was to violate what Hume had considered to be a cardinal principle of reasoning – that causes should always be proportioned to their effects. In Miller's reply, an evangelical faith was fused with an enthusiasm for geology to deprive Hume of the last word. The fossil record revealed new forms of life as one passed from each great epoch to the next. To study them was to enjoy that experience of creations that Hume had deemed impossible.

More ingeniously, Miller pointed out that to base one's conception of creative power on the evidence of the first epoch would, on Hume's principles, lead to a false result. This was because each succeeding epoch revealed a progressively greater complexity of form. To follow Hume one would have had to surmise that the creative force was limited to fishes – only to discover that reptiles were within its power. And likewise in the progression from reptiles to mammals to men. In retrospect the producing Cause had, in Miller's words, been working 'greatly under its strength'.[28] Where faith still burned, natural theology could most certainly survive and in the most intimate union with the sciences. The form that it took and, viewed in retrospect, its vulnerability to future developments were both rooted in time and place. Only two years elapsed between the publication of Miller's *Testimony of the Rocks* (1857) and Darwin's *On the Origin of Species* (1859).

Natural Theology and the Promotion of Religion

Historians who have reflected on the use of the design argument in religious apologetics have often reached conclusions that can only be described as unsympathetic.[29] A sympathetic assessment is not helped by the prevalence of arguments that seem worse than quaint.

In one of the classic texts of physico-theology, William Derham observed that five feet was just the right height for the human race. If we had been much smaller we would have been food for birds; much larger and we would have been tyrants in creation, treading on everything else.[30] To the suggestion that this might sound naive to later ears, Derham would have replied that we do at least have ears, that they are in the right place, and that there are two of them, in case one should go wrong.[31]

But the case for an unsympathetic assessment rests on more than this. It is often said that the eighteenth-century vogue for physico-theology diverted attention from God the Redeemer to God the Creator. Echoing Pascal, the objection is that arguments for a personal God based on impersonal forces were bound to lead to a bankrupt religion. The more Christian apologists implied that the existence of God could be established independently of revelation, the more they encouraged the deists in their belief that revelation could be dispensed with altogether. A negative evaluation would stress still other respects in which natural theology might dig its own grave. Arguments for divine wisdom based on the intricate designs of organic structures, the perfect design of a woodpecker's beak or a kangaroo's throat, were the arguments that would prove most vulnerable to the Darwinian critique.[32] Strategies to highlight a sense of the sacred in nature were often the very ones to backfire.[33] In common with Boyle, Newton employed an old analogy to make belief in an active deity seem reasonable. If our minds are able to move and control our limbs, if mind can act on matter in this way, why should not God be able to move and control the matter of the universe?[34] More sophisticated variants of this analogy are still in use;[35] but it could imply that the universe is the body of God and one would then be on a slippery slope to pantheism. What these and many similar examples show is that arguments used to render divine activity credible can all too easily invite their own refutation. In retrospect we can see only too clearly the kind of circularity that such arguments involved.

Apologists would sometimes appeal to the universality of Newton's law of gravitation to establish the unity of the universe and thence the unity of the Creator, oblivious of the fact that Newton had already grounded the universality of his law in a monotheistic, voluntarist theology.[36] Newton's premise had been that space was to be regarded as the sensorium of a God who immediately perceived all things in it. Presupposing that the laws of motion arose from the will of this same God, Newton had concluded that they may be of universal extent.

It may, nevertheless, seem hard on physico-theology to blame it for generating *atheism*. That it did so has, however, been argued with some subtlety by Michael Buckley.[37] He insists that atheism takes its meaning from the particular form of theism it rejects. This dialectical relationship is nicely captured in the remark of the atheist Charles Bradlaugh who once declared: 'I am an Atheist, but I do not say that there is no God; and until you tell me what you mean by God I am not mad enough to say anything of the kind.'[38] One consequence of taking this dialectical relationship seriously is that to understand the origins of modern atheism it is no good looking only at the history of atheism. It is also essential to examine the history of theism. Only then can we find the kind of theism to which modern atheism was an appropriate response. Buckley finds it in the theism of those who, as advocates of physico-theology, had ostensibly reduced the deity to an architect and craftsman. Buckley's point is how easy it was for physico-theology to engender atheism. It happened with Diderot, who in his *Pensées* had already said that a physico-theology provided the *only* road to God. With the collapse of that one road there was simply nothing left.[39]

But was the use of natural theology to promote religious belief as disastrous as such negative verdicts suggest? We might ask whether Christian apologists did routinely present the design argument as if it were the only one worth considering. Critics of natural theology would isolate it in this way; deists might adopt such a stance; but the few Boyle lecturers who did use the design argument, such as William Whiston and Samuel Clarke, were not so reductionist. The perfect exemplar for Buckley's thesis would be the character of Cleanthes in Hume's *Dialogues*. Hume makes Cleanthes say that it is by the design argument, the argument *a posteriori*, 'and by this argument alone' that 'we prove at once the existence of a Deity, and his similarity to human mind and intelligence'.[40] And as if to anticipate Buckley's thesis, Hume has Demea reply: 'What! No demonstration of the Being of a God! No abstract arguments! No proofs *a priori*.' Surely, Demea continues, 'by this affected candour, you give advantage to Atheists'. Even Demea in this context fails to mention arguments that the Boyle lecturers had in fact used in their defence of Christianity. Whiston, for example, had replied to the deists' assault on revelation by pointing, as Newton had, to the fulfilment of biblical prophecy. The beauty of this argument was that fulfilled prophecies 'seemed to demonstrate God's continuing agency in nature without – apparently – involving him in disrupting it'.[41]

It seems a little hard on Newton and the Boyle lecturers that Buckley should blame them for a welling up of atheism which undoubtedly had many springs. The transfer to nature of powers and predicates traditionally reserved for God had preceded the efforts of the Boyle lecturers to put a stop to monistic and materialistic schemes. For example, Giordano Bruno's translation of the infinity of God into the infinity of nature had preceded them by a hundred years.[42] A predisposition towards deism and atheism could be engendered by internal strife within the churches, by moral revulsion against the intolerance of established religions and by the perception that political expediency often lay behind the adoption of religious positions.[43] Moreover, it would be inaccurate to suggest that either Newton or the Boyle lecturers had reduced the Christian religion to the design argument. Their apologias were richer and far more diverse than this. Newton publicly warned that to reject the prophecies of Daniel was to reject the Christian religion: 'For this religion is founded upon his Prophecy concerning the Messiah.'[44] Newton did not say that it was founded on the evidence for design.

The use of science in religious apologetics can take a quite different form. It is sometimes necessary to counter the criticism that a particular scientific theory destroys the credibility of belief. The typical riposte might be that even if the theory were true it would not have the implications for belief that the sceptic or atheist maintains. In this way one pulls the teeth of one's attacker. Some of the excessive burden placed on the sciences arose in this way. Once this is recognised a more sympathetic account than Buckley's becomes possible. The old adage that no-one had doubted the existence of God until the Boyle lecturers undertook to prove it will not really do. To some extent it was they who were reacting to a series of existing challenges, of which deism was certainly one. Deists such as Anthony Collins and the republican John Toland were using Newton's science in a manner that appeared subversive of Christianity. Collins saw in Newton's gravitational force proof that matter had its own source of activity. Toland took a similar view, drawing on the heretical naturalism of Bruno. Toland conceded that, by making gravity an innate property of matter, he was interpreting it differently from Newton.[45]

Once the issue became how the new science was to be interpreted, it was difficult for Christian apologists to ignore the challenge of deistic and other subversive interpretations. William Whiston, in common with Newton and Samuel Clarke, had unorthodox views on the Trinity, but he would not let the deists get their way. The gravitational force had to be the interposition of God's 'general, immechanical, immediate power'.[46] A heavy burden was placed on the sciences because Christians and their critics fought over their implications. A dialectical process could cut both ways. In ascribing the origins of modern atheism principally to an act of negation made possible by a new theistic stance, Buckley might also be criticized for glossing over the social and political changes that conferred different elements of power on particular groups of protagonists. On a dialectical explanation alone, it is not clear why Paris rather than London should have experienced the most concentrated assault on the sacred.

Another important consideration is that arguments for design, despite the bad press they have today, had a long career because they were not always overstated. To present them as a decisive proof, akin to a geometrical demonstration, would be asking for trouble. But among more sophisticated advocates, such as the *Bridgewater Treatises* authors Thomas Chalmers and William Whewell, their limitations were freely acknowledged.[47] A modest and qualified natural theology had the capacity to survive and for reasons that the historian can perhaps uncover.

We suggested earlier that it can be a mistake to isolate the theistic proofs from the contexts in which they served the interests of a particular religious group. The sermons of Whewell make an interesting case-study because they reveal a commitment to natural theology, but within an Anglican Christian piety that also committed him to qualifications. A natural theology, whether based on science or not, would always have subordinate status because, in his words, 'the end of our wisdom is to make us wise to salvation'.[48] No amount of scientific knowledge could produce that kind of wisdom. In a devotional context, reflection on the wonders of nature had real value, not to produce belief, but to confirm and enhance a pre-existing faith. As he put it, scientific pursuits could 'feed and elevate ... devotion when it exists'.[49] To trace law and order in the natural world was a way of confirming more general notions of law and order that were applicable in the moral sphere.

Whewell certainly did not believe that rational argument opened the portals of belief. 'Demonstration', he declared, 'produces a result far short of its claims.' Men and women were brought to God through the 'foolishness of preaching' not through invincible argument.[50] If the arguments were invincible what place was left for the initiative of God? Whewell was perfectly aware that the sciences were being overburdened if they were supposed to provide proof. There was even a practical defect in demonstrative appeals to nature. The uncomfortable fact was that the more one grew accustomed to the regularities of nature, the greater the danger of spiritual indifference. Whewell made the point in a sermon of 1849, just after Cambridge had been smitten with cholera. During the previous epidemic in 1832, it had still been common for Low Churchmen and Methodists to see divine judgement visiting inebriates and reprobates with stiletto precision. But since the Master of Jesus College had just died, that was hardly an option for Whewell. Instead he observed that 'the very frequency and regularity of the occurrences which *should* speak to us of God's providence produces upon us a contrary effect'.[51] He could then account for the pestilence. It was an 'extraordinary' visitation designed to heighten a waning sense of dependence.

The example of Whewell shows that we should avoid denigrating the design argument, as if it always appeared without qualification. Evidence for the coherence of nature could raise questions to which a Christian theism gave what Whewell considered the best answer. The intricacy of organic structures *illustrated* the wisdom and skill of their Maker but, in his own words, 'they suggest nothing as to a *moral* author of the world'.[52] If design arguments survived well into the nineteenth century it was because they could be useful, even whilst lacking demonstrative pretensions. They could be used as a source of edification, to evoke a sense of wonder, to confirm an existing faith.[53] As we shall see in chapter 6, they were used rhetorically to win over the waverer. They could be used apologetically to combat claims like that of the French materialist La Mettrie who had said that the study of nature made only unbelievers. A natural theology could help to control deviancy within a specific religious tradition and, in a missionary context, offered the prospect of common ground between one religious culture and another. These are all functions within the domains of religious practice and it is possible to add more.[54] But there was another informal role that design arguments could play. This was in the promotion not of religion but of science.

Natural Theology and the Promotion of Science

The pursuit of experimental science has not always been applauded. Those who know their *Gulliver's Travels* may recall Jonathan Swift's satire of the scientific Academy:

> The first man I saw was of a meagre aspect, with sooty hands and face, his hair and beard long, ragged and singed in several places. His clothes, shirt and skin were all of the same colour. He had been eight years upon a project for extracting sun-beams out of cucumbers, which were to be put into vials hermetically sealed, and let out to warm the air in raw inclement summers. He told me, he did not doubt in eight years more, that he should be able to supply governors' gardens with sun-shine at a reasonable rate; but he complained that his stock was low, and intreated me to give

> him something as an encouragement to ingenuity, especially since this
> had been a very dear season for cucumbers. I made him a small present,
> for my Lord had furnished me with money on purpose, because he knew
> their practice of begging from all who go to see them.[55]

In eighteenth-century England, public lecturers on science could put on a good show of electrical sparks but they too attracted criticism from censorious High Churchmen. From the city of dreaming spires an eventual bishop of Norwich, George Horne, complained in 1753 about the 'stupid admiration' shown to those making experiments that degraded 'the philosopher into the mechanic'.[56] His specific target was the experimental philosophy of the Newtonians. Another anti-Newtonian was Andrew Michael Ramsay, who from 1724 was tutor to the Pretender, Charles Edward Stuart. Ramsay particularly lamented the solace given by Newton and Clarke to the deists: 'Some ... deny there is a God, laugh at virtue and vice, call them only political inventions to impose on the mob; and pretend that all religion is a cheat. Others assert that spirit and matter are the same, that man is composed of ten yards of gut, and that his supreme felicity consists in filling and emptying them by turns.' Still others 'spend all the force of their mind in the speculations of Algebra and geometrical curves, or in metaphysical quibbles ... so as to forget the great end of their creation'.[57] In such remarks we can see how particular forms of natural science and their practitioners could easily be held in suspicion. The design argument was not confined to the defence of religious belief. It could assist the promotion of innovative science in the face of religious suspicion.[58]

This happened in Scotland in the late eighteenth century when James Hutton published his *Theory of the Earth* (1795). Hutton was concerned with the physical processes that were pre-conditions for the support of life. At rock bottom there had to be soil, and this ultimately came from the erosion of mountains. But the processes of erosion were continuous and this implied that over millions of years there would have to be mountain building as well as decay. The power house for the elevation of land came from the earth's subterranean heat, of which volcanoes were evidence. Hutton used teleological language in his book. It was as if the system had been designed. But his recurring cycles carried a time bomb.

In his own famous words, he could find no evidence of a beginning, no prospect of an end. Those who liked to see Revelation confirmed by science greeted Hutton's scheme with suspicion. In the immediate aftermath of the French Revolution it was easy to accuse his geology of subversion. One of his most vicious critics, Richard

Kirwan, did exactly that. Kirwan wanted a geology that in his own words established 'the credit due to Moses on mere philosophic grounds'.[59] In such circumstances Hutton needed friends. He had one in the Revd John Playfair, professor of mathematics and later of natural philosophy at the University of Edinburgh. Was Hutton's system atheistic? Absolutely not, said Playfair. To deny that geology could supply evidence of a beginning or prospect of an end was not to deny either beginning or end. It was simply good scientific prac-tice not to exceed the limits of an inductive method. Hutton had not discussed ultimate origins because that question was off limits. The crucial point, however, is Playfair's recourse to natural theology in order to grant Hutton his reprieve. Had not natural theology been strengthened by Newton's understanding of the cyclic motions in the heavens? The same was surely true of the Huttonian cycles. Hutton's own references to the wisdom and economy of nature allowed Playfair to insist on an overtly theistic reading. He claimed that what Hutton himself had valued most in his system was the new evidence for design. It was this addition to our knowledge of *final causes* that he had 'contemplated with greatest delight'.[60]

It is probably true to say that until Darwin published his *Origin of Species* (1859), geology was the science most likely to generate suspi-cion. In certain contexts it became imperative to allay the fears. From the second decade of the nineteenth century William Buckland had the delicate task of promoting geology in Oxford. There is no doubting his enthusiasm for the science. It was said that he carried his hammer up his sleeve 'in order not to shock the feelings of the Scotchmen on Sunday'.[61] In order to avoid shocking feelings in Oxford he set out to vindicate his science from the charge of irreli-gion. One of his best known strategies was to argue for a universal flood. The phenomena, such as smooth U-shaped valleys, that we explain with reference to a recent ice age Buckland explained with reference to a recent deluge. Far from destroying the credibility of Revelation, geology confirmed the Mosaic flood.[62] The reconstruc-tion of fossil species provided another route to the affirmation of design. As cumbersome a beast as the giant sloth might not look like the perfect example of divine panache. But when the British Association for the Advancement of Science met in Oxford, Buckland kept his audience almost to midnight as he waxed eloquent on the animal's design.[63] The forelimbs might look grotesque, but for a sloth they were just the thing for digging up roots and other food.

The sciences were decidedly overburdened in having to maintain the fabric of design, but one reason for the burden was the need to avert suspicion. In contexts where this was imperative, an overstatement of the argument was often the result. In 1819 Buckland had claimed that geology would have required a universal flood even if Genesis had not.[64] It was that sort of exaggerated claim that would soon prove embarrassing. Buckland's opposite number in Cambridge, Adam Sedgwick, was offering his own recantation as early as 1831.[65]

There was, however, another attraction of natural theology: it could be discussed without necessarily compromising religious doctrines.[66] In fact this may be another reason why it survived in polite society. It could provide a common discourse in which it was not necessary to probe more deeply into contentious doctrinal or political matters.[67] This was especially true in face-to-face encounters. A recent study of the London 'season' of 1845 has shown how the subjects of Creation and natural law were acceptable conversational gambits.[68] The anonymity of Robert Chambers' *Vestiges*, only recently published, added a certain spice. Even the young Florence Nightingale discussed it at a polite dinner party at which the Nightingale family was introduced to a leading Tory diplomat, Baron Ashburton, and his American wife. Florence recorded her conversation with Anne Louisa: 'She is an American, and we swore eternal friendship upon Boston. ... She has a raspberry-tart of diamonds upon her forehead worth seeing. Then Mesmerism, and when we parted, we had got up so high into *Vestiges* that I could not get down again, and was obliged to go off as an angel.'[69] Natural theology could be the medium for this kind of elevation.

The role of natural theology in the popularisation of science is particularly conspicuous in the success enjoyed by the *Bridgewater Treatises*. This series of eight books published in the 1830s all made reference to design and in most cases possessed a high scientific content. Chalmers, Buckland and Whewell were among the authors, as were the anatomist Charles Bell, the physiologist Peter Mark Roget, the entomologist William Kirby and the chemist William Prout. The *Treatises* have often been discussed as the last feeble flowering of the argument for design. But to treat them as the epitome of a moribund theology is to miss their historical significance. As the author of a recent study reminds us, they rank among the scientific best-sellers of the early nineteenth century.[70] In Henry Brougham's campaign for popular education, the natural theology helped to counter the politically militant elements within working class radicalism. But it was the science itself in which so much hope was placed by many educational reformers. The hope in Brougham's circle was that if the working classes were given a scientific education they would be drawn out of shallowness and sensuality into placid and upright citizens.

The success of the *Bridgewater Treatises* as scientific texts may have surprised some of the authors. But it would not have disappointed them. Even the most evangelical among them, Thomas Chalmers, valued the edifying role of science itself. Writing on popular education he had held that there 'obtains a very close affinity between a taste for science, and a taste for sacredness'. They were both 'refined abstractions from the grossness of the familiar and ordinary world'. The mind that relishes either has 'achieved a certain victory of the spiritual or the intellectual, over the animal part of our nature'. His conclusion was that 'the two resemble in this, that they make man a more reflective and less sensual being, than before'.[71] We are a long way here from the use of design arguments to construct a formal proof of God's existence. The relevance of science to religion is more subtle. It is argued in terms of taste, of intellectual parallels and of convergent paths towards moral refinement.

There is a conclusion here that is difficult to escape. We must be suspicious of the claim that arguments for design were rendered obsolete by the philosophical critiques of Hume and Kant. Until their diplomatic functions were compromised they had a continuing role in the promotion of science itself.[72] A full analysis would have to explore their political connotations as well. There can be no doubt that natural theology was a vehicle by which the clerical scientists of Oxbridge tried to slam the door on political agitation. William Whewell explicitly associated political instability with those countries that had failed to bring science and religion into union, where superstition had given way to irreverence.[73] Without respect for the divine Mind there would be no respect for human authority. We saw in chapter 1 how Adam Sedgwick preached resignation to some three or four thousand colliers on Tynemouth beach in 1838 when the British Association was in town.[74] In his Easter sermon for 1848, and now installed as Dean of Westminster, William Buckland put the matter in a nutshell: 'equality of mind or body, or of worldly condition, is as inconsistent with the order of nature as with the moral laws of God'.[75] A fortnight earlier every precaution had been taken to protect the Abbey from a potentially unruly Chartist meeting.

Examples of this kind might encourage the view that there was a direct correlation between natural theology and political sentiment. The exciting work of Adrian Desmond has gone a long way towards endorsing that view.[76] A natural theology redolent of Oxbridge values could easily become the butt of satire when radical agitators and reformers of scientific as well as political institutions had their say. Thomas Wakley, his face set against the nepotism of the Royal College of Surgeons, would lampoon powerful figures of the old guard. He was merciless in his mimicry of the *Bridgewater Treatise* author Charles Bell, who 'never touches a phalanx and its flexor tendon, without exclaiming, with uplifted eye, and reverentially-contracted mouth, "Gintilmin, behold the winderful eevidence of *desin*"'.[77] In 1826 Wakley had attacked another surgeon, Sir Anthony Carlisle, who had proclaimed that same 'winderful eevidence' in the anatomy of an oyster. Wakley's report was a devastating retort: 'whilst tearing asunder its bivalves, lacerating its ligaments, and inflating its rectum, [he] piously observed, that the benevolence of an omnipotent power is exhibited in all the works of nature'. Wakley considered the remark at least ill-timed and added: 'we are inclined to believe that had the oyster spoken, it would have given a flat denial of the Orator's proposition'.[78]

The political complacency of many texts on natural theology certainly invited radical censure. The map is not, however, as simple as it may seem. Some eighteenth-century champions of natural theology had been anything but conservative. The Unitarian minister Joseph Priestley is a striking example, given his sympathies with American independence and the French Revolution.[79] Yet by the 1830s, natural theology may have become an emblem of political conservatism. The Scotsman Robert Knox dubbed the *Bridgewater Treatises* 'Bilgewater Treatises',[80] a sentiment that was repeated in radical literature. But it would be wrong to interpret it as inherently or invariably conservative and there are many shades of conservatism. The anthropologist Clifford Geertz has observed how systems of religious symbols can be either models *of* or models *for* social systems.[81] In line with that distinction it is possible to distinguish between a quiescent and a prophetic strain within references to natural order.[82] In the quiescent strain, current social and political structures are naturalised by reference to the transcendent. But in the prophetic strain the *status quo* is seen as a deviation from the natural, thereby legitimating reform.

Priestley's natural theology had been of the prophetic type. Once the Trinitarian obstacle had been removed, Priestley had envisaged a rational dialogue between Christianity and Islam, that would, as a matter of fact, lead to the triumph of his rational Christianity. It is a measure of his optimism that he thought 'less than a century' might suffice.[83] A simple polarity between natural theology and radical reform can miss the prophetic use of alternative concepts of the 'natural'. As editor of the *Poor Man's Guardian*, James O'Brien protested in 1833–4 that the current distribution of wealth was anything but natural. 'Fellow countrymen!', he exclaimed:

> Turn with scorn from the selfish hypocrites who connect the name of God with the present cannibal system, with a view to reconcile you to its abominations. If ... He who created us had ordained that one part of the human race should grow rich and fat on the sighs and sufferings, the tears, the toil and the blood of the other, then should we bend the knee to our fate ...; but we deny – utterly deny – the blasphemous doctrine.[84]

This forthright denial was not grounded in atheism or in materialistic forms of science but in a natural theology that celebrated the bounties of nature. A beneficent deity had ordained that there was enough to go round, that there need not be poverty, if only wealth and property were more evenly distributed. It was the *status quo* that was unnatural.

There are other reasons why attempts to correlate natural theology with political preferences can be frustrated. One is that, irrespective of their intentions, authors could lose control of how their texts were read. There is a striking example in Buckland's *Bridgewater Treatise*. The author went to great pains to explain why a great age for the earth need not jeopardise the Genesis text and therefore the authority of his Church. But he could not prevent readings in which this was seen as infidelity in disguise. Buckland carefully explained how geology and Christianity were still in harmony, but he could not prevent the atheist William Chilton from using him to exemplify the 'cowardice and dishonesty of scientific men'. Buckland's account of progressive creation made it perfectly clear that a Creator had been involved in replacing lost species with new ones, but he could not prevent the Owenite 'Shepherd' Smith from welcoming his book as a boon to pantheism. Buckland had insisted that progressive creation was a pious alternative to theories of organic transmutation. But he could not prevent Robert Chambers from using his book and his name to further exactly that subversive programme.[85] Reactions to Chambers's own book also reveal the contingency of relations between natural theology and politics. In the months following the publication of *Vestiges* it was great sport to speculate on the identity of the anonymous author. The striking point is that two of the prime suspects were poles apart in the political spectrum. One was the arch-Tory Sir Richard Vyvyan, who had led the opposition to the Reform Bill of 1832. The other was Byron's daughter, Countess Ada Lovelace, who was known to move in liberal Whig circles.[86]

Given the political uses of natural theology, it would be surprising if there were not divisions between exponents of the design argument.[87] And these divisions could be reflected in divergent forms of the argument itself. In fact it is possible to distinguish at least four different constructions of nature in the 1850s, each susceptible of a teleological interpretation. Paley's argument was still to be found, even in the changed and changing world revealed by the study of fossil forms. One could still argue, as Buckland had, that each species had been well adapted for the conditions in which it had endured. For Robert Chambers and the young Charles Darwin, the teleology took the form of designed laws. These were laws that had the purpose of producing the highest good, which Darwin identified with the development of complex organic forms.[88] The third kind of teleology was that advanced by Whewell and Richard Owen as they contemplated the suitably modified instantiations of a skeletal archetype. There was in their view a pattern common to the skeletons of

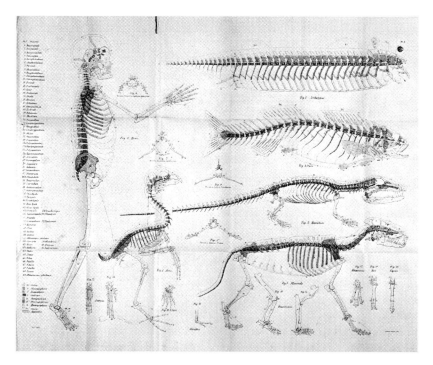

Figure 18: An illustration from Richard Owen's *On the Nature of Limbs* (1849) depicting Owen's skeletal archetype and the relationship it bears to actual vertebrates supposedly modelled on it. Reproduced by courtesy of the Syndics of Cambridge University Library.

all vertebrates. This represented an idea in the Mind of the Creator who had modified it for the needs of each species.[89] In the 1850s a fourth construction was offered by Hugh Miller who focused on the beauty of fossil forms and how they anticipated human architecture.[90] We shall return to this aesthetic argument in chapter 7. For the moment, the crucial point is that, largely as a result of developments within science itself, the argument for design had diversified before the Darwinian blow was struck.[91]

The Darwinian Challenge to Natural Theology

Darwin himself recognised the challenge his theory posed to orthodox Christian belief. Man may see himself as worthy the attention of a creator, Darwin wrote, but it is more accurate and more humble to recognise his continuity with the animals.[92] The damaging implications for religious belief were often made the basis of humour. Apes at the London Zoo allegedly asked, 'Am I my keeper's brother?' Darwin's theory did show how nature could counterfeit design, and sensitive Christian analysts saw the point only too clearly.[93] The Princeton theologian Charles Hodge described neither Darwin himself nor evolutionary theories in general as atheistic. But the specific mechanism proposed by Darwin he had to conclude was effectively atheistic, in that it left no room for design.[94]

It would, of course, be bizarre to suggest that Darwin's theory was not a profoundly disturbing revelation. There were fears for the stability of society if men and women were encouraged to behave like animals. Satirical cartoons, showing the loss of a monkey's tail, cashed in on the prospects for the animals: 'cut it off short Tim; I can't afford to await developments before I can take my proper position in Society'.[95] At a more sophisticated level there would seem to be at least three major shifts that symbolise what has become known as the Darwinian revolution.

One was the breakdown of any kind of consensus on how scientific and religious beliefs were to be related and integrated. Members of the same religious tradition would react in widely differing ways. At Princeton James McCosh became an advocate of theistic evolution despite the reservations voiced by Hodge.[96] When Henry Drummond presented his scheme of theistic evolution to a Northfield conference in 1893, his evangelical audience was not amused. 'Many fell upon me and rent me', he complained.[97]

A second shift was the often painful process of readjustment to the idea that apes and humans have a common ancestor. Scientists could be as sensitive on this matter as theologians. Neither Charles Lyell, the eminent geologist, nor Alfred Russel Wallace, Darwin's co-founder of the theory of natural selection, could finally accept that the powers of the human mind were adequately explained by natural selection.

A third shift concerned the character of scientific texts. By the end of the nineteenth century it would be extremely rare to find references to divine design, direction or control in scientific texts on evolution. Peter Bowler has observed that, although Darwin's mechanism of natural selection was itself involved in a struggle for survival by the end of the nineteenth century, the theoretical alternatives under discussion had all the appearance of being completely naturalistic.[98] This had not been the case in the middle years of the century. Even Darwin had used what he described as *Pentateuchal* language in the concluding section of the *Origin*.[99]

Does it make sense then to say that with Darwinism came the death of God? In fact it would be fairly easy to show that the Darwinian theory was not an efficient murder weapon. After all, Darwin never presumed to explain the ultimate origins of the earth or even of the first living forms. But his theory undoubtedly was effective in adding to the burden of qualifications with which the concept of a divine being was lumbered. The issue as seen by Darwin's disciple George John Romanes was how one could possibly square the goodness and omnipotence of God with a creative process that involved such carnage and extinction.[100] Conversely, one might claim, as did Asa Gray, to see more clearly how waste and suffering were part and parcel of all creative processes. Gray wrote that 'Darwinian teleology has the special advantage of accounting for the imperfections and failures as well as for successes. ... It explains the seeming waste as being part and parcel of a great economical process.'[101] For Gray there was no inconsistency between natural selection and natural theology because, without competing multitudes, there would have been no 'survival of the fittest', and, without that, no progression from lower to nobler forms.

Given such diversity of response, it may be more rewarding to ask not whether Darwin's theory demanded the death of God, but how it affected images of the deity. If we pursue this more subtle question it soon becomes clear that two images of God took a beating. One was that of the magician who had conjured up new species out of the mud. Such a deity was clearly rendered obsolete. We should note, however, that the death of this God could be a cause for celebration. The Christian socialist Charles Kingsley was one of the first clergymen to give an appreciative response to Darwin's work. There had once been an interfering God who made all things. But now there was a God so much wiser who could make things make themselves.[102] Kingsley even claimed to see the Christian ideal of self-sacrifice underwritten by Darwinian naturalism.[103]

The image of God as artisan or mechanic also took a beating. This had had its classic formulation in Paley who had marvelled at the craftsmanship in the human eye. The epiglottis, too, was a wonderful contrivance. How few aldermen had choked at feasts! With good reason Darwin insisted that this watchmaker God had been made redundant by his theory.[104] He had, after all, provided an alternative account of how such adaptations had come about by gradual refinement over immense periods of time. It is not clear, however, that the loss of this watchmaker God was a theological disaster. There had always been those who thought that the God of physico-theology looked a bit too much like a God created in the image of man, and of British industrial man to boot.[105] Paley's construction of nature invited one to look on the bright side. It was, in his own words, a happy world after all. Long before Darwin's theory appeared, he had been attacked by Christian writers for insensitivity to the poor and suffering.[106] His mechanistic models of nature had another disadvantage: they had certainly been compatible with a deism in which a remote clockmaker was preferred to the demanding God of Christian theism.

In post-Darwinian natural theology there is a gradual death of the artisan God; but a re-birth perhaps of God the artist. Instead of seeing nature as a great machine, it was seen by some commentators as a great canvas on which many creative strokes were discernible. This image left room for an evolving landscape as it were, with the artist enjoying an ongoing and intimate relationship with that which was being created. One scholar who would develop this analogy between the work of Providence and the work of an artist was the Jesuit modernist George Tyrrell. Writing in the early years of the twentieth century, Tyrrell found it hard, just as Darwin had, to see some single overriding cosmic purpose working itself out through nature. Natural disasters, such as the earthquake that hit Southern Italy in 1908, could not be slotted into a single all-embracing end. But if the universe were conceived as a canvas or a keyboard, then each picture or each melody might have a worth in itself, apart from all the rest.

We might not like the idea, but it shows that we are not seeing so much the death of God as a recasting of images. For Tyrrell, the Darwinian metaphor of a branching tree was turned to theological advantage. He wanted to say that the alternative to a single cosmic purpose was not blind materialism:

> Rather [the universe] teems with aims and meanings, although it has no
> one aim or meaning. It is like a great tree, that pushes out its branches,
> however and wherever it can, seeking to realize its whole nature ... in
> every one of them, but aiming at no collective effort. This is its play, this
> is its life, this is, if you will, its end.[107]

There is a further respect in which it would be misleading to say that
God and evolution became mutually exclusive. Darwin's achievement was to show how the process of speciation could be understood
as a natural process obeying the same kinds of law that operated in
any branch of the sciences. This is why another casualty was the god-
of-the-gaps who had traditionally survived in the crevices of scientific
ignorance, only to be squeezed out as scientific knowledge increased.
But this was not enough to annihilate the God of the monotheistic
religions because their God was pre-eminently a law-giver. Everything
hinged on the interpretation placed on the law metaphor.[108] There
was of course the problem whether the law of natural selection is the
kind of law one would have chosen if one had been God. But popular
religious writers could still look on the bright side if they wished.
Nature might be red in tooth and claw, but for Henry Drummond,
the fact remained that it was better to have lived and been eaten than
never to have lived at all. When discussing the problem of waste in
nature, Darwin could even come to one's aid. Frederick Temple,
who eventually became Archbishop of Canterbury, could argue that
'the inevitable operation of this waste, as Darwin's investigation
showed, has been to destroy all those varieties which were not well
fitted to their surroundings, and to keep those that were'.[109] As early
as 1860 Temple had jettisoned a god-of-the-gaps in favour of an
extension of natural law. The establishment of natural laws made the
existence of moral laws more, not less, credible.[110]

Darwinism has often been credited with turning the Creator into
a remote and distant figure who at most designed the initial swirl of
cosmic dust so that it would eventually produce such a universe as we
inhabit. T. H. Huxley, for all his agnosticism, could not take exception to such a 'wider teleology', as he called it, because it was 'actually
based upon the fundamental proposition of Evolution'.[111] This was
that 'the whole world, living and not living, is the result of the mutual
interaction, according to definite laws, of the forces possessed by the
molecules of which the primitive nebulosity of the universe was
composed'.[112] But the striking point is that, for less secular minds,
the name of Darwin was sometimes invoked to support the image of
a more immediate God, constantly working through the laws of
nature. For some theologians at least, traditional images of a totally
transcendent God had been overdrawn. Their view was that the

notion of an immanent God – a God involved within the world – was actually rendered *more plausible* by Darwinian evolution.

A late-nineteenth-century exponent of this view was Aubrey Moore, a contributor to a collection of theological essays with the title *Lux Mundi*. Moore wrote the striking words that, under the guise of a foe, Darwin had done the work of a friend. He had made it impossible to accept the image of an absentee landlord who interfered on rare occasions. This was a kind of semi-deism no longer sanctioned by science. Darwin, to his credit, had sharpened up the choice: it was a question now of all or nothing. God was an active participant, immanent in the world, or completely absent. It is no coincidence that Moore and other contributors to *Lux Mundi* were committed to a theology that stressed the importance of the Incarnation in Christian theology: a God who dwelled with humanity in the person of Christ and who shared in earthly suffering.[113]

In early drafts of his theory Darwin himself had retained teleological language. We even catch a glimpse of a new theodicy. Darwin was deeply sensitive to the more gruesome features of creation. What a book, he exclaimed, might be written by a devil's chaplain on the horribly cruel and wasteful processes of nature.[114] He had in mind such gory examples as the insects that lay their eggs in the bodies of caterpillars. But might the deity be spared immediate responsibility if such creatures were by-products of an evolutionary process that had not been predetermined in all its details? Darwin entertained though did not systematically develop such a theodicy. Later theologians did.

The idea sat quite comfortably with other developments in late-nineteenth-century Christian theology, especially an exploration of what it meant to say that God's power had been deliberately limited in the context of relations with humanity. The most celebrated example of this nuance was in the context of Christology where Charles Gore spoke of *kenosis*: in becoming man God the Father had relinquished certain powers and qualities.[115] A similar idea could work in the context of a creative role in nature: God might have deliberately set limits to omnipotence by choosing to work through natural agencies rather than override them. It might then be possible to refer to incidental features of a creative process that God, in self-limitation, had chosen not to nullify.[116] This was how the Cambridge philosopher and theologian F. R. Tennant developed the argument in the early years of the twentieth century. In a manner reminiscent of the early Darwin, Tennant suggested that 'many of the details accompanying the execution of the plan are not essential parts of it but only necessarily incidental'.[117] Earthquakes, floods, the indiscriminate distribution of disease and other ills, all had to be possible in the kind of world in which it had also been possible for sensitive and intelligent life to emerge. The influence of Darwinism on theology was an issue that Tennant specifically discussed and it certainly left its mark on his own. Thus he took strong exception to the view that every form of suffering had been a premeditated means to a particular end. To suggest that it had been would be to attribute devilishness to the deity.[118] That was precisely the dilemma that Darwin had addressed.

Epilogue

Our theologies today tend to be less theocentric than they were in the second half of the nineteenth century. But concerns about the environment or about the status of animals are, for many, ultimate concerns that carry ideological freight as did the concerns of nineteenth-century theists. A question sometimes arises concerning the implications of Darwinism for our attitude towards animal suffering. The answer is far from straightforward. On the one hand Darwin stressed our kinship with the animal creation: 'we are all netted together', he wrote in a famous jotting in his transmutation notebooks.[119] For those who like to set up an antithesis between an anthropocentric and a biocentric view of nature, Darwin's authority seems to help. On the other hand, the mechanism of natural selection sets one species against another and its own members against each other. Extinction almost becomes a way of life. And if it is part of the natural order, why get sentimental about it? The question 'Why should animals be treated with respect?' cannot therefore be given an unequivocal answer in Darwinian terms. A sense of the mutuality of living things was arguably more in evidence in earlier, pre-evolutionary, constructions of natural history where a sense of divine design did prevail.[120] But an argument, recently aired by the philosopher Alan Holland, suggests that the God of pre-Darwinian natural theology is still alive, or at least walking as a ghost.

The argument goes that one ground on which animals might be respected would be if they truly were God's creatures, separately designed and created in just the way Darwin denied. It is acknowledged that for most philosophers such a justification will not do because, for them, such a God *is* dead. But then comes the subtle move: it is of the very essence of the Darwinian theory that it explains why animals appear as if they had been so meticulously designed. Even if organisms are not fixed but are dynamically changing, they still appear as if they were designed by a God if only such a God were there.[121]

This is not as phoney as it may sound. Even the most ruthlessly Darwinian authors find it difficult to avoid the language of design. Daniel Dennett has remarked that the brain of Johann Sebastian Bach was 'exquisitely designed as a heuristic program for composing music'.[122] He is as adamant as Richard Dawkins that the design does not imply a designer. But the argument we are considering for clemency towards animals does not require that it should. That they are as finely wrought as if they had been designed may be sufficient, so it is argued, to persuade us that they are intrinsically precious and to be valued.[123] They are the kind of thing God would have designed had there been such a God to do it.

Because this chapter has been devoted to natural theology and the history of science, we have said nothing about the complex relations between the natural sciences and the 'science' of biblical criticism. But here is another story waiting to be told. However one interprets Genesis, it tells of human sinfulness in throwing nature out of joint. In the context of environmental concerns some have found a resurrection of meaning in the text. Have we not, through human greed, polluted the world? In the writing of another contemporary philosopher of biology is to be found this striking passage:

> The biologist is sure that whatever nature is in itself, today and for millennia past, its fundamental character has nothing to do with human sinfulness. Yet the biologist, in consensus with the theologian, now does fear that human sin can henceforth throw nature out of joint. Both can agree that nature does now need to be redeemed on that account. Sin pollutes the world. An ancient insight is breaking over us anew. We had almost thought that geology, biology and anthropology had drained the truth out of the Genesis stories. But then we discover that these stories contain a profound myth of aboriginal community and the human fall from it.[124]

What the text tells us, on this account, is that 'we are made for fellowship at multiple levels: with God, with persons, with the Earth. When that sense of community breaks, the world begins to fall apart.' Such sentiments may help us to understand why, in the USA at least, there can be a 'Joint Appeal from Religion and Science' on behalf of the environment.[125]

NOTES

1 W. Whewell to G. Morland, 15 December 1815, in *William Whewell: An Account of his Writings with Selections from his Literary and Scientific Correspondence* (ed. I. Todhunter), 2 vols., London, 1876, ii, 10.

2   R. Yeo, *Defining Science: William Whewell, Natural Knowledge and Public Debate in Early Victorian Britain*, Cambridge, 1993, 56–61.

3   D. Brewster, 'Review of Whewell's *History of the Inductive Sciences*', *Edinburgh Review*, 66 (1837), 110–51, especially 147–51.

4   Whewell to G. B. Airy, 28 October 1837, in Todhunter, op. cit. (1), ii, 263. On the strained relations between Whewell and Brewster over an extended period, see J. H. Brooke, 'Natural theology and the plurality of worlds: observations on the Brewster–Whewell debate', *Annals of Science*, 34 (1977), 221–86.

5   For an introduction to the many facets of Whewell's idealist philosophy of science, see the various essays in *William Whewell: A Composite Portrait* (ed. M. Fisch and S. Schaffer), Oxford, 1991.

6   R. Yeo, 'William Whewell, natural theology and the philosophy of science in mid-nineteenth-century Britain', *Annals of Science*, 36 (1979), 493–512.

7   W. Whewell, *Philosophy of the Inductive Sciences*, 2nd edn., 2 vols., London, 1847, Cass reprint edn., London, 1967, i, 619–21. Whewell insisted that 'this Idea of Final Cause is not deduced from the phenomena by reasoning, but is assumed as the only condition under which we can reason on such subjects at all'. Despite Immanuel Kant's critique of physico-theology, Whewell could capitalise on Kant's assertion to the effect that an organised product of nature is that in which all the parts are mutually ends and means. *Ibid.*, i, 619.

8   *Ibid.*, i, 625.

9   For both sympathetic and critical perspectives on these new physico-theologies, see *Physics, Philosophy and Theology: A Common Quest for Understanding* (ed. R. J. Russell, W. R. Stoeger and G. V. Coyne), Vatican, 1988; and *Chaos and Complexity: Scientific Perspectives on Divine Action* (ed. R. J. Russell, N. Murphy and A. Peacocke), Vatican, 1995.

10 Al-Ghazali, 'The Jerusalem Tract', translated and edited by A. L. Tibawi, *Islamic Quarterly*, 9 (1965), 97–8, on 98. Cited by J. Clayton, 'Piety and the proofs', *Religious Studies*, 26 (1990), 19–42, on 22.

11 Clayton, *ibid.*, 23.

12 For the contextualising of Anselm see J. Clayton, 'The otherness of Anselm', *Neue Zeitschrift für Systematische Theologie und Religionsphilosophie*, 37 (1995), 125–43.

13 H. Fisch, 'The scientist as priest: a note on Robert Boyle's natural theology', *Isis*, 44 (1953), 252–65; M. Hunter, *Science and Society in Restoration England*, Cambridge, 1981; *idem.*, 'The conscience of Robert Boyle: functionalism, "dysfunctionalism" and the task of historical understanding', in *Renaissance and Revolution: Humanists, Scholars, Craftsmen and Natural Philosophers in Early Modern Europe* (ed. J. V. Field and F. A. J. L. James), Cambridge, 1993, 147–59; T. Shanahan, 'Teleological reasoning in Boyle's Disquisition about Final Causes', in *Robert Boyle Reconsidered* (ed. M. Hunter), Cambridge, 1994, 177–92.

14 P. M. Rattansi, 'The social interpretation of science in the seventeenth century', in *Science and Society, 1600–1900* (ed. P. Mathias), Cambridge, 1972, 1–32, on 21.

15 J. Redwood, *Reason, Ridicule and Religion: The Age of Enlightenment in England, 1660–1750*, London, 1976.

16 J. Wilkins, *Of the Principles and Duties of Natural Religion*, London, 1675, Preface.

17 *Ibid.*

18 R. Hooke, *Micrographia*, London, 1665, 2.

19 *Deism: An Anthology* (ed. P. Gay), Princeton, 1968, 157–8.

20 Voltaire, *Elémens de la Philosophie de Neuton*, Amsterdam, 1738; P. M. Rattansi, 'Newton and the wisdom of the ancients', in *Let Newton Be!* (ed. J. Fauvel, R. Flood, M. Shortland and R. Wilson), Oxford, 1988, 185–201, especially 191–2.

21 J. Butler, *The Analogy of Religion* (1736), New York, 1961, 127; J. H. Brooke, 'Natural theology in Britain from Boyle to Paley', in *New Interactions Between Theology and Natural Science*, Milton Keynes, 1974.

22 Clayton, op. cit. (10), 19; *idem.*, 'Thomas Jefferson and the study of religion', an Inaugural Lecture, University of Lancaster, 18 November 1992.

23 M. Shortland, 'Hugh Miller's contribution to the *Witness*: 1840–56', in *Hugh Miller and the Controversies of Victorian Science*, Oxford, 1996, 287–300, especially 294.

24 D. Macleod, 'Hugh Miller, the Disruption and the Free Church of Scotland', in *ibid.*, 187–205.

25 H. Miller, 'The Disruption', *The Witness*, 20 May 1843.

26 C. Gibbon, *The Life of George Combe*, 2 vols., London, 1878, i, 209–25, 235–64; R. Cooter, *The Cultural Meaning of Popular Science: Phrenology and the Organization of Consent in Nineteenth-Century Britain*, Cambridge, 1984.

27 H. Miller, 'Editorial', *The Witness*, 17 September 1845. For access to the literature on Chambers see J. A. Secord, 'Introduction' to R. Chambers, *Vestiges of the Natural History of Creation and Other Evolutionary Writings*, Chicago, 1994, ix–xlv.

28 Brooke, op. cit. (21), 49. Miller repeated his argument in *The Testimony of the Rocks* (1857), Edinburgh, 1869, 184–5.

29 A classic example would be J. Dillenberger, *Protestant Thought and Natural Science*, London, 1961.

30 W. Derham, *Physico-Theology: Or a Demonstration of the Being and Attributes of God, from His Works of Creation* [1713], London, 1754, 288–90.

31 *Ibid.*, 113–14.

32 W. F. Cannon, 'The bases of Darwin's achievement: a revaluation', *Victorian Studies*, 5 (1961), 109–34; P. J. Bowler, 'Darwinism and the argument from design: suggestions for a revaluation', *Journal of the History of Biology*, 10 (1977), 29–43; R. Dawkins, *The Blind Watchmaker*, New York, 1986.

33 J. H. Brooke, 'Science and the fortunes of natural theology: some historical perspectives', *Zygon*, 24 (1989), 3–22.

34 In an early essay, Newton wrote that his object was to show that 'God may appear to have created the world solely by the act of will just as we move our bodies by an act of will alone; and, besides, so that I might show that

the analogy between the divine faculties and our own is greater than has formerly been perceived by philosophers.' R. S. Westfall, *Force in Newton's Physics*, London, 1971, 340.

35 A. Peacocke, 'God's interaction with the world', in Russell, Murphy and Peacocke, op. cit. (9), 263–87, especially 282–7.

36 The examples of William Whiston and Colin Maclaurin are discussed in Brooke, op. cit. (21), 23–4. On Newton's grounding the universality of his gravitation law in his voluntarist theology, see Westfall, op. cit. (34), 397.

37 M. J. Buckley, *At the Origins of Modern Atheism*, New Haven, 1987.

38 *Ibid.*, 15.

39 *Ibid.*, 194–250.

40 D. Hume, *Dialogues Concerning Natural Religion* [1779], in *Hume on Religion* (ed. R. Wollheim), London, 1963, 116.

41 J. E. Force, *William Whiston: Honest Newtonian*, Cambridge, 1985, 70.

42 F. Yates, *Giordano Bruno and the Hermetic Tradition*, Chicago, 1964; R. S. Westman and J. E. McGuire, *Hermeticism and the Scientific Revolution*, Los Angeles, 1977.

43 See, for example, W. Stephens, *An Account of the Growth of Deism in England* (1696), with an introduction by J. E. Force, Los Angeles, 1990.

44 Newton, *Observations upon the Prophecies of Daniel and the Apocalypse of St. John*, London, 1733, 25; Force, op. cit. (41), 71.

45 M. C. Jacob, *The Newtonians and the English Revolution, 1689–1720*, Ithaca, 1976, ch. 6.

46 W. Whiston, *Astronomical Principles of Religion, Natural and Revealed*, London, 1717, 111.

47 T. Chalmers, *On the Power, Wisdom and Goodness of God as Manifested in the Adaptation of External Nature to the Moral and Intellectual Constitution of Man*, 2 vols., London, 1833, ii, 282–93; J. H. Brooke, 'Indications of a Creator: Whewell as Apologist and Priest', in Fisch and Schaffer, op. cit. (5), 149–73.

48 W. Whewell, Sermon, February 1827, Whewell papers, Trinity College Cambridge, R6 17.13.

49 *Ibid.*

50 W. Whewell, Sermon (undated) 1843, Whewell papers, Trinity College, Cambridge, R6 17.55.

51 W. Whewell, *A Sermon Preached before the University of Cambridge on the Day of General Thanksgiving*, Cambridge, 1849, 10.

52 Brooke, op. cit. (47), 154.

53 *Ibid.*, 162–4.

54 Clayton, op. cit. (12), 133–5; Brooke, op. cit. (47).

55 J. Swift, *Gulliver's Travels* [1728], London, 1952, part 3, ch. 5, 197.

56 G. Horne, *A Fair, Candid, and Impartial State of the Case between Sir Isaac Newton and Mr. Hutchinson*, Oxford, 1753, 54; cited by L. Stewart, 'Seeing through the Scholium: religion and reading Newton in the eighteenth century', *History of Science*, 34 (1996), 123–65, on 145.

57 Cited by Stewart, *ibid.*, 147.

58 J. H. Brooke, 'The natural theology of the geologists: some theological

strata', in *Images of the Earth: Essays in the History of the Environmental Sciences* (ed. L. J. Jordanova and R. S. Porter), Chalfont St. Giles, 1979, 39–64.

59 C. C. Gillispie, *Genesis and Geology* [1951], New York, 1959, 53.

60 J. Playfair, *Illustrations of the Huttonian Theory of the Earth*, Edinburgh, 1802, 132–3; Gillispie, op. cit. (59), 76.

61 E. O. Gordon, *The Life and Correspondence of William Buckland D.D.*, London, 1894, 34.

62 W. Buckland, *Vindiciae Geologicae; Or the Connexion of Geology with Religion Explained*, Oxford, 1820; *idem.*, *Reliquiae Diluvianae; Or Observations on the Organic Remains Contained in Caves, Fissures, and Diluvial Gravel, and on Other Geological Phenomena Attesting the Action of an Universal Deluge*, London, 1823.

63 W. Buckland in *Report of the British Association for the Advancement of Science, 1832*, London, 1833, 104–6; N. A. Rupke, *The Great Chain of History: William Buckland and the English School of Geology 1814–1849*, Oxford, 1983, 240–8; J. H. Brooke, 'Scientific thought and its meaning for religion: the impact of French science on British natural theology, 1827–1859', *Revue de Synthèse*, 4 (1989), 33–59.

64 Buckland, *Vindiciae Geologicae*, op. cit. (62), 38.

65 As President of the London Geological Society, Sedgwick conceded that 'we ought, indeed, to have paused before we first adopted the diluvian theory, and referred all our old superficial gravel to the action of the Mosaic Flood. For of man, and the works of his hands, we have not yet found a single trace among the remnants of a former world entombed in these deposits.' Gillispie, op. cit. (59), 142–3.

66 Brooke, op. cit. (58), 42–5.

67 When Adam Sedgwick addressed the 1833 meeting of the newly formed British Association for the Advancement of Science he specifically warned that 'if we transgress our proper boundaries, go in to provinces not belonging to us, and open a door of communication with the dreary wild of politics, that instant will the foul demon of discord find his way into our Eden of Philosophy'. Such utterances show how natural theology might help to preserve the naturalist's Garden of Eden. Brooke, op. cit. (58), 44–5.

68 J. A. Secord, 'Conversations on Creation', paper presented to the conference on Robert Chambers and *Vestiges* held at the Wellcome Centre for the History of Medicine, London, November 1994.

69 Cited in *ibid.*, 13.

70 J. Topham, 'Science and popular education in the 1830s: the role of the *Bridgewater Treatises*', *British Journal for the History of Science*, 25 (1992), 397–430.

71 T. Chalmers, 'On mechanic schools, and on political economy as a branch of popular education', in *On the Christian and Civic Economy of Large Towns*, 3 vols., Glasgow, 1821–26, iii, 378–408, on 378–9; Topham, op. cit. (70), 406.

72 On the further question whether a preoccupation with design affected the theory and practice of science, see J. H. Brooke, *Science and Religion: Some Historical Perspectives*, Cambridge, 1991, 213–25.

73 W. Whewell, *On the Principles of English University Education*, London, 1837, 48–52.

74 *The Life and Letters of the Reverend Adam Sedgwick* (ed. J. W. Clark and T. Hughes), 2 vols., Cambridge, 1890, i, 515–16.

75 Gordon, op. cit. (61), 243–5.

76 A. Desmond, *The Politics of Evolution: Morphology, Medicine and Reform in Radical London*, Chicago, 1989; *idem.*, 'Artisan resistance and evolution in Britain, 1819–1848', *Osiris*, 3 (1987), 77–110; *idem*, 'Lamarckism and democracy: corporations, corruption, and comparative anatomy in the 1830s', in *History, Humanity and Evolution* (ed. J. R. Moore), Cambridge, 1989, 99–130.

77 Cited by Desmond, *The Politics of Evolution*, op. cit. (76), 111–12.

78 *Ibid.*, 112.

79 *Motion Toward Perfection: The Achievement of Joseph Priestley* (ed. A. T. Schwartz and J. G. McEvoy), Boston, 1990.

80 P. F. Rehbock, *The Philosophical Naturalists: Themes in Early Nineteenth-Century Biology*, Madison, 1983, 36–55; Desmond, *The Politics of Evolution*, op. cit. (76), 20.

81 C. Geertz, 'Religion as a cultural symbol', in *Anthropological Approaches to the Study of Religion* (ed. M. Banton), London, 1966, 1–46.

82 J. R. Topham, ' "An infinite variety of arguments": the *Bridgewater Treatises* and British natural theology in the 1830s'. PhD dissertation, Lancaster University, 1993, 207.

83 J. H. Brooke, ' "A sower went forth": Joseph Priestley and the ministry of reform', in Schwartz and McEvoy, op. cit. (79), 21–56, especially 36.

84 Topham, op. cit. (82), 235.

85 We are indebted to Jonathan Topham for each of these examples, which he has discussed in an as yet unpublished paper: 'Beyond the "common context": the readership of the *Bridgewater Treatises*', paper presented to the conference on Robert Chambers and *Vestiges* held at the Wellcome Centre, London, November 1994.

86 Secord, op. cit. (68). A recent study of foreign translations of *Vestiges* has revealed a similar contingency. The first German translation was made by Adolf Friedrich Seubert, who clearly valued the book as a work of natural theology. He even interleaved passages from Whewell's *Indications of a Creator*, which had been intended by Whewell as a refutation. As Nicolaas Rupke has pointed out, Seubert was the last person to harbour underground republican aims. He was a military man who rose to the rank of colonel. During the revolution of 1848 he fought against the rebels. But *Vestiges* could appeal to rebels too. The translator for a second German edition was the materialist Carl Vogt who valued a cosmology in which nature ran autonomously according to pre-established laws. Vogt could argue by analogy that society should not be subject to the arbitrary whim of an autocratic king. N. A. Rupke, 'The *Vestiges* in translation: Dutch and German', paper presented to the conference on Robert Chambers and *Vestiges* held at the Wellcome Centre, London, November 1994.

87 The divisions between Whewell and Brewster are discussed in detail in Brooke, op. cit. (4).

88 J. H. Brooke, 'The relations between Darwin's science and his religion', in *Darwinism and Divinity* (ed. J. Durant), Oxford, 1985, 40–75, especially 46–7.

89 Owen's use of the archetype in his battling with T. H. Huxley is discussed by A. Desmond, *Archetypes and Ancestors: Palaeontology in Victorian London 1850–1875*, London, 1982. See also N. A. Rupke, *Richard Owen, Victorian Naturalist*, New Haven, 1994.

90 H. Miller, *The Testimony of the Rocks*, Edinburgh, 1857.

91 J. H. Brooke, 'Between science and theology: the defence of teleology in the interpretation of nature, 1820–1876', *Journal for the History of Modern Theology*, 1 (1994), 47–65.

92 G. de Beer, 'Darwin's Notebooks on transmutation of species', *Bulletin of the British Museum (Natural History)*, Historical Series, 2 (1960), parts 2–5, entry 196.

93 For the image of nature counterfeiting design see N. C. Gillespie, *Charles Darwin and the Problem of Creation*, Chicago, 1979. There is an extensive literature on religious responses to Darwin's theory, summarised in Brooke, op. cit. (72), 393–9. Particularly recommended are O. Chadwick, *The Victorian Church*, 2 vols, London, 1966–70; A. Ellegard, *Darwin and the General Reader*, Göteborg, 1958; F. Gregory, 'The impact of Darwinian evolution on Protestant theology in the nineteenth century', in *God and Nature: Historical Essays on the Encounter between Christianity and Natural Science* (ed. D. C. Lindberg and R. L. Numbers), Berkeley, 1986, 369–90; D. N. Livingstone, *Darwin's Forgotten Defenders*, Edinburgh, 1987; J. R. Moore, *The Post-Darwinian Controversies: A Study of the Protestant Struggle to Come to Terms with Darwin in Great Britain and America 1870–1900*, Cambridge, 1979; J. H. Roberts, *Darwinism and the Divine in America: Protestant Intellectuals and Organic Evolution, 1859–1900*, Madison, 1988.

94 C. Hodge, *What is Darwinism?*, New York, 1874, 48–52; Livingstone, op. cit. (93), 102–5.

95 *Harper's Bazaar*, 16 September 1876.

96 Livingstone, op. cit. (93), 106–9.

97 J. R. Moore, 'Evangelicals and evolution', *Scottish Journal of Theology*, 38 (1985), 383–417.

98 This is not to deny, however, that variants of Lamarckism, with its admission of inherent tendencies towards complexification, had proved (and were continuing to prove) attractive to proponents of theistic evolution. P. J. Bowler, *The Eclipse of Darwinism*, Baltimore, 1983, ch. 3.

99 C. Darwin to J. D. Hooker, 29 March 1863, in *The Life and Letters of Charles Darwin* (ed. F. Darwin), 3 vols., London, 1887, iii, 17–18. For instructive comment on this letter, see Gillespie, op. cit. (93), 134–7.

100 G. J. Romanes, *Thoughts on Religion*, London, 1895; Brooke, op. cit. (72), 316.

101 A. Gray, *Darwiniana* (ed. A. H. Dupree), Cambridge, MA, 1963, 310–13.

102 Kingsley often referred to the older image as that of the 'master-magician'.

The effect of Darwin was to re-structure one's theological choices: 'between the absolute empire of accident, and a living, immanent, ever-working God'. B. Colloms, *Charles Kingsley*, London, 1975, 236. See also *Charles Kingsley: His Letters and Memories of His Life* (ed. F. E. Kingsley), London, 1883, 245, 309–10.

103 Kingsley, *ibid.*, 318.

104 *The Autobiography of Charles Darwin* (ed. N. Barlow), London, 1958, 87.

105 N. C. Gillespie, 'Divine design and the industrial revolution: William Paley's abortive reform of natural theology', *Isis*, 81 (1990), 214–29.

106 P. Corsi, *Science and Religion: Baden Powell and the Anglican Debate, 1800–1860*, Cambridge, 1988, 68, 179; Brooke, op. cit. (72), 223–4.

107 G. Tyrrell, 'Divine fecundity', in *Essays on Faith and Immortality*, London, 1914, especially 252–73. For this reference we are indebted to Professor James C. Livingston who discusses Tyrrell in ch. 5 of a major study provisionally entitled *Reconceptions of a Theological Tradition: British Religious Thought, 1860–1910*.

108 J. H. Brooke, 'Natural law in the natural sciences: the origins of modern atheism?', *Science and Christian Belief*, 4 (1992), 83–103.

109 F. Temple, *The Relations between Religion and Science*, London, 1884, 165.

110 F. Temple, *The Present Relations of Science to Religion: A Sermon Preached on July 1, 1860 before the University of Oxford*, Oxford, 1860.

111 T. H. Huxley, 'On the reception of the "Origin of Species"', in F. Darwin, op. cit. (99), ii, 179–204, on 201.

112 *Ibid.*

113 These aspects of Moore's theology are discussed by A. Peacocke, 'Biological evolution and Christian theology – yesterday and today', in Durant, op. cit. (88), 101–30, especially 110–11. Moore had no compunction in saying that the new view of nature was fatal to traditional models of teleology. But he could appeal to Darwin's 'deeper and wider view of purpose' to suggest that every species could be given a rationale within a unified evolutionary process. Each had had its place in the genealogical tree.

114 The local and political connotations of the term 'devil's chaplain' are fully explained by A. Desmond and J. Moore, *Darwin*, London, 1991, 70–3.

115 C. Gore, *Dissertations*, London, 1895, 95.

116 Variations of this theme are sensitively discussed by Livingston, op. cit. (107), ch. 5.

117 F. R. Tennant, *The Origin and Propagation of Sin*, Cambridge, 1902, 124–33.

118 F. R. Tennant, 'The influence of Darwinism upon theology', *Quarterly Review*, 211 (1909), especially 428–40; *idem.*, *Philosophical Theology*, 2 vols., Cambridge, 1930, ii, 203. For further commentary on Tennant's handling of the theodicy problem, see N. Smart, *Philosophers and Religious Truth*, 2nd edn., London, 1969, 139–62.

119 F. Darwin, op. cit. (99), ii, 5–9. A more authoritative and comprehensive transcription was subsequently published by G. de Beer, *Bulletin of the British Museum*, Historical Series, 2 (1960), 23–200 and 3 (1967), 129–76. For commentary on Darwin's first branching diagrams of the tree and

coral of life, see D. Kohn, 'Theories to work by: rejected theories, repro-duction, and Darwin's path to natural selection', *Studies in the History of Biology*, 4 (1980), 67–170, especially 94–5; and for his early incorporation of man into a unitary scheme, see J. R. Durant, 'The ascent of nature in Darwin's *Descent*', in *The Darwinian Heritage* (ed. D. Kohn), Princeton, 1985, 283–306, especially 287–92.

120 C. Glacken, *Traces on the Rhodian Shore: Nature and Culture in Western Thought from Ancient Times to the End of the Eighteenth Century*, Berkeley, 1967, 427; K. Thomas, *Man and the Natural World*, Harmondsworth, 1984, 180.

121 It was arguably the same insight that lay at the heart of Cannon's argument in op. cit. (32).

122 D. Dennett, *Darwin's Dangerous Idea: Evolution and the Meanings of Life*, New York, 1996, 512.

123 We are indebted to Alan Holland of the Philosophy Department, Lancaster University, for permission to cite this argument, which he is currently developing.

124 H. Rolston, 'Does nature need to be redeemed?', *Zygon*, 29 (1994), 205–29, on 226. For a related discussion of the bearing of human 'fallenness' on environmental sensibilities, see C. A. Russell, *The Earth, Humanity and God*, London, 1994, 136–40.

125 W. J. Wildman, 'The quest for harmony: an interpretation of contemporary theology and science', in *Religion and Science: History, Method, Dialogue* (ed. W. M. Richardson and W. J. Wildman), New York, 1996, 41–60, especially 60, note 1.

6
The Language of Natural Theology

Natural theology has traditionally been contrasted with revealed theology; the former appealing to reason, the latter to God's revelation, especially as manifested in the sacred texts. Although the scope of the former is often taken to include wider concerns about our knowledge of God and His attributes, the following discussion centres on one specific, but recurrent, aspect of natural theology: the argument from design, which gave rise in Europe to a flourishing genre from the late seventeenth century to the mid nineteenth and beyond. (Throughout this chapter the term will be used in this restricted sense, not the wider one as employed by Lord Gifford.[1]) With its popularity spanning two centuries, perhaps longer, the design argument constitutes a major topic in the field of 'science and religion'. As indicated in the preceding chapter, natural theology was not monolithic but fulfilled many different functions; hence the historian should be sensitive to its various modalities. But the focus of the present chapter moves discussion in a rather different direction, for we shall examine the historical significance of the design argument by analysing it as a form of rhetoric. Many historians of science, literary historians and sociologists of science have recently found common cause in attempting to understand science from the standpoint of rhetoric. Studies of narrative style and rhetorical form have been directed to such diverse productions as Darwin's *Origin of Species*, papers on chemistry in specialist journals, and astronomy lectures intended for public consumption.[2] Presentations of the design argument are also amenable to such analysis.

To the modern reader many examples of the design argument appear naive, perhaps even absurd. Even Isaac Newton – the most sophisticated of theoreticians – made theological capital out of the undisputed fact that we have two arms, two legs, two eyes and two ears. Such symmetry, he proclaimed, was surely a sign of design![3] That we possess one heart which is located off-centre did not seem to trouble him. Although this and many other examples may seem unsophisticated, even worthless, we are in danger of trivialising the design argument if we fail to push our historical analysis further. We should surely try to appreciate the significance of the design argument in its heyday. Why were so many natural theology texts on the list of best-sellers? What were its social resonances? Our aim in this chapter is to show how the historian can use rhetorical analysis to expose some of the social functions of natural theology.

Appeals to design long predate the writings of Boyle and Newton and are to be found among the writings of the ancient Greeks and Romans. However, it is no coincidence that the design argument gained a new lease of life during the 'Scientific Revolution' of the seventeenth century. Many of the leading natural philosophers of that period conceived the universe as providentially designed and enthusiastically recognised nature, and especially the many recently-discovered laws and phenomena, as God's handiwork. As Kepler wrote, 'order exists [in the universe], not chance; there is pure mind and pure Reason'.[4] Towards the close of that innovative century the sub-title of John Ray's *The Wisdom of God Manifested in the Works of Creation* proclaimed that his survey encompassed 'the heavenly BODIES, ELEMENTS, METEORS, Fossils, Vegetables, Animals, (Beasts, Birds, Fishes, and Insects) ... the Body of the Earth, its Figure, Motion, and Constitution; and ... the admirable Structure of the Bodies of Man and other Animals; as also in their Generation, &c'.[5] In this magnificent and broadly-conceived survey of creation Ray identified numerous signs of God's wisdom and goodness writ large. His book, which passed through many editions, became the paradigmatic British treatise on natural theology.

The best-known work in the genre is doubtless Archdeacon Paley's *Natural Theology* (1802), which trumpeted a similar message. Other familiar examples are the *Bridgewater Treatises* of the early 1830s whose authors divided nature into eight extensive topics, devoting one widely-read publication to each.[6] Although contributions to the genre continued apace for some decades after the *Bridgewaters*, we can with hindsight appreciate several indications of decline even before the publication of Darwin's *Origin of Species* in 1859.[7] The great age of natural theology had long passed by the time Adam Lord Gifford penned his will in 1885, but remnants of the argument from design continue to lurk in the corners of science, such as in the Anthropic Principle discussed in John Barrow's 1988 Gifford Lecture. There are even claims for its revival, as in the writings of John Polkinghorne.[8]

Although the design argument now receives relatively little scholarly attention, we misconstrue its history if we accept Richard

Dawkins' incisive but derogatory judgement that in the light of evolutionary theory Paley's argument 'is wrong, gloriously and utterly wrong'.[9] We also limit our understanding of natural theology if we follow Clarence Glacken who paid excessive attention to the great philosophers, like Hume and Kant, but downplayed the numerous lesser mortals who contributed so much to the genre.[10] While many of the 'greats' have written on the design argument, often critically, it is important to recognise the genre's social significance since, through sermons, lectures and numerous publications, it was addressed to the wider public and not just to a handful of philosophers. That many works in this genre passed through numerous editions confirms the popularity of natural theology among the book-buying public, however difficult it may be to ascertain whether and how these books were read. While it would be fascinating to know who, if anyone, was persuaded by the natural theologians' arguments, internal evidence provides us with some clues about how authors conceived their books would be read. Most importantly, these natural theologians deployed rhetorical devices to persuade the reader or listener of the existence of God and also of some of God's attributes.

At the outset it will be helpful to introduce briefly one specific example. In 1718 a Dutch work by Bernard Nieuwentijt appeared in an English translation with the appropriate title, *The Religious Philosopher: or, the Right Use of Contemplating the Works of the Creator.* This substantial book, which surveyed in detail many aspects of the Creation, soon attracted attention, rapidly passing through several editions. Of the numerous evidences for design paraded by Nieuwentijt, we shall concentrate on his discussion of the structure and functions of the eye. Like other writers who found compelling evidences for design in the eye, Nieuwentijt dwelt on its refined optical characteristics, its ability to accommodate to different distances, the wonderful design of the lens system which focused light on the retina, and much else. His chapter on the eye ended with the following meditation:

> Now whosoever is a reasonable Person, and does plainly comprehend all that we have been saying about [the intricate structure and functions of] the Eye, ought he not to be astonish'd, that there was a Lucretius among the Ancients, so there are likewise in our Age Men that pretend to be Philosophers and Enquirers after Truth, and yet will not allow that the Maker of all these things, which contribute towards the forming of a good Sight, had any wise Purposes or Designs in forming the same?[11]

There are several features of this long and rather convoluted sentence that deserve attention. First, it is in the form of a rhetorical question addressed directly to the reader. Second, the reader is accepted as a reasonable person who will readily appreciate that the eye has been crafted by God. Third, Nieuwentijt elicits the reader's astonishment that anyone could possibly deny this manifestly true proposition. Finally, he portrays Lucretius and certain phoney modern philosophers as unreasonable men since they arrogantly deny such striking evidence of purpose and design.

A few further introductory comments are in order before we return to discuss these rhetorical aspects of natural theology. The notion of genre will be central to this chapter, but it is not easily defined and literary theorists are divided over its meaning. Some theorists, drawing on Wittgenstein's *Philosophical Investigations*, liken a genre to a game with its own rules. One advantage of this way of analysing genre is that it emphasises strategy, especially the strategic use of rhetoric to win over an audience – a point to be developed below. However, there is a danger that the game analogy positions genre above and apart from its constituent texts, as if every literary work naturally conforms to some pre-ordained genre. A more helpful way of envisaging genre is to accept that 'works manifest genres rather than exist in a particular one'.[12] Thus a specific text might exhibit more than one genre. Moreover, although literary theorists are divided over the question whether genre transcends history or is historically localised we shall adopt the latter position.

The strength of the notion of genre is that it groups together texts that bear some generic similarity. In discussing natural theology as a genre we shall employ the term to refer to a collection of texts that engage recognisably similar subjects in a common manner. Most importantly, writers who adopted this genre perceived themselves building on a shared foundation and they self-consciously drew on a common (but ever-expanding) collection of canonical works. Thus later natural theologians saw themselves standing on the shoulders of John Ray, William Derham and William Paley, often quoting from them extensively but not always agreeing with the details of their arguments. We must also recognise that genres develop and that this development is partly through internal criticism and partly from external stimuli, such as the engagement with critics or by the influence of social and political events. The design argument was remarkably malleable and was moulded in response to both the Industrial Revolution and the French Revolution. Nor should we overlook the diversity within the genre: Natural theologians often disagreed among themselves. Among the many contentious problems were the following: Were physical laws – such as Newton's law of gravitation – particularly compelling proofs of design? Could God legitimately be compared to an artisan? Were (what we might now call) theoretical entities, such as atoms or the luminiferous ether, evidence of design? Did the structure of the human body offer more persuasive evidence than did celestial mechanics? While opposing views were expressed on all these issues, such differences represent disagreements within the genre. By contrast, natural theologians were united in confronting their commonly-agreed enemies, variously identified as the infidel, the deist and the atheist. Consensus over the opposition was important in helping to define and delimit the genre and also played a significant role in its historical development. Thus in the early nineteenth century many British natural theologians responded with hostility to Laplace's nebular hypothesis which they considered materialistic and a serious threat to Christianity.

One final point of contention. There was much dispute over the legitimacy and proper deployment of the design argument since many Christians, particularly High churchmen and evangelicals, considered it inferior to Revelation as a means of access to the nature of God. Unlike the Bible, the argument from design had little or nothing to say about the Trinity or about God's covenants with humanity. As we considered in the preceding chapter, it might even prove dangerous since deists could exploit it to legitimate a minimalist and decidedly non-Christian notion of the deity. Thus, for many, the design argument was not an unsullied blessing. Having recognised its disputed status among Christians we now examine its rhetorical, suasory dimensions.

Natural Theology as Rhetoric

Put simply, using evidence gleaned from the physical, biological and (sometimes) mental worlds, natural theologians deployed the argument from design to persuade their audiences to accept the existence of God and also some of His attributes, especially His power, wisdom and goodness. The argument rested on empirical evidence – such as the readily-observed complex structure of a flower, the wonderful workmanship of the eye, or the size of the earth's orbit. Such evidence was manifested by nature and had therefore to be accepted as true and incorrigible. Thus one of the argument's major attractions lay in the visibility, incorrigibility and ubiquity of nature. Irrespective of education or social background, anyone could observe and appreciate the numerous instances of design displayed by the natural world – the intricate structure of the thistle or the rose (whether of the Lancashire or Yorkshire variety). The Book of Nature was open for all to read. As one natural theologian noted, 'every person possessed of an ordinary share of understanding, and whose organs of sensation are in a sound state, is capable of acquiring all the leading truths of the most useful sciences'.[13] The design argument was firmly based on an empirical bed-rock, which is why David Hume considered it so worthy of refutation.

In the light of the preceding chapter it is important to re-emphasise that natural theologians did not deploy such evidence to 'prove' (in the strong, deductive sense) the existence and attributes of God. As eighteenth-century philosophers appreciated, deduction possesses very limited applicability outside mathematics and mechanics. By contrast, the empirical sciences – such as physical optics, chemistry, electricity and natural history – were recognised as inductive sciences. Inductive forms of inference deal with arguments where a conclusion does not follow necessarily from the premises. Here we are concerned with matters of degree – of likelihood rather than certainty. For example, suppose that Rangers have beaten Celtic at football on the last seven occasions. From this impressive record we might argue that Rangers are likely to win again next year. However, the argument is not watertight and does not lead to the untenable conclusion that Rangers must definitely win. The conclusions of inductive arguments may carry weight, but not certainty.

The design argument was generally accepted as an inductive argument. As one evangelical noted, 'the principles of Baconian philosophy' can be applied extensively in natural theology since many of God's attributes are 'demonstrable *a posteriori*'.[14] The conclusion of the design argument was deemed a 'moral' truth – one that admits of degrees. As a contemporary writer on rhetoric claimed, 'In moral reasoning we ascend from possibility, by an insensible gradation, to probability, and thence, in the same manner, to the summit of moral certainty.'[15] One factor affecting the strength of an argument was the amount of evidential support; the more evidence offered and (perhaps) the greater its diversity, the stronger the inference. By piling on examples of design natural theologians considered that they had reached the 'summit of moral certainty'.

Concern with inductive inferences and with the persuasiveness of arguments suggests a close similarity between natural theology and the proceedings in a courtroom. In their numerous sermons, lectures and texts natural theologians treated their audience like a jury. Just as a prosecuting advocate would use every available argument to convince the jury of the guilt of the defendant, so the theologian would deploy any argument and hone any rhetorical device that would help persuade the audience that examination of the empirical evidence leads inexorably to the Designer. Persuasion was therefore the name of the game. The major weapons in the theologians' armoury were a quiver of rhetorical devices. Most importantly, they appealed directly to the testimony of nature. Nature sat in the witness box and was encouraged to spin her own forceful narrative, speaking of creation and intelligent design. In the dock stood the atheist who cut a sorry figure since he had perversely refused to be swayed by this most persuasive natural evidence. While the analogy can doubtless be extended, the relation between the advocate and jury can be seen as the key feature of the courtroom; the advocate's role being to persuade the jury by the appropriate use of rhetoric.

Rhetoric is concerned with appeals to the imagination and the emotions as well as to the faculty of reason. Thus in his *Discourse on Natural Theology* (1835), Henry Brougham identified the pleasures and advantages to be gained from studying natural theology, which he considered to be much greater than those arising solely from the pursuit of science. He proceeded to characterise natural theology as 'an exercise at once intellectual and moral, in which the highest faculties of the understanding and the warmest feelings of the heart alike partake, and which ... without ceasing to be a [natural] philosopher the student feels as a man'.[16] This quotation conveys the wide range of mental faculties that Brougham considered should be empoyed by the natural theologian. Writers in this genre also frequently appealed to the non-rational functions of the mind. For example, in his *Bridgewater Treatise* published two years earlier William Whewell rejected the nebular hypothesis because it provided no 'resting place or satisfaction for the mind'.[17] In the light of such concerns about the affective connotations of natural theology, it would be inappropriate to reduce this complex genre to the domain of logic and ignore its intended influence on the other mental faculties, especially the imagination.

If the natural theologian's immediate aim was to persuade his listeners or readers, his objective was to induce waverers to alter their ways by acknowledging God in their lives and by thus encompassing a fuller Christian perspective. In the last chapter we cited the Cambridge philosopher and physicist William Whewell who considered that natural theology should nudge men 'towards richer perceptions of their life; not rationally propelled'. Likewise, in one of his sermons Whewell appealed to the feelings that natural theology should evoke: 'We ought to feel that all the Laws of the Universe are so woven together that we cannot separate or disentangle them, and [we] are necessarily by any thread drawn to the highest point: the Judge and Purifier of all.'[18] Like Whewell, many other writers emphasised the usefulness of natural theology since it not only evinced the power, wisdom and goodness of God, but also fulfilled moral, as well as intellectual, purposes. For John Ray natural theology served to 'stir up and increase in us the Affections and Habits of Admiration, Humility, and Gratitude'. In similar vein Paley argued that natural theology not only paves the way for receiving the truths of Revelation but carries the reader far beyond the mere intellectual acceptance of its propositions. He wrote: 'It is one thing to assent to a proposition of this sort; another, and a very different thing, to have properly imbibed its influence.' By imbibing the full significance of the conclusions of natural theology the soul comes to appreciate God's presence in everything and is thereby encouraged to lead a more fulfilling religious life.[19]

The status of rhetoric in the eighteenth and early nineteenth centuries requires a little more by way of introduction. Although based on the writers of antiquity, especially Cicero, Aristotle and Quintilian, the so-called 'New Rhetoric' moved the subject beyond its classical roots. Such books as George Campbell's *The Philosophy of Rhetoric* (1776), Hugh Blair's *Lectures on Rhetoric and Belles Lettres* (1783) and Richard Whately's *Elements of Rhetoric* (1828) sought to base the theory and practice of rhetoric on the philosophical assumptions of British empiricism, broadly defined.[20] For example, Campbell, who was Professor of Divinity at Marischal College, Aberdeen, drew on Thomas Reid's philosophy of common sense. In the universities – especially the Scottish universities – rhetoric was widely taught. Hence university-educated clergymen would have received a grounding in the subject. The importance of presenting religious arguments in the most persuasive manner was urged by Campbell, among others, who noted that religion 'gives scope for the exertion of all the highest powers of rhetoric'.[21] According to Campbell, the verbal or written communication should not only appeal to the reasoning faculty; it should also 'please the imagination, ... move the passions, or ... influence the will', which were, he claimed, 'the handmaidens of reason'.[22] Although rhetoric played no role in deductive arguments, Campbell considered that in all other forms of discourse rhetoric was required in order to produce conviction in an audience. Since the preacher's job was to delight, to move and to teach his congregation, he would have little impact on his listeners if he appealed only to their intellects. Instead, insisted Campbell, a preacher would gain their attention by exciting their imagination through the use of analogies and metaphors. Likewise, the congregation's passions must be appropriately aroused, particularly if a preacher is seeking to change their lives; the 'primary intention of preaching' being 'the reformation of mankind'.[23]

Stimulating the Imagination

As Campbell noted in his *Philosophy of Rhetoric*, the role of the imagination was crucial in constructing any suasory discourse. He proceeded to specify 'vivacity, beauty, sublimity, and novelty' as the four main qualities that 'gratify the fancy'.[24] We shall illustrate these in turn, before examining three familiar tropes – analogy, metaphor and antithesis.

1)   *VIVACITY*: In part the 'vivacity' of natural theological narratives arises from their direct appeal to the reader who is, as it were, taken on a Cook's tour of the physical universe, introduced to its various parts, exhorted to appreciate the design manifest throughout and then led to the conclusion that a beneficent designer is responsible. To increase the argument's vigour, it was often addressed *ad hominem*. For example, in Paley's celebrated work the interlocutor – 'I' – is present in many sections of the text and Paley thus invites the direct participation of the reader. His often-cited opening sentence begins: 'In crossing a heath, suppose I pitched my foot against a *stone*, and were asked how the stone came to be there; I might possibly answer . . .'. The encounter with a stone, then a watch, trades on the shared experience of stones and watches and also encourages the reader to join Paley on his literary journey. But the reader, as much as the interlocutor, is led to answer the questions posed by Paley: How did the stone come to be there? 'Can anything be more decisive [evidence] of contrivance' than the human eye? Encouraged by Paley the reader is directed to the only feasible answer.[25] Again, to take an earlier example, when Derham dilated on the necessity and uses of the atmosphere he exclaimed, 'Who can but own this to be the Contrivance, the Work of the great Creator?'[26] The serious reader cannot but concur.

Many other strategies were employed to enliven natural theological discourse, such as rhetorical questions, exclamations and the use of italics and capital letters.[27] Some natural theology texts were profusely illustrated, none more so than William Buckland's

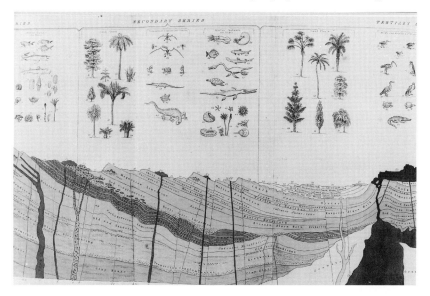

Figure 19: A small part of William Buckland's impressive geological section that forms plate 1 of his *Geology and Mineralogy Considered with Reference to Natural Theology* (1836).

Bridgewater Treatise with its 69 plates, the first of which was a massive double fold-out in several colours, measuring 120cm in length, which showed a section through the earth in order to display the different geological strata and their fossils. Although critical assessments of this *Treatise* varied, it was widely hailed as a major contribution to geology, the reviewer in *The Times* declaring it 'the most valuable and eloquent discourse that has appeared upon the science of geology since the time of the learned Burnett'.[28]

2)   *BEAUTY*: As will be emphasised in the next chapter, it is important to recognise the aesthetic grounding of the design argument. Many natural theologians directed their readers to appreciate the beauty observable in all parts of God's creation. Whatever its intrinsic attraction, the mere apprehension of beauty provided but a weak argument against the atheist, whose sense of beauty was generally thought to be stunted. The appeal to beauty was therefore connected with other, less superficial qualities revealed by the contemplation of nature. Derham beheld the 'Harmony of this lower World', and 'an Œconomy worthy of the Creator'. Turning to the generation and conservation of species 'we find every Thing in compleat Order; the Balance of *Genera*, Species and Individuals

always proportionate and even; the Balance of the Sexes the same'.[29] Likewise Buckland perceived the 'exquisite symmetry, beauty, and minute delicacy of structure' of ammonites, while William Kirby, the author of another *Bridgewater Treatise*, argued that the 'great object of the Creator is the maintenance of the whole system of creation in order and beauty'.[30] As these examples show, the notion of beauty was intimately connected with the ideas of design, order, coherence, harmony, unity and symmetry – that were thought to please the imagination and soothe the mind. In such examples the aesthetics of natural theology was directed more to the mind's eye than to the eye itself.

Natural theologians invariably accepted that nature was a divinely-ordained economy manifesting unity and coherence. The various component parts fit together to form an harmonious whole, and means are appropriate to ends. Buckland dilated on the compound eye of the trilobite, which contains nearly four hundred microscopic lenses, all suitably adjusted. 'It appears impossible to resist the conclusions as to Unity of Design in a common Author, which are thus attested by such cumulative evidences of Creative Intelligence and Power ... transcend[ing] the most perfect productions of human art'.[31] The harmony, order and coherence identified by natural theologians assured readers that they are not alone but that a mindful protector has established order in the universe. Even the most threatening forces in nature could be tamed and rendered safe. Thunder and lightning, Whewell affirmed, are 'parts of a great scheme, of which every discovered purpose is marked with benefi- cence as well as wisdom'.[32] Likewise Derham dilated on the moral implications to be drawn from the existence of 'fierce, poisonous, and noxious Creatures'. These, he insisted, were created for a purpose – they 'serve as Rods and Scourges to chastise us' and can also provide valuable food and medicines.[33] For William Prout, the existence of poisonous metals did not furnish an argument against God's design but rather manifested His power.[34] Properly deployed within the language of natural theology all of nature – even its least congenial elements – could be interpreted as indispensable parts of the providential plan. The scientist was therefore in a privileged position, being better able than the layperson to appreciate God's providence.

Natural theologians generally painted nature in optimistic colours. Even if humankind was sometimes unable to perceive God's provi- dence and benevolence, they assured their readers that all aspects of the physical world are ordered and designed by God. These opti- mistic natural theologians found that the amount of pleasure far outweighed the amount of pain, and argued that even the relatively little pain that exists was introduced by God for specific – and ultimately beneficial – purposes. Thus Buckland argued that when rightly understood, apparent cases of evil – such as carnivores eating the weaker members of other species – were examples of universal good. He also conceived that under divine providence joy and happiness were maximised; thus the oceans were filled with teeming fish enjoying themselves.[35] Paley likewise argued that in the vast majority of instances design is beneficial and he even portrayed society as a smooth-running system and not in need of change. Not surprisingly, evangelicals complained that he was far too complacent about human nature while radicals saw his natural theology as providing uncritical legitimation of the *status quo*.[36]

3)   *SUBLIMITY*: Many eighteenth and early-nineteenth-century writers on 'psychology' and aesthetics drew a sharp distinction between beauty and the sublime. Indeed, Edmund Burke, among others, not only contrasted the feelings of the sublime and the beautiful but also attributed them to different causes. For Burke the perception of beauty occurs when the mind is soothed, whereas the sublime is founded on terror and sets the mind in a modified state of tension.[37] Natural theologians made extensive use of the sublime by evoking those aspects of the natural world which most inspire wonder, awe and reverence.

Astronomy was an unrivalled source for imagery of the sublime. Viewing the heavens Alexander Crombie declared: 'How magnificent, how sublime a spectacle ... the imagination is confounded'. Likewise, in his popular book on *Celestial Scenery* Thomas Dick surveyed the solar system and asserted that contemplation of the heavens 'impress[es] on our minds ... an overpowering sense of the *grandeur* and *Omnipotence* of the Deity'.[38] As these examples indicate, the sublime in nature was readily serviceable to natural-theological narratives.

4)   *NOVELTY*: In his *Natural Theology* (1829) Crombie complained that familiarity with the natural objects around us tends to deaden their impact on the mind. Moreover, this mental lethargy leaves us prey to atheism. We must therefore repeatedly be made to recognise that the natural world overflows with wonders. Only by appreciating these wonders do we become convinced that the Creation manifests God's wisdom.[39] Crombie's emphasis on the importance of novelty in stimulating the imagination was echoed in the writings of other natural theologians who portrayed the whole world as overflowing

with exciting novelties. The reader was therefore deluged with vast amounts of titillating information.

One specific strategy was to draw attention to extraordinary facts about the physical world, such as the size of the solar system or the intricate structure of the smallest of insects. That ice is less dense than water enables aquatic creatures to survive in winter beneath a protective barrier of ice. The protective scales of the armadillo, the aggressive fangs of the viper and the bulk of the earth (being 260,000,000,000 cubic miles) are among the many novel facts aimed at enlivening the imagination.[40] But perhaps no instances of novelty can match the tribes of exotic but extinct creatures described in Buckland's *Bridgewater Treatise.* Even among these marvels one stood head and shoulders above the rest, the ungainly form of the megatherium which Buckland portrayed as 'nearly allied to the Sloth, and, like the Sloth, presenting an apparent monstrosity of external form, accompanied by many strange peculiarities of internal structure'. Described in detail over 25 pages and depicted on three pages of plates, this monstrous 'Leviathan of the Pampas' captured the public imagination.[41]

A second strategy was to argue that the novel fact possessed profound significance, for had the world been only slightly different from its present state, then destruction would have occurred. This extended sense of novelty is apparent in many discussions of the distance of the earth from the sun. Natural theologians argued that if the distance were less than its present value, then we would all fry, but had it been greater, then the world would have been too cold and therefore unsuitable for all forms of life. From this stand-point the radius of the earth's orbit takes on a new significance that illuminates the theme of design, for although an arbitrary magnitude, the observed size of the orbit was chosen by the Designer in preference to other possible values.[42] Although God is a free agent, able to cast the earth into any orbit, He chose just the right one.[43] Some works in this genre made excessive, even bizarre, use of this strategy. Thus in his *Religious Philosopher* Nieuwentijt dilated on the senses and why they would have been inadequate had they been made either more or less sensitive; why every plant and animal would have died without water; why the earth is not 'render'd Loathsome by Filth and Nastiness'; and the 'Inconveniences that would befal us, if there were no such thing as Fire in the World' – to mention but a few possible scenarios.[44] The scope for conjuring up conceptually possible but emotionally repulsive worlds was immense, but they served to show the reader how each facet of the creation had been selected for a recondite purpose.

Thirdly, a refined level of novelty was achieved by showing that, when considered together, the facts and laws of nature – as exciting as they may be by themselves – displayed a coherence and even more profound meaning. The fang of the viper was no sport of nature but a perfectly designed piece of machinery for wounding its enemy.[45] William Derham likewise considered the atmosphere suited 'to many Uses of our Globe, and its great Convenience to the whole: and, in a Word, that it answereth all the Ends and Purposes that there can be for such an Appendage'.[46] Appeals to the adaptation of means to

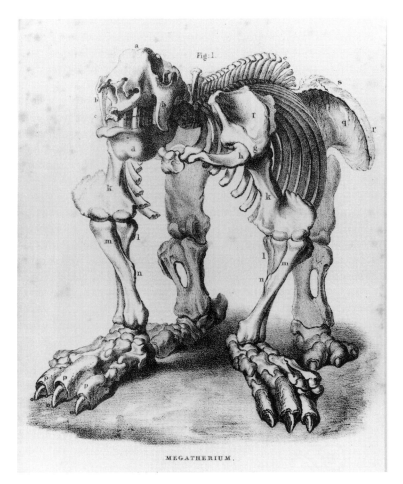

Figure 20: The 'Leviathan of the Pampas'. William Buckland considered that the Megatherium impressively illustrated adaptation and therefore provided strong evidence of God's design. From plate 5 of Buckland's *Geology and Mineralogy Considered with Reference to Natural Theology* (1836).

ends, the conformity between structure and function, and the coherence of the parts, all contributed to the perception of novel relationships within the universe. Even the hulking megatherium was shown by Buckland not to be the misfit it might appear at first sight. Instead, when all the bones were considered in relation to one another in the light of Cuvier's morphological theories, the megatherium emerged as a structurally coherent creature.[47] The ultimate meaning of such perceived interrelationships was that all parts of the universe – even the long-extinct megatherium – were included in the Designer's blueprint.

5)   *ANALOGY*: According to Campbell, who drew selectively on Butler's *The Analogy of Religion* (1736), analogical evidence is 'at best but a feeble support, and is hardly ever honoured with the name of proof. Nevertheless, when the analogies are numerous, ... it doth not want its efficiency'.[48] This scepticism about the power of a single analogy and the implicit need to multiply instances may help explain why natural theological texts abound with examples of design. In works like Ray's, Derham's and Paley's the analogies are amassed, sometimes several to a page, and the argument appears to gain inductive strength from the accumulation of instances especially when chosen from several different domains.

The fundamental form of analogy employed four terms arranged in two pairs. One pair included a man-made artefact – such as a telescope – and its maker; the other a specific part of the natural world – for example, the eye – and its Maker. Just as the telescope was constructed by the optician, so the eye was forged by the Creator; in both cases design implied a designer and craftsman. The analogy may be expressed in the following form:

$$\frac{\text{artefact}}{\text{artisan}} :: \frac{\text{natural object}}{\text{God.}}$$

Sometimes a non-specific artefact was chosen. For example, Whewell portrayed the luminiferous ether simply as a complex machine, 'as skilfully and admirably constructed' as the atmosphere – which he considered to be another machine.[49] More specific artefacts were usually cited, often reflecting widely-available modern technologies. Clocks and watches were frequently evoked long before Paley fantasised about finding one on a heath. Heat and steam engines also sometimes provided analogues, and even in the early 1710s Derham had discussed the role of the atmosphere, and particularly the rain cycle, by appealing to its analogy with a 'Pneumatick Engine'.[50]

While natural theologians often described the human body as a

machine – 'that wonderful machine' according to Kirby[51] – mechanism rarely played so central a role as in Paley's *Natural Theology*.
Imbued with an optimistic utilitarian and progressivist ethic Paley
appealed to mechanistic analogies and identities throughout his
book. Not surprisingly, he claimed that muscular motion is mechanical and it 'is as intelligible as the adjustment of the wires and strings
by which a puppet is moved ... and is as accessible as the mechanism
of the automaton in the Strand'.[52] When discussing the circulation
of the blood the Archdeacon drew an analogy with another kind of
mechanical system – the water supply to a city, which requires a
central pump. He insisted that the argument from design could be
made all the more rhetorically appealing to his readers – and all the
more comprehensible – by identifying much of the body with
familiar forms of machinery. Paley's enthusiasm for locating mechanical contrivances in nature sometimes resulted in strange
locutions, as when he declared that 'every [bird's] *feather* is a mechanical wonder'![53] Ironically, the claim that the world is or is
analogous to a machine evoked the very term – mechanism – that
had often been associated with the atheists' conception of a self-
sustaining godless universe. To distance himself from such
mechanical reductionism Paley was at pains to insist that a piece of
mechanism, such as a watch, no matter how well contrived, is not
self-acting but requires an external source of power. Although we
can identify a mechanical structure in nature, 'living, active, moving,
productive nature, proves also the exertion of a[n external]
power'.[54] Therefore Paley's God not only designed the world-
machine but was also its mover.

Although mechanistic analogies were dominant, authors often
deployed analogies derived from other domains. Even Paley recognised that the animal body was not completely reducible to a
machine and on several occasions turned to chemistry to account for
natural phenomena that were not susceptible to mechanical analysis.
He noted that mechanical systems often terminate in chemical ones
and characterised the stomach as 'the great laboratory', likening
digestion to the chemical process of fermentation operating in the
manufacture of cider.[55] Although such processes were not well
understood he conceded that they were law-like and must therefore
be accepted as signs of design. In one of the very few natural theological works that engaged chemistry, Prout contrasted the limited
knowledge and abilities of the most proficient chemist with 'the
great Chemist of nature'. God therefore emerges as the 'great
Chemist' possessing super-human skill.[56] Other authors likened God
to a sculptor fashioning a statue or an architect designing a house.

When contemplating the way each animal species depended on the appropriate kind of food, Derham described God as a 'most prudent Steward and Householder', thus emphasising the economy of the natural world.[57] Whewell, however, made use of legal terminology, since in stressing that nature is law-governed he was claiming that the laws of nature are 'remarkably adapted to the office which is assigned them; and thus offer evidence of selection, design and goodness'. God was therefore not only the Creator but also the 'Legislator'.[58] Close analysis of these various analogies indicate subtly different conceptions of God and of His relation to the world. Yet, for all its literary ornament, natural theology in the eighteenth and early nineteenth centuries lacked the clear, incisive analysis to be found in the most competent scholastics, such as Aquinas, and tended towards anthropomorphic images of the deity.

If we want to find an accomplished nineteenth-century theologian we need look no further than Thomas Chalmers, the Scottish Evangelical. Although critical of natural theology earlier in his career, he had made some accommodation to it by the early 1830s. Of particular interest is his response to those writers who portrayed God as the lawmaker. However effective this analogy, Chalmers was concerned that it could readily be subverted by atheists who claimed that laws were natural and not of divine origin. He therefore argued that in constructing a watch an artisan does not create elasticity in its mainspring but rather fashions the spring and the other components, so as to form an integral, working whole. The artisan is not a lawmaker but one who carefully and thoughtfully shapes and positions the material objects according to a plan. By analogy 'we behold the finger of God', not in the properties of matter but in its dispositions; not in the law of gravity but in the location of the planets round the sun. Indeed, had both matter and laws been created but the matter had been incorrectly distributed throughout the universe, then chaos would have resulted, not order.[59] The point that emerges from Chalmers' intervention is that analogy can be subject to contradictory interpretations. A recurrent theme within the genre of natural theology was how to elaborate such analogies as effective rhetorical devices while preventing them from being hijacked by the deist or atheist.

6)   *METAPHOR*: Tropes, such as metaphor, metonymy and synecdoche, feature prominently in both classical and modern studies of rhetoric such as those by Campbell and Whately who emphasised that, appropriately deployed, metaphors and other tropes add greatly to the energy and effectiveness of an argument.[60] Natural

theological texts abound with such tropes. For example, when Derham referred to the 'Almighty hand' and Paley to the 'hands of the Creator', they were using a conventional synecdoche in which a part – a 'hand' or 'hands' – is taken to stand for God and his actions.[61] However, less familiar examples were also employed and one of these bears closer examination since it contains crucial insights into the way the argument from design was articulated. In his chapter on the length of the year Whewell stated that 'The vegetable clock-work is so set as to go for a year.'[62] The conjunction between 'vegetable' and 'clock-work' immediately produces a tension since vegetables are normally classed as organic and are thus usually contrasted with mechanical devices. However, the effectiveness of the metaphor is due to the more conventional appeal to the regularity of the planetary motions. The earth takes a year to orbit the sun and the seasons are 'set … to go for a year'. What the metaphor achieves is the introduction of celestial clockwork into the vegetable realm. The life of plants takes on the characteristics of orderliness and regularity, cohering with the time-period governing the earth's annual movement. But the image also binds together these two often-contrasted domains of the physical universe and shows them to be interlocking, synchronous parts of the Divine plan.

7)   *ANTITHESIS*: According to writers on rhetoric the judicious use of antithesis is 'calculated to add greatly to [the] Energy [of a narrative]. Every thing is rendered more striking by contrast; and almost every kind of subject-matter affords *materials* for contrasting expressions. Truth is [to be] *opposed* to error.'[63] Natural theologians frequently generated a stark opposition between the existing situation and other possible, but thoroughly uncongenial, worlds. Thus Whewell claimed that if the earth had been as large as Jupiter, gravity would be eleven times greater than its current value and we would be flattened against the ground. Thus 'for man to lift himself upright, or to crawl from place to place, would be a labour slower and more painful than the motions of a sloth'. Surely no intelligent deity would have made that mistake! Likewise, when discussing the role of the luminiferous ether Whewell conjured up two contrasting possibilities – either a world without ether, in which case 'all must be inert or dead', or a living world vitalised by the ether.[64]

As these examples from Whewell's treatise indicate, one rhetorical device available to natural theologians was to confront their readers with two opposing scenarios. However, the most frequently deployed and most effective contrast was between a world that manifests order and one that is chaotic. A seminal text indicating how this opposition had been perceived in the seventeenth century is *Paradise Lost*. In the opening lines of the first book Milton portrayed Genesis as teaching 'how the heav'ns and earth/ Rose out of Chaos' and he then proceeded to characterise Chaos as the dark hell where Satan resides. In book 2 Satan visits the gates of hell where he encounters Chaos, 'next him high arbiter/ Chance governs all'. In this 'wild abyss' nature is in a state of confusion.[65] Like Milton, later natural theologians considered Satan's allies to be the 3 'Cs' – Chaos, Chance and Confusion – the terms used to characterise the picture of the universe conjured up by atheistical materialists. If Milton's evocation of hell touched the deepest chords of Christian consciousness, natural theologians exploited this prevalent mythology to discredit their opponents by aligning the atheist (and often the infidel) with Satan. At the very heart of Western religious mythology lies the choice between evil and good, between a world of chaos and a God-created one. For natural theologians the argument from design posed this existential choice in its starkest form, for to refuse to acknowledge design was to court Satan in the guise of the atheist.

The possibility that atomism might be hijacked by the atheist was repeatedly identified as a major threat to a Christianised natural philosophy. Most famously, Newton conjured up the image of the atheistical materialist and sought to confute him in the 'Queries' to the *Opticks* and the 'General Scholium' added to the second (1713) edition of the *Principia*. The argument was also repeated by Roger Cotes in the preface added to that edition. In the final 'Query' of the *Opticks* Newton poured scorn on the idea that the world could 'arise out of a Chaos by the mere Laws of Nature' – 'blind Fate' could not account for the meticulously calculated orbits of the planets and comets.[66] Similar strategies were adopted by many other writers in the natural theological tradition. For example, Richard Bentley devoted a significant part of his Boyle Lectures, entitled *The Confutation of Atheism from the Origin and Frame of the World* (1693), to showing that the 'Atheistical Hypothesis of the World's production' was untenable. Not only did he argue against the eternity of matter, but he also showed that a chaos of atoms was inadequate to produce the present state of the physical world: or, as he stated the leading question; 'whether a World like the Present could possibly without a Divine influence be formed in it or no?' Facing the reader with this stark choice Bentley marshalled numerous incisive arguments against his adversaries ('supine unthinking Atheists'), thus demonstrating that the world has been providentially created by God.[67]

In these examples natural theologians conjured up visions of horrendous, dysfunctional worlds that seem to have much in common with the worst 'B' movies. Perhaps like such films, these narratives were intended to scare and produce revulsion, but their main rhetorical function was to create a stark comparison between such nightmare universes and the one we inhabit – which, by implication, appears safe, ordered and attractive. If chance is accepted, then chaos reigns and we are lost; whereas if the theistic option is true, then readers open their hearts to the Christian message and ultimately to salvation. A long, hard look at the physical world should convince the waverer that the world is designed and that the atheistical scenario cannot be a viable possibility. Faced with these two possibilities, any impartial judge is bound to accept the theistic alternative and totally reject the atheistical one. Only the perverse would opt for the latter, those devoid of reason.

United in Opposition

Natural theologians repeatedly identified atheists and their fellow travellers as the main opponents of Christianity. As in our earlier quotation from Nieuwentijt, Lucretius and his modern disciples were often cast as the enemy. A surprising amount of energy was expended on Epicurus, Lucretius and other long-dead writers whose frequently-reprinted books continued to disseminate their theories – Creech's English translation of Lucretius's *De Rerum Natura* passed through six editions between 1682 and 1722. The list of perceived enemies of Christianity was subsequently extended to include Spinoza, David Hume, Diderot, d'Holbach, Lamarck and Laplace, among others. Thus of the many adversaries cited by Thomas Chalmers, David Hume and Jean-Baptiste de Mirabaud – the nom de plume adopted by Paul Henri d'Holbach – feature prominently in his *Bridgewater Treatise*.[68] It is also clear that, during the latter decades of the eighteenth century but especially after the Revolution, British theologians generally identified materialism and atheism with France. Denis Diderot's later writings, particularly his *Rêve de d'Alembert*, and d'Holbach's *Système de la Nature* (1770) were viewed as seditious and atheistical works that had contributed to the revolutionary spirit in France and had begun to infiltrate Britain. As Chalmers noted, the circulation of d'Holbach's book 'has been much extended of late by the infidel press of our own country – where it is, we understand, working mischief among the half-enlightened classes of British society'.[69] It is difficult to overestimate the impact of the French Revolution on all aspects of British life, natural theology included, and it helps explain the renewed vigour of the genre in the ensuing decades. Atheism was no longer just a philosophical enemy but was demonstrated as an insidious plot to overthrow the established order by the labouring classes. The marked increase in radical, anti-clerical agitation in the decades following the French Revolution fuelled the impression that atheism was rampant in Britain and posed a serious threat to church and state. This provides the context for the assertion in 1794 by John Adams, the Royal Mathematical Instrument Maker, that the design argument was Britain's strongest defence preventing the French cancer from crossing the Channel.[70]

The more scientific *Bridgewater* authors were, however, more selective in their condemnation of the French, since by the 1830s no branch of science could be pursued without acknowledging substantial contributions by Frenchmen. For example, in his *Treatise* on the form and structure of animals William Kirby borrowed extensively from Lamarck's works and adopted much of his classificatory system. However, in his extensive introductory essay this High Church Tory vehemently chastised both Lamarck and Laplace for disregarding 'the word of God, and for seeking too exclusively their own glory'. He was particularly critical of Lamarck's view that material particles form the basis of living creatures. In his opinion the Frenchman had revived Epicureanism which portrayed nature as a blind, self-regulating and inhospitable principle of order that acts by chance, not design. Moreover, Kirby claimed that Lamarck had displaced God and instead had insinuated 'nature' onto His throne.[71] Kirby therefore devoted his two volumes to reinstating God as the Creator and ruler of the world.

Although there is much evidence of deism during the eighteenth and early nineteenth centuries and also some examples of more extreme forms of atheism in Britain, 'the atheist' presents the historian with a problem. The repeated references to Epicurus, Democritus and Lucretius, the paradigmatic materialists, suggest that we are dealing more with enemies on paper than with evil men likely to assault the casual visitor in the dark alleys of Glasgow or Leeds. Moreover, despite the claims by natural theologians that they were trying to convert the atheist, card-carrying atheists do not seem to be their main target. While not denying that atheists – especially political agitators – might have been thought to lurk at every street corner, their identity is not our principal concern here. Instead, from the linguistic perspective developed in this chapter we would suggest that *the atheist* fulfilled specific rhetorical functions within natural theological discourse.

The figure of the atheist (and likewise the infidel) is a familiar one in Christian mythology since he shares many of Satan's characteristics. He radiates evil and threatens to seduce the unwary away from the path of righteousness. He is the Antichrist who seeks to subvert the social order, which he was seen to have achieved in revolutionary France. He is the power lurking in the human mind that wilfully refuses to acknowledge manifest evidence of divine design. Among its various functions natural theology could provide valuable support to the clergy in pursuing their calling which required them to battle for the souls of men and women. In this struggle for souls the aim of natural theology was not only to win over the atheist (real or imagined) but, perhaps more importantly, to strengthen the resolve and commitment of those already receptive to the Christian message and particularly the waverer. For example, in his preface to Nieuwentijt's book John Theophilus Desaguliers warned that 'the Weak and Ignorant' were particularly at risk.[72] A century later Alexander Crombie devoted eighty pages of his two-volume *Natural Theology* to examining the causes of atheism. Yet his analysis was addressed primarily to the wavering Christian, since he warns his readers not to be seduced by the misuse of words, the writings of the sceptics, their own arrogance or deference to the judgement of others. Indeed, on this last issue he cautioned against the authority of well-known atheists – Epicurus, Democritus, Spinoza, Diderot and Laplace – and asserted that when deciding the question whether the eye is constructed for seeing, a peasant is as competent a judge as a trained scientist.[73]

As constructed in these narratives the atheist cuts a pathetic figure since, when confronted by the argument from design, he denies design and thereby flies in the face of both evidence and reason. Chris Kenny has claimed that for defenders of Christianity atheism 'could not by its very nature be philosophical and any attempt to clothe infidelity by means of philosophical coverings was a mere exercise in the art of concealment'.[74] Thus although often proclaiming to be a champion of rational argument, the atheist's deployment of reason had to be shown by theologians to be a sham. The atheist is thus revealed naked as a monster. Derham dismissed him as 'a Monster among rational Beings ... a Rebel against human Nature and Reason' since he 'is under the Power of the Devil, under the Government of Prejudice, Lust, and Passion, not right Reason'. Samuel Clarke likewise chastised atheists as ignorant, stupid, debauched, corrupt and hardly superior to animals.[75] Employing the language of deviance, madness and monstrosity natural theologians portrayed atheists as beyond the pale of rational civilised society

since they perversely refused to comprehend that nature unflinch-
ingly testifies to its Creator.

What is particularly fascinating about the history of natural
theology is its symbiotic relationship with its proclaimed antagonists.
Although natural theologians tried desperately to keep their opponents at arms length the two sides shared much – perhaps too much
– in common. Natural theology was therefore vulnerable to subversion by deists who accepted that the world appeared to be ordered
but rejected the inference to a biblical God still intimately
concerned with creation. Hence natural theologians were forced to
defend the genre by repeatedly policing its boundaries so as to
exclude the taint of deism. For example, Whewell moved onto the
defensive in his chapter on Laplace's nebular hypothesis, which
offered a naturalistic account of the development of the solar system.
He proceeded to dismiss all such theories which purported to offer
the 'ultimate cause[s]' of phenomena and which thereby inhibited
the search for divine meaning in the universe. If such causes 'claim
a place in our Natural Theology, as well as our Natural Philosophy;
we conceive that their pretensions will not bear a moment's examination'.[76] For Whewell, then, the nebular hypothesis and other purely
naturalistic theories were monstrosities that had to be barred,
refuted and distinguished clearly from the legitimate domain of
natural theology.

Even language was a shared resource. As Michael Buckley has
noted, atheism was 'necessarily dependent upon theism for its vocabulary, its meanings, and its embodiments'.[77] However, although
Christians, deists and atheists drew on a common vocabulary, that
vocabulary was constantly being refined and contested. This point is
well illustrated by d'Holbach's *Système de la Nature*, which Henry
Brougham claimed had made a far greater impact on the British
public than any other atheistical work.[78] D'Holbach adopted a hard-
headed style in trying to undermine the arguments of theologians,
particularly natural theologians. Thus he ruled out of court any
appeal to the perceived wonders of nature which he dismissed as
merely the result of a 'heated imagination'. For him this misplaced
feeling of wonder did not form part of the natural world but was an
indicator of the prevalent nonsense encouraged by theologians.
There are, he claimed, neither 'wonders nor miracles in nature'.
Instead he argued that if we discern nature clearly then such feelings of wonder are dissipated and we come to recognise that all
physical phenomena are produced by the regular course of nature
governed by the laws of matter.[79] By dismissing the feeling of
wonder as an inadequate and inappropriate response, d'Holbach

sought to undercut one of the natural theologians' main rhetorical strategies.

He deployed a similar strategy to neutralise the traditional opposition between order and chaos (or confusion) which natural theologians had used to create a sharp antithesis between their own providentialist view of nature and the atheists' chaos of atoms. D'Holbach, however, redefined these terms so as to dissolve this contrast. He argued that both 'order' and 'confusion' are not to be found *in* nature but are terms imposed by humans: when we can identify causes – such as the regular motion of the planets – then we perceive order, but when we fail to do so – as in cases of drought, plague, earthquake and (in earlier times) comets – then we proclaim confusion and pray to God for deliverance. Yet, for d'Holbach, plagues, droughts and earthquakes were as natural as the planetary motions, although we might not, at present, know the laws by which they are governed. Nature was redefined to include not only the finely-sculpted chrysanthemum but also the disastrous Lisbon earthquake of 1755. Sounding all too much like his opponents, d'Holbach dismissed the term 'chance' as 'a word devoid of all sense' whose function is 'to cover ... [man's] ignorance of those natural causes which produce visible effects'. For d'Holbach the customary but improper meaning of the word 'chance' stands in opposition to intelligence. Moreover, theologians had illegitimately transferred the notion of intelligence from its human reference to an hypothetical intelligent being who, they claimed, has ordered the universe. As with the previous example, d'Holbach declared this dichotomy false and argued that both chance and intelligence are not in the natural world but are merely products of an erroneous theistic perspective. When correct meanings are appreciated, 'nothing is given to *chance*, nothing to a blind cause; but every thing he [mankind] beholds is attributed to real, to known [physical] causes, or to such as are easy of comprehension'.[80] All ultimately resolves into nature and the laws of matter, not into God and His laws.

D'Holbach's book was just one of an increasing number of attempts from the mid eighteenth century onwards to attack natural theology by weapons from its own armoury. The linguistic approach suggests that we should not simply concentrate on the arguments used by the warring parties or on their social and political contexts. Rather the texts and their rhetorical structure should be savoured. The central claim of this chapter has been that we can recover from such texts the dynamics of the design argument (and that of its opponents). To do so we need to appreciate that in its heyday theologians utilised all the rhetorical strategies at their disposal to hone the design argument for consumption by the wider public. In particular they conceived it as a genre that could rescue waverers and bring them back into the Christian fold. Thus we misinterpret the significance of the design argument if we simply dismiss it as either wrong or trivial and easily undermined by the philosophically sophisticated.

Epilogue

Finally, we wish to broach a related issue of contemporary relevance. Despite the recent renaissance of interest in natural theology, the decline of the design argument in the later decades of the nineteenth century has left a major lacuna that has not been adequately filled. So much of modern science is directed to the solution of either theoretical problems or practical ones arising from the requirements of business, industry and the military. Hence science is now usually justified to the public either in terms of expanding the frontiers of human knowledge or as the goose that lays the golden egg. The first may be the source of great satisfaction to the scientist, while the latter only impinges rather indirectly, perhaps via technology, on the woman on the Hillhead omnibus. Neither of these rationales appears particularly persuasive at a time when many sections of the public manifest little interest in science and science courses in many universities are significantly undersubscribed. The scientific community has therefore sought to remedy the situation by encouraging scientists to communicate with those outside their own milieu – for example in Britain through the many ventures organised by the Committee for the Public Understanding of Science, such as the aptly-named Faraday Award.

By contrast, in nineteenth-century Britain the public, or at least large sections of the reading public, evinced considerable interest in science. Their interest was stimulated by public lectures and by a wide variety of texts including textbooks, articles in the periodical press and works on natural theology. In many of these science was not simply presented as a series of facts about the universe but the wider significance of scientific knowledge was exploited. One recurrent theme was the alliance between science and natural theology, as in the *Bridgewater Treatises*. This alliance manifested two important features so lacking in modern science. First, it provided a bridge between the scientist and the wider public. Such a bridge is now more needed than ever before. Second, it was an expansive form of discourse that communicated the broader meanings of the scientific enterprise in ways that could touch people's lives. This issue was addressed as follows by George Fownes in a mid-nineteenth-century natural theology text:

> What is the object of all science? Is it to procure the means of increased indulgence and refinement in the luxuries and the arts of life that we seek to extend the boundaries of natural knowledge[?] Is it the discovery of abstract principles only desirable on account of the possible application of these principles to the attainment of wealth and power? It cannot be by such considerations that the philosopher [scientist] is urged forward in his painful and thorny path of discovery. It is rather by an irresistible impulse, an instinct of his nature, which prompts him to rejoice in the contemplation of physical truth for its own sake, and to take delight and pleasure in its development.

A few lines later Fownes states that the primary aim of science is 'the elevation and improvement of the mind itself'.[81] He does not mean simply the acquisition of knowledge but he also included improvement of our moral, religious and ethical condition and understanding. For Fownes and many other writers in this genre natural theology made science edifying. Science was not therefore just an end in itself or a means of attaining wealth. Through natural theology science became a morally elevating discourse that celebrated nature and provided a glimpse through nature to its Creator. The term 'the wonders of nature' may have adopted a deeper, more vibrant, ring when nature was perceived through the lens of natural theology. Today, we live in increasingly technological, man-made and rather sterile environments and all too rarely can we glimpse the natural world (however defined). We may also have lost our sense of wonder and our appreciation of the poetry of natural theology.

In part science was responsible for this change. But it was not just evolution and materialistic theories in physics, biology and psychology that are relevant to this story. Professionalisation placed a premium on specialisation, utilitarianism and a sometimes myopic vision of the scientist's role. Partly as a result, the hiatus between the scientist and the public has increased considerably throughout the twentieth century. Moreover, science has become a business and the strings of bureaucratisation often inhibit the wellsprings of science that lie deep in the human spirit. Whatever the causes, few non-scientists can appreciate the poetry of science. Even scientists may be experiencing increasing difficulty in seeing beyond the limited scope imposed by an ends-means research programme.

In the decline of natural theology something very valuable has been lost, perhaps never to be regained. In dissociating itself from natural theology science lost a powerful ally and a potentially humanising force. Yet natural theology was not all light and we must not mourn its passing without drawing attention to one of the seeds of its own destruction. In emphasising order in the universe most natural theologians were unable to cope adequately with disorder, chaos or evil. The very optimism apparent in so much natural theology has not survived into the late twentieth century. After two devastating world wars, the Holocaust and the Atom Bomb, few can perceive design in history. In science the main locus of the design argument is pushed far back from our daily lives to the first few seconds of creation. Yet one of the main aims of this chapter has been to show that until the middle of the nineteenth century the design argument was a thriving, dynamic and popular genre.

For most of the twentieth century science could manage without the help of natural theology. In many countries science has seemed secure, progressive and appreciated by its political masters. However, in Britain the tide began to turn in the late 1970s when the scientific community found its budget cut and realised its lack of political friends and public support. The battle cry 'Save British Science' has been heard in the land. After a long period of neglect the public is again being actively wooed by the scientific community. Yet there is much disagreement about how a new rapport can be achieved. While large sections of the scientific community have sought secular responses to their predicament, natural theology might be reconstructed for this purpose. Many of the old arguments are no longer serviceable and the old edifice will have to be substantially refurbished if this programme is to become viable. But how should it be reconstituted? Should the burgeoning new natural theology be concerned principally with God's selection of the physical parameters at Creation? Or is a more active and immanent God required? Most importantly, could a new natural theology inject the sense of social responsibility which the Chernobyl disaster and the BSE scandal have shown to be so lacking but so necessary?

NOTES

1 See preface.
2 G. Beer, *Darwin's Plots: Evolutionary Narrative in Darwin, George Eliot and Nineteenth-Century Fiction*, London, 1983; J. Golinski, *Science as Public Culture: Chemistry and the Enlightenment in Britain, 1760–1820*, Cambridge, 1992; S. Schaffer, 'Natural philosophy and public spectacle in the eighteenth century', *History of Science*, 21 (1983), 1–43.

3   I. Newton, *Opticks or a Treatise of the Reflections, Refractions, Inflections &
    Colours of Light*, reprint edn. New York, 1952, 402–3.

4   Quoted by R. S. Westfall, 'The rise of science and the decline of orthodox
    Christianity: A study of Kepler, Descartes, and Newton', in *God and Nature.
    Historical Essays on the Encounter between Christianity and Science* (ed. D. C.
    Lindberg and R. L. Numbers), Berkeley, 1986, 218–37, on 221.

5   J. Ray, *The Wisdom of God Manifested in the Works of Creation*, 10th edn.
    London, 1835, title page. See also N. C. Gillespie, 'Natural history, natural
    theology, and social order: John Ray and the "Newtonian ideology"', *Journal
    of the History of Biology*, 20 (1987), 1–49.

6   J. R. Topham, '"An infinite variety of arguments": The *Bridgewater Treatises*
    and British natural theology in the 1830s', PhD dissertation, University of
    Lancaster, 1993; *Idem.*, 'Science and popular education in the 1830s: The
    role of the *Bridgewater Treatises*', *British Journal for the History of Science*, 25
    (1992), 397–430.

7   See chapter 7; J. H. Brooke, 'The natural theology of the geologists: some
    theological strata', in *Images of the Earth* (ed. R. Porter and L. Jordanova),
    Chalfont St Giles, 1979, 39–64.

8   J. Barrow, 'Inner space and outer space: The quest for ultimate expla-
    nation' in *Humanity, Environment and God: Glasgow Centenary Gifford Lectures*
    (ed. N. Spurway), Oxford, 1993, 48–103, esp. 71–5; J. D. Barrow and
    F. J. Tipler, *The Anthropic Cosmological Principle*, Oxford, 1988; J. C.
    Polkinghorne, *One World: The Interaction of Science and Theology*, London,
    1986; *Idem.*, *Science and Providence: God's Interaction with the World*, London,
    1989.

9   R. Dawkins, *The Blind Watchmaker*, Harlow, 1986, 5.

10 C. J. Glacken, *Traces on the Rhodian Shore*, Berkeley and Los Angeles, 1967,
    525 and 537.

11 B. Nieuwentijt, *The Religious Philosopher: or, the Right Use of Contemplating the
    Works of the Creator*, 3rd edn. London, 1724, 132.

12 L. Hunter, *Modern Allegory and Fantasy. Rhetorical Stances of Contemporary
    Writing*, Basingstoke, 1989, 15. Hunter is here discussing the position of T.
    Todorov.

13 T. Dick, *On the Improvement of Society by the Diffusion of Knowledge*, New York,
    1833, 71.

14 Anonymous review of T. Chalmers' *The Evidence and Authority of Christian
    Revelation*, in *Christian Observer*, 14 (1815), 247–8.

15 G. Campbell, *The Philosophy of Rhetoric*, 2 vols., Edinburgh, 1808, i, 107.

16 H. Brougham, *Natural Theology: Comprising a Discourse of Natural Theology,
    Dialogues on Instinct, and Dissertations on the Structure of the Cells of Bees and on
    Fossil Osteology*, London, n.d., 125.

17 W. Whewell, *Astronomy and General Physics, Considered with Reference to Natural
    Theology*, London, 1833, 185.

18 J. H. Brooke, 'Indications of a Creator: Whewell as Apologist and Priest', in
    William Whewell: A Composite Portrait (ed. M. Fisch and S. Schaffer), Oxford,
    1971, 149–74, esp. 167 and 163.

19 Ray, op. cit. (5), preface. Original in italics; W. Paley, *Natural Theology; or,*

Evidences of the Existence and Attributes of the Deity. Collected from the Appearances of Nature, 20th edn. London, 1820, 298.

20 N. Johnson, *Nineteenth-Century Rhetoric in North America*, Carbondale, 1991, esp. ch. 2.

21 Campbell, op. cit. (15), i, 228–33.

22 *Ibid.*, 22 and 160.

23 *Ibid.*, 233.

24 *Ibid.*, 163.

25 Paley, op. cit. (19), 1 and 15.

26 W. Derham, *Physico-Theology: or, a Demonstration of the Being and Attributes of God, from his Works of Creation*, 6th edn, London, 1723, 25.

27 J. M. Robson, 'The fiat and the finger of God: The *Bridgewater Treatises*', in *Victorian Faith in Crisis. Essays on Continuity and Change in Nineteenth-Century Religious Belief* (ed. R. J. Helmstadter and B. Lightman), Basingstoke, 1990, 71–125, esp. 84–8.

28 *The Times*, 15 November 1836, cited by Topham, op. cit. (6), 170.

29 Derham, op. cit. (26). 27, 144 and 244.

30 W. Buckland, *Geology and Mineralogy Considered with Reference to Natural Theology*, 2 vols., London, 1836, i, 335; W. Kirby, *On the Power, Wisdom and Goodness of God as Manifested in the Creation of Animals and in their History, Habits and Instincts*, 2 vols., London, 1835, i, 135.

31 Buckland, op. cit. (30), i, 403.

32 Whewell, op. cit. (17), 112.

33 Derham, op. cit. (26), 55–7.

34 W. Prout, *Chemistry, Meteorology and the Function of Digestion Considered with Reference to Natural Theology*, London, 1834, 155.

35 Buckland, op. cit. (30), i, 131 and 292.

36 B. Hilton, *The Age of Atonement: The Influence of Evangelicalism on Society and Economic Thought 1785–1865*, Oxford, 1988, 4; A. Desmond, *The Politics of Evolution: Morphology, Medicine, and Reform in Radical London*, Chicago and London, 1989.

37 E. Burke, *A Philosophical Enquiry into the Origin of our Ideas of the Sublime and Beautiful*, (ed. J. T. Boulton), London, 1958; S. H. Monk, *The Sublime: A Study of Critical Theories in XVIII-Century England*, New York, 1935.

38 A. Crombie, *Natural Theology; or Essays on the Existence of Deity and of Providence, on the Immateriality of the Soul, and a Future State*, 2 vols., London, 1829, i, 433; T. Dick, *Celestial Scenery: or, the Wonders of the Planetary System Displayed; Illustrating the Perfections of Deity and a Plurality of Worlds*, London, 1838, 384.

39 Crombie, op. cit. (38), i, 69–79.

40 Ray, op. cit. (5), 336; Paley, op. cit. (19), 138; Derham, op. cit. (26), 43.

41 Buckland, op. cit. (30), i, 139–64; ii, plates 5 and 6; Desmond, op. cit. (36).

42 Whewell, op. cit. (17), 10.

43 Modern cosmologists likewise argue that the earth would not have been habitable had certain physical constants been slightly different from their present values. See J. D. Barrow, *Theories of Everything: The Quest for Ultimate Explanation*, Oxford, 1991, 162–71.

44 Nieuwentijt, op. cit. (11).

45 Paley, op. cit. (19), 138.

46 Derham, op. cit. (26), 25.

47 Buckland, op. cit. (30), i, 139–64.

48 Campbell, op. cit. (15), i, 125.

49 Whewell, op. cit. (17), 139.

50 Derham, op. cit. (26), 26.

51 Kirby, op. cit. (30), 8.

52 The wonders of modern technology were displayed at the Strand Gallery.

53 Paley, op. cit. (19), 45, 84 and 121; N. C. Gillespie, 'Divine design and the industrial revolution. William Paley's abortive reform of natural theology', *Isis*, 81 (1990), 214–29.

54 Paley, op. cit. (19), 234.

55 *Ibid.*, 51 and 148.

56 Prout, op. cit. (33), 155. See also chapter 10.

57 Derham, op. cit. (26), 213.

58 Whewell, op. cit. (17), 9 and 12; C. Bell, *The Hand: Its Mechanism and Vital Endowments as Evincing Design*, London, 1833, xi; P. M. Roget, *Animal and Vegetable Physiology Considered with Reference to Natural Theology*, London, 1834, 2 and 560.

59 T. Chalmers, *Natural Theology*, 2 vols., Edinburgh, 1850, i, 188–228. See also D. Cairns, 'Thomas Chalmers's astronomical discourses: a study in natural theology', *Scottish Journal of Theology*, 9 (1956), 410–21, and C. Smith, 'From design to dissolution: Thomas Chalmers' debt to John Robison', *British Journal for the History of Science*, 12 (1979), 59–70. Interestingly Robert Chambers subsequently tried to undermine this kind of argument by showing that the positions followed a law-like distribution; Cf. J. A. Secord's edition of Chambers, *Vestiges of the Natural History of Creation and other Evolutionary Writings*, Chicago, 1994, 10–11.

60 Campbell, op. cit. (15), ii, 321–34; R. Whately, *Elements of Rhetoric*, 7th edn, London, 1882, 181–6.

61 Derham, op. cit. (26), p.80; Paley, op. cit. (19), 19.

62 Whewell, op. cit. (17), 22.

63 Whately, op. cit. (60), 209.

64 Whewell, op. cit. (17), 49 and 141.

65 J. Milton, *Paradise Lost* in *The Poetical Works of John Milton*, London and New York, 1896, 104 and 150. Robson (op. cit. (27), 97) notes that Milton is cited in four of the eight *Bridgewater Treatises*.

66 Newton, op. cit. (3), 402.

67 R. Bentley, *A Confutation of Atheism from the Origin and Frame of the World* partly reprinted in *Isaac Newton's Papers & Letters on Natural Philosophy and Related Documents* (ed. I. B. Cohen), Cambridge, Mass. 1958, esp. 316, 326 and 332.

68 Derham, op. cit. (26), 271; Nieuwentijt, op. cit. (11), ix–xiv; Crombie, op. cit. (38), i, 39; Chalmers, op. cit. (59), i, 163.

69 *Ibid.*, i, 163. See also M. J. Buckley, *At the Origins of Modern Atheism*, New Haven and London, 1987; M. Moriarty, 'Figures of the unthinkable: Diderot's materialist metaphors', in *The Figural and the Literal: Problems of*

Language in the History of Science and Philosophy 1630–1800 (ed. A. E. Benjamin, G. N. Cantor and J. R. R. Christie), Manchester, 1987, 147–75.

70   J. Adams, *Lectures on Natural and Experimental Philosophy*, 5 vols, London, 1794, i, vii–xiii.

71   Kirby, op. cit. (30), xx and xxv–xxxvii. See also L. Jordanova, 'Nature's powers: A reading of Lamarck's distinction between creation and production', in *History, Humanity and Evolution* (ed. J. R. Moore), Cambridge, 1989, 71–98.

72   Letter prefacing Nieuwentijt, op. cit (11), v.

73   Crombie, op. cit. (38), i, 1–79, esp. 48.

74   C. Kenny, 'Theology and natural philosophy in late seventeenth and early eighteenth-century Britain', PhD dissertation, University of Leeds, 1996.

75   Derham, op. cit. (26), 429; S. Clarke, *A Demonstration of the Being and Attributes of God. More Particularly in Answer to Mr. Hobbs, Spinoza, and their Followers*, 8th edn, London, 1732, 2–3.

76   Whewell, op. cit. (17), 190.

77   Buckley, op. cit. (69), 17.

78   Brougham, op. cit. (16), 144.

79   P. H. Thiry, Baron d'Holbach, *The System of Nature: or, Laws of the Moral and Physical World*, Boston, 1889, 35.

80   *Ibid.*, 33–9.

81   G. Fownes, *Chemistry, as Exemplifying the Wisdom and Beneficence of God*, London, 1844, 156–7. This work was awarded the Actonian Prize, instituted in 1838, for 'the best essay illustrative of the wisdom and beneficence of the Almighty'. The Prize was administered by the Managers of the Royal Institution.

7

From Aesthetics to Theology

To encounter a picture of the kind illustrated in colour is almost certainly to raise the question: is this a work of art? An affirmative reply might not seem out of place. Another, actually more correct, answer might be that it is neither a work of art nor of science. Yet, in the production of the image, science played a crucial role because we are looking at penicillin crystals through the privileged 'eye' of an electron microscope. If nature itself were 'seen' as a work of art, then the answer would be even more complex; for the image might then be said to be both a work of art and of science.

We are perhaps more familiar with attempts to introduce sharper lines of demarcation between art and science. In George Steiner's book *Real Presences* there was an explicit contrast between scientific and aesthetic discourse. He wrote of the latter that 'no interpretative-critical analysis, doctrine or programme is superseded, is erased, by any later construction'. In science it is otherwise: 'The Copernican theory did correct and supersede that of Ptolemy. The chemistry of Lavoisier makes untenable the earlier phlogiston theory.'[1] This contrast is one of several that Steiner drew between science on the one hand; poetry, music and art on the other. What he called the gravity and constancy at the heart of major forms of art were even said to be religious in that they enact 'a root-impulse of the human spirit to explore possibilities of meaning and of truth that lie outside empirical seizure or proof'.[2] The tacit contrast with the scientific effort was again obvious. Modelling in science, according to Steiner, aims at mastery and ownership. In aesthetic appreciation we are put in touch with the transcendent, 'with matters "undreamt of" in our materiality'.[3]

It is a nice question whether Steiner was not perhaps caricaturing science in order to sustain his antithesis. What about the role of aesthetic appreciation within science itself? What of the claims of the Copernican astronomers to be offering a more elegant picture of the cosmos than was possible with the Ptolemaic system? The argument of this chapter is that an uncovering of beauty in nature and an

Penicillin crystals under an electron microscope. Image taken from vol. iv of
Storia delle Scienze, Milan, 1994; courtesy of the Electa archive, Milan.

appreciation of beauty in the scientist's constructions of nature have been prominent goals of scientific enquiry, with edifying, humanising effects. Statements about beauty in nature have also graduated into religious discourse, not least because analogies between the natural world and works of art, music or literature have been frequently used to elucidate what it means to speak of divine activity in the world. The practice of science was edifying for many of its founders precisely because it helped to bring out harmonies and beauties in nature that might otherwise be missed.

It is important to stress that we are not thinking primarily of references to simplicity. There is a complexity in nature that has dashed many theories premised on criteria of simplicity. Indeed, philosophers of science have produced cogent reasons why we should not expect the simplest organising principles to deliver truths about the natural world.[4] But the lure of an aesthetic vision can survive that inconvenience. There is a longed-for elegance and beauty in the reconstruction of nature that has often been at the heart of scientific endeavour. A beautiful theory may be discarded as a fantasy, only to be replaced by another in which an unexpected beauty gleams. With what reluctance did Kepler abandon circular motion for the planets. To lose the music of the spheres was an intolerable deprivation. Playing with oval curves for the planetary orbits Kepler compared them to a cart-load of 'dung'.[5] And yet he could not believe that nature was so foul. In due course he was rewarded with the elegance of the ellipse – new music to his ears and a new music of the spheres.[6] There would seem to be a kind of methodological aestheticism in the pursuit of science. The quest for economy, elegance and beauty may often be frustrated, may often be a poor guide to the merits of a particular theory; but the quest is always there, regulating scientific enquiry and the construction of theories. For many scientists this would have no transcendental implications. For others it has. In other words there is an issue here that belongs to the discussion of science and religion.

There are several constituencies for whom the aesthetic dimensions of science are of topical interest. Among some philosophers of religion there has been renewed concern to find a way of speaking of the beauty of God. In Patrick Sherry's *Spirit and Beauty*, attention is drawn to the fact that the word 'beautiful' is not used of material things alone. It is also predicated of the immaterial, of ideas, of scientific theories.[7] At a more popular level, religious writers have sought to recapture the domain of artistic appreciation, determined that it should not be the exclusive preserve of a surrogate religion. In Richard Harries's discussion of *Art and the Beauty of God*, there are echoes of John Keble: in earthly beauty may be discerned the glow of the divine.[8] Resurrecting an old association between beauty and wisdom, Harries places the patterns disclosed by the scientist alongside those of the artist, both displaying characteristics of beauty, order and rationality.[9] References to the tantalising quality of beauty and the longing it may evoke have also appeared in essays that deal explicitly with the theme of 'science and religion'. In 1993 Anthony O'Hear wrote that science and religion should not be seen as conflicting discourses.[10] Because he wrote as a non-believer his remarks on the relationship between aesthetic and religious experience are particularly striking. The religious impulse, he suggested, might be seen as a 'response to the experience of a natural object or work of art as beautiful: in which we see a thing not just as [a] "fragment of nature" (in Wittgenstein's phrase), but as something which mediates between our own longing for perfection and some other world in which that perfection is actually realised'.[11] He also admitted to a 'transcendent sense of rightness one sometimes has in the experience of something beautiful'.[12]

Philosophers of science have been particularly active in reappraising the role of aesthetic considerations in scientific argument. In his book *The Scenes of Inquiry*, Nicholas Jardine has given perhaps the best account to date of the different ways in which aesthetic arguments can function in the sciences. His thesis is that 'aesthetic appeal and response are ... deeply involved in all aspects of inquiry in the sciences: in the marshalling and deployment of evidence; in the promotion of new methods and practices; in the presentation and adjudication of factual and theoretical claims'.[13]

A useful feature of Jardine's analysis is a taxonomy that distinguishes three types of aesthetic appraisal. Type 1 covers the direct ascription of an aesthetic virtue to a theory or hypothesis and is extremely common in scientific discourse, where adjectives such as 'economical', 'harmonious', 'elegant' are applied to explanatory schemes. This must, however, be distinguished from type 2 where a theory may be favoured if it 'brings out' certain aesthetic virtues in the phenomena it purports to explain. A familiar example would be the retrograde motion of the planets, which took on a very different aspect when viewed through the lens of Copernican theory. If the earth is not a stationary observatory but moves with the other planets around the sun, then the wayward motion of Mars becomes less so because its apparent backtracking simply reflects its being 'overtaken' by the observer on a faster inside track. Jardine himself suggests that one's experience of the night sky just after sunset, and of the configuration of the planets in particular, can be directly enhanced by visualising their orbits fixed on the sun rather than the earth.[14] A third type of aesthetic appraisal refers to the visual language of science – to the rhetoric inscribed within diagrams, maps and illustrations. Here the scientist opts for theories or

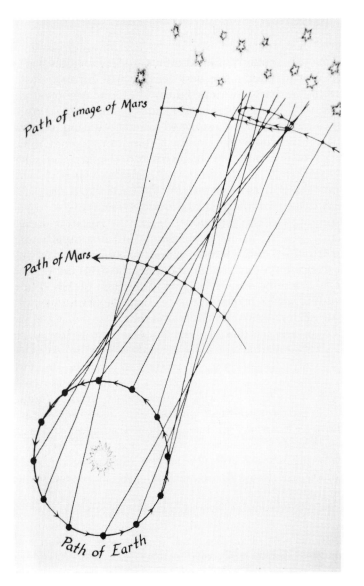

Figure 21: The observed retrograde motion of the planets elegantly explained by the Copernican system.

hypotheses that bring out certain virtues in *representations* of the phenomena they explain. In the representation of phenomena analysed by scientific methods, art and science have frequently come together, sometimes to remarkable effect. The large circular cavity in Galileo's depiction of the moon assisted his case for an imperfect, mountainous surface, but also tempted Kepler to speculate that so arresting a circle must imply the abode of extra-terrestrial life.[15]

If there is a rekindled interest in the aesthetic dimensions of science we can certainly ask whether historical analysis has anything distinctive to offer. At the very least it can furnish examples to support and perhaps even extend the kind of taxonomy that Jardine has proposed. How often, for example, has the scientist's first interest in an object been awakened by its captivating beauty? Robert Boyle was entranced by the beauty of gem-stones; Hugh Miller by the beauty of fossil forms. The historian will also recognise a kind of theory appraisal that measures virtue in terms of consistency with other prevailing theories or with metaphysical expectations. We shall return to this type towards the end of the chapter.

By bringing out the aesthetic elements in scientific creativity the historian can also correct uninformed and unsympathetic perceptions of science.[16] One sometimes wonders how many youngsters are put off by presentations that deliberately leave out the very elements that make scientific enquiry so rewarding. The lifeblood of science, the wrestling with a problem, the personal involvement in finding a solution, the creative imagination that this requires, and the aesthetic experience that may convince us that we are on the right track – all these features of a life in science must be reaffirmed. The historian can help to recover them, and to focus on the aesthetic is one way of doing so. In a famous series of Gifford Lectures, Michael Polanyi drew on history as well as personal experience to emphasise the human rather than the de-personalising aspects of science. In his book *Personal Knowledge* an intimacy between beauty and truth was a recurring motif: the affirmation of a great theory, he wrote, 'is in part an expression of delight'. Such a theory has 'an inarticulate component acclaiming its beauty, and this is essential to the belief that the theory is true'.[17]

Whether we can today so readily speak of 'truth' in such contexts is a difficult issue but, as Polanyi recognised, aesthetic considerations often carried weight in the past because they mediated between statements about nature and statements about God. It is this phenomenon that invites further investigation. Among innumerable examples would be Tycho Brahe's resistance to Copernican astronomy as he contemplated the great chasm between the furthest planet and the nearest star that the absence of stellar parallax would imply. Insisting that 'decent proportion' had to be preserved, Tycho explained that this was 'because God, the author of the universe, loves appropriate order, not confusion and disorder'.[18] There used to be a debate between those who saw seventeenth-century science as a form of asceticism and those who saw in it an expression of hedonism.[19] As a form of pious hedonism the aesthetic pleasure derived from natural philosophy could transcend that dichotomy. For some students of nature that may even have been part of its appeal.

If we take seriously the role of aesthetics in the 'Scientific Revolution', there are important consequences. In reconstructions of the path to modernity the new astronomy of Copernicus and the mechanical philosophy of Descartes are routinely coupled to explain how humanity came to be dethroned. A population explosion among extra-terrestrials, of the kind envisaged by Giordano Bruno, has also been invoked to give the explanation an extra air of plausibility.[20] But a strong case can be mounted against the usual line on the dethronement of humanity. Because many of the grounds on which such decentring might be asserted were ultimately aesthetic, prominently so in the defence of Copernicanism, they served to exalt rather than diminish what was distinctive in humankind. This was not only the ability to reason but also to appreciate the beauty and scope of Creation.

The point stands out in one of the early treatments of physico-theology – Walter Charleton's *Darkness of Atheism Dispelled by the Light of Nature* (1652). Having enthused about the 'exquisite' beauty of nature Charleton observed that it would be to no purpose were it not for man to admire.[21] As for the intuitive view that Copernican astronomy must have relegated man from the centre of creation, the argument could as easily go the other way. At the centre of the Aristotelian cosmos humankind was at the centre of corruption, living in a garbage bin – the sink of all refuse, as Galileo put it.[22] To be placed in the heavens along with the planets could be a kind of promotion. In an exegesis of Psalm 115, the Dutch pastor and Copernican Philip Lansbergen insisted that to be placed in the central planetary orbit was to occupy the 'most dignified place of the first heaven'.[23] In important respects the human race was not dethroned by the 'Scientific Revolution'. For those able to appreciate the new theories the status of the aesthete, privileged to reinterpret God's creation, was enhanced.

Aesthetic Preference and the 'Scientific Revolution'

One of the principal tasks of the astronomer, according to Copernicus, was to reveal the order and symmetry of God's Creation. In the Preface to his great book of 1543 he suggested that he had done so more successfully than his predecessors. His was a system in a way that Ptolemy's was not. His predecessors had been unable to discern what Copernicus called the principal thing, namely the 'design of the universe and the fixed symmetry of its parts'. It was 'as though one were to gather various hands, feet, head and other members, each part excellently drawn, but not related to a single body, and since they in no way match each other, the result would be monster rather than man'.[24] He felt justified in using such rhetoric because, in the Ptolemaic scheme, the planetary orbits would be treated separately. They could be independently scaled in size. But in his system the relative sizes of the planetary orbits were fixed with respect to each other in a unified whole.[25] Within this new system was real order and symmetry because there was a clear relationship between the period of a planet and the size of its orbit. The further the planet from the sun, the greater its period. There was a harmony here that Kepler later captured in precise mathematical terms.

When speaking of aesthetic preference there is always the question 'Whose aesthetics?' In the case of Copernicus, an answer has been given. His image of current astronomy as a monstrous body is reminiscent of a classical text on the art of poetry. This was the *Ars Poetica* of Horace, which, in Italy, was attracting extensive commentary during the first half of the sixteenth century. The opening lines of Horace also speak of a monstrous body: 'If a painter chose to join a human head to the neck of a horse ... and to spread feathers of many a hue over limbs picked up now here now there, so that what at the top is a lovely woman ends below in a black and ugly fish, could you, my friends, if favoured with a private view, refrain from laughing?'[26] That reference to 'my friends', to an audience, indicates a central theme in Horace: it is that which moves, delights or persuades an audience that makes for good poetry. Copernicus's Preface was a similar exercise in rhetoric addressed to the Pope. In supporting the claim that Copernicus drew on the aesthetic canons of Horace, Robert Westman has said that 'the central theme emphasized by Horace and noticed by his Renaissance commentators was the principle of "fittingness" or "belongingness". Style must fit its characters; characters must preserve decorum, appropriateness.'[27] He can then say that 'Copernicus tacitly transferred the Horatian ideal of good poetry into the domain of astronomical practice.'[28]

The argument of Copernicus was that his heliostatic system was the more appropriate, the more fitting for a system made by God.

Taking the sun, not the earth, as the fixed point of reference created such harmony for both Copernicus and Kepler that new epistemological claims seemed appropriate. A true knowledge of the celestial order was, after all, possible.[29] But it was only possible because of the shift of vantage point, the shift of perspective. And here another connection with Renaissance mannerism has been made. The shift in vantage point that turned monstrosity into elegance was a prominent theme in contemporary theory and practice of art.[30] References to symmetry in Copernicus relate to the unified body that the heliocentric planetary system now became and have therefore invited comparison with the symmetry explored by the painter Albrecht Dürer in his drawings of the human body.[31] As Fernand Hallyn has put it: 'if the Renaissance artist is often called a god, Copernicus's God creates like a Renaissance artist'.[32]

In both Copernicus and Kepler there is a sense of excitement at the disclosure of a hidden beauty. This does not mean that their only arguments for the earth's motion were aesthetic.[33] Once there was a grasp of an orderly system of planets focused on the sun, causal connections could be made between planetary motions and the sun as their motor. Kepler would think in terms of magnetic spokes radiating from a rotating sun. Among the Copernicans different balances were struck between aesthetic and physical arguments.[34] But the aesthetic were always prominent. This was because different aesthetic nuances were applicable to different aspects of the theory. There was economy in that a rotating earth saved the gigantic heavens from turning. There was unification in that the planetary orbits could be analysed in relation to each other, rather than separately as in the Ptolemaic scheme. There was the aesthetic purchase Copernicus gained from his exclusion of a technical device of Ptolemy – the equant – which violated the ancient precept of uniform circular motion. There was the elegance with which an orbiting earth could account for the retrograde motions of the exterior planets; and there was harmony in the correlation of planetary periods with planetary distances from the sun. England's first Copernican, Thomas Digges, echoed precisely these virtues. Once recognise the correlation between orbital period and orbital size and 'the orderly and most beautiful frame of the heavens doth ensue'.[35]

For Kepler this harmony was music to his intellect if not to his ears. Each planet had its own melody as it orbited the sun. The more slowly it moved the lower the pitch. As it approached the sun and accelerated so it sang a higher note. The combined choir might not make a wonderful sound now, but at the time of the Creation all was perfection. Kepler even thought it might be possible to determine the age of the world. One would simply extrapolate each planet's motions backwards in time until that perfect consonance was recovered.[36] In such arguments there was graduation from aesthetic preference into theological discourse. The aesthetic appreciation of a work of art has often been described as a dwelling in the mind of its creator.[37] In appreciating the artistry within nature, the mathematical structure within the world, Kepler effectively claimed that he was thinking God's thoughts after him.

Routine accounts of the decentring of humanity usually combine the Copernican innovation with a dehumanisation of nature that accompanied the mechanical philosophy. In chapter 3 we have already criticised the way this move is made in New Age historiography. It will complement that critique if we reflect on the role of aesthetic argument in the mechanical construction of nature. At first sight the mechanical philosophies of Gassendi and Descartes, of Charleton, Boyle and Hooke, would seem to be poor soil for the cultivation of aesthetic sensibilities. It was the corpuscularian ontologies that would later bring down the wrath of Romantics who accused them of removing all splendour from the world.[38] It was surely difficult to celebrate the beauty of the real world when that world was redefined in terms of the primary qualities of microparticles that were not even visible. As Joseph Glanvill put it in his *Scepsis Scientifica* (1665), 'we cannot profound into the *hidden things* of Nature, nor see the first springs and wheeles that set the rest agoing'.[39]

It would be difficult perhaps to find a stronger objection to the primacy of aesthetic considerations – unless we could uncover a shift in sensibility that conferred some kind of beauty on the arrangement of particles. Joseph Needham used to remark on the peculiar fondness for particles in Western natural philosophy compared with the resistance to them in the organic philosophies of China.[40] What is it that makes one fond of particles? In the case of Robert Boyle they allowed him to speak of economy and simplicity in the workings of nature.[41] And when he listed the virtues of his mechanical philosophy, he included some that might be applied to the evaluation of a work of art: clarity, intelligibility and the kind of comprehensibility that comes from visual representation.[42]

To *explain* an upsurge in popularity of the mechanical philosophies it would be insufficient to invoke a new aesthetic sensibility. Historians have been careful to avoid giving too intellectualist an explanation for a process that arguably had its social roots in a renegotiation of the relationships between mathematical practitioners, instrument makers and philosophers of nature.[43] The diversity of purpose to which mechanical metaphors were put also makes it impossible to find a unilateral explanation for their new prevalence. At one extreme they would be used by deists and other radicals who wished to mechanise the soul. At the other, they would be used to reconstruct the boundaries of a natural order, allowing genuine miracles to stand out.[44] For the English Catholic Thomas White, the success of philosophers in giving naturalistic accounts of nature's machinery was part of his case against a sceptical philosophy that called all knowledge claims into question.[45]

Notwithstanding such diversity in the contexts of use, we can see certain trends in the expression of a new aesthetic sensibility. Two of these demand our attention and can, in the first instance, be contrasted. In one the stress fell on the grandeur of the cosmic machinery. As with Darwin in the nineteenth century, an aesthetic of grandeur could have secular connotations, especially when joined with the view that not everything was made for humankind alone. The less secular aesthetic might be called one of precision rather than grandeur, in that one could celebrate the filigree work of the divine mechanic. In both these trends it would be possible to detect a liberation from anthropocentric theologies; but an alternative reading must also be considered. Even the more secular trend encouraged anthropocentric views to survive. As the perceivers of grandeur humans were ennobled. 'Do you think you have humbled me', asks the Marquise in Fontenelle's *Conversations on the Plurality of Worlds,* 'by telling me the Earth moves around the Sun?'. 'I swear to you', says the lady to the philosopher, 'I don't have any less self-esteem.' And the philosopher replies: 'Good Lord, no madame! ... I know full well that people are less jealous of their place in the universe than in a drawingroom.'[46]

In the second half of the seventeenth century an aesthetics of precision was clearly facilitated by the microscope. In Robert Hooke's *Micrographia* (1665) there was explicit reference to the beauty of the microscopic world.[47] As unpromising a subject as the scale of a fish turned out to be remarkably fine, prompting Hooke to comment that 'here in fishes, as well as other animals, nature follows its usual method, framing all parts so, as that they are both useful and ornamental in all its composures'.[48] Beauty was mingled with utility but not yet derived from it. Compared with the filigree precision of nature, human artifacts made a sorry sight: 'the more we see of their shape', Hooke observed, 'the less appearance will there be of their beauty'.[49] The edge of a razor, when magnified,

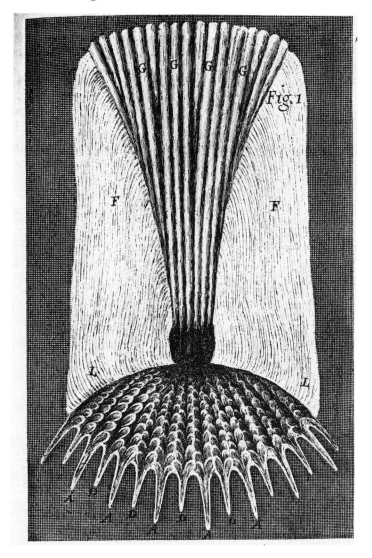

Figure 22: The magnification of fish scales reveals their beauty. From Robert
Hooke's *Micrographia*, first published in 1665.

was observed 'to be of all kinds of shapes, except what it should
be'.[50] The argument was not entirely perfect. Ladies examining
their skin under the microscope were not usually delighted with
what they saw.[51]

Nevertheless nature's invisible realm did possess a beauty that
natural philosophers created for it. The architecture of matter was

patterned on what was known of visible micro-structures – many of high perfection. A snow crystal might not look perfect by the time it landed on one's sleeve; but Hooke was sure these 'pretty figured stars of snow, when at first generated might be ... very regular and exact'.[52] Boyle, following Gassendi, came to believe that external crystal shape was built up by a pleasingly regular arrangement of angular particles.[53] Nehemiah Grew even had plant forms constructed from angular saline particles.[54] Several years before Hooke tickled his audience with magnified fleas, Charleton had already discussed their proboscis. There was more industry 'in its delicate and sinuous perforation, than all the costly aqueducts of Nero's Rome'. In fine 'the meanest piece of nature throws disparagement and contempt upon the greatest masterpiece of art'.[55] Yet this did little to diminish human significance. Charleton insisted that the deity 'adorned the universe' principally for man's sake – not exclusively, for there was always the question of God's own Glory.[56]

There was, potentially at least, a less sacred aesthetic in Descartes's philosophy. There was still beauty in his mechanised world. The Cartesian vortices put into pictorial form a fact that Newton would find pleasing in itself – that the planets orbited the sun in the same direction and almost the same plane. In his *Principles of Philosophy* (1644) Descartes explicitly introduced aesthetic terms. A grand conception of the Creator's power should eliminate any fear that we imagine his works to be 'too vast, too beautiful, too perfect'.[57] And the grandeur of the universe did mean that we must not think too proudly of ourselves. Modesty required that we should not imagine everything to have been created for our sake. It also meant that we should not presume to know the ends that God had in view. A letter written from the Hague in June 1647 shows again how the grandeur of the universe could be a vehicle of release: 'We may say that all created things are made "for us", inasmuch as we can derive some utility from them; but I do not see that we are obliged to think man is *the* end of creation.'[58]

The contents of this letter can be seen as a perfect summation of Descartes' critique. He even allows for the possibility of extraterrestrial intelligence as a further signal. But his argument does not pull in one direction only. In fact he makes an important distinction that leads, in the end, to an elevation of the human self. His distinction is between 'those advantages which can be diminished through others' enjoying similar ones, and those which cannot'.[59] Virtue, knowledge, and health, for example, are in no way lessened in ourselves because they might be found in others. The same could be said of aesthetic sensibility. In this respect we are not diminished in the Cartesian universe: dethronement in one sense meant re-enthronement in another. As Descartes put it himself: 'if we love God and for his sake unite ourselves in will to all that he has created, then the more grandeur, nobility and perfection we conceive things to have, the more highly we esteem ourselves, as parts of a whole that is a greater work'.[60] This almost holistic identification with the immensity of creation shows perhaps a rather different side to Descartes than the customary profile of a detached spectator and exploiter of nature. It chimes with our earlier remarks about the inadequacy of much New Age historiography. The twin facets of Descartes's position were neatly captured by Fontenelle. The narrator observes that most people admire nature only because they believe she has a kind of magic at her command: the minute they begin to understand her she loses all their respect. But not so the Marquise who registers a 'much higher regard' for nature once she knows the world is like a watch.[61]

It was, of course, with Newton rather than Descartes that the scientific movement of the seventeenth century reached its climax. The ancient Pythagorean correlation of musical tones with the lengths and tensions of strings meant that for Newton, as for Kepler, references to the harmony of creation were not merely metaphorical. Enthralled by the problem of dividing the octave, Newton appears to have relished a correlation between the seven tones of the scale, the seven colours of his spectrum and the seven planets of the solar system.[62] Newton also believed that the elegance of his inverse-square law of gravitation had been known to Pythagoras for whom the pursuit of cosmic harmony had been a means of spiritual purification.[63] Instead of separating out Newton's interests according to modern criteria, the historian cannot ignore the connections that, for Newton himself, bound them together. There was a holistic character to Newton's interests because 'a true understanding of the uses of language enabled [him] to introduce astronomical calculation into his chronological writings, and to complete his mathematical arguments with theological references'.[64] In one of his theological manuscripts Newton chose to recall the Wisdom of Solomon: the omnipotent God had 'in ye beginning of his divine wisdom created ye things of the heaven & of ye earth in weight number and measure, depending upon most wonderful proportions & harmony to serve ye time wch he hath appointed'.[65] Aesthetic considerations and their grounding in a primitive theism were not embellishments of Newton's science. They were at the heart of his understanding of the world and of his role in it.

Science and the Dethronement of Humanity

When Keith Thomas published his *Man and the Natural World* in 1983, he could say that the late-seventeenth-century dethronement of man represented one of the great revolutions in modern western thought, but one to which historians had scarcely done justice. Both in detail and sweep he then gave an illuminating account. A charming detail came from the Civil War sectary who affirmed that God 'loved toads as well as the best saints'.[66] Symbolising the sweep was John Ray's remark in his *Wisdom of God*: 'It is a generally received opinion that all this visible world was created for Man [and] that Man is the end of the Creation, as if there were no other end of any creature but some way or other to be serviceable to man. But though this be vulgarly received, yet wise men nowadays think otherwise.'[67]

We have been hinting in this chapter that there was also a counter-point to this theme. The aesthetic grounds on which wise men now thought otherwise only served to highlight the uniqueness of man as an aesthete. A not dissimilar point was made by Polanyi in his *Personal Knowledge*: 'Copernicus gave preference to man's delight in abstract theory, at the price of rejecting the evidence of our senses. . . . In a literal sense, therefore, the new Copernican system was as anthropocentric as the Ptolemaic view, the difference being merely that it preferred to satisfy a different human affection.'[68] The reflex-ivity whereby the appreciation of beauty reflected back on human self-perception is not just an ingenious invention. It can be found in the primary sources. One of the ironies is that Ray could accuse the Cartesians of being too anthropocentric: 'Those philosophers indeed, who hold man to be the only creature in this sublunary world, endued with sense and perception, and that all other animals are mere machines or puppets, have some reason to think that all things here below were made for man.'[69]

It is by no means clear, however, that Ray's position was as radical as it seems. In the *Wisdom of God*, as in most of the primary sources that Keith Thomas cited, the form of words is that not everything was made for man *alone*.[70] 'For my part', Ray declared, 'I cannot believe, that all the things in the world were so made for man, that they have no other use.'[71] This formula can be read as an invitation to consider the more radical possibility that some things were not made for man at all. That may even have been the intention of some who used it. But it is not what the formula says. In fact when Ray clarifies his position, the balance shifts in favour of a more conservative resol-ution. Objects that appear to be of no human use now, may well be to future generations. It remained true that 'all the creatures in the world may be some way or other useful to us'.[72] At the very least they exercised our wits and, by contemplating them, one was led to admire their Maker. Ray did make room in his universe for angels and other rational beings, but there was a profound sense in which a plurality of worlds did not entail human diminution. To say that other worlds had been made for their inhabitants both reflected and reinforced the assumption that this earthly world was made for us. It was still a long way to Thomas Hardy's deduction in *Two on a Tower* that because the invisible stars were not made for us, nothing was. Indeed the choicest symbol of a surviving anthropocentrism occurred at the front of the very book which, at a popular level, might have done most to deflate it. As late as 1821, an edition of Fontenelle's *Conversations* appeared, duly updated to include the planet Uranus. But when the curtains were rolled back, there, still

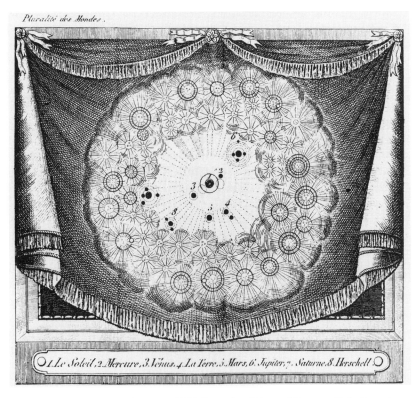

Figure 23: Illustration from an 1821 French edition of Fontenelle's *Entretiens sur la Pluralité des Mondes*. Taken from Steven J. Dick, *Plurality of Worlds: the Extra-Terrestrial Life Debate from Democritus to Kant*, Cambridge, 1982; courtesy of Cambridge University Press.

centre stage, was our own sun.[73]

The reconstruction of nature that we associate with the seventeenth century did not leave humanity displaced. As the aesthetes who could appreciate the grounds on which the reconstruction had been achieved the natural philosophers were still in touch with their Maker. It is not clear that they felt compelled to assume an objectivist view of beauty. In his Boyle lectures, Richard Bentley could sound strangely relativistic: 'All pulchritude is relative; and all bodies are truly physically beautiful under all possible shapes and proportions.'[74] This was, however, immediately qualified with the conditions that they must be 'good in their kind' and 'fit for their proper uses and ends'. To describe mountains as barren and misshapen was to neglect their use in making the plains fertile – an argument that still worked for John Ruskin one hundred and fifty years later.

For Newton, the harmony of creation as revealed by physical theory was decidedly a divine gift – the pivot on which a discourse of natural philosophy could become one of moral philosophy.[75] Another gift, still intact, was its beauty as perceived by the senses. Whether the beauty was of colour, sound or human architecture, Newton clearly believed there were underlying mathematical ratios. He advised the Oxford student John Harington to pursue them because such an exercise would 'exemplify the simplicity in all the works of the Creator'.[76] Newton was inclined to believe that 'some general laws of the Creator prevailed with respect to the agreeable or unpleasing affections of all our *senses*; at least the supposition does not derogate from the wisdom or power of God'.[77] Divinely ordained laws were involved in the perception as well as the structure of all that was beautiful. Creature and Creator were still tied by the very possibility of appreciating beauty. This was a form of anthropocentrism that science would find it hard to abolish because there was a sense in which it depended upon it.

The Scientist as Aesthete

During the Enlightenment there were many attacks on established religion, but among natural philosophers a sense of the artistry in creation was rarely lost. The discovery of economy or beauty in nature did not always point beyond itself but in many instances it did. In astronomy James Ferguson was prepared to populate comets because their paths provided ever changing vistas on the beauty of creation.[78] In the life sciences, the conviction of a natural order that could be displayed through taxonomic categories remained strong, even when it proved elusive. The art of classification certainly had a transcendental meaning for Linnaeus who was nicknamed the second Adam because of his penchant for naming new species. In chapter 6 we showed how natural theology could function as an apology for science or for religion. In Linnaeus it did both. Because humans alone were able to appreciate the economy and beauty in nature he concluded that they had been made 'for the purpose of studying the Creator's works that [they] may observe in them the evident marks of divine wisdom'.[79] For most of his life Linnaeus believed that one mark of that divine wisdom was the fixity of species. It is therefore tempting to suppose that when the first evolutionary theories came along, there would be inevitable damage to aesthetic sensibilities. Yet some of the earliest evolutionary schemes were premised on a gradual ascent up the 'great chain of being', one of the most durable and aesthetically pleasing of all taxonomic ideals.[80] Charles Darwin's earliest drafts of his evolutionary theory would embrace the aesthetically pleasing notion that evolution was nature's way of preserving adaptation to a changing environment.[81]

Even in chemistry – the science of material change – aesthetic sensibilities continued to find expression and, in striking cases, with religious overtones. Early in the nineteenth century Humphry Davy used Lavoisier's new, anti-phlogistic chemistry more, he said, for its beauty than its truth.[82] A belief in the ultimate unity of matter was aesthetically so attractive to Davy that he resisted Dalton's indivisible atoms in the hope of reducing a burgeoning list of elements. It was his peculiar misfortune to keep discovering more; but this did nothing to dampen his spirits. As his most recent bio-grapher has observed, 'God for Davy was the guarantor of a simple, harmonious and ultimately intelligible world, making science a reasonable acitivity, as it would not be if the world were governed by pure chance.'[83]

What of the earth sciences, which in the nineteenth century did so much to shake the foundations of popular Christian belief? Even here there were expressions of awe and wonder, an appreciation of grandeur and beauty that were not always secular in tone. Hugh Miller loved to talk about the beauty of fossil forms and their resem-blance to human architecture. The interior arches of an ammonite shell reminded him of the 'groined ribs of a Gothic roof'. Amid the coal measures he found the ornately carved columns of the Sigillaria, examples of delicate work more exquisite in their finish than those of Westminster Abbey or Canterbury Cathedral. Every human design that had proved to be pleasing had been anticipated in previous

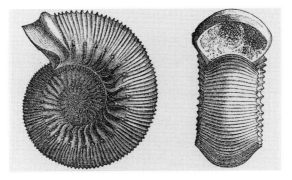

Figure 24: The beauty of an ammonite. From Hugh Miller's *The Testimony of the Rocks*, first published in 1857.

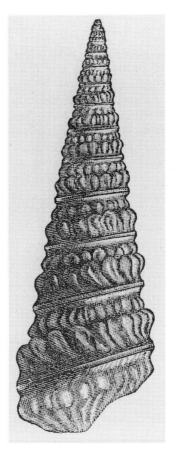

Figure 25: Fossilised architecture in *Murchisonia bigranulosa*, also from Miller's *Testimony of the Rocks.*

organic structures. Miller's point was not that architects had consciously imitated nature but that the same architectonic principles were visible in their work and that of their Maker. They evidently shared the same aesthetic sensibilities. For Miller this was evidence that man had been made in the image of God. And because they were of like mind they could work together on the improvement of nature.[84]

The graduation of aesthetic into theistic discourse has been a recurrent theme with many variations. But the historian should be the last to suggest that there has been no modulation and no negation of the theme. It is clear from the post-Darwinian controversies that an emphasis on utility and natural selection did, for some, strip the world of beauty. Structures that Hugh Miller had found captivating were seen in a new light. It was their usefulness in the struggle for existence that accounted for their form. An anonymous contributor to the *Monthly Journal of Science*, writing in April 1879, expressed the sadness that would afflict a sensitive mind when the woods and fields no longer offered a 'soothing contrast to the exchange, the workshop, or the battlefield'. Neither lavish, nor liberal, 'Dame Nature' had become 'more penurious than the wife of the thriftiest peasant-proprietor in rural France'. The reduction of beauty to utility, orchestrated by the Darwinians, marked the passing of an era: 'Those colours which so fascinated the poet or artist, and which seem to be spread in such royal lavishment over copse and meadow and heath, have all their purpose to fulfil; they have to serve as an attraction to insects which effect the fertilisation of the flower.'[85]

It would be tempting to conclude that Darwin killed the beautiful and the sublime. Late in life he complained of the atrophy of an aesthetic sensibility in himself.[86] But those who have studied his writing carefully have concluded that he had preached a 'naturalist reconciliation of the sublime and the beautiful'.[87] His famous image of a tangled bank was part of a theodicy of landscape. Certainly he had not been insensitive to the sublime. As a young man he had been lured by images of the Brazilian rain forest. When he finally arrived, his language, too, had graduated from the aesthetic to the religious: 'Twiners entwining twiners, ... tresses like hair – beautiful lepidoptera – Silence – hosannah'.[88] Later, when he had a theory to promote, he still spoke of a 'grandeur' in his vision of nature where the production and extinction of species were due to secondary causes. The laws that governed their operation were still ascribed, albeit ambiguously, to a Creator.[89] The experience of the sublime was not for Darwin an acceptable argument for the existence of God, any more than the powerful feelings excited by music.[90] But he did acknowledge that the state of mind which 'grand scenes' had excited in him had been 'intimately connected with a belief in God'.[91]

In twentieth-century physical science, references to the harmony and beauty disclosed by theoretical structures have been no less prominent than in previous centuries. When Einstein announced his field equations in 1915 he wrote of a 'magic' that was inescapable for anyone who fully understood his theory – a magic which consisted in the harmonious coherence of its mathematical structure.[92] A respected biographer of Einstein has written that an 'overriding urge for harmony' directed his scientific life as much as it did that of Max Planck.[93] Einstein's famous quip that 'when judging a physical theory, I ask myself whether I would have made the Universe in that way had I been God'[94] was too presumptuous for Niels Bohr and may indeed go beyond the pantheism that Einstein himself professed. One must also allow for the jocular. Nevertheless, Einstein was surely earnest in saying that the emotional state which enables great scientific achievements to be made is 'similar to that of the religious person or the person in love'.[95] One facet of that state could be resistance to the ugly. Reminiscing about Einstein, Hermann Bondi said that 'when I put down a suggestion that seemed to me cogent and reasonable, he did not in the least contest this, but he only said, "Oh, how ugly." As soon as an equation seemed to him to be ugly, he really rather lost interest in it.... . He was quite convinced that beauty was a guiding principle in the search for important results in theoretical physics.'[96] There was certainly nothing intrinsically ugly about $e = mc^2$.

The achievements of modern physics have been associated with an ethereal beauty that can be experienced only by the mathematically literate. There have even been references to the 'unreasonable effectiveness of mathematics' in elucidating the structure of the physical world. Elaborating what he meant by 'unreasonable', Eugene Wigner even used the word 'miracle': 'The miracle of the appropriateness of the language of mathematics for the formulation of the laws of physics is a wonderful gift that we neither understand nor deserve.'[97] Responses to this sense of a 'gift' have varied enormously, but there is one that is not uncommon. It surfaced in a remark made by the physicist Frank Close when asked to describe the most thrilling moment his work had given him. His reply was 'the first time an experiment confirmed my theory and I felt humbled by having "caught Nature at it" '.[98] The fact that Nature already 'knew' about *his* equations was 'an eerie and mystical experience'. It was an 'incredible surprise that quarks were for real!' And so from the interviewer came the inevitable question: 'Do you believe in a god?' To which came the conventional reply: 'Not in a conventional sense.'

The stuff we are made of might be merely flotsam on a sea of dark matter. And yet this could itself evoke a sense of awe, an experience that Close was prepared to describe as 'religious'.

Some Exegetical Problems

The graduation from aesthetic appreciation into religious discourse could be illustrated with many more examples. Werner Heisenberg spoke of a spirit of humility in which one had to accept the gift of 'an incredible degree of simplicity' in the mathematical abstractions of physical theory. These beautiful interrelationships could not be invented: 'they have been there since the creation of the world'. His wife recorded that he had once said to her: 'I was lucky enough to look over the good Lord's shoulder while He was at work.'[99] To interpret such remarks is, however, a difficult matter. It would be surprising were the religious apologist not to seize them because they seem to show a congruity between the practice of science and some kind of belief in the transcendent. Press such claims too hard, however, and they are likely to burst. There are problems with this kind of apologetic and the historian is in a good position to assess them.

Thus it might be objected that the only tests that ultimately carry weight are those concerning the fruitfulness of a theory, the control it gives, and its ability to withstand attempts at falsification. It is not always obvious that a beautiful theory is any the less beautiful after being slain. Nor could anyone conversant with the history of science possibly pretend that beauty (or simplicity for that matter) is a guarantor of truth. In the case of simplicity or economy, there is the pragmatist's objection that the simpler a theory is, the simpler it is to use. Relationships apparently elected for their simplicity may also turn out to be grounded in some other theoretical constraint, invisible to the superficial glance.[100] To complicate matters still further, the idea that aesthetic criteria may arbitrate between contending theories fails to recognise that each may have its own distinctive appeal, with a resulting impasse if the aesthetic components provide the sole criterion for choice.

How serious are these complications for the religious apologist seeking to capitalise on perceptions of beauty in scientific work? The problem of the impasse if aesthetic criteria alone are given weight is perhaps more hypothetical than real given that they are rarely deployed in isolation from other constraints.[101] As we have noted, Tycho Brahe had aesthetic objections to the expanded Copernican

universe because it created an unseemly chasm between the outer-
most planet and the nearest star. But he also had physical and
biblical objections to a moving earth, eventually focussing his attack
on the alleged inadequacy of Copernicus's observations.[102] An apologist might also refer to those celebrated cases where a theory *has*
withstood attempts at falsification, *has* proved fruitful, and, as in the
case of general relativity, *has* retained an elegance on which there
seems to be consensus. In such cases the survival of the aesthetic
component may, for some scientists, if not a majority, generate a
sense of contact with those verities not of their making and which, in
Heisenberg's phrase, have been there since the creation of the
world. If there is consensus on the beauty of relativity theory this also
suggests that prescriptions can be given that would allow an aesthetic
experience to be shared, thereby nullifying the objection that it
would be confined to the first moment of formulation or
'discovery'.[103] Religious apologists might, therefore, feel that they are
not thwarted by the obvious objections. Writing as both physicist and
Christian theologian, John Polkinghorne provides an excellent
example of how a response to beauty can mediate between the practice of science and the affirmation of a religious orthodoxy. For
Polkinghorne the abstract beauty of a scientific theory does more
than convert into an argument for scientific realism. It also points to
a mystery beyond itself. In his terms, it is the Creator's joy in creation
which lies behind the human experience of beauty.[104]

   This kind of affirmation clearly survives; but the question may still
remain whether the pages of history are not littered with beautiful
delusions. Much of Kepler's work, for example, appears to have been
inspired and sustained by what, in retrospect, was the forlorn hope
of correlating the arrangement and spacing of planetary orbits with
what they would be if they were wrapped around the regular Greek
solids. It may also be correct to speak of delusions when referring to
Newton's belief in a unified harmonic theory of light and colour, or
Faraday's belief in the interconvertibility of gravitational and electrical forces, or even Einstein's refusal to admit the implications of
the indeterminacy principle as interpreted by Heisenberg and Bohr.
But in each case the belief in some kind of unity and harmony in
nature had inspired brilliant work of enduring significance.

   It therefore seems appropriate to ask whether the historically-
based objection adds up to anything more than that science is a
fallible process? It would surely only do so if it could be shown that
conjectures based on aesthetic considerations had, on balance, been
more fallible historically than those in which such considerations
had played no part. When discussing the role of guiding principles

in science a distinction is usually drawn between treating them as dogmas and as methodological prescriptions. It is a distinction that has often been made when discussing the scope of 'reductionist' models in the life sciences, and indeed in other academic disciplines.[105] Reductionism as a research strategy can be distinguished from reductionism as an epistemological claim. The attempt to analyse wholes in terms of the behaviour of their parts does not commit one to the claim that the concepts, theories or laws applicable to one level of analysis can be derived from those that pertain to another. Nor does reductionism as a principle of method commit one to the kind of ontological reductionism assumed in claims that a living system is 'nothing but' a collection of physical and chemical processes. But if we may speak of 'methodological reductionism' there seems no good reason to exclude a category of 'methodological aestheticism'. Delusion – and success – have accompanied both. The distinction might even be of service to the apologist. It would allow one to say that the quest for economy, elegance and beauty does usually regulate scientific enquiry without denying that it has produced fantasies as well as facts.

A rather different objection to the apologetic moves might, however, arise at this point. When scientists speak of harmony and beauty in their maps of the natural world, is not this a rhetorical ploy in the specific context of communicating with a wider audience? This is a pertinent objection because insufficient attention is generally paid to the kind of text in which such terms are used. As we observed in chapter 1, scientists undoubtedly do adopt different conventions when writing for their peers and for the general populace. Yet it would surely be wrong to suggest that affirmations of elegance and beauty are merely an affectation.[106] They may be an attractive way of engaging an audience, of making science seem more like an art form. But there is more to it than this. There is ample evidence that words like beauty and elegance are heard within laboratories and not merely in works of popularisation. A physical chemist might speak of beautiful spectra, of the internal harmony of a molecular crystal, of the resemblance between polymer structures and minimalist music.[107] Whether the scientist in question be Faraday, Darwin or Einstein, aesthetic motives in the quest for a unified theory were a driving force and not an excrescence.[108] It might be objected that the intellectual coherence achieved by Darwin's theory, its imposition of order on a complex web of biogeographical and paleontological data, cannot offer the same kind of aesthetic experience as the mathematical formalism of relativity theory. But no-one could pretend that the aesthetic experience derived from an immersion in the *Ring* cycle of Wagner is of the same kind as that derived from a finely spun melody of Bellini.

We are still left with the most powerful objection with which a religious apologist has to contend. This concerns the move from aesthetic appreciation to theistic reference. Surely any inference from the nature of the finite to the nature of the transcendent remains susceptible to Hume's critique? The objection may also take a theological as well as a philosophical turn in that the experience of beauty, either directly in nature itself or through the mediation of scientific theory, may lack potency in drawing those affected to the kind of deity favoured by the apologist. Writing in the nineteenth century, when the beauties of creation had been extolled by the nature poets as never before, Thomas Chalmers noted, with regret, that to be so moved was not necessarily to be moved in the right direction.[109] There is a thesis that the emotional states associated with aesthetic experience are closely allied to those accompanying the awareness of a trans-temporal reality. But a more recent critic than Chalmers has recalled the aphorism that many have mistaken the vibrations of a 32-foot organ pipe for the witness of the Holy Spirit.[110] Joking apart, the issues here are exceedingly subtle. No one could have been more forceful than Karl Barth in renouncing attempts to reason from the harmonies of creation to the existence and attributes of the deity.[111] Yet in Mozart's music Barth claimed to hear harmonies *analogous* to the harmony of God's good creation and *parables* of God's free grace.[112] It must be clear that there is no kind of 'proof' that would take one from aesthetic experience to a transcendent deity. A compatibility of aesthetic with religious experience is, however, another matter, as it clearly was for Barth.

Theologising about the experience of beauty in science (or in the arts) has finally to contend with a mundane problem. Apologetic inferences may be too narrowly conceived if they gloss over alternative secular philosophies of science in which the appreciation of elegance or beauty becomes an end in itself. The intellectual pleasure derived from science certainly can be a form of hedonism; and the pleasure itself can be intensified if plausible scientific models happen to fit a metaphysical preference. The conformity of scientific discovery to a metaphysical expectation offers an experience that has itself been called aesthetic.[113] This is an important point because it means that scientific naturalists, atheists and materialists have had their pleasure too. Think what delight T. H. Huxley took in Darwin's theory when he realised that it conformed to his hope and expectation. His hope had been that a theory would emerge to displace the recourse to divine intervention. He could

therefore celebrate Darwin's *Origin of Species* as a triumphal fulfilment of the metaphysical principles of nature's continuity and
uniformity.[114]

The Conformity of Science to Metaphysical Expectation

Michael Polanyi spoke of Neo-Darwinism as a theory that 'beautifully
fits into a mechanistic system of the universe'.[115] This was a tacit
acknowledgement that the accordance of theories with general
metaphysical principles can indeed be a source of aesthetic satisfaction. The question then becomes whether the theist, who sees in
certain scientific advances a corroboration of theism, enjoys an
essentially different experience from the materialist who might make
a similar claim. A topical example comes from modern cosmology.
In the fine-tuning of the universe, theists may discover features of
their world that bring intense pleasure: they conform to what one
would expect if the universe had been in some sense planned.[116] But
it is always open to the sceptic or atheist to protest that our universe
may be only one of whole families of universes, perhaps the only one
which, by chance, had the necessary parameters to survive.[117]

For the sceptic or atheist this extension of Darwinian natural selection to universes themselves can surely yield a comparable pleasure.
To judge from some reviews of Daniel Dennett's book *Darwin's
Dangerous Idea*, this is emphatically the case. Dennett's discussion of
the cosmological theory that whole families of universes have been
'born' out of black holes is described by one reviewer as 'deliciously
up to date'.[118] It is that word 'deliciously' that catches the eye. There
is evidently pleasure to be had when a topical theory rebuffs the
claim that only by reference to a designer God can one possibly
explain the propitious features of our universe. The theist may claim,
as Richard Swinburne continues to do, that a monotheistic explanation for the unity of the universe is objectively the simplest as well
as the most pleasing.[119] But that does not settle the matter because
of comparable meta-level pleasures available to the sceptic on the
basis of alternative schemata. Thus we find Richard Dawkins, in a
vehement reply to Swinburne, complaining that a deity who keeps a
billion fingers on a billion electrons is about the most complicated
hypothesis one could envisage.[120]

The historian finds such exchanges arresting precisely because, in
the past, the debate has not always revolved around easily cate-
gorised scientific advances, some favourable to theism others to
atheism. Historically it has often been the same advances that have

given solace to both parties.[121] Polanyi's reference to a 'mechanistic system of the universe' may conceal the fact that a system, initially conceived as a way of reinforcing Christian theism, in later hands became an instrument of aggression against the Christian Churches.[122] The fact is that such key terms in the reconstruction of nature as 'mechanism', 'law', 'power', 'conservation', natural 'selection', and many more, are metaphors susceptible of competing meanings – some theistic, some entirely naturalistic.[123]

There is an example of this susceptibility in recent discussions of evolutionary theory. Writers prepared to embrace a form of theistic evolution often dwell on the creative interplay of law and chance. This is true of Arthur Peacocke who has given special weight to the disclosure from thermodynamics that organic molecules have the power to organise themselves. In this discovery is seen a reinforcement of *theistic* evolution, in that it is what one might expect to find if some kind of creative evolution had been intended.[124] John Bowker has made the same point:

> We have now moved in a short space from near zero probability to inevitability in the origin of life. Although the former might seem to offer the clearest opportunity to invoke the agency of God (as one who is necessary to bring about the near-impossible), that is simply another instance of the 'God-of-the gaps' argument. It is the latter – the very fact of regularity which compels the argument to search (successfully) for inevitability – which supplies the most powerful illustration of the coherence of the appeal to personal agency.[125]

But would not the materialist claim a similar coherence? If matter has within itself the powers that have made evolution possible, if there has been a form of necessity endemic in the process, why need there be an appeal to a deity at all? Certainly in the seventeenth century, the notion of such *self*-organising matter was eschewed by Christian writers precisely because it *was* thought to imply the autonomy of nature.[126] Conversely, the contingencies in the evolutionary process have been harnessed for both theistic and atheistic purposes.[127] Where the theist might celebrate elements of spontaneity in a process of continuous creation, the atheist rejoices in the opportunity to ascribe our presence in the world to 'chance'.

To sample the satisfaction of the atheist we might consider an address to the South Place Ethical Society given by the Oxford chemist Peter Atkins. In polemical vein he spoke of the simplicity discoverable through the sciences as epitomising a cultural goal in opposition to the complexities of religion and superstition.[128] It is not a little ironic that extremes appear to come together in that both

Atkins and Swinburne favour an objectivist account of simplicity. The greatest aesthetic satisfaction, according to Atkins, should come from the revelation, through science, of the unity and simplicity of nature. His diatribe against 'religion' (as so often reduced to a thing) concludes with an antithesis typical of a rationalist sermon: 'Religion regards human intelligence as too puny to master understanding, and urges us to resort to elaborated superstition. Science, in contrast, respects the power of human comprehension and shows the supreme power and joy of rational, public testable investigation.'[129]

When he claims that 'religion emerged from magic' Atkins seems not to know that the same could be said of science.[130] When he says that philosophers have contributed little to our understanding of nature, he seems to forget that Newton would have called himself a philosopher. When he says that theologians have contributed nothing, he neglects that distinguished lineage of theologians who have been advocates of science. The original architect of the natural sciences tripos at Cambridge was one: William Whewell, whom we met in earlier chapters. When Atkins speaks of the unity and simplicity of nature as if these terms belong to scientific discourse alone, he seems not to know that they have been constitutive of an extensive literature of natural theology in which the beauty of the world pointed beyond itself. It was the unity of the world both presupposed and revealed in Newtonian mechanics that helped persuade William Paley and his predecessors of the case for monotheism. It was the unity of the evolutionary process that in the nineteenth century persuaded Asa Gray and Frederick Temple of the plausibility of theistic evolution.

The effect of Atkins' dogmas is to create a cultural dichotomy: science, high on its pedestal; the arts down and out on the floor. One would have hoped that his awareness of aesthetic sensitivity within the sciences might have encouraged greater subtlety. If scientists have frequently studied nature as if it were a work of art, the dichotomy is surely too crude. When Einstein gave a memorial address in honour of the physicist Karl Schwarzschild, he perfectly captured this aspect of scientific endeavour: 'The mainsprings of Schwarzschild's motivations in his restless theoretical quests seem less from a curiosity to learn the deeper inner relationships among the different aspects of Nature than from an artist's delight in discerning delicate mathematical patterns.'[131] By contrast, when scientific rationalists declare, as Atkins does, that 'science appears to be omnicompetent', that scientists 'see further into truth than any of their contemporaries',[132] this may not be the most tactful way of promoting the public understanding of science. It is certainly not the most effective because it fuels expectations of infallibility which controversy between experts then belies.

For those like Atkins who wish to pit science against religion the crucial goal appears to be an explanation of how the universe came out of absolutely nothing. But it is very doubtful whether such an explanation would have the desired effect because religious beliefs are not simply substitutes where scientific knowledge is lacking. They provide resources, myths and symbols that, for many, give inspiration and meaning to life in the here and now. How something might have come out of nothing before there was time is an enthralling question but is likely to remain tangential to our existential and moral concerns. Nor is it clear that theists would have to admit defeat if it could be shown that universes are born out of black holes or nothing at all. They might argue that explanations given within the terms of the natural sciences cannot escape certain 'givens'.[133] References to the quantum fluctuation of a vacuum, for example, still presuppose what were once called laws of nature and a reality that behaves accordingly. The atheist's response might be to say that it is inappropriate to speak in this way because the laws came with the universe and the task is to explain why they were as they were. But in the theory that might finally give the rationalists what they want, is it not likely that others will find an elegance, a beauty even, that will continue to beckon to that unfathomable beyond?

It is not our contention that theology can do any better than science when probing these 'limit questions'. Our examination of aesthetic discourse within the sciences nevertheless lends support to what John Hick has called the 'religious ambiguity of the universe'.[134] Arguments drawn from nature, and from nature as reconstructed through the sciences, simply cannot decide the question between theism and naturalism. The choice has to be made on other grounds but, once made, may affect in the deepest way possible the meaning seen in nature's powers. As historians we find ourselves drawn to Hick's conclusion, which is not as negative as it may seem. At the very least it stands in judgement over excessive and misplaced dogmatism of the kind one finds in both popular religious and scientistic affirmation.

NOTES

1 G. Steiner, *Real Presences*, London, 1989, 76.
2 *Ibid.*, 225.

3   *Ibid.*, 227. In a much publicised lecture which opened the 50th Edinburgh Festival, Steiner appeared to have changed his tune, lamenting the impotence of a culture in which sensibilities are shaped by aesthetics, by their identification with fictions and by an enchantment with the past. It is the sciences, he now claimed, that should have prominence in the festivals of tomorrow. Indeed, he briefly alluded to the 'criteria of elegance, of beauty, of harmony in mathematics as old as Pythagoras or Plato but now hidden from all who cannot master the languages, dare one say, the poetry of algebra'. *Idem.*, 'A festival overture', 11 August 1996, Edinburgh, 1996, 1–15, on 14.

4   N. Cartwright, *How the Laws of Physics Lie*, Oxford, 1983, especially 52–3, 165.

5   A. Koestler, *The Sleepwalkers*, Harmondsworth, 1964, 334.

6   The frustrations experienced by Kepler along his tortuous route to the ellipse have served to underline the inadequacy of both inductivist and hypothetico-deductivist accounts of scientific 'discovery'. N. R. Hanson, *Patterns of Discovery*, Cambridge, 1958, ch. 4.

7   P. Sherry, *Spirit and Beauty: An Introduction to Theological Aesthetics*, Oxford, 1992, 35–6.

8   R. Harries, *Art and the Beauty of God: A Christian Understanding*, London, 1993, 15.

9   *Ibid.*, 75 and 102.

10   A. O'Hear, 'Science and religion', *British Journal for the Philosophy of Science*, 44 (1993), 505–16, on 512.

11   *Ibid.*, 513.

12   *Ibid.*

13   N. Jardine, *The Scenes of Inquiry: On the Reality of Questions in the Sciences*, Oxford, 1991, 208–9.

14   *Ibid.*, 210–11.

15   S. Y. Edgerton, 'Galileo, Florentine "Disegno" and the "strange spotted-nesse" of the moon', *Art Journal*, Fall 1984, 225–31; S. J. Dick, *Plurality of Worlds: The Extraterrestrial Life Debate from Democritus to Kant*, Cambridge, 1982, 75–6, 130, 179–80.

16   J. O'Neill, 'Science, wonder and the lust of the eyes', *Journal of Applied Philosophy*, 10 (1993), 139–46.

17   M. Polanyi, *Personal Knowledge: Towards a Post-Critical Philosophy*, London, 1958, 133.

18   A. Blair, 'Tycho Brahe's critique of Copernicus and the Copernican system', *Journal of the History of Ideas*, 51 (1990), 355–77, on 364.

19   R. Merton, *Science, Technology and Society in Seventeenth-Century England*, New York, 1970, first published in *Osiris*, 4 (1938), 360–632; L. S. Feuer, *The Scientific Intellectual: The Psychological and Sociological Origins of Modern Science*, New York, 1963.

20   Dick, op. cit. (15), 61–70.

21   W. Charleton, *The Darkness of Atheism Dispelled by the Light of Nature: A Physico-Theological Treatise*, London, 1652, 168.

22 Galileo, *Sidereus Nuncius*, Venice, 1610, translated by S. Drake, *Discoveries and Opinions of Galileo*, New York, 1957, 21–58, on 45.

23 The reasoning behind Lansbergen's position is discussed most fully by K. J. Howell, 'Copernicanism and Biblical Interpretation in Early Modern Protestant Europe', PhD dissertation, Lancaster University, 1995, ch. 5. Further comments on the ambivalence of the Copernican innovation in its implications for the status of humanity will be found in J. H. Brooke, *Science and Religion: Some Historical Perspectives*, Cambridge, 1991, 82–116.

24 N. Copernicus, *De Revolutionibus Orbium Coelestium*, Nuremberg, 1543, Preface.

25 O. Gingerich, ' "Crisis" versus aesthetic in the Copernican Revolution', in *Vistas in Astronomy* (ed. A. Beer and K. Strand), 17 (1975), 85–95.

26 Cited by R. S. Westman, 'Proof, poetics, and patronage', in *Reappraisals of the Scientific Revolution* (ed. D. C. Lindberg and R. S. Westman), Cambridge, 1990, 167–205, on 182.

27 *Ibid.*

28 *Ibid.*, 182–3.

29 N. Jardine, *The Birth of History and Philosophy of Science: Kepler's A Defence of Tycho against Ursus, with Essays on its Provenance and Significance*, Cambridge, 1984.

30 M. Kemp, *The Science of Art: Optical Themes in Western Art from Brunelleschi to Seurat*, New Haven and London, 1990, 49–50. This is a particularly rich resource for examining the multiplicity of uses, including the religious, to which anamorphic images could be put. For example, Kemp shows how two seventeenth-century theorists, the Minim fathers Jean-François Nicero and Emmanuel Maignan, used geometrical artifice to achieve effects analogous to natural magic: 'Their images of saints were insinuated by optical means into frescoes which appeared in the guise of peculiar landscapes when viewed from the front. The saints thus manifested the hidden spiritual order of God's creation, which to the casual eye merely seems a chaos of disparate forms.' *Ibid.*, 211.

31 F. Hallyn, *The Poetic Structure of the World: Copernicus and Kepler*, New York, 1993, 97–103.

32 *Ibid.*, 94.

33 E. McMullin, 'Rationality and paradigm change in science', in *World Changes: Thomas Kuhn and the Nature of Science* (ed. P. Horwich), Cambridge, MA, 1993, 55–78.

34 Howell, op. cit. (23), ch. 5.

35 T. Digges, *A Perfect Description of the Celestial Orbs*, London, 1576; M. B. Hall, *Nature and Nature's Laws*, London, 1970, 26–7.

36 M. Caspar, *Kepler*, London, 1959, 282–4. For Kepler's enduring preoccupation with a geometrical harmony of the heavens, see J. V. Field, *Kepler's Geometrical Cosmology*, London, 1988.

37 Polanyi, op. cit. (17), 142–5.

38 P. M. Rattansi, 'Art and science: the Paracelsian vision', in *Science and the Arts in the Renaissance* (ed. J. W. Shirley and F. D. Hoeniger), London, 1985, 50–58, especially 50.

39 J. Glanvill, *The Vanity of Dogmatizing: The Three 'Versions'*, with a critical introduction by S. Medcalf, Harvester Renaissance Library: 1, Hove, 1970, xxiii.

40 J. Needham, *The Grand Titration: Science and Society in East and West*, London, 1969, 21–2, 323–8.

41 R. Boyle, 'About the excellency and grounds of the mechanical philosophy' (1674), in *Selected Philosophical Papers of Robert Boyle* (ed. M. A. Stewart), Manchester, 1979, 138–54.

42 On the rhetorical force of appeals to intelligibility, see K. Hutchinson, 'What happened to occult qualities in the Scientific Revolution?', *Isis*, 73 (1982), 233–53. Among other epistemic virtues, Boyle valued the extensiveness of mechanical explanations, in that the variables of matter and motion were sufficient to explain diversity. A mechanical philosophy was commended because it was applicable to the minute particles of bodies, removing the need for the more opaque concept of substantial form. Boyle also recommended it for its universality, in that mechanical principles were suited to the accommodation rather than exclusion of any other hypothesis founded on nature. And if these were not virtues enough, Boyle added self-consistency for good measure. When justifying his claim that a mechanical philosophy could be extended to the microstructure of matter, Boyle made explicit appeal to human artifacts: 'yet an artist, according to the quantity of the matter he employs, the exigency of the design he undertakes, and the magnitude and shape of the instruments he uses, is able to make pieces of work of the same nature or kind, of extremely different bulks where yet the like art, contrivance and motion may be observed'. Boyle, op. cit. (41), 143.

43 J. A. Bennett, 'The mechanics' philosophy and the mechanical philosophy', *History of Science*, 24 (1986), 1–28.

44 On the diversity of use of mechanical philosophies, see Brooke, op. cit. (23), 117–91.

45 B. C. Southgate, *"Covetous of Truth": The Life and Work of Thomas White, 1593–1676*, Dordrecht, 1993, 79, 115, 123. White's crypto-Protestant bid to purge the doctrine of purgatory was also helped by a mechanistic psychology: J. Henry, 'Atomism and eschatology: Catholicism and natural philosophy in the Interregnum', *British Journal for the History of Science*, 15 (1982), 211–39. It is difficult to disagree with Henry's conclusion that 'the mechanical philosophy could be (and was) used to provide a philosophical foundation for almost any ideological standpoint'. *Ibid.*, 237.

46 B. Fontenelle, *Entretiens sur la Pluralité des Mondes* [1686], English edn., Berkeley, 1990, 17.

47 For an analysis that stresses the pressure on Hooke to construct an apposite aesthetic discourse, see J. T. Harwood, 'Rhetoric and graphics in *Micrographia*', in *Robert Hooke: New Studies* (ed. M. Hunter and S. Schaffer), Woodbridge, 1989, 119–47.

48 R. Hooke, *Micrographia*, London, 1665, 162.

49 *Ibid.*, 2.

50 *Ibid.*, 4.

51 Spinoza even turned the argument upside down, observing how ugly the

hand looked under the magnification: W. Tatarkiewicz, *History of Aesthetics*, 3 vols., The Hague, 1970, iii, 369.

52 Hooke, op. cit. (48), 91–2.
53 N. E. Emerton, *The Scientific Reinterpretation of Form*, Ithaca, 1984, 145.
54 *Ibid.*, 149.
55 Charleton, op. cit. (21), 66–7.
56 *Ibid.*, 81.
57 R. Descartes, *Philosophical Writings: A Selection* (ed. E. Anscombe and P. T. Geach), London, 1954, 222.
58 Descartes to Chanut, 6 June 1647, *ibid.*, 292. An ingenious appeal to Genesis helped at this point. Since the creation narrative had been written for human understanding, and since the Holy Ghost had seen fit to give those particulars that were principally of human concern, the impression of anthropocentricity given by the biblical text was hardly surprising. *Ibid.*, 295.
59 *Ibid.*, 295.
60 *Ibid.*, 296.
61 Fontenelle, op. cit. (46), 12.
62 P. Gouk, 'The harmonic roots of Newtonian science', in *Let Newton Be!* (ed. J. Fauvel, R. Flood, M. Shortland and R. Wilson), Oxford, 1988, 101–25.
63 J. E. McGuire and P. M. Rattansi, 'Newton and the pipes of Pan', *Notes and Records of the Royal Society*, 21 (1966), 108–43.
64 S. Mandelbrote, ' "A duty of the greatest moment": Isaac Newton and the writing of biblical criticism', *British Journal for the History of Science*, 26 (1993), 281–302, on 300.
65 Newton, Keynes MS 33, Cambridge University Library; *ibid.*, 301.
66 K. Thomas, *Man and the Natural World*, Harmondsworth, 1984, 166.
67 *Ibid.*, 167.
68 Polanyi, op. cit. (17), 3–4, 148.
69 J. Ray, *The Wisdom of God Manifested in the Works of Creation*, 7th edn., London, 1717, 176.
70 Thomas, op. cit. (66), 168–9.
71 Ray, op. cit. (69), 176.
72 *Ibid.*, 177.
73 Dick, op. cit. (15), 127.
74 R. Bentley, *A Confutation of Atheism*, Sermon preached on 7 November 1692, in *Isaac Newton's Papers and Letters on Natural Philosophy* (ed. I. B. Cohen), Cambridge, MA, 1978, 389.
75 In Query 31 of his *Opticks*, Newton wrote that 'if natural philosophy in all its parts ... shall at length be perfected, the bounds of moral philosophy will be also enlarged. For so far as we can know by natural philosophy what is the first cause, what power he has over us, and what benefits we receive from him, so far our duty toward him, as well as that toward one another, will appear to us by the light of nature.' *Newton's Philosophy of Nature: Selections from his Writings* (ed. H. S. Thayer), New York, 1953, 179.
76 Newton to Harington, 30 May 1698, in *Correspondence of Isaac Newton* (ed.

A. R. Hall, J. F. Scott, L. Tilling and H. W. Turnbull), 7 vols., Cambridge, 1959–77, iv, 274.

77 *Ibid.*, 275.

78 S. S. Genuth, 'Devil's hells and astronomers' heavens: religion, method, and popular culture in speculations about life on comets', in *The Invention of Physical Science: Intersections of Mathematics, Theology and Natural Philosophy since the Seventeenth Century* (ed. M. J. Nye, J. L. Richards and R. H. Stuewer), Dordrecht, 1992, 3–26, especially 11–12.

79 C. Linnaeus, *Reflections on the Study of Nature* [1754], cited in D. C. Goodman, *Buffon's Natural History*, Milton Keynes, 1980, 18.

80 A. O. Lovejoy, *The Great Chain of Being* [1936], reprint edn., New York, 1960. The appeal of linear models of evolution, with the process consummated in humankind, is discussed with particular reference to Herder and Goethe by Jardine, op. cit. (13), 34, 40–3, 193.

81 D. Kohn, 'Theories to work by: rejected theories, reproduction, and Darwin's path to natural selection', *Studies in the History and Philosophy of Biology*, 4 (1980), 67–170, especially 81–113; D. Ospovat, *The Development of Darwin's Theory*, Cambridge, 1981; J. H. Brooke, 'The relations between Darwin's science and his religion', in *Darwinism and Divinity* (ed. J. R. Durant), Oxford, 1985, 40–75. For later, critical reflections on what Darwin meant by 'perfect adaptation', see D. Kohn, 'Darwin's ambiguity: the secularization of biological meaning', *British Journal for the History of Science*, 22 (1989), 215–39.

82 D. M. Knight, *Humphry Davy: Science and Power*, Oxford, 1992, 68.

83 *Ibid.*, 78.

84 J. H. Brooke, 'Like minds: the God of Hugh Miller', in *Hugh Miller and the Controversies of Victorian Science* (ed. M. Shortland), Oxford, 1996, 171–86.

85 Anon, 'Is Nature perfect?', *Monthly Journal of Science*, London, 1879, 271–6.

86 *The Life and Letters of Charles Darwin* (ed. F. Darwin), 3 vols., 3rd. edn., London, 1887, i, 311–12.

87 Kohn, 'Darwin's ambiguity', op. cit. (81), 234. See also Jardine, op. cit. (13), 212–24.

88 A. Desmond and J. Moore, *Darwin*, London, 1991, 122.

89 Kohn, 'Darwin's ambiguity', op. cit. (81), 238.

90 Darwin, op. cit. (86), i, 312.

91 *Ibid.*

92 S. Chandrasekhar, *Truth and Beauty: Aesthetics and Motivations in Science*, Chicago, 1987, 64–73, 166. Chandrasekhar rightly warns of the dangers of dilettantism in the explication of what it means to say of a theory that it is beautiful. It must, he suggests, have a certain strangeness, an exceptional quality, which means that, as one follows the reasoning of its author, one experiences the same sense of a veil being lifted. Polanyi, too, spoke of an unfamiliar beauty when discussing Einstein's construction: Polanyi, op. cit. (17), 144.

93 A. Pais, *'Subtle is the Lord': The Science and the Life of Albert Einstein*, Oxford, 1982, 27.

94 Chandrasekhar, op. cit. (92), 68.

95 Cited by Pais, op. cit. (93), 27.

96 This anecdote, taken from G. J. Whitrow, *Einstein: The Man and his Achievement*, appears in *Einstein: A Centenary Volume* (ed. A. P. French), London, 1979, 79.

97 E. P. Wigner, 'The unreasonable effectiveness of mathematics', in *Mathematics: People, Problems, Results* (ed. D. M. Campbell and J. C. Higgins), 3 vols., Belmont, Calif., 1984, iii, 116–25, on 124.

98 F. Close: Interview reported in *The Daily Telegraph*, 3 November 1993.

99 Chandrasekhar, op. cit. (92), 22.

100 A classic example would be the atomic theory of John Dalton, who assumed that when two elements can produce more than one compound, the first in the series must be of the form A + B rather than 2A + B or A + 2B. This looks like the perfect example of a simplicity axiom at work, though with a less than perfect result since the formula for water, on this basis, had to be HO. Closer analysis suggests that Dalton's choice was regulated by a theoretical consideration of a different kind. Dalton believed that identical atoms were surrounded by identical heat envelopes and that between them would be repulsion. Consequently a compound of the form 2A + B would be less stable than one of the form A + B because of repulsion between the A atoms. This example, which shows how a 'simple' hypothesis can be deceptive, false and yet fruitful is discussed by W. H. Brock, *The Fontana History of Chemistry*, London, 1992, 136–47.

101 E. McMullin, 'The shaping of scientific rationality: construction and constraint', in *Construction and Constraint: The Shaping of Scientific Rationality* (ed. E. McMullin), Notre Dame, 1988, 1–47.

102 Blair, op. cit. (18).

103 Thus Polanyi made the point that the data that become more beautiful in the light of a particular theory are also likely to be the 'facts' that assume a greater interest for a scientific *community* and not merely for the person who first constructed the theory: Polanyi, op. cit. (17), 135, 145.

104 J. Polkinghorne, *Serious Talk: Science and Religion in Dialogue*, London, 1996, 8, 38, 56, 110.

105 A. R. Peacocke, *An Introduction to the Physical Chemistry of Biological Organization*, Oxford, 1983, 12–13, 268–72; *idem.* (ed.), *Reductionism in Academic Disciplines*, Guildford, 1985; I. G. Barbour, *Religion in an Age of Science: The Gifford Lectures 1989–1991*, i, London, 1990, 165–8.

106 The same riposte is made by Jardine, op. cit. (13), 205.

107 P. Laszlo, *La Parole des Choses*, Paris, 1993, 181–218.

108 G. Cantor, *Michael Faraday: Sandemanian and Scientist*, London, 1991, 168–74, 245–58; F. H. T. Rhodes, 'Darwin's search for a theory of the Earth: symmetry, simplicity and speculation', *British Journal for the History of Science*, 24 (1991), 193–229; Pais, op. cit. (93), 31–4, 138–47.

109 D. Cairns, 'Thomas Chalmers' *Astronomical Discourses*: a study in natural theology', *Scottish Journal of Theology*, 9 (1956), 410–21, reprinted in *Science and Religious Belief* (ed. C. A. Russell), Milton Keynes, 1973, 195–204, on 203.

110 E. J. Sharpe, Review of F. D. Martin, *Art and the Religious Experience*, in *Religious Studies*, 11 (1975), 381–3.

111 E. Brunner, *Natural Theology*, transl. P. Fraenkel, comprising Brunner's 'Nature and Grace' and Karl Barth's reply 'No!', London, 1946.

112 R. J. Palma, *Karl Barth's Theology of Culture*, Allison Park, Penn., 1983; T. F. Torrance, 'The transfinite significance of beauty in science and theology', in *L'Art, La Science et La Métaphysique* (ed. P. Lang), L'Académie Internationale de Philosophie de l'Art, Berne, Berlin, New York and Paris, 1993, 393–418.

113 J. W. McAllister, 'Truth and beauty in scientific reason', *Synthèse*, 78 (1989), 25–51.

114 T. H. Huxley, 'On the reception of the "Origin of Species"', in *The Life and Letters of Charles Darwin*, op. cit. (86), ii, 179–204, especially 197–8.

115 Polanyi, op. cit. (17), 136.

116 Polkinghorne, op. cit. (104), 68–72; J. D. Barrow and F. J. Tipler, *The Anthropic Cosmological Principle*, Oxford, 1988.

117 J. Leslie, 'How to draw conclusions from a fine-tuned universe', in *Physics, Philosophy and Theology: A Common Quest for Understanding* (ed. R. J. Russell, W. R. Stoeger and G. V. Coyne), Vatican, 1988, 297–311.

118 J. Gribbin, *Sunday Times*, 24 September 1995.

119 R. G. Swinburne, *The Existence of God*, Oxford, 1979, 141–2; *idem.*, *The Christian God*, Oxford, 1994, 126, 155, 167–8, 170, 232, 237.

120 R. Dawkins, 'God only knows', *Sunday Times*, 4 February 1996.

121 J. H. Brooke, 'Science and the fortunes of natural theology: some historical perspectives', *Zygon*, 24 (1989), 3–22.

122 Brooke, op. cit.(23), 117–51.

123 For the metaphor of 'selection', this point was forcefully made by R. M. Young, *Darwin's Metaphor: Nature's Place in Victorian Culture*, Cambridge, 1985, 126–63.

124 Peacocke, op. cit. (105), 216, 263–4; *idem.*, *Creation and the World of Science*, Oxford, 1979, 92–111; *idem.*, 'Biological evolution and Christian theology – yesterday and today', in *Darwinism and Divinity*, op. cit. (81), 101–30.

125 J. Bowker, 'Did God create this Universe?', in *The Sciences and Theology in the Twentieth Century* (ed. A. R. Peacocke), London, 1981, 98–126, on 118.

126 A classic example would be R. Boyle, 'An essay, containing a requisite digression, concerning those that would exclude the deity from intermeddling with matter' (1663), in *Selected Philosophical Papers of Robert Boyle*, op. cit. (41), 155–75.

127 On the side of theism, C. S. Peirce argued that the execution of predetermined ends is a purely mechanical process, leaving no room for development or growth. The recognition of chance and contingency in biological evolution meant for Peirce that the process was inseparable from the idea of a personal Creator. See *Philosophers of Process* (ed. D. Browning), New York, 1965, 57–109. An atheistic response to the high degree of contingency is clearly visible in J. Monod, *Chance and Necessity*, New York, 1971. In an unpublished commentary Ernan McMullin has argued that however much contingency might be identified in evolutionary processes, however overwhelming the dearth of *recognisable* design, this is of no consequence for those who wish to affirm divine purposes in

the world – as long as the doctrine of God's eternality is maintained. E. McMullin, 'Evolutionary contingency and cosmic purpose', a discussion paper presented to the Consultation on Science and Theology, Center for Theological Inquiry, Princeton, May 1996.

128 P. Atkins, 'What is science for? To free us from irrationality and superstition', *New Humanist*, 109 (July 1993), 9–12.

129 *Ibid.*

130 See the various contributions to *Occult and Scientific Mentalities in the Renaissance* (ed. B. Vickers), Cambridge, 1984. The emergence of Atkins' own science, chemistry, has been traced to a dialectical relationship between the natural magic of the Paracelsians and humanist critiques of the kind offered by the Lutheran Andreas Libavius. O. Hannaway, *The Chemists and the Word: The Didactic Origins of Modern Chemistry*, Baltimore, 1975.

131 Quoted by Chandrasekhar, op. cit. (92), 16s7.

132 Atkins, op. cit. (128).

133 See the discussion of 'limit questions' in W. Drees, *Religion, Science and Naturalism*, Cambridge, 1995; *idem.*, *Beyond the Big Bang: Quantum Cosmologies and God*, La Salle, 1990.

134 J. Hick, *An Interpretation of Religion*, London, 1989, 85–6, 94, 123–4.

Section IV: *Structuring Experience*

8
Biographical Narratives

There are many levels at which science and religion can be seen to interact. Yet commentators have usually discussed this interaction in terms of key concepts that bridge scientific theories and theological propositions. For example, Francis Oakley and others have demonstrated the role of voluntaristic theology in early modern science.[1] Although this bridging strategy deserves a central place within the science–religion domain, it should not exclude other approaches. One of the aims of this chapter is to move the focus away from the history of ideas and instead engage the life and experience of the individual, since it is through our life experiences that we directly engage both science and religion. If the self is accepted as a site worthy of study, then biography offers an appropriate genre for understanding the construction of science–religion relationships.

In writing biography the historian or biographer seeks to identify the various strands that mould the biographical subject. Religious background and sensibilities are often accorded prominence; indeed, contributors to the *New Dictionary of National Biography* are instructed to include information on their subjects' affiliation and degree of religious adherence. For a scientist a further important constituent will be the choice of career and research topic, together with the pressures generated in pursuing a life in science. Biography has also to engage the social and political currents that toss the individual. Both unities and disjunctions are often revealed as we witness the unfolding of an individual's life. Thus through biography we might come to appreciate the existential tensions encountered by scientists as they struggle to cope with the demands made both by science and by religion. Equally, both the theory and practice of science may express a person's celebration of God through the appreciation of lawlikeness and harmony perceived in the universe.

Despite the widespread popularity of biographies among the book-buying public, some academics remain rather reticent towards them. Until recently many historians of science eschewed scientific biography, perhaps considering it a genre more suited to retired scientists than to sophisticated scholars. For example, Alexandre Koyré, whose idealist and anti-Marxist views profoundly influenced the post-war generation of British and American historians, wrote extensively on Newton and Galileo but never attempted a biography of either. His most celebrated article, which is entitled 'The significance of the Newtonian synthesis', contained the absolute minimum of biographical detail about Newton. Instead, Koyré argued incisively that Newton's significance lay in his mathematisation of the cosmos and he particularly directed attention to Newton's innovative ways of conceptualising space, time and causality.[2] In Koyré's hands 'Newton' was not a person, in the conventional sense, but a peg from which to hang a clutch of scientific theories and metaphysical notions. Although Koyré's idealist approach was later challenged by a new generation of sociologically-informed historians they also downplayed biography but for a very different reason. They conceived individual lives subsumed within and explained by broader social and institutional forces. Despite being concerned with social background, these social historians of science tended to portray Newton or Darwin as cyphers representing certain social interests. More recent fashions, such as deconstruction and the analysis of 'laboratory life', have likewise decentred scientific biography.

However, over the last decade or two there has been a greater willingness to accept biography as an exacting genre that raises a host of demanding historiographical problems. Several academic meetings have recently been held on the subject and the first volume of collected essays devoted specifically to analysing scientific biography was published in 1996.[3] There are also some excellent exemplars in print, such as Richard Westfall's portrait of 'restless' Newton, Janet Browne's insightful treatment of Darwin's personality, the more heady politicised account of Darwin by Adrian Desmond and James Moore, and the portrayal of Lord Kelvin as the son of industrial Glasgow, by Crosbie Smith and Norton Wise.[4] All these biographies are weighty tomes. Indeed, to portray adequately a rich and varied life spanning three score years and ten seems now to require several hundred, if not a thousand, pages. While the thickly-textured approach to biography possesses many advantages, this is not the place to explore the lives of individual scientists in so much depth and detail. Instead the brief biographies offered in this chapter are more akin to pencil sketches than to full-length portraits in oil.

Turning from science to religion we likewise find no shortage of biographies. Indeed, despite the problems of recovery, the lives of Jesus and Mohammed are often accepted as exemplary by the Christian and the Muslim respectively. The lives, thoughts and deeds of religious men and women – from Martin Luther to Martin Luther

King, and from Saint Thérèsa to Mother Teresa – have been recounted on numerous occasions.[5] While there is no one message to be read from the many volumes of religious biography, the biographical subject's religious experiences and moral attributes are frequently emphasised. Thus to quote James McClendon, biography has a major role to play in Christian theology since the recounting of 'singular or striking lives ... may serve to disclose and perhaps to correct or enlarge the community's moral vision'. McClendon also argues that biography is a proper vehicle to teach Christian ethics by example and thereby transform theology. 'Biography at its best', he claims, 'will be theology.'[6] If McClendon's use of biography sails rather too close to hagiography for comfort, many critical, scholarly biographies are to be found in religion as well as in science. It is also interesting to note that the philosopher Richard Rorty has advocated the study of biographies since they 'take us out of our old selves by the power of strangeness, to aid us in becoming new beings'. Although Rorty adopts a secular position, he, like McClendon, emphasises that reading biographical narratives can be a major source for personal renewal.[7]

In this chapter we shall illustrate the uses of biography by briefly sketching four Victorian lives: those of an Anglican, a dissenter, a Catholic and an agnostic. Each came from a different religious tradition; each had different educational experiences; each practised a different science and each conceived the science–religion nexus differently. Yet despite these contrasts their life-lines were not so isolated or distinct. They shared the environment of early Victorian Britain and their lives were buffeted by many of the same social, political, religious and scientific forces. Like other contemporary thinkers all four took firm stands on the pressing question of the interrelation between science and religion.[8] In this chapter we shall return to Charles Darwin's *Origin of Species* since its publication in 1859 provides a common locus for these biographical sketches. How our four subjects responded to this widely-discussed book can be understood in terms of their individual biographies.

One final point must be made before we meet these Victorians. Biographers and their publishers sometimes claim that they are offering the 'definitive biography' of some well-known character – usually a literary lion or a film star. Such a claim implies that the purchaser will be buying the master-narrative that follows the writer or film star from the cradle to the grave (and perhaps beyond). Yet, as with other historical genres, there is no single biographical story but rather a welter of contending narratives. To cite the example of Newton, biographers have offered us Newton the hero of science,

Newton the alchemist, Newton the autocrat who orchestrated the Royal Society, Newton the closet theologian who believed that he possessed a special and close personal relationship with God, and, of course, Newton the neurotic.[9] Many words may have been written on Newton, but never the last word.

John Tyndall (1820–1893), Agnostic

From a biographical stand-point Tyndall's Protestant Irish background is all-important. His father was an Orangeman and throughout his life John Tyndall consistently supported the Unionist

THE SCIENTIFIC VOLUNTEER.

"If ever I have to choose . . . . I shall, without hesitation, shoulder my rifle with the Orangeman."—*See Professor Tyndall's Reply to Sir W. V. Harcourt.* "*Times*," Feb. 13, 1890.

Figure 26: John Tyndall as depicted in *Punch* (1890).

cause. As to religious commitment he was less constant. Although he later related that as a child he was 'well versed in Scripture; for I loved the Bible, and was prompted by that love to commit large portions of it to memory',[10] he soon found that he could use this sharp mind to score points against Catholicism, which he viewed as the bastion of reaction and oppression. Thus in letters written to his father in 1841 he claimed that he was engaged in refuting the arguments for transubstantiation with the aid of a modicum of logic.[11] There are also indications that from early in his career he adopted an anti-supernaturalist position and insisted that humankind should stand on its own without expecting assistance from any divine agency. Having undermined Catholicism to his satisfaction, he then deployed the same critical apparatus to question his own religious tradition and in particular the doctrine of resurrection. As he later recalled, one major doctrinal difficulty was that he could not imagine how the particles composing one human body could be reassembled after having been dispersed at death, subsequently forming many different mixtures or compounds. Thus a particular atom that once formed a person's hand might combine with other atoms to form a flower, and later an insect or a worm. A most extra-ordinary concourse would be required at the Resurrection to reunite that atom perfectly with its neighbours so as to recompose the orig-inal hand. For the young Tyndall such a miracle seemed too far-fetched to be credible.[12]

His early social experience is also highly relevant. As a young man working with the Ordnance Survey in Preston he was deeply shocked to witness the massacre of a number of impoverished workers by soldiers during a bread riot.[13] Shortly thereafter he was sacked from the Survey for complaining about the conditions to which he and other employees were subjected. Fired by 'a burning zeal against injustice and oppression', he often aligned himself with the spirit, although not always with the policies, of the radicals.[14] Thomas Carlyle's *Past and Present* was a significant and early influence on Tyndall who particularly sympathised with Carlyle's insistence on the dignity of man and the paramount need to pursue truth. In his later writings he frequently cited Fichte, Goethe, Emerson and particularly Carlyle, with whom he shared a close friendship.[15] Carlyle's recognition of the nobility of the human spirit appealed to him greatly: 'I could see that his contention at bottom always was that the human soul has claims and yearnings that physical science cannot satisfy.' According to Carlyle, man possesses the ability to transcend this mundane life and to participate in the 'ethical and ideal side of human nature', which is the source of our strength and moral identity.[16] In accepting the ethical and transcendental side of human nature, Tyndall's soul was filled with the ideals of Romanticism, not Christianity.

Coming from a poor family Tyndall entered science by a circuitous route. At the end of the great railway boom he failed to obtain a satisfactory post as a surveyor but was hired in 1847 as a teacher at Queenwood College, which Robert Owen had earlier founded as a Socialist institution. A year later he proceeded to the University of Marburg where he sat at the feet of the eminent chemist Robert Wilhelm von Bunsen and several other leading scientists. By dint of hard work he completed his PhD in two years – rather than the normal three. Tyndall then returned to Queenwood in 1851 desperately seeking a scientific post while trying to make contacts in the scientific community and writing research papers. His break occurred in February 1853 when he delivered a lecture at the Royal Institution which was very well received and brought him to Michael Faraday's attention. Later that year he was hired as its Professor of Natural Philosophy. Although his low salary forced him to accept a great deal of outside work, including the editorship of the *Philosophical Magazine*, he now possessed a key post in Metropolitan science. He was a paradigm example of the Victorian self-made man.

While working in Marburg Tyndall studied the behaviour of crystals in a magnetic field and related their behaviour to modifications in the crystal's molecular arrangement. His subsequent work on heat and light was likewise directed to elucidating molecular structures. Tyndall increasingly found himself 'compelled to regard not only crystals, but organic structures, the body of man inclusive, as cases of molecular architecture, infinitely more complex … than those of inorganic nature, but reducible, in the long run, to the same mechanical laws'.[17] This was the basis of the materialistic creed that Tyndall espoused so vehemently in his 1874 Presidential Address before the British Association in Belfast.[18] For him the cutting edge of science lay in its ability to account for phenomena in terms of material particles and the laws governing their behaviour.

This public and widely-reported Address raised a storm and he was accused of preaching the atheistical doctrine of materialism. Yet such criticism failed to recognise that Tyndall's materialism was restricted to answering questions about the material universe. While the human body is material, Tyndall viewed the soul as decidedly non-materialistic and not reducible to matter. If we concentrate on the issue of materialism we are liable to overlook other religious issues raised by Tyndall's Address. The local context is particularly important since in returning to the country of his birth Tyndall took the opportunity to attack the Catholic authorities' attempts to control their flock by denying them an education in science. His anti-Catholic guns blazing, Tyndall recounted an appeal made the previous year by seventy students and ex-students of the Catholic University of Ireland who complained that the University failed to teach modern developments in the sciences, including the works of Lyell, Darwin and Huxley. Tyndall saw this as a typical example of censorship by the Catholic Church.[19]

Frequently engaged in skirmishes, Tyndall became a skilled and effective controversialist. On several occasions he crossed swords with that celebrated Glaswegian, William Thomson, later Lord Kelvin. In the midst of one controversy Peter Guthrie Tait, the professor of Natural Philosophy at Edinburgh, wrote to Thomson: 'I think we ought to crush Tyndall at once ... Such a nuisance must be abated, even at the risk of becoming [a] Commissioner of Sewers.'[20] This antipathy was exacerbated by their religious differences, especially Tyndall's dismissal of the design argument which both Thomson and Tait considered so important to science. Indeed, when invited to edit William Prout's *Bridgewater Treatise* he refused, claiming that 'if no better Deity than this can be purchased for the eight thousand pounds of the Earl of Bridgewater, it is a dear bargain'.[21] Yet, despite Tyndall's willingness to publicly challenge organised religion and Christian – especially Catholic – cant and dogma, he counted a number of churchmen among his friends, such as Dean Arthur Stanley, David Brewster, Louis Rendu and Françoise Moigno, the last two being French Catholics. In reviewing J. B. Mozley's 1865 Bampton Lectures on miracles he claimed that 'It is my privilege to enjoy the friendship of a select number of religious men, with whom I converse frankly upon theological subjects.'[22] With characteristic generosity, humour and honesty he subsequently related an unexpected encounter with Canon Henry Liddon, of St. Paul's, who, he claimed, must previously have

> pictured me ... as a creature with hoofs and horns. But we parted very cordially .... There is something wonderfully kind and sympathetic in the Canon's eye. The world will be better when such men rely upon their natural impulses instead of tacking on to them the tag, rag and bobtail of an impossible religion.[23]

The main reason why he considered Christianity 'impossible' was that it posited an interventionist supernatural being. Instead Tyndall insisted that humankind must be self-sufficient and not look for support from some hypothetical divine hand.

The Yale historian Frank Turner has labelled Tyndall one of the leading Victorian 'naturalists' – naturalism, in this instance, being contrasted with supernaturalism.[24] Another revealing insight into his religious sensibilities can be gained from an early letter to his friend Thomas Archer Hirst in which he reported an encounter with two 'Methodist fanatics' who were distributing pamphlets in the street. Although he denied any intellectual sympathy with their religious cause, he admitted deep admiration for 'the working of that spirit which keeps the world out of mud'.[25] Here we see an instance of the power of the human spirit that Tyndall the Romantic found so essential and so congenial. Tyndall's biographers rightly insist that he was not an atheist and instead suggest that he should be labelled an agnostic since he rejected the claims of both scientists and theologians who allowed science to be debased by ungrounded speculations. Yet he also readily admitted that our scientific knowledge is limited and he accepted that an incomprehensible power suffuses all of nature, ourselves included.[26] This deeply-held Romantic perception of nature distances Tyndall from Huxley and other more trenchant agnostics who took every opportunity to attack both the institutional and anti-materialistic aspects of religion.

Since most of his research was in physics Tyndall was not directly concerned with the implications of Darwin's theory of evolution for biology. Nevertheless, in a number of his essays and public lectures he championed evolution as a great stride in the search for truth and as a prime example of the freedom of thought. Here was an account of species, humankind included, that required no supernatural cause but was naturalistic through and through. Here also was a fine example of a truly scientific theory firmly underpinned by evidence and analogy. While Tyndall cautioned against claiming too much for the theory, he was bitterly opposed to those theologians who dismissed its powerful insights either from prejudice or from inadequate knowledge of the subject. Darwin's theory was, he claimed, concerned solely with the laws governing the organisation of matter, particularly the 'germs' that give rise to diverse organic forms. The theory had to be assessed critically by rational scientific criteria, against which it would either prove successful or be shown inadequate. He could see no relevant theological objections and argued that evolutionary biologists 'have as little fellowship with the atheist who says there is no God, as with the theist who professes to know the mind of God'.[27]

Moreover, as a fellow practitioner, Tyndall respected Darwin for his hard work and intellectual honesty. According to him Darwin 'shirks no difficulty' but 'moves over the subject with the passionless strength of a glacier', usually overcoming the objections of his opponents.[28] As one of the pioneers of glaciology Tyndall knew just how slowly and unrelentingly glaciers travelled!

St George Jackson Mivart (1827–1900), Catholic

Despite his hostility to Catholicism, Tyndall was certainly correct in pointing out how few Catholics adorned the ranks of British science. Among contemporary Catholic scientists none was better known than St George Jackson Mivart, the Professor of Comparative Anatomy at St Mary's Hospital Medical School in London. Another ardent polemicist, Mivart wrote extensively on the relationship between evolutionary theory and Catholicism but adopted positions and conclusions starkly opposed to Tyndall's.

According to his biographer, Mivart's father, who owned Mivart's Hotel (now Claridges), was a cosmopolitan man with a zest for learning. A Fellow of the Zoological Society, he presented his young son with a copy of Buffon's *Histoire Naturelle* and also encouraged his boyhood enthusiasm for collecting monkeys and reptiles.[29] If his father fostered his scientific leanings, his mother's evangelical commitments nurtured his youthful religious sensibilities. Although brought up in the Anglican communion, in his mid-teens he met a number of Tractarians and was carried on their wave of fervour. However, the aesthetics of architecture seems to have played a major role in driving him towards Catholicism. In particular, young Mivart was inspired by Augustus Pugin's vision of Gothic architecture in the service of Catholicism. Thus his biographer claims, 'it was the externals of the Church – its rituals, its language and its architecture – which chiefly concerned' Mivart, while his son stressed that his 'keen sense of the beauty of Gothic architecture brought him quickly to realize the sublimer beauty of Catholic ritual'.[30] After reading Pugin he toured several neo-Gothic Catholic churches, ending at St Chad's, Birmingham, where he received his first communion at the tender age of sixteen and a half. Now unable to proceed with his earlier intention of entering Oxford he joined several other recent converts at Oscott College, Birmingham, under Nicholas Wiseman's presidency.

Although Mivart later trained as a lawyer, science became his vocation, his two mentors being Richard Owen and Thomas Henry Huxley, who offered exciting but sharply contrasting ways of understanding living organisms. From Owen he learnt his zoology and particularly the skill of identifying structural homologies between the bones of different species. Mivart subsequently pursued this

Figure 27: Interior of St Chad's Cathedral, Birmingham, designed by Pugin,
that captivated young Mivart; courtesy of the Administrator, St Chad's
Cathedral, Birmingham.

programme in his own research on the comparative anatomy of
primates and, like Owen, envisaged archetypal structures reflected in
different species. This early passion for architecture and his highly-
developed aesthetic sensibility may help explain why he emphasised
teleological and architectonic principles in his anatomical

researches. The 'architecture of the universe' became his subject of study and he readily perceived God as its architect.[31] The importance to Mivart of aesthetic judgements in both science and religion is a further illustration of the theme explored in the preceding chapter.

Through Huxley Mivart was drawn into the Darwinian circle and shared in the excitement generated by Darwin's innovative theory. The evidence concerning his attitude to Darwinism in the early 1860s is somewhat contradictory. Although he declared in 1897 that he had initially withheld his vote either for or against the theory of natural selection – 'I was neither its opponent nor convinced it was untenable' – in an earlier article he maintained that he rapidly became 'a hearty and thoroughgoing disciple of Mr Darwin, and I accepted from him the view that Natural Selection was "*the* origin of species" '.[32] However strong his initial attraction to orthodox Darwinism, he later became its most persistent and able critic. So abrasive were his criticisms that Darwin devoted a new chapter principally to them when the sixth edition was published in 1872.

Why did Mivart change his mind and become Darwin's bitter opponent? In part the answer lies in broader changes within both science and the Catholic Church. Mivart's initial interest in Darwin's theory occurred at a time when many Catholics in Britain were optimistic and looked forward to the Church providing positive encouragement for science. This optimism was, however, short-lived. In 1863 Pius IX promulgated the Munich Brief that required science to be subservient to theology. Moreover, a conservative backlash within Catholicism resulted in increasing emphasis on scholasticism and on papal infallibility and authority. Mivart, who repeatedly sided with Newman and other liberals, found himself in an increasingly isolated position within the Church and also under mounting pressure to oppose Darwinism. Confronted with these divergent demands Mivart sought a new synthesis between science and religion that would honour both. Yet, he could only achieve this synthesis by rejecting not only the reactionaries within the Catholic Church but also the faction around Huxley who were bent on making anti-religious capital out of the theory of evolution.

A scientifically-literate Catholic priest named William Roberts, who was also on close terms with Huxley, appears to have played a crucial role in Mivart's biography. In 1868 Roberts seems to have persuaded him that evolution is incapable of accounting for the origin of the human mind. Moreover, over the next two or three years Mivart became increasingly concerned that Darwin's theory implied that man and the apes were descended from a common ancestor. Although he had mentioned his disaffection to Huxley two years earlier, Mivart's public declaration of his withdrawal from Darwinian orthodoxy came in 1871 with a hard-hitting review of Darwin's *Descent of Man*, in the *Quarterly Review*, and his book *On the Genesis of Species*.

In the former he argued that although there are a number of apparent continuities between brutes and men, man alone possesses self-consciousness and reasoned thought. In particular he pointed to the moral sense and the use of language as setting man apart from other animals.[33] The crux of his argument was that if man were different in type from other species – as Mivart believed he had demonstrated in his anatomical researches – then natural selection was inadequate in explaining the evolution of our minds. He nevertheless acknowledged that evolution could account for our physical form. However, this review also makes manifest his concern that scientists do not overstep their authority. The first half of the article is devoted to showing that Darwin was not infallible – indeed, according to Mivart, he was often inconsistent and even downright wrong. Moreover, he accused Darwin of having largely abandoned the theory of natural selection; instead the mechanism of sexual selection was attributed a far more central role in Darwin's *Descent of Man* (1871). Mivart was also deeply troubled by the way Darwinism had become the new orthodoxy. Indeed, he complained that 'starting at first with an avowed hypothesis, [Darwin then] constantly asserts it as an undoubted fact, and claims for it, somewhat in the spirit of a theologian, that it should be received as an article of faith'.[34] Science was in danger of becoming a new religion.

On the Genesis of Species, which was based on articles published in a Catholic periodical, enabled Mivart to mount a frontal assault on the mechanism of natural selection, while maintaining that species had undergone change. For example, he raised a forceful objection based on the observation that distinct species sometimes manifest very similar organic structures. Claiming that these species were of independent origin, Mivart argued that their convergence could not be explained solely by the mechanism of natural selection. Moreover, he conceived that natural selection is incompatible with saltationism,[35] which he claimed was strongly supported by diverse evidence. Although he was committed to evolutionary change, he argued that natural selection was insufficient to account for the evolution of species and that there must be other forces at work. While acknowledging that external factors were relevant, he believed that 'an *internal power* is a great, perhaps the main, determining agent' for directing changes in organisms and producing convergence to common structures.[36]

The second aim of his book was to demonstrate that organic change, by whatever mechanism, was perfectly compatible with Catholicism and posed no threat to religion. Thus the widely-perceived conflict between Darwinism and religion 'has arisen through a misunderstanding'.[37] Properly understood, the creation of new species through intermediate law-like causes (as postulated in the theory of evolution) was perfectly compatible with God being the creator of those causes. Hence evolution was 'Divine action by and through natural laws'.[38] While Mivart resented the criticism of evolutionary theory by scientifically illiterate men claiming to speak for theology, he particularly cautioned his readers that Darwin had gained 'a chorus of more or less completely acquiescing disciples' who were totally uncritical of the theory.[39] Mivart's book was greatly appreciated by his mentor Cardinal Newman who expressed satisfaction in finding that a Catholic had written 'the first real exposition of the logical insufficiency of Mr Darwin's theory'. Catholics, added Newman, 'may be better reasoners than [are the] philosophers'.[40]

The ferocity of Mivart's attack in the *Quarterly Review* stung Darwin, who took his criticisms personally. Writing to Hooker he claimed that Mivart 'shows the greatest scorn and animosity towards me .... He makes me the most arrogant, odious beast that ever lived. I cannot understand him; I suppose that accursed religious bigotry is at the root of it.'[41] In response to these attacks on Darwin and his henchmen Mivart was marginalised, isolated and bitterly attacked, especially by Huxley who likewise attributed Mivart's opposition to Darwinism to his Catholicism, which Huxley despised. According to another member of their circle, Huxley intended 'to "pin out" Mr. Mivart, for his insolent attack on Mr. Darwin'.[42] Forced to defend himself in print Mivart overreacted, striking out wildly at the immorality he perceived implicit in Huxley's scientistic philosophy:

> the principles he advocates cannot but tend, by a fatal necessity ... to produce results socially, politically, and morally, which he [Huxley] would be the first to deplore. They tend in the intellectual order to the degradation of the mind, by the essential identification of thought with sensation, and in the political order to the evolution of horrors worse than those of the Parisian Commune. I refrain from characterising their tendency in the moral order.[43]

Moderation was never Mivart's forte. Soon Huxley formally terminated their friendship.

For Mivart, Catholicism did not specify a unitary, infallible truth; even the judgements of the Pope and bishops were open to question. Since Scripture had to be mediated by fallible men there was always

Figure 28: Portrait of St George Jackson Mivart, by permission of the Linnean Society, London.

room for genuine, informed disagreement. Moreover, he believed that truth is not static but is continuously emerging as part of the natural evolutionary process. What most distressed him was the possibility that reactionary forces within the Church would prevent it from achieving its historical destiny. In particular, he feared a repeat of the Galileo affair if the Church prohibited the theory of evolution:

> In this important matter [the Galileo affair] it was the man of science that was right and ecclesiastical authority that was wrong. The latter sought to

impose, and more or less succeeded in imposing, an erroneous belief as to God's word, from which erroneous belief science has delivered us.[44]

The Galileo affair had not only resulted in the suppression of scientific truth but it had also greatly damaged his Church. To prevent a similar imbroglio over the theory of evolution, he cautioned ignorant clerics not to pronounce on Darwin's theory. Instead, the Church would be strengthened by encouraging those Catholics, like himself, who possessed a God-given vocation for science.

As an outspoken liberal, Mivart was attacked with increasing frequency in the Catholic press. Paradoxically the issue that triggered his excommunication had little direct connection with science but instead turned on a theological doctrine with implications for the Church's authority. In 1892 he launched an outright attack on the doctrine of eternal damnation which he found distasteful because it smacked of pagan barbarism and because it did not cohere with his progressivist view of Catholicism. Moreover, he complained that incarceration in hell seemed doctrinally flawed since it offered the soul no means of redemption.[45] That he published his views in a non-Catholic periodical doubtless fanned the flames of controversy. Mivart soon found many powerful members of the Catholic hierarchy arraigned against him. Hell was unmoved and the Church proved unmoveable; instead his articles on the subject were placed on the Index of prohibited books in 1893. A further blow came in the same year with the encyclical *Providentissimus Deus,* which was intended to foster study of the Bible but which also favoured a literalist interpretation of Scripture while discouraging scientific biblical criticism, which Mivart had publicly championed.

During the late 1890s he found himself in an increasingly isolated and desperate situation as his rift with Rome increased. Further estrangement resulted from the French Church's questionable involvement in the Dreyfus case and the Pope's failure to intervene. Mivart viewed this as evidence that the Vatican was morally bankrupt and complacent.[46] Also, in reviews published in January 1900 he was sharply critical of a Church which, in his opinion, had taken refuge behind a facade of biblical literalism and had become unresponsive to the challenges of the modern world.[47] Having experienced several years of torment by leading clerics Mivart was excommunicated in 1900. He felt considerable relief in parting from the Church which he believed had so signally failed to grasp its evolutionary destiny. However, his relief was short-lived, since a few weeks later he died from a heart attack and was buried in unconsecrated ground.

What conclusions can be drawn from Mivart's biography? Perhaps too many and too many inconsistent ones. Had we asked Huxley or Tyndall they would have identified Catholicism as the problem and unquestioningly attributed Mivart's desertion from the Darwinian camp to his (untenable) religious beliefs. By contrast, many Catholics championed Mivart when he attacked Darwin's theory but abandoned him when he became a thorn in the Church's flesh.[48] That he survived so long without censure is testimony to the patronage of Newman and even of Pope Leo XIII.

But we reach a different conclusion if we read events from his standpoint. Indeed, the biographical perspective is particularly instructive precisely because it shows how an individual can be riven by conflicting loyalties. At one level the conflict was internal: Mivart was torn between his allegiances to both science and religion. However, we must also recognise that far from subscribing to the conflict thesis he firmly believed that science and religion must be in harmony. He therefore devoted much of his own writings to criticising both anti-scientific Catholics and those scientists who freely deployed science for anti-religious purposes. In his opinion both sets of opponents were blinkered dogmatists who set their pet views about both religion and science beyond rational criticism. Likewise both misused their authority. As he wrote in one of his later essays, the proper attitude of scientists 'is emphatically a questioning attitude, while for consistent Theists doubt has a distinctly religious character'.[49] From this standpoint the discord lay not with Mivart but with the gatekeepers of both science and religion who frustrated his personal quest. They excommunicated him twice – first from the Huxleyite chapter of the scientific church and later from the Catholic Church. In his dealing with both communities Mivart found himself at odds with powerful Mafiosi. It must also be remembered that changing external circumstances are highly relevant since not only did Catholicism become distinctly more reactionary and conservative during the closing decades of the nineteenth century, but the scientific community was becoming increasingly professional and authoritarian, but also less tolerant of dissent.

William Benjamin Carpenter (1813–1885), Dissenter

Our third biographical subject is William Benjamin Carpenter whose scientific research was centred on physiology, but also covered oceanic studies, zoology and psychology. Despite some worthy contributions to research, he was generally considered a competent

Figure 29: William B. Carpenter; frontispiece to W. B. Carpenter, *Nature and Man. Essays Scientific and Philosophical. With an Introductory Memoir by J. Estlin Carpenter* (1888).

compiler of other people's ideas rather than a creative, original thinker. Partly for financial reasons and also as an adjunct to his various teaching posts he published a number of textbooks, including several works on physiology and a frequently-reprinted book on the microscope.[50] Although Carpenter's work will probably be little-known to a present-day audience, he was a respected Victorian who became Registrar at London University and a Vice-President of the Royal Society.

Carpenter was the fourth child of the Revd Dr Lant Carpenter, a leading figure in the Unitarian movement who wrote copiously on religious, moral and educational issues. The elder Carpenter was also one of the founders of the Bristol Philosophical and Literary Institution and included many scientists of note among his personal friends. The Carpenter home has been described as earnest but 'not oppressive, only healthful and bracing, and abundant room was given for the free play of every activity'.[51] However, James Martineau, who became one of Lant Carpenter's pupils, later claimed that he had 'never seen in any human being the idea of duty, the feeling of right, held in such visible reverence .... Of the discipline enjoined upon his house – its early rising, its neatness, its courtesy, its golden estimate of moments – he himself [Lant Carpenter] was the model.'[52] As a child William was imbued with the values of virtue, duty and public service. On the surface he was a solid Victorian, who strove to accomplish all the goals he set himself or which were set by others. A workaholic by temperament, he seems to have filled almost every waking moment, occasionally finding relief in music or a vacation. Continually aware of the difficulty of living up to the highest standards preached by his father, he expressed the fervent wish 'that in my moral character I had more of his spirit'.[53] Even his achievements in science were not sufficient and on one occasion he confided to his mother that those committed Christians – like his father and younger brothers – who devote their lives to saving sinners do 'a far higher work' than the scientific textbook writer or the research scientist.[54] A supreme example of his faithfulness to duty was his insistence on delivering a scheduled lecture to students at University College London less than an hour after receiving news of his mother's death.[55] The great personal demands he made on himself also took their toll and sometimes resulted in frustration. Writing to his sister Mary in 1850 he complained that his work was frequently interrupted: 'I try to exercise Christian charity towards the many people who bother me; but it is really very difficult to do so when one feels driven to desperation by the want of power to fulfil one's engagements, to say nothing of having one's trains of thought interrupted.'[56]

The great engine directing his life was his search for truth. As R. K. Webb has stressed, early Unitarians were imbued with a strong sense of intellectual independence; so that, having carefully weighed the evidence, each was expected to make an informed decision on any issue in science, religion, society or politics.[57] This emphasis on the judicious use of reason coloured the Unitarian response to science. Moreover, the Church's history included Joseph Priestley and many other scientists of note who avidly championed science in the name of truth. As Carpenter insisted, 'In the pursuit of truth', we should 'faithfully, strictly, and perversely ... *fix our attention on the goal*, not allowing ourselves to be distracted by the temptations of self-interest' or timidity.[58] His commitment to science was based on his belief that it provided one sure road to truth, the other being religion. 'I have the greatest confidence in the ultimate prevalence of truth', he told one of his brothers.[59] This optimistic creed suffused not only his science but also his socio-religious outlook, and, like Joseph Priestley, he confidently predicted that science would lead to an increasingly bright future and the perfectibility of humankind.

Much of Carpenter's science was inspired by his belief that the physical world constitutes an harmonious unity. Thus in his earliest researches he sought to unify the animal and vegetable domains by exploring their structural and functional analogies. Again, in his paper 'On the mutual relations of the vital and physical forces' (1850) he developed William Grove's view that mechanical motion, heat, light, electricity, and so forth are mutually related forms of force, by claiming that these physical forces are interrelated to vital forces, such as the force produced in the nerves. This search for unity led, almost naturally, to a reassessment of God's role. Thus he speculated whether 'all the physical forces of the universe ... [are] the direct manifestation of the Mental force of the Deity'. Moreover, in a passage reminiscent of Newton's speculations about the universe being the sensorium of God, Carpenter conjectured whether 'the phenomena of the material universe [may be] considered as the immediate expression of the Divine will'.[60]

Although he was prone to these pantheistic speculations about the role of force, Carpenter insisted that the laws of nature were manifested as observable uniformities in phenomena. By identifying the laws of nature he sought to demonstrate that 'Science and Religion are manifestly in harmony'. Thus in a series of eighteen articles published in 1845 in a leading dissenting newspaper, the *Inquirer*, he engaged the science–religion issue under the explicit title 'On the harmony of science and religion'. Here he argued that through the discovery of laws we become convinced that the world is constructed according to the divine plan implemented at the Creation:

[A] true appreciation of the Laws of Nature leads us to put aside the idea of *continual interference* on the part of the Deity, [and] it is equally opposed to the idea that the Laws can operate without His *continual sustaining action*; and they can only be regarded as simple forms of expressing the *modes* and *conditions*, in which the Deity *appears* to operate in the material and moral world. [Indeed,] every step which we gain in our [scientific] generalizations, is really a step in our ascent towards Him.[61]

Lawlikeness was not only to be found in astronomy and the physical sciences but also in the biological sciences and in psychology. All branches of science were therefore founded on laws that proclaim God's omnipotence and omniscience. Contrary to the reactions of many of his religious contemporaries, Carpenter asserted that even the nebular hypothesis was the 'greatest contribution that Science has made to Religion'. He even endorsed much of the scientific argument of the *Vestiges of the Natural History of Creation* (1844), insisting that, if properly considered, the author's argument would lead to a theistic conclusion.[62]

Carpenter's essays in the *Inquirer* provoked one critic to complain that he seemed prepared to throw out Revelation when it conflicted with our admittedly limited knowledge of the natural world: 'His philosophy may be compared to a flowery, but fruitless, creeper, twining round a hollow trunk, whose mouldering structure it endeavours to conceal, and whose well-known character it attempts to disguise.'[63] This critic correctly identified Carpenter's tendency to emphasise reason over faith, science over Revelation; for although he often asserted the complete coherence between science and Revelation he avoided any close, analytical engagement with the Bible. For Carpenter, science was the dominant mode and he even envisaged a time when 'the fundamental truths of religion will rest on the generalizations of science'.[64] As the historian of the Metaphysical Society has commented, Carpenter attempted 'to make religion scientific and science religious'.[65] If he successfully maintained an insistent providentialism in respect to the latter, his notion of religion became all too circumscribed under the sway of science. In adopting this position Carpenter was reflecting a significant change evident among contemporary British Unitarians, spearheaded by his lifelong friend James Martineau. Unlike earlier generations that had constructed their religion with close attention to the Bible, Martineau relegated Biblical authority and instead emphasised the dominant role of reason and conscience in shaping the human spirit.[66] Likewise, Carpenter's writings on science and religion extolled reason and feeling at the expense of Revelation.

Carpenter expressed the heartfelt hope that he might 'be of some use as a mediator in the conflict which has now distinctly begun between science and religion'.[67] Yet compared with Mivart's tortuous path, Carpenter trod an intellectually undemanding road and displayed little awareness of the deeper and more challenging problems facing contemporary science and religion, and their interrelationship.

The foregoing discussion should prepare us for his response to evolution. He reviewed the *Origin of Species* favourably and Darwin was gratified that a physiologist of Carpenter's standing had supported him. However, Darwin confided to Charles Lyell that although Carpenter's review was 'very good and well balanced', it was 'not brilliant'.[68] Indeed, with characteristic caution Carpenter did not go quite far enough on the question whether vertebrates were descended from one ancestor.

Although Carpenter's reviews were principally concerned with the scientific aspects of Darwin's work, he briefly engaged religious issues in a manner that would both have pleased Darwin but also did not go as far as Darwin might have hoped. Possibly reflecting his earlier brushes with the critics of science, Carpenter felt the need to defend evolution against unnamed theological opponents. He presumed that these critics would claim that the theory of natural selection removed God's action from the physical world. Such an objection he considered 'simply absurd' since the truth of Darwin's theory was a scientific and not a theological issue. Moreover, as he pointed out, botanists had long been concerned with tracing slow changes in plant species without raising a theological storm.

Although Carpenter initially appeared to distance Darwin's work from theology, he also conceived an underlying harmony. Denying that God's interaction with the physical world had ended at the Creation, he portrayed nature as in a continual state of progressive development under God's creative power. However, the question remained whether God had to intervene, periodically, to eliminate some species and replace them by new ones, or whether the new species had developed through the modification of the old. The question was easily settled since special creation was unacceptable to Carpenter, who considered that it required God to act in a mysterious and incoherent manner. By contrast, Darwin's theory appealed to him precisely because it employed natural selection which operated according to natural law. He asserted that since evolutionary theory connoted 'order, continuity, and progress' it was commensurable with the acceptable notion that God 'knows no variableness, neither shadow of turning'. Since Carpenter had long accepted the world as ordered and progressive and God as a rational agent, he took Darwin's theory in his stride and did not consider it a threat to religion. Indeed, he could not envisage how theology could offer any challenge to science. Instead he labelled those theologians who rejected the theory as obscurantists, and argued that in time they would come to accept it just as their predecessors had eventually accepted the Copernican theory. Darwin's theory was clearly on the side of progress and provided it encapsulated physical law – which it did – Carpenter could accept it as yet another example of God's lawlike governance of the physical world.[69]

Adam Sedgwick (1795–1873), Anglican

Unlike the other three scientists discussed in this chapter, Adam Sedgwick was not only a product of Cambridge University but spent most of his adult life in Cambridge. Entering Trinity College in 1804 at the relatively advanced age of 19, he rose through a College Fellowship to become the Woodwardian Professor of Geology in 1819 and Vice-Master of Trinity in 1845. Although a leading and respected member of that isolated Anglican community Sedgwick was no grey, conformist clergyman and academic but displayed some of the proud independence of his Yorkshire background. Like his father, the vicar of Dent, he was strongly opposed to the slave trade; he supported Catholic emancipation, the abolition of religious tests and championed many other aspects of university reform. Although a leading don, he remained ambivalent towards the University and often felt constrained by its reactionary ethos. It may be no coincidence that when in Cambridge his health usually deteriorated, whereas his vigour returned on geological fieldtrips, particularly when pursued in the neighbourhood of Dent.

But there is another strong sense in which he was deeply marked by his rural, Yorkshire roots. Late in life he recounted his childhood, emphasising the assiduity, stability and moral rectitude of the Dentdale population. This ideal community was financially sustained by smallholdings, sheep farming, textile manufacture and mining. However, the world he had known as a child had largely disappeared by the mid nineteenth century owing principally to the forces of mechanisation which rendered traditional industries uneconomic. Poverty became widespread, the indigenous population fell sharply and lawlessness increased. The economic and moral decline of Dentdale affected Sedgwick profoundly.

Sedgwick possessed great personal charm and evoked deep feelings of love and admiration from his many friends. He could certainly bear grudges (for example, against his ex-co-worker Roderick Murchison who, he believed, had gratuitously undermined some of his innovations in geology), but most of his letters overflow with warmth, humour and sympathy. He could readily share his friends' joys and sorrows; his letters comforting the bereaved are especially poignant. Although he never married – much to his regret – he pursued long-term correspondence with several younger women, such as his nieces, towards whom he adopted the role of an avuncular confidant. The vein of humanity found in his letters was an expression of his practical Christianity. As a lecturer he inspired great affection, evidenced by the following comment by one of his auditors at an anniversary meeting of the Geological Society: 'Sedgwick made the great speech of the evening. By turns he made us cry and roar with laughter, as he willed. His pathos and wit are equally admirable.'[70] But Sedgwick's eloquence was not reserved for High Table at Trinity or the Geological Society of London. He was President of the Kendal Natural History and Scientific Society (Kendal being some 15 miles from his family home at Dent); he lectured to an audience of 1200 at the Leeds Mechanics' Institute and, most famously, in 1838 he delivered an impromptu address on the geology and economy of coal 'on the sea-beach at Tynemouth to some 3000 or 4000 colliers and rabble (mixed with a sprinkling of their employers), which has produced a sensation such as is not likely to die away for years'.[71]

When he accepted the Woodwardian Chair in 1819 he knew little about geology. Soon, however, he undertook expeditions to Matlock, the West of England including Cornwall, the Yorkshire coast, the Isle of Wight, Hampshire, Oxfordshire and the Lake District. He was quickly recognised as a leading geologist, and played a central role in the 'golden age' of British geology, spanning the 1820s to 1850s, when the basic fieldwork and theories were pursued in a spirit of novelty and excitement.[72]

If geology was his passion, his theological concerns appear more sporadic. Indeed, according to his biographers, as a young man 'he had no very decided inclination' to enter the Church.[73] Only in 1817, when he was in danger of dismissal from his Fellowship if he did not take orders, did he secure his position at Cambridge by seeking ordination. A further seventeen years passed before he was appointed by Henry Brougham to a prebendary stall at Norwich Cathedral which, worth £600 per annum, provided reasonable financial security. However, this position required him to spend two months each year in Norwich. With typical dedication he was the model of a hard-working cleric dedicated to the spiritual and pastoral care of his flock. He was foremost a practical Christian involved in the daily duties of a hard-pressed cleric but relatively unconcerned with controversial issues in theology. When offered the deanery of Peterborough in 1853 he declined, preferring his regular duties at Norwich to advancement. By that time in his life his earlier career ambitions had long been satisfied.

Despite his evangelical leanings Sedgwick emphasised toleration. Thus shortly after taking up his post at Norwich he sought 'to bring together more heretics and schismatics within my house' than had ever entered since the Cathedral had been built – Independents, High Churchmen and Quakers attended.[74] Likwise, there was a degree of self-reference when he described Charles Simeon as 'a devout and faithful man, who stuck to his principles ... and ended by gaining the love and good-will of all men about him'. What he appreciated most about Simeon was the steadfastness of his faith and his emphasis on Christianity as a biblically-inspired way of life.[75] Although brotherly love came before all other commandments, Sedgwick's toleration was severely strained by many High Churchmen and he particularly deplored Newman and the Tractarians who had split the Church of England on issues of doctrine. 'I pity their delusion, I despise their sophistry, and I hate their dishonesty', he wrote. Their defection to Rome had, he believed, been delayed far too long and had damaged his beloved Anglican Church.[76]

Sedgwick was committed to liberal causes and was widely recognised as one of the most solid Whigs in Cambridge. In matters of religion he is more difficult to characterise, but on many issues he was most closely akin to the moderate evangelicals. For example, at a time of rapid social change and dislocation Sedgwick viewed Christian morality as a stabilising force and as proof against the depravity to which he believed humankind was so easily prey. As Boyd Hilton has emphasised, during the first half of the nineteenth century Anglican evangelicals reacted strongly against the utilitarianism of the age, which they rejected as conducive to atheism. In place of the utilitarian theory of mind they constructed a providentialist moral economy commensurate with their Christian beliefs.[77]

Like many of his Cambridge contemporaries, Sedgwick stands firmly in this tradition; for example, in his 1833 *Discourse on the Studies of the University*, he attacked William Paley for denying the moral sense and for championing a utilitarian theory of ethics.[78] While utilitarianism was a common enemy recognised by all evangelicals, Sedgwick deployed his heaviest artillery against those who sought to undermine Christianity by mobilising materialistic interpretations in science. Thus in his review of Chambers's *Vestiges* in the *Edinburgh Review* and in an overly-long preface to the fifth edition of his *Discourse* (1850) he sought to repudiate the increasing number of scientific writers who, he claimed, sought to propagate

materialism, atheism and pantheism in their various forms.[79] Yet his
intention was not only to refute such works but to provide an alternative and (in his opinion) correct value-system, particularly in the
realm of education.

Sedgwick's need to live within the framework of Christian morality
is best captured by the following declaration contained in one of his
letters: 'I wish to live and die with the hopes of a Christian. If these
hopes were away, what would the remnant of my life be good for? A

Figure 30: The 'finished moral scavenger'; frontispiece to vol. i of J. W. Clark
and T. M. Hughes, *The Life and Letters of the Reverend Adam Sedgwick* (1890).
Painted by Thomas Phillips, 1832.

stammering remnant of a babbler's dream.'[80] As Senior Proctor, Sedgwick was directly responsible for enforcing moral standards among Cambridge students who were easy prey to drink and prostitutes. On appointment to the post in 1827 he pictured himself 'strutting about and looking dignified, with a cap, gown, cassock, and huge pair of bands; the terror of all academic evil-doers – in short a *finished moral scavenger*'.[81] He appears to have carried out his duties with great efficiency and commitment. Moral education was also the central theme of his *Discourse* in which he argued that a university education had to be grounded firmly on Christian ethical principles. Again, he conceived his geological lectures at Cambridge as possessing 'the power of producing a *good moral influence* by raising my voice against a kind of dreamy pantheistical philosophy which tries to lift up its head among academical men'.[82] This quotation is of particular interest since it makes clear the moral role he attributed to geology.

As he emphasised in his *Discourse*, the study of science should not be an end in itself but must serve moral purposes. Not only do scientific studies lead to intellectual improvement but they also help to inculcate self-control and function as an antidote to arrogance and pride. Those trained in science should manifest the qualities of 'simplicity of character, humility, and love of truth'. But the main moral significance of science lay in natural theology. Science was not an end in itself – a 'cold and uninviting' subject – or merely a means for material progress. Rather, its main purpose was to enrich us, both emotionally and intellectually. The study of Newtonian science, for example, 'teaches us to see the finger of God in all things animate and inanimate, and gives us an exalted conception of his attributes'. He therefore urged his auditors to use their scientific studies

> to believe yourselves in the perpetual presence of God – to adore him in the glories of his creation – to see his power and wisdom in the harmony of the world – his goodness and his providence in the wonderful structure of living beings ....[83]

What is so striking about this passage is Sedgwick's appeal *ad hominem* through the use of the reflexive verb. He portrayed science as continually enhancing one's appreciation of God's relation to His creation, ourselves included.

Reflecting on the relationship between science and revelation, Sedgwick envisaged that 'these two kinds of truth, embodied in physical history and revealed religion, so far from being conflicting, were entirely in unison and harmony, if we investigate the one, and read the other, in a right spirit'.[84] Thus he conceived that both science and Revelation were in agreement in confirming the earth's finite age and man's recent habitation on the earth. Moreover, his early geological papers display an enthusiasm for Werner's neptunist theory with its emphasis on the role of water in precipitating the various strata of rocks, that were identified by their mineral content,[85] and in 1825 he argued that 'a great diluvian catastrophe [had occurred] during a comparatively recent period in the natural history of the earth'. Although he insisted that this was a legitimate inference from scientific observations and not an illegitimate attempt to frame *a priori* a Mosaic geology, he was clearly delighted that science and revealed religion concurred in this conclusion.[86]

However in his 1830 Presidential Address to the Geological Society he argued strenuously against those geologists who strove to reconcile science with a literal interpretation of Mosaic history. Not only was this an inappropriate way to pursue an inductive science but any mistake in the scientific argument might lead readers to doubt the truth of Scripture. Moreover, he stressed that geology was a new science in which excessive theorising was premature. Instead, the subject needed to be constructed on a firm basis of observed facts from which laws could be inductively inferred.[87] In line with this empiricist approach much of Sedgwick's geological writings stressed natural (rather than revealed) theology and the moral value of the inductive sciences. In the following year he recanted his diluvialist leanings before the Geological Society, expressing caution about specifying any tight connections between geological theory and the biblical narrative.[88]

While adamantly opposed to scriptural geology, Sedgwick's responses to both *Vestiges* and Darwin's *Origin of Species* should be interpreted as part of his ceaseless moral crusade against those who used science for atheistical purposes. Like many scientists of the period, Sedgwick had no shortage of scientific objections to *Vestiges* but it is clear that the underlying thrust of his argument was the author's immorality and the book's unacceptable implications for moral philosophy. As he wrote to Charles Lyell, 'what shall we say of [the author's] morality and his conscience, when he tells us he has "destroyed all distinction between [the] moral and [the] physical" . . .? If the book be true, the labours of sober induction are in vain; religion is a lie; . . . morality is moonshine; . . . and man and woman are only better beasts!'[89] Some fifteen years later he read Darwin's book through the same moralistic lens, yet he considered the *Origin* even more dangerous because it was far better argued and contained fewer errors than the *Vestiges*.

It is clear that the moral implications of materialism lay at the heart of Sedgwick's objection to evolution. While he chastised Darwin for 'utterly repudiat[ing] final causes', it was not only the absence of teleological arguments that distressed him. Worse still, evolutionary theory 'indicates a demoralized understanding on the part of its advocates' who portray the human condition devoid of all morality and decency. The word 'demoralized' implies the denial of moral evidence and the rejection of our higher faculties, especially our conscience and religious feelings. Darwin had thereby stripped humankind of its moral faculties and degraded its members to the level of beasts. This deeply offended Sedgwick's sensibilities and threatened his world-view in which he conceived humankind as part of the providential scheme. As he wrote to Darwin immediately after reading the *Origin*, there 'is a moral or metaphysical part of nature, as well as a physical'. Moreover, Darwin had impugned the proper practice of science, which should lead the scientist and the scientific reader to a richer appreciation of God's providence.[90] However, just as the Dentdale of his childhood had been largely swept away by industrialisation, so Darwin threatened to reduce Sedgwick's *Weltanschauung* to 'A stammering remnant of a babbler's dream.'

Concluding Comments

Not surprisingly, the attitudes of our four biographical subjects were deeply affected by their backgrounds and subsequent experiences. Thus Tyndall's Protestant, Irish upbringing coloured his attitude not only to Catholicism but ultimately to all religious systems. Carpenter grew up at the centre of the Unitarian community and throughout his life espoused the values so deeply inculcated by his father. Likewise, Sedgwick's childhood in rural, idyllic Dentdale influenced his responses both to Cambridge University and to industrialisation. Despite Mivart's trajectory being the least easy to chart, his cosmopolitan London background is highly relevant to his biography.

Although all four were marked by their social, political and religious backgrounds, one of the main uses of biography is to challenge stereotypes and to show that the experience of the individual is often far more complex and interesting than the stereotype will allow. Thus Tyndall was not the atheistic materialist portrayed by his opponents but was imbued with Carlyle's Romanticism. This provided him with strong religious (although not specifically Christian) sensibilities and emphasised the creative power of the human spirit. Likewise, although Mivart was influenced by the Tractarian movement and converted to Catholicism, he was not a submissive representative of Rome but fought for the liberal, progressive brand of English Catholicism advocated by his mentor Cardinal Newman. Even Sedgwick, who usually projected a calm and confident exterior, was deeply affected by contemporary events and in a letter admitted that 'To my friends I shew my best face; but by myself I am often oppressed with miserable spirits, and with the consciousness of doing so little of what I ought to do.'[91]

On the crucial issue of Darwin's theory of evolution there was also much diversity. While Tyndall and Carpenter accepted evolution without reserve, Sedgwick bitterly attacked the theory for challenging the doctrine of providential design and for threatening Christian morality. From a biographical stand-point the responses of these three authors could have been predicted from their reactions to such earlier theories as Laplace's nebular hypothesis, Lamarck's transformationism and Chambers' *Vestiges*. Yet biographical analysis is also useful for illuminating cases which do not display such outward constancy. Here the example of Mivart is particularly informative since he initially welcomed Darwin's theory; later, however, he increasingly opposed the theory of natural selection whilst continuing to proclaim a broad-based evolutionist philosophy.

The most important general issue raised by the preceding biographical sketches is that they challenge a form of analysis frequently encountered in discussions of science and religion. In the opening chapters we characterised 'the essentialist position' which attributes fixed defining qualities to both science and religion. Essentialists then proceed to postulate a unique relationship between them. However, it should be clear that this approach is thoroughly a-historical and flies in the face of the diversity displayed through the study of history.

Essentialism likewise underpins many of the attempts to construct taxonomies that characterise the various ways science and religion have been interrelated. For example, a recent and sophisticated taxonomy appears in Ian Barbour's sociologically-informed *Religion in an Age of Science* where four 'stances' are postulated. 'Conflict' claims that there is a necessary opposition, such as between a naturalist and a supernaturalist account of the origin of humankind. Secondly, 'independence' consigns science and religion to different, non-interacting domains. 'Dialogue' postulates that science and religion share certain similarities – such as both are tentative or use metaphorical language – so that there can be negotiation. Finally, there are various forms of 'integration' where there is an interfusion between the scientific and religious beliefs; for example, the argument from design mixes these two ingredients.[92] While Barbour does not appear to be committed to essentialism, his taxonomy may encourage this position and each of his four options can be, and has been, read as connoting the essence of the science–religion relationship.

From the historian's point of view, we find Barbour's taxonomy problematic if each of his four stances is taken as an exclusive alternative, each mapping on to an essentialist definition of both science and religion. Instead we wish to emphasise the role of human agency working in history and in society. Biography is particularly useful in sustaining this approach, since in the preceding case-studies we see that individuals were not restricted to any single essentialist position. Instead, in each case the scientist made use of more than one of Barbour's stances. This is not to imply inconsistency, but rather to emphasise the complex and diverse ways in which the science–religion interrelation can be manipulated.

The example of Mivart is especially instructive since he employed all four of Barbour's stances. He perceived 'conflict' between the Darwinians' overstated commitment to natural selection and his understanding of the human condition in which mental and moral attributes were important but could not be explained by natural selection. Likewise he used an 'independence' strategy when arguing that the Galileo affair should teach us that science is for scientists and theology for theologians. Each had its own proper domain. Yet he also conceived a form of dialogue when arguing that both science and religion are rational activities; he insisted that neither scientists nor theologians should forsake their critical faculties. Finally, much of his own research was empowered by specific integrationist strategies. Thus he perceived the world framed by the divine architect and he directed his research to elucidating archetypes. His integrationist programme greatly inflamed Huxley and other proponents of scientific naturalism.

In studying Mivart's biography it should be clear how an individual can – and often does – make use of a variety of different arguments. Yet this very diversity and complexity casts doubt on the usefulness of trying to capture the contingent and changing relations between science and religion along any single essentialist axis. Indeed, in opposition to the essentialist programme we would argue that the individual must be treated as an active agent who deploys different strategies creatively. In the case of Mivart, who was desperately trying to maintain his participation in both science and Catholicism in the face of determined opposition from both communities, much resourcefulness was required. He cannot be understood as exemplifying any single essentialist position but as actively constructing his understanding of the mutual bearings of science and religion at a specific time and place.

Biography is important precisely because it focuses on such specificity. Both religion and science are thereby particularised in terms of how they were experienced by the biographical subject. As the historian Thomas Söderqvist has written, biography 'is primarily a genre through which we try to bring to life again the unique individual'.[93]

NOTES

1 F. Oakley, 'Christian theology and the Newtonian science: The rise of the concept of the laws of nature', in *Creation: The Impact of an Idea* (ed. D. O'Connor and F. Oakley), New York, 1969, 53–84; C. Kaiser, *Creation and the History of Science*, London and Grand Rapids, 1991.

2 A. Koyré, 'The significance of the Newtonian synthesis', in Koyré, *Newtonian Studies*, Chicago, 1965, 3–24.

3 *Telling Lives in Science: Essays on Scientific Biography* (ed. M. Shortland and R. Yeo), Cambridge, 1996.

4 R. S. Westfall, *Never at Rest: A Biography of Isaac Newton*, Cambridge, 1980; J. Browne, *Charles Darwin: Voyaging*, London, 1995; J. Moore and A. Desmond, *Darwin*, London, 1991; C. Smith and M. N. Wise, *Energy and Empire: A Biographical Study of Lord Kelvin*, Cambridge, 1989.

5 To take just a few examples: E. H. Erikson, *Young Man Luther*, New York, 1958; D. L. Lewis, *Martin Luther King: A Critical Biography*, London, 1970; J. Lafrance, *My Vocation is Love: St. Thérèsa of Lisieux*, Slough, 1991; M. M. Pond, *Mother Teresa: A Life of Charity*, New York, 1992; A. Sebba, *Mother Teresa: Beyond the Image*, London, 1997.

6 J. W. McClendon, Jr., *Biography as Theology. How Life Stories can Remake Today's Theology*, Nashville and New York, 1974, 37–8.

7 R. Rorty, *Philosophy and the Mirror of Nature*, Princeton, 1980, 360.

8 The three who lived in London belonged to the Metaphysical Society which was devoted to this topic. See A. W. Brown, *The Metaphysical Society. Victorian Minds in Crisis, 1869–1880*, New York, 1947.

9 See R. S. Westfall, 'The changing world of the Newtonian industry', *Journal of the History of Ideas*, 37 (1976), 175–84; D. Brewster, *Memoirs of the Life, Writings, and Discoveries of Isaac Newton*, 2 vols., Edinburgh, 1855; Koyré, op. cit. (2); Westfall, op. cit. (4); F. E. Manuel, *A Portrait of Isaac Newton*, Cambridge, Mass., 1968.

10 J. Tyndall, 'Professor Virchow and evolution', in Tyndall, *Fragments of Science: A Series of Detached Essays, Addresses, and Reviews*, 8th edn. 2 vols., London, 1892, ii, 373–418, on 381.

11 A. S. Eve and C. H. Creasey, *Life and Work of John Tyndall*, London, 1945, 7.

12 Tyndall, op. cit. (10), 381–2.

13 J. Tyndall, 'On unveiling the statue of Thomas Carlyle', in Tyndall, *New Fragments*, London, 1892, 392–7.

14 Eve and Creasey, op. cit. (11), 11.

15 On Tyndall's Romanticism and especially his connection with Thomas Carlyle see R. Barton, 'John Tyndall, pantheist. A rereading of the Belfast Address', *Osiris*, 3 (1987), 111–34; A. T. Cosslett, 'Science and value: The writings of John Tyndall', in *John Tyndall. Essays on a Natural Philosopher* (ed. W. H. Brock, N. D. McMillan and R. C. Mollan), Dublin, 1981, 181–92.

16 Tyndall, op. cit. (10), 382.

17 *Ibid.*, 385.

18 J. Tyndall, 'The Belfast address', *ibid.*, ii, 135–201; Barton, op. cit. (15); D. N. Livingstone, 'Darwinism and Calvinism. The Belfast–Princeton connection', *Isis*, 83 (1992), 408–28.

19 J. Tyndall, 'Apology for the Belfast address', in Tyndall, op. cit. (10), ii, 202–23, especially 210–18.

20 J. T. Lloyd, 'Background to the Joule–Mayer controversy', *Notes and Records of the Royal Society of London*, 25 (1970), 211–25, on 217.

21 Eve and Creasey, op. cit. (11), 56. For readings of the *Bridgewaters* see J. Topham, ' "An infinite variety of arguments": The *Bridgewater Treatises* and British natural theology in the 1830s', PhD dissertation, University of Lancaster, 1993. See also chapter 10.

22 J. Tyndall, 'Miracles and special providences', in Tyndall, op. cit. (10), ii, 8. Mozley was a High Churchman and Fellow of Magdalen College, Oxford.

23 Eve and Creasey, op. cit. (11), 201.

24 F. M. Turner, *Between Science and Religion: The Reaction to British Naturalism in Late Victorian England*, New Haven, 1974.

25 Eve and Creasey, op. cit. (11), 70.

26 *Ibid.*, 283.

27 J. Tyndall, 'Scientific use of the imagination', in Tyndall, op. cit. (10), ii, 101–34, on 132.

28 Tyndall, op. cit. (18), 179.

29 J. W. Gruber, *A Conscience in Conflict. The Life of St. George Jackson Mivart*, New York, 1960; F. St G. Mivart, 'Early memories of St. George Mivart', *Dublin Review*, 174 (1924), 1–27. St G. Mivart's *An Introduction to the Elements of Science*, London, 1894, opens with a short appreciation of Buffon's *Histoire Naturelle*.

30 Gruber, op. cit. (29), 11; F. St G. Mivart, op. cit. (29), 27. For his later and more critical views on Gothic architecture see St G. Mivart, *Contemporary Evolution*, London, 1876, 224–54.

31 St G. Mivart, op. cit. (29), 17.

32 St G. Mivart, 'Some reminiscences of Thomas Henry Huxley', *Nineteenth Century*, 42 (1897), 985–98, especially 992; St G. Mivart, 'Specific Genesis', in Mivart, *Essays and Criticisms*, 2 vols., London, 1892, ii, 103–26, on 104–5.

33 St G. Mivart, 'Darwin's *Descent of man*', *Quarterly Review*, 131 (1871), 47–90, reprinted in *Essays and Criticisms*, ii, 1–59. The uniqueness of man was explored in greater detail in his *Man and Apes*, London, 1873.

34 Mivart, 'Darwin's *Descent of man*', *ibid.*, 8.

35 The theory that organic change does not occur smoothly but by sharp transitions.

36 St G. Mivart, *On the Genesis of Species*, London, 1871, 227. Emphasis added.

37 *Ibid.*, 262.

38 *Ibid.*, 261.

39 *Ibid.*, 10.

40 J. H. Newman to Mivart, 9 December 1871, in *The Letters and Diaries of John Henry Newman* (ed. C. S. Dessain et al), 31 vols., Oxford, 1961–77, xxv, 446.

41 C. Darwin to J. D. Hooker, 16 September 1871; *More Letters of Charles Darwin* (ed. F. Darwin), 2 vols., London, 1903, i, 333.

42 L. Huxley, *Life and Letters of Sir Joseph Dalton Hooker*, 2 vols., London, 1918, ii, 128.

43 St G. Mivart, 'Evolution and its consequences: A reply to Professor Huxley', *Contemporary Review*, 19 (1872), 168–92, reprinted in op. cit. (32), ii, 60–102, on 101. As with Bishop Wilberforce at the 1860 BAAS meeting, the rhetorically-skilful Huxley could bring out the worst in his opponents.

44 St G. Mivart, 'Modern Catholics and scientific freedom', *Nineteenth Century*, 18 (1885), 30–47, on 39. See also W. W. Roberts, *The Pontifical Decrees against the Doctrine of the Earth's Movement, and the Ultramontane Defence of them*, 2nd edn., Oxford and London, 1885.

45 St G. Mivart, 'Happiness in hell', *Nineteenth Century*, 32 (1892), 899–919.

46 Letter in *The Times*, 17 October 1899.

47 St G. Mivart, 'The continuity of Catholicism', *Nineteenth Century*, 47 (1900), 51–72; *Idem.*,'Some recent Catholic apologists', *Fortnightly Review*, 67 (1900), 24–44.

48 W. J. Schoenl, *The Intellectual Crisis in English Catholicism. Liberal Catholics, Modernists, and the Vatican in the late Nineteenth and early Twentieth Centuries*, New York and London, 1982, 89–94; *Letters from a 'Modernist'. The Letters of George Tyrrell to Wilfrid Ward 1893–1908* (ed. M. J. Weaver), Shepherdstown, 1981, 25 and 166.

49 Mivart, 'Some . . .', op. cit. (32), 987.

50 W. B. Carpenter, *Principles of General and Comparative Physiology*, London, 1838; *Idem., Principles of Human Physiology*, London, 1842; *Idem., Manual of Physiology*, London, 1846; *Idem., The Microscope and its Revelations*, London, 1856.

51 J. E. Carpenter, *The Life and Work of Mary Carpenter*, 2nd edn., Macmillan, London, 1881, 2.

52 Quoted in R. L. Carpenter, *Memoirs of the Life and Work of Philip Pearsall Carpenter, Chiefly Derived from his Letters*, London, 1880, 8.

53 W. B. Carpenter, *Nature and Man. Essays Scientific and Philosophical. With an Introductory Memoir by J. Estlin Carpenter*, London, 1888, 29.

54 *Ibid.*, 70.

55 *Ibid.*, 72.

56 *Ibid.*, 48.

57 R. K. Webb, 'The faith of nineteenth-century Unitarians: A curious incident', in *Victorian Faith in Crisis. Essays on Continuity and Change in*

Nineteenth-Century Religious Belief (ed. R. J. Helmstadter and B. Lightman), Basingstoke, 1990, 126–49.

58   Carpenter, op. cit. (53), 135.

59   *Ibid.*, 118.

60   *Ibid.*, 52–3.

61   W. B. Carpenter, 'On the harmony of science and religion', *The Inquirer*, 4 (1845), 183.

62   *Ibid.*, 231, 358 and 454–5.

63   *Ibid.*, 4 (1845), 228.

64   Carpenter, op. cit. (53), 37.

65   Brown, op. cit. (8), 50.

66   H. Gow, *The Unitarians*, London, 1928, 107–31.

67   Carpenter, op. cit. (53), 117.

68   D. L. Hull, *Darwin and his Critics. The Reception of Darwin's Theory of Evolution by the Scientific Community*, Cambridge, Mass., 1973, 87–8. Carpenter's reviews appeared as 'The theory of development in nature', *British and Foreign Medico-Chirurgical Review*, 25 (1860), 367–404, and 'Darwin and the origin of species', *National Review*, 10 (1860), 188–214.

69   Hull, op. cit. (68), 83–4. Carpenter derived the phrase 'no variableness, neither shadow of turning' from the New Testament: James, 1:17.

70   H. H. Woodward, *The History of the Geological Society of London*, London, 1907, 172.

71   J. W. Clark and T. M. Hughes, *The Life and Letters of the Reverend Adam Sedgwick*, 2 vols., Cambridge, 1890, i, 515–16. The quoted passage is taken from a letter written by John Herschel to his wife. Sedgwick would not have described his audience as 'colliers and rabble'.

72   M. J. S. Rudwick, *The Great Devonian Controversy. The Shaping of Scientific Knowledge among Gentlemanly Specialists*, Chicago, 1985; J. A. Secord, *Controversy in Victorian Geology. The Cambrian–Silurian Dispute*, Princeton, 1986.

73   Clark and Hughes, op. cit. (71), i, 103.

74   *Ibid.*, ii, 437.

75   *Ibid.*, ii, 122. See also *ibid.*, i, 220; ii, 20–1 and 115. Sedgwick had been reading W. Carus, *Memoirs of the Life of the Rev. Charles Simeon*, London, 1847. On Simeon see also H. E. Hopkins, *Charles Simeon of Cambridge*, London, 1977; D. W. Bebbington, *Evangelicalism in Modern Britain. A History from the 1730's to the 1980's*, London, 1989.

76   Clark and Hughes, op. cit. (71), ii, 93 and 115.

77   B. Hilton, *The Age of Atonement. The Influence of Evangelicalism on Social and Economic Thought, 1795–1865*, Oxford, 1988.

78   A. Sedgwick, *A Discourse on the Studies of the University*, Cambridge, 1833, 48–69.

79   A. Sedgwick, Review of *Vestiges* in *Edinburgh Review*, 82 (1845), 1–85; *Idem.*, *A Discourse on the Studies of the University*, 5th edn., Cambridge, 1850. For the broader political context of transformationist theories before Darwin see A. Desmond, *The Politics of Evolution. Morphology, Medicine, and Reform in Radical London*, Chicago, 1989.

80   Clark and Hughes, op. cit. (71), ii, 299.

81   *Ibid.*, i, 306. Emphasis added. See also 319 and Moore and Desmond, op. cit. (4).

82   *Ibid.*, ii, 249. Emphasis added.

83   Sedgwick, op. cit. (78), 10–12 and 27.

84   Clark and Hughes, op. cit. (71), ii, 151.

85   Secord, op. cit. (72), 64, portrays the Wernerian influence on Sedgwick as limited.

86   A. Sedgwick, 'On the origin of alluvial and diluvial formations', *Annals of Philosophy*, 9 (1825), 241–57 and 10 (1825), 18–37.

87   A. Sedgwick, 'Presidential address to the Geological Society [1830]', *Proceedings of the Geological Society of London*, 1 (1826–33), 187–212, on 207–8. Here he was explicitly criticising A. Ure's *A New System of Geology, in which the Great Revolutions of the Earth and Animated Nature are reconciled at once to Modern Science and Sacred History*, London, 1829. See also Clark and Hughes, op. cit. (71), ii, 343 and 76–80.

88   A. Sedgwick, 'Anniversary address [1831]', *Proceedings of the Geological Society of London*, 1 (1826–33), 281–316.

89   *Ibid.*, ii, 84.

90   Sedgwick's review in the *Spectator* is reprinted in Hull, op. cit. (68), 159–66. Also letter to Darwin, *ibid.*, 157–9, and Clark and Hughes, op. cit. (71), ii, 356–60.

91   *Ibid.*, ii, 55.

92   I. G. Barbour, *Religion in an Age of Science*, London, 1990, 1–30. A similar set of categories has been employed by J. F. Haught, *Science and Religion. From Conflict to Conversation*, New York, 1995.

93   T. Söderqvist, 'Existential projects and existential choice in science: Science biography as an edifying genre', in Shortland and Yeo, op. cit. (3), 62.

9

'A Taste for Philosophical Pursuits' – Quakers in the Royal Society of London

Although science is often viewed as a body of well-tested knowledge, it can also be studied fruitfully as a social activity. Indeed, much recent scholarship in the history and sociology of science has been directed to analysing the institutions in which scientists operate. The institutions of science include such formal organisations as universities, the Institute of Physics and the Glasgow Philosophical Society, but also informal groups of researchers with scientific interests in common. A similar perspective can be applied to the study of religion since much religious activity takes place within institutions, such as mosques, synagogues, churches, the Salvation Army, the *Tablet* and the Ecumenical Movement.

If both science and religion can be viewed as social practices associated with institutions, the science–religion interrelation is likewise open to social and institutional analysis. Such an approach might compare and contrast scientific and religious institutions in any of a number of ways; for example, in terms of their aims, functions, authority, recruitment, organisational structure and openness to outsiders. In some instances the relationship will be convergent, in other cases divergent. An example of the former is the use of the term 'scientific clerisy' to describe early members of the British Association for the Advancement of Science who implemented Samuel Taylor Coleridge's vision of a new clerisy that would provide intellectual leadership for the nation. The application of the term 'clerisy' to scientists also acknowledges that by the 1830s science had become a powerful institution within society.[1] By contrast, other writers have repudiated any apparent similarity between science and ecclesiastical institutions. In noting that a narrow-minded consensus had developed within the scientific community at the turn of the twentieth century, the Austrian physicist/philosopher Ernst Mach expressed his strong disapprobation. Hence his complaint that '[s]cientists have now become a church and I do not regard it as an honour to be a member of this or of any church'.[2]

In this chapter we shall be concerned with the interrelation between a particular scientific institution – the Royal Society of London – and a religious institution – the Society of Friends (otherwise known as the Quakers). Although George Fox had been attracting followers for several years, 1652 is usually taken as the start of the Quakers as an independent religious movement, while the Royal Society, which can be traced to earlier groupings, received its Charter of Incorporation from Charles II in 1662. If we examine their subsequent histories, one evident connection between these two Societies is the number of Quakers who have been honoured by a Fellowship of the Royal Society (henceforth FRS). The chemist John Dalton, Thomas Young (of wave theory fame) and Lord Lister come readily to mind – although of these three only Dalton remained a Quaker throughout his life. In our own century we can cite the astronomer Arthur Stanley Eddington and the crystallographer Kathleen Lonsdale (the latter being one of the first two women elected to the Royal Society in 1945).

Historians have not only been impressed by the major contributions made by these and other Quaker scientists, but have also claimed that an impressively large number of Quakers were elected to the Royal Society when compared with the small proportion of Friends in the total population. Indeed, according to one frequently-cited statistic, in the latter half of the nineteenth century the probability of a man being elected an FRS was approximately forty-six times higher 'if he was a Quaker, or of Quaker descent, than was the case if he belonged to the general population'.[3] This is an impressive figure that appears to identify Quakers as statistically significant within the Royal Society. This statistic is also usually taken as evidence that Quakers were particularly productive members of the British scientific community. However, after reworking the data we find this figure to be incorrect in two important respects. First, as Fig. 31 indicates, the foregoing figure approached 35 (not 46) at the turn of the century but was also considerably smaller during the immediately-preceding decades. Second, the cited figure is also misleading because the proportion varied considerably over time, not rising above 5 until the third quarter of the nineteenth century. Indeed, prior to the second decade of the eighteenth century, only one FRS was a practising Quaker. In the light of these criticisms Quaker involvement in the Royal Society requires reanalysis.

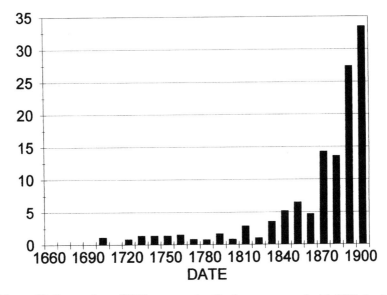

Figure 31: Proportion of FRSs among the Quakers compared with FRSs in the general population; for each decade 1670–1900.

Before proceeding with our own investigation we must specify its limitations. In the ensuing discussion we have identified those Quakers who had gained their Fellowships by the beginning of the twentieth century. Moreover, by adopting this criterion we have included all those Quaker FRSs born before or during the year 1861, a date which possesses some significance in Quaker history since it marks a major change in the membership rules, especially in respect to inter-marriage, which had previously resulted in numerous exclusions.

The problem of deciding who is to be counted as a Quaker turns out to be more difficult and more convoluted than one might expect. Considerable care is necessary since earlier analyses contain a high proportion of inaccuracies, especially in the first century of Quakerism, and these misidentifications have often been adopted uncritically by later writers.[4] In compiling Appendix 1 we have sought to remedy some of these defects. However, the available data have still not always enabled us to determine unequivocally which Fellows of the Royal Society were Quakers. Nevertheless, proceeding cautiously and using the best evidence available, we have listed 56 Quaker FRSs born before 1862.

However, there is a further problem with the identification of Quakers. By the beginning of the eighteenth century a high propor-tion of Quakers were 'birthright Quakers'; that is, of Quaker parentage; indeed, nearly all of the men on our list were birthright Quakers. During the eighteenth and nineteenth centuries the Society of Friends attracted relatively few who were not of Quaker parentage. This route was taken by only two on our list – Martin Barry and William Pengelly.[5] By contrast, in each generation disownment resulted in a significant loss of members. According to one recent analysis relating to the mid nineteenth century 'between a quarter and a third of all who married at all' married out and were therefore disowned.[6] The proportion of those who left or were disowned varied and it may not be very helpful to compound figures over a period of two and a half centuries, yet 29 of the 56 FRSs (i.e. 52%) were disunited at the time of their deaths. This proportion is probably somewhat higher than for the Quaker body overall, but we should be careful not to draw the premature conclusion that dabbling in science was a significant cause of exclusion. Indeed, on closer inspection there is no evidence that participation in science resulted directly in any exclusions. Moreover, as Fig. 32 shows, the proportion of our small sample who were disowned varied considerably over two centuries. That fewer disownments occurred in the

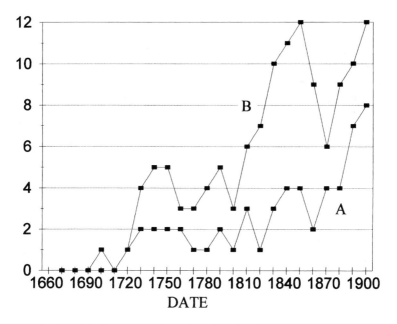

Figure 32: Line A indicates number of Quakers in the Royal Society, and line B shows the sum of Quakers *and* ex-Quakers. The vertical distance between these lines indicates the number of ex-Quakers (i.e. those who had been disowned). Graph points for each decade 1670–1900.

closing decades of the nineteenth century reflects a more general trend after the organisational changes in 1861.

Intermarriage was certainly the major reason for disownment,[7] although many Quakers were excluded for other deviations. For example, Thomas Young was disowned in 1798 for 'having attended places of public diversion' and for subsequently attempting to justify his behaviour when interviewed by a deputation of elders. A close friend of Young, Hudson Gurney, 'reacted strongly against [his] strict Quaker upbringing ... [and was] disowned by the Society in 1803 for making [a] contribution to a fund for military purposes at a time of danger of French invasion'.[8] Disownment also sometimes resulted from schisms within the Society. For example, during the Beacon controversy of 1836 an evangelical group seceded that included the meteorologist Luke Howard and his son John Eliot Howard, who studied the properties of quinine.[9] At some points in our analysis we shall have to distinguish those who remained within the Society throughout their lives from those lapsed Quakers, like Young, Gurney and the two Howards. We shall refer to this latter group as *ex-Quakers*. In Fig. 32 the difference between the two lines indicates the number of ex-Quaker FRSs at the start of each decade. However, the group of ex-Quakers is far from homogeneous since although some firmly rejected their religious upbringing others remained in close contact with the Quaker movement and even continued to attend meetings. For example, the Liberal politician William Forster 'retained the deepest interest in all' aspects of Quakerism after being excluded for marrying Matthew Arnold's daughter. Following his death in 1886, a memorial service was held in Westminster Abbey but Forster was subsequently accorded a 'simple Quaker funeral' and was buried near his home in Yorkshire.[10]

Compiling a list of Quaker FRSs forces the historian to confront other problems, one of which can be illustrated by the example of William Penn who was proposed for Fellowship by the tea merchant John Houghton in 1681, shortly before he set sail for America. Penn is not included in Appendix 1 because, in the strict sense, he was not an FRS; for although his name appears in the published register of Fellows he was never formally admitted to the Society, never attended a meeting nor paid his dues. Despite Penn's evident support for the Society's aims and his subsequent assertion that he was 'a Greshamist throughout',[11] his direct involvement with the Royal Society was minimal.[12]

It is also important to note that, until the latter decades of the nineteenth century, the Royal Society contained numerous Fellows who did not actively pursue scientific research. Indeed, the high proportion of members who made no contribution to scientific knowledge was emphasised by the reformers who sought to change the Society's constitution in the second quarter of the century. Yet prior to the mid-century most of those elected to the Society did not possess any scientific credentials or publications. For many it was just another London club and one with the added attraction of a Royal Charter. However, there is evidence that a far higher proportion of Quakers was active scientifically within the Royal Society than among their non-Quaker counterparts.[13] These data also suggest that a relatively smaller proportion of Quakers joined the Royal Society for purely social reasons. We should also note that although the new statutes of 1847 sought to deter those lacking a scientific reputation, members of 'the privileged class' continued to be granted admission to the Society. Two of our number who were Privy Councillors, the Rt Hon William Edward Forster (FRS 1875) and the Rt Hon Lord Justice Sir Edward Fry (FRS 1883), obtained membership by this less rigorous route.

It has to be stressed that much first-rate science was pursued outside the sometimes dreary and unedifying proceedings of the Royal Society. Moreover, certain identifiable groups, such as amateur botanists, which included many Quakers, were not well-represented among FRSs. Membership was restricted in other ways. Women were categorically excluded until 1945, while many of those who could not afford the substantial subscription may also have been deflected.[14] Hence we must be careful not to assume that any conclusions about the Royal Society apply to the broader scientific community.

Absence of Quakers to *c.* 1710

The first Quaker FRS was Edward Haistwell, a wealthy London merchant who earlier in his career had been amanuensis to George Fox. Apart from serving on Council for one year Haistwell was not active in the Royal Society and his scientific interests – if any – remain obscure.[15] Except for Haistwell and the problematic case of Penn, there were no Quaker FRSs during the Society's first half century. The reason for this almost complete absence is to be found in the movement's early character when Friends constituted what one historian has called 'a group of vagrant and sometimes naked preachers and their ecclesiastically subversive followers'.[16] Opposition to Fox and his acolytes was often violent and numerous early Quakers were imprisoned or suffered at the hands of the mob.

During its early history the Society of Friends was principally involved in preaching its religious message, in gaining converts and in cementing its network of followers. Most early Quakers would not have encountered the grandees in London who controlled the Royal Society. The 'Royal' designation may also have deterred them because of its social and political connotations with royalty and the establishment. One of the few extant comments on the Royal Society by an early Quaker came from the pen of Isaac Penington who, in 1668, addressed a short theological work to the Society. He commended the Society for 'seeking after the excellency of Nature and Learning' but warned that such a project should be subsumed within a programme for obtaining religious understanding. He therefore cautioned the Fellows not to limit themselves to studying nature but urged them to 'know and partake of true wisdom, and feel union with God in ... [their] own [Lives]'.[17]

It is difficult to know whether Penington's views were typical of the early generations of Quakers. However, a few early Friends positively encouraged the study of nature as a morally elevating activity suitable for Quakers and as an appropriate subject for instruction. For example, Fox urged that schools should teach natural history and emphasise the usefulness of God's creation. Like other Quakers who crossed the Atlantic, Penn could but marvel at the profusion of God's works – 'Strawberry's ripe in the woods in Aprill ... Peas, beans, Cherrys & Mulberrys ... The sorts of fish in these parts are excellent and numerous ... Mineral[s] here is [in?] great store.'[18] Moreover, Thomas Lawson, the Cumbrian botanist, practised science extensively and earned a substantial reputation. However, when he visited London in 1677 Lawson made no attempt to contact the Royal Society, although he subsequently corresponded with John Ray and other Fellows. Lawson's interest was instead directed towards collecting botanical specimens and meeting fellow Quakers.[19]

Perhaps the most intriguing link between the early Royal Society and the Quakers is to be found in a draft of Penn's *Frame of Government for Pennsylvania* where he urged that certain matters in the Pennsylvania legislature should 'be determined by a balloting box as it is now used in the Royal Society at Gresham College'.[20] Clearly impressed by the way members were elected to the Royal Society by secret ballot, Penn suggested that the same procedure should be adopted in his new Quaker state. Although the passage did not appear when the *Frame of Government* was printed in 1682, it offers an example of how organisational structures can traverse subject domains.

Wealth and Social Respectability

After minimal contact for half a century, a cohort of three practising Quakers and four ex-Quakers was elected to the Royal Society between 1711 and 1734. During this period Newton and (from 1727) Hans Sloane sat in the Presidential chair. We shall be using the members of this group – especially those who remained Friends – to introduce the main themes in this chapter; the first being wealth and social respectability.

Quaker persecution declined markedly after 1685 and the Toleration Act of 1689 provided another significant moment in their social legitimation. By the early eighteenth century Quakers had 'settled down ... as a highly respectable and rather exclusive "connection"'.[21] They were still readily recognisable by their clothing; they maintained their own customs and were subject to discrimination and even imprisonment for failing to pay tithes and church rates. However, general attitudes towards the Quakers were changing as was the Society itself, with increasing emphasis on family connections and on the organisational structure of the movement. While there were certainly a few wealthy Friends in the seventeenth century, such as Haistwell, the opening decades of the eighteenth witnessed not only a significant improvement in their economic position, but more importantly in the eyes of contemporaries they became increasingly respectable.

Silvanus Bevan and Peter Collinson were early Quakers with commercial interests who were accepted as gentlemen and welcomed into the Royal Society. Bevan was admitted to the Society of Apothecaries in 1715 and rapidly built up the highly successful Plough Court Pharmacy just off Lombard Street in the City of London. Ten years later he was elected to the Royal Society. Collinson, the son of a woollen draper, took over his father's business but also began trading in seeds and plants particularly from America. Although his interest in botany had started as a hobby, he was elected to the Royal Society in 1728 and by the mid 1730s he had worked up a flourishing business with extensive contacts on both sides of the Atlantic. Collinson played a key role in providing British collectors with exotics from America, often obtained from his Quaker contacts in Pennsylvania.[22]

Contemporary accounts emphasise that both Collinson and Bevan were not only economically secure but also respected gentlemen. Partly owing to their business successes and partly to financially-advantageous marriages they both lived well and used their wealth judiciously to earn the respect of others. One visitor was greatly impressed by Bevan's 'beautiful garden' in Hackney which contained 'every kind of flowers, plants, and vegetables ... [and] the noble statue of the Gladiator ... In the house [were] a variety of curious paintings and rich old china ... He is visited by most great men of taste.'[23] Likewise Collinson cultivated his own attractive gardens at Peckham and later at Mill Hill that were admired by many visitors. He counted numerous gentry and nobility among his clients and also supplied plants and seeds to the Apothecaries' Gardens at Chelsea and the Royal Gardens at Kew. The substantial houses owned by Collinson and Bevan and their ornamental gardens well-stocked with unusual imported plants are indications not only of their wealth but also of their cultivated and respectable lifestyle.

Many later Quaker and ex-Quaker FRSs were also wealthy. They were often the sons of successful Quaker families that had accrued considerable affluence (and often land) through business, through manufacturing and through banking . Luke Howard, for example, was the son of an affluent tin-plate manufacturer from whom he received a settlement of £10,000, and he also married into a wealthy family of city merchants. Richard Phillips, the chemist, and his geologist brother William were from a family with substantial investments in mining and country property. Thomas Young inherited a house, a library, paintings and approximately £10,000 following the death of a kinsman, Dr Richard Brocklesby, in 1797. Robert Were Fox hailed from a family with extensive banking and manufacturing interests in Devon and Cornwall.[24] Yet there were some apparent counter-examples that, on closer examination, often confirm the preceding generalisation. Thus although Silvanus P. Thompson was the son of a schoolmaster at Bootham, his grandfather was a manufacturing chemist in Liverpool and his mother hailed from the well-established Tatham family who owned a successful pharmaceutical business in Settle.[25] One of the few genuine exceptions was John Dalton who gained financial security only after receiving a Civil List Pension of £150 per annum in 1833, rising three years later to £250.[26]

Career patterns are also highly relevant. Many of the Quaker and ex-Quaker FRSs had attended schools set up by Friends for the sons of Friends, such as Grove House (in Tottenham), Wigton (Cumbria), Ackworth and Bootham (in Yorkshire).[27] Although Quakers controlled their own schools, which often emphasised science subjects, subsequent career choices and educational opportunities were limited. Many proceeded into the so-called 'innocent trades' such as iron smelting, food production and medicine. Of the three traditional professions – the clergy, the law and medicine – only the last was open and particularly attractive to Quakers.

Occupational patterns did however change, with the legal profession becoming an increasingly viable option in the nineteenth century. Moreover, although in the late eighteenth century a few ex-Quakers entered Parliament, it was not until 1833 that the first practising Quaker was elected. Six Members of Parliament are included in our list of FRSs, and it may be no coincidence that all six were disowned by the Friends.[28] Perhaps due to its strong involvement in worldly matters a political career did not sit easily with Quaker practice? Less easily, it seems, than a career in science.

All branches of the medical profession proved attractive to Quakers. In almost every town and city where there was a sizeable meeting house Quaker physicians, surgeons and apothecaries were in evidence, often playing a major role in founding hospitals and dispensaries. However, Quakers could not gain degrees at either Oxford or Cambridge until the Test Acts were repealed in 1871. Although the zoologist J. J. Lister was the first practising Quaker on our list to obtain a Cambridge degree (BA 1880), Thomas Young had commenced studies at Cambridge several months before his disownment in 1798. Probably the main attraction of a Cambridge degree was that it enabled him to obtain a Fellowship at the Royal College of Physicians.[29]

Prior to Cambridge Young had conformed to Quaker norms by studying at London, Edinburgh and on the Continent. It is interesting to note that many Quakers, including several other FRSs, followed a similar educational trajectory. Thus in the 1730s the eminent physician Dr John Fothergill had studied at Edinburgh and St Thomas's Hospital in London, where he subsequently practised.[30] Some Quaker doctors also studied for a time on the Continent – Leyden being popular until the early nineteenth century; thereafter Paris or one of the German universities. It has even been suggested that the Test Acts help to explain the success of Quakers in science and medicine during the eighteenth and early nineteenth centuries since they were thereby spared an Oxbridge education and instead attended universities that often offered a far superior education in science.[31]

Apothecaries feature significantly on our list of Quaker FRSs. To become an apothecary required extensive training including attendance at medical lectures while serving an apprenticeship under an established apothecary. Apprenticeship was expensive, parents paying about £250 in the late eighteenth century to place a son in a respectable London establishment.[32] The Plough Court Pharmacy, with its strong tradition in developing and manufacturing pharmaceuticals, is important since it produced six Quakers who were elected to the Royal Society.[33] It may not only have been modesty but also a sense of social hierarchy that caused Daniel Hanbury to express the 'feeling that it would be invidious were the honour of membership [of the Royal Society] conferred on a pharmaceutist who had really accomplished so little for science'.[34] The pharmacy at Plough Court also offers a microcosm of Quaker society with its nexus of business and family connections. The families of these pharmacists frequently inter-married and were also involved in joint business ventures. The firm of Allen and Hanbury, which still exists, was founded by two of these Quaker dynasties.

Medicine and pharmacy were often related to the themes of philanthropy and social reform.[35] One of the earliest FRSs on our list, John Bellers, was an ardent reformer and devised schemes for the education of poor children and for prison reform. In 1714 he published a small book containing elaborate plans for an extensive national health service which, he argued, was necessary for the physical, economic and moral health of the nation. This project was to be funded by the state which was also required to endow the Royal Society generously, 'the better to Enable them to carry on that Useful and Grand Design, of improving Men in the Knowledge of NATURE ... of which MEDICINE is the principal Branch'. Thus the Royal Society was accorded a crucial role in his visionary plan for the advancement of medicine and medical care. The Royal Society was also expected to reward with prizes those who made new discoveries. Needless to say none of these proposals was adopted. Later, however, Karl Marx was greatly enamoured with Beller's writings and celebrated him as one of the precursors of communism.[36]

Subsequent Quaker FRSs were also heavily involved in philanthropic schemes. In the second half of the eighteenth century Fothergill, Lettsom and the ex-Quaker Dimsdale were major proponents of mass inoculation against smallpox, with Lettsom particularly involved in both the Society for Inoculating the Poor and the General Dispensary, which was better able to deliver preventive medicine to the less affluent population of London. Fothergill supported John Woolman's anti-slavery campaign and John Howard's work on prison reform. Lettsom was likewise active in the prison reform movement, freed his slaves on Tortola, and was a prime mover in the Royal Humane Society. Fothergill was the founder of a medical society (*c.* 1752) and Lettsom was one of the founders in 1773 of the Medical Society of London, which challenged the Royal Colleges and their vested interest in retaining the professional separation between physicians, surgeons and apothecaries.[37] Likewise, in the cruel 1790s the pharmacist William Allen founded a soup kitchen to help feed the poor in London and served on Count Rumford's committee of the Society for Bettering the Condition of the Poor. Soon he was also involved in propagating Jenner's views on vaccination. One of his reasons for pursuing science was that he conceived it as the handmaiden to his philanthropic activities. For example, scientific knowledge was required in order to produce cheap, nutritious soup and curative medicines.[38] Later in life Allen retired from his pharmaceutical business in order to devote himself to philanthropic projects. He became a roving envoy founding schools for the poor and trying to resolve international conflicts.

A major change in the Royal Society occurred around the mid nineteenth century when a concerted move was made to undercut the traditional system of patronage by limiting membership to those who had made contributions to science.[39] Over the ensuing decades the proportion of FRSs who were not scientifically productive fell significantly. Although interested amateurs continued to join, they were increasingly displaced by those who held scientific posts, especially in universities. This trend is strongly reflected by several late Victorian academics who appear in Appendix 1, including William Miller, William Harvey, Joseph Lister, Edward Tylor, Daniel Oliver, the Brady brothers, John Cash and Silvanus Thompson.[40] Of those Quaker and ex-Quaker FRSs living at the turn of the century the only representative of the continuing amateur tradition was the lawyer and botanist Edward Fry.

Social Construction of the Quaker FRS

In the preceding chapter we sought to interrelate science and religion through biographical narratives. Although the biographies of individuals play only a minor role in studies of institutions, there are some apposite questions to be asked about the relation between an institution and the personal qualities of its members. Certain personal characteristics may be fostered by an institution, while those people who are seen as deficient are often excluded. In the Society of Friends much emphasis is placed on personal responsibility and the importance of developing Quakerly values and virtues. Although Quakers do not subscribe to a creed, much of their literature, from Fox's writings to the current edition of *Quaker Faith and Practice*, emphasises discipline and contains prescriptions for individual behaviour. Thus the social norms of the Society of Friends are relevant to this study, particularly those that can be related to science.

William Allen's diary is a breathtaking document. He appears to have possessed boundless energy and to have crammed a vast amount into his three-score years and ten. Quaker meetings, spiritual meditations, science, philanthropy, business and travels abroad – together with three marriages – seem to have occupied his every moment. Reflections on what he must achieve even invaded his nights: 'On waking at night', he wrote on 1 March 1823, 'my mind was sweetly contrited and comforted in the feeling of divine goodness and my own nothingness. Dedicated myself afresh to the service of my dear Lord and Master.'[41] Yet his diary not only provides an account of his own life but also indicates how a devout Quaker was expected to behave. It is noticeable that many of the other Quakers on our list were vigorous men who not only filled their lives profitably but refused to waste time. For example, the London surgeon Jonathan Hutchinson wrote to his wife claiming that he had been busy all morning and was feeling energetic: 'It seems a general impression that my attempt to resuscitate the London Hospital reports will fail. Oh the lack of zeal [on the part of others]!' He then recounted the views of Dr John Rutty, an eighteenth-century Quaker surgeon in Ireland. 'He used to bewail the sloth of the Dublin Apothecaries, who would not meet him at six o'clock in the morning ... I think I shall write an essay on Zest of Existence, Appetite of Life, or some such title.' In a later letter the puritanical Hutchinson succinctly summed up his attitude: 'All waste is sin, whether of time, energy, or material.'[42]

This requirement to live life to the full was coupled with the demand that the Quaker should not be capricious but present a serious demeanour. From the start of the movement frivolous activities were proscribed. Thus in his *Apology for the True Christian Divinity*, first published in 1676, Robert Barclay warned against participating in 'gambling, diversions, and frolicsome pleasures ... to play cards, roll dice, and dance ... to sing, fiddle, or pipe ... to use stage-plays and comedies'. Instead, Quakers were exhorted to be humble, dress modestly and spend their time wisely and usefully.[43] Religious observance and, increasingly throughout the latter part of the eighteenth century, good works were accepted as the marks of a devout Friend. With many other avenues closed to them, science was highly acceptable to many Quakers precisely because it was a sober endeavour that not only led to truth but also displayed the hand of a rational, providential designer. A high degree of commitment and determination often accompanied the Quaker scientist's sober pursuit of truth. As Hudson Gurney wrote in his memoir of Thomas Young:

His parents were ... [among] the strictest of a sect, whose fundamental principle it is, that the perception of what is right and wrong, to its minutest ramifications, is to be looked for in the immediate influence of a supreme intelligence, and that therefore the individual is to act upon this, lead where it may, and compromise nothing. To the bent of these early impressions he [Young] was accustomed in afterlife to attribute, in some degree, the power he so eminently possessed of an imperturbable resolution to effect any object on which he was engaged, which he brought to bear on every thing he undertook ... .[44]

This seriousness and goal-directedness could sometimes be over-bearing. Caroline Fox, a 'gay Quaker' and the daughter of the scientist Robert Were Fox, received the following account from the French physicist Dominique Arago. Arago had met John Dalton at a social gathering and described him as a strait-laced and rather traditional Quaker who 'could not take a joke at all. Once when Dalton had taken a glass of wine, Arago, who does not drink any, remarked, "Why, you are quite a debauchee compared to me."' Dalton took this remark 'very ill' and apparently never recovered from it all evening.[45]

Despite adopting an earnest approach to their science, many Quakers appreciated that neither science nor business should be viewed as their ultimate goals. Repeatedly Quakers were warned that while they should be *in* this world they should not be *of* the world. Science, business ventures or any other worldly activity could lead members to compromise their religious fidelity. The young William Allen was cautioned by an elderly woman at his Meeting House who warned

lest my ardent desire for knowledge, even with laudable intention of bene-fiting mankind, should eclipse the lustre of that inestimable gift, which she believed was bestowed upon me. Her discourse was delivered with great affection, and enforced with energy. O! could I believe that I should ever attain – that I should struggle through the briars and thorns, how would my soul rejoice! But the sickening prospect of those who have failed by the way, and the humiliating sense of my own weakness and unworthy-ness, at times almost weigh me down.

In many of his early diary entries he expressed similar concerns. Thus after delivering a successful lecture at the Royal Institution he wrote: 'May I be preserved and never give up my principles, for the empty applause of the world, which, in a trying hour, will yield no support!'[46] Likewise, having recently obtained his Bachelor of Arts degree at London University, the over-confident nineteen-year-old Silvanus Thompson was deflated by John Bright, the eminent Liberal politician and Quaker, who rebuked him with the words: 'Nature provides a very convenient safety-valve for knowledge too rapidly acquired!' However, Thompson subsequently admitted that he recognised the wisdom of Bright's admonition. Like several of the other Quaker FRSs on our list Thompson became a minister and elder in the Society of Friends. He enjoyed a successful career in science and science education – he was the biographer of both Faraday and Kelvin and served as Principal of Finsbury Technical College. Yet he remained a modest, humble Quaker who was greatly involved in the sect's affairs and played a major role in the 1895 Manchester Conference at which a new synthesis of tradition and modernity was hammered out.[47]

Those Quakers covered in this study appear not to have viewed scientific knowledge as a threat to their religion but to have acknowledged a high degree of convergence between these two domains. For example, Thompson claimed that his science and his Quakerism were mutually supporting; the search for truth was paramount in both activities. Thus in his 1915 Swarthmore Lecture entitled *The Quest for Truth*, he argued that since science is one of the surest roads to Truth, the pursuit of science was an important, worthwhile activity for a devout Quaker. Moreover, he claimed that, owing to the method of experimental verification by independent workers, science provides a much higher standard of truth than is found in most other domains.[48]

The status of the Bible has been a matter of contention throughout Quaker history, but for many the Bible has been more a source of inspiration than the canonical basis for religion. The individual must heed his or her inner light and accept the responsibility to decide what is true and how to lead a moral, worthwhile life. This lack of dogma seems to have enabled Quakers not only to pursue science but to pursue it in a relatively unencumbered manner. Thus, for example, Quaker schools have generally evinced more enthusiasm for science education than have their Anglican counterparts. But there is a related point worth making concerning the organisational structure of the Society of Friends. Despite the emphasis on discipline, each member is encouraged to form his or her own views on any subject. In the search after religious truth Quakers have usually emphasised toleration and the need to hear all viewpoints in meetings; the aim of the meeting being to try to forge a consensus acceptable to all parties. Although this ideal has not always worked in practice, it may have helped inculcate a similarly open attitude towards science. From this perspective scientific theories are acknowledged as tentative and, at best, stations on the road to truth, not immovable dogmas that have to be defended against all criticism. Moreover, from the earliest days of the movement there was a deep suspicion of systems, whether in theology, philosophy or science.

This thesis is corroborated if we examine how our Quakers responded to Darwin's theory of evolution, which caused such ructions in the Victorian religious world. The admittedly limited evidence to hand suggests that Quaker scientists (like Unitarians and, perhaps, certain other dissenters) were more prepared to entertain Darwin's theory than their Anglican counterparts and did not encounter religious scruples in accepting it. For example, in an early essay dating from 1871 Silvanus Thompson asserted that as a Quaker he found nothing upsetting in Darwin's theory since it did not conflict with religion, when both scientific theory and religious understanding were correctly interpreted. Rejecting biblical creationism as untenable, he insisted that religion must be a rational enterprise. He also welcomed evolution because, like other scientific theories, it displayed God's design and purpose in the physical world.[49] The lawyer and amateur botanist Edward Fry responded similarly to Darwin's theory. As he later recounted, the publication of the *Origin of Species*

> caused great uneasiness in the minds of many good people, who felt that Darwin's teaching, and still more the suggestions that arose from his teaching, to be inconsistent with the teachings of the Bible and their hopes of immortality for the human race. I gave a good deal of attention, as every one did, to those new views ... but I did not, like so many good people, feel distressed at the influence of Darwin's theory upon my religious views.[50]

He subsequently wrote a small book of essays in which he urged that science posed no threat to religion; indeed, in his own view, science must lead to 'a sublime spirituality'. The anthropologist and early Gifford Lecturer Edward Tylor offers a further example, but a somewhat problematic one since he and his wife resigned from the Quakers in 1864. Tylor encompassed the theory of evolution soon after Darwin's book was published and he also shared with the Darwinians a naturalistic perspective and methodology which he applied to the development of human societies. The influence of his Quaker background may nevertheless be apparent in his commitment to the idea of progress and his rejection of ritual and superstition as degenerate.[51]

A different type of evidence is to be gleaned from the Certificates of Election to the Royal Society which show that Charles Darwin supported both Tylor and the Quaker botanist George Brady. Likewise Thomas Henry Huxley recommended four Friends, and Joseph Hooker added his support for five. Such examples of patronage within the Royal Society suggest that the Darwin circle viewed these Quakers as allies.[52] While Quaker responses to Darwinism need to be researched in greater depth, the preceding evidence suggests that Quaker scientists did not perceive Darwin's theory as a threat to religion, but welcomed it as a potential step on the path to truth. Moreover, this attitude to evolution may be indicative of a more general willingness not to encumber science with religious doctrine.

Networking

We turn now to the social structures that have been such a crucial part of the Society of Friends. Not only is the meeting house the centre of Quaker life but Quakerism is an essentially social religion since the individual is locked into a complex organisation with its Monthly Meetings, Quarterly Meetings, Yearly Meetings and Meetings of Sufferings. Responsibility is shared but each individual has a duty to support the organisation. Moreover, the strength of communal Quakerism emphasises the need for the individual to interrelate with others in order to maintain the organisation's fabric. These social and networking functions appear to have been readily carried over into their activities within secular institutions, such as the Royal Society.

It has often been noted how Quakers supported one another in business.[53] The same is true of Quaker FRSs, many of whom were linked by business and familial ties. Moreover, in the election of Fellows to the Royal Society, a similar support system operated among Quakers and ex-Quakers. Prior to 1731 a potential member was first proposed by a current FRS. At a subsequent meeting a secret ballot would be held. If successful at the ballot, the new member would be admitted after signing a bond. Bevan proposed both Collinson and the ex-Quaker mathematician Benjamin Robins.[54] Beginning in 1731 a new system was introduced. A certificate was now displayed in the Society's rooms for a specified length of time and signed by existing Fellows who wished to support the prospective candidate. Election could only proceed if enough signatures were collected.[55] Thus we possess a record showing that Quakers (and ex-Quakers) often endorsed the candidature of other Quakers and ex-Quakers. For example, William Allen's signature appears on the certificates of Willan, Gurney, Luke Howard, Prichard, J. J. Lister and Barry, while Dillwyn, Young, Oliver and Hanbury each supported the applications of two or more fellow Quakers (or ex-Quakers). Since certificates were signed by a number of supporters – often a dozen or more – the Quaker vote was not decisive but it does indicate that the Quaker network operated within the Royal Society. Moreover, a supporting statement was required, although during the eighteenth and early nineteenth centuries this was often a variant of the formula: 'A gentleman well versed in various parts of natural knowledge.' Although some Quakers (and particularly ex-Quakers) were supported by this conventional formula, in many instances a far stronger case was mounted. Thus in the certificate that preceded his election in 1821 Howard was described as the 'Author of the Climate of London and several other Meteorological Papers'.[56]

It is striking what a central role Quakers and, particularly, ex-Quakers have played in maintaining the Royal Society's organisation. If we turn first to those elected in the 1710s–1730s, Thomas Birch's career illustrates how a less affluent ex-Quaker could obtain respect, trust and social status through connection with the Royal Society. The son of a coffee-mill maker from Clerkenwell, he was educated by Quakers and served as an usher at Quaker schools until 1726. His exclusion would have predated his marriage to a curate's daughter in 1728, two years before he was baptised. Although he subsequently made his career in the Church of England, rising to the Presidency of Sion College, his reputation rested primarily on his various literary ventures, his Secretaryship of the Royal Society (1752–65) and the major role he played in founding the British Museum. Birch's most recent biographer has emphasised that he was a hard-working 'self-made man' who 'must have been very aware of the indolence of those of superior station. However, he had a genius for friendship.'[57] This description could equally apply to John Bellers, Collinson or Bevan. All four worked hard to achieve their positions but were also highly successful in their dealings with others and cultivated acquaintances from a wide range of occupations and social positions. The emerging sense of family and community among the Quakers may have given these men a social advantage in dealing with other people in a kindly and generous manner. Moreover, their Quaker background may have proved helpful in distancing them from contemporary political and religious controversies so that they could be accepted by protagonists on all sides.

It is important to stress the centrality of this small group of Quakers and ex-Quakers in maintaining the organisational structure of the Royal Society. Not only was Birch one of the Secretaries for a thirteen-year period, but he served on Council for a total of eighteen years, while John Bellers, Silvanus Bevan, John Collinson and the ex-Quaker instrument maker George Graham also served on Council, the last two on a number of occasions. The three practising Quakers in this group must have looked conspicuous in their plain, black dress and broad hats. During the period from 1720 to the mid-1760s there was an almost continuous presence of Quakers and ex-Quakers on the twenty-one man Council; indeed for twelve years two of them served.[58] The effect of these Quakers and ex-Quakers on the running of the Royal Society has yet to be ascertained, but their presence is a reflection of their standing as honest, respected and respectable Fellows. Their names also appear in connection with other aspects of the Society's activities. For example, Collinson and Birch were among the eight Fellows who signed Benjamin Franklin's membership certificate, while Graham worked on the construction of John Harrison's chronometers and played a significant role in defining and producing the standard yard; both major practical projects directed by the Society.[59]

The Royal Society offered many attractions to these Quakers and ex-Quakers. Through the Society Collinson, Bevan, Birch and Graham all found customers for their business ventures selling (respectively) plants, medicines, books and instruments. But the social advantages gained through this connection were even more important. Birch in particular aligned his career with the Royal Society, becoming not only one of its two secretaries but also the author of its four-volume *History* and Robert Boyle's biographer and editor.[60] There is also much evidence that Collinson and, to a lesser extent, Bevan expanded their business and personal connections well beyond the Quaker community through their contacts at the Royal Society. Moreover, these Quakers would have found the Royal Society a congenial venue since the Society officially espoused a non-denominational and non-political ideology.

This tradition of service to the Royal Society continued into the nineteenth century. Over that period Quakers and ex-Quakers were twice as strongly represented on Council when compared with the overall membership. Following Thomas Birch's example, four other ex-Quakers became officers of the Society; Thomas Young was Foreign Secretary from 1804 until his death in 1829, William Miller held the Vice-Presidency and was also Treasurer, Henry Head was Vice-President in 1916–17, and Lord Lister, after two years as Foreign Secretary, was President from 1895 to 1900. That five ex-Quakers became officers of the Society may indicate the perpetuation of social commitments instilled during their Quaker upbringing. Another form of service is seen in the case of Henry Bowman Brady who bequeathed to the Royal Society his books and papers on Protozoa together with the sum of £800.

Although the Royal Society had been the only major scientific society in England during the early decades of the eighteenth century, a number of other scientific societies existed by the mid nineteenth. Many of these, like the Linnean and Geological Societies, were London-based and were limited to a specific subject area, while outside the metropolis there existed a mixture of generalist and specialist groups. Quakers were often prominent in these organisations. Two examples will suffice. Jonathan Hutchinson 'presided over the Hunterian [Society in 1869], in 1879 over the Pathological, and in 1883 over the Opthalmological. Then in 1887 he was president of the Neurological, in 1890 of the Medical, and in 1894 of the Royal Medical and Chirurgical Society.' He was also President of the Royal College of Surgeons in 1889–90. Not surprisingly, he did not attend meetings of the Royal Society regularly, although he valued his Fellowship greatly.[61] The second example is the botanist John Gilbert Baker, whose role curiously parallels that of Peter Collinson more than a century earlier. When the London Botanical Society went into abeyance in the late 1850s Baker, who was one of its leading lights, maintained one of the Society's key functions from his home in Thirsk. A founder member of the Thirsk Natural History Society, he turned this small local group into a botanical exchange club with a national clientele. Until a disastrous fire at his premises destroyed his stock eight years later, he played a major organisational role in British botany.[62]

Although we do not wish to claim that all the 56 Quaker and ex-Quaker FRSs were good networkers, many possessed this quality and used it effectively in the confined domain of the Royal Society. Moreover, a number of these FRSs made considerable use of their networking skills both within and without the scientific community. William Allen again provides a prime example since he was continually meeting people of different religious persuasions, different political colours and from diverse social backgrounds. A similar point is made by the biographer of the Cornish scientist Robert Were Fox who claimed that 'Strong as his own religious convictions [were] they did not prevent agreeable and profitable communion with men of every form of religious belief.'[63] As the diaries of Fox's son and daughter make clear, the family home was an open house not only for leading literary figures of the day, such as the Mills and Hartley Coleridges, but also for a wide cross-section of the scientific community. When in London or at a British Association meeting the

Foxes were engaged in an almost continuous round of socialising with other scientists.[64] A further example comes from Michael Foster's obituary notice of the botanist Henry Bowman Brady, whom he characterised as 'a friend and a helpmate ... His wide knowledge of many branches of scientific inquiry and his large acquaintance with scientific men made the hours spent with him always profitable.'[65]

The Significance of Natural History, Especially Botany

The Appendix listing 56 Quaker and ex-Quaker FRSs contains some surprises. The only mathematician is Benjamin Robins. Moreover, physics, which by the 1830s had become highly mathematical and the cutting edge of science, is vastly under-represented. Since Cambridge was the main breeding ground for mathematically-trained physicists this under-representation may be due in part to Cambridge University's refusal to award degrees to Dissenters throughout most of the century. Chemistry is rather better-represented, especially if its connection with pharmacy is acknowledged. But the subject that occurs most frequently on the list is botany, not only among those who were professionally engaged in botany but also among the many others who displayed a keen amateur enthusiasm for the subject. Over a third of those listed joined the Linnean Society, founded in 1798. Among the membership of the Linnean Society were many Quakers – often seedsmen and amateur botanists – who had no contact with the Royal. Likewise at least 5.4% of the 371-strong Botanical Society of London were practising Quakers. The significance of this figure becomes clearer when we remember that at this period Quakers constituted less than 0.1% of the population of England and Wales. However, of these twenty Quakers only three became Fellows of the Royal Society.[66]

An interest in botany can be traced back to the early Quakers. For example, George Fox urged that children should be taught the 'nature of herbs, roots, plants and trees' while William Penn, who made contributions to horticulture, likewise considered that Quakers should become competent naturalists.[67] Collinson and Fothergill are among the best-known eighteenth-century botanists, but there were numerous other Quakers during that period who practised botany. This tradition appears to have continued through the nineteenth century down to John Baker, Daniel Oliver and into our own century. Nor was botanical education ignored in Quaker schools; for example, Bootham School, York, developed a strong tradition in the sciences and could boast a Natural History Society from 1834 while children at Ackworth were encouraged to tend their own gardens.[68]

A vigorous amateur tradition existed. Returning to William Allen's journal we find a number of references to botany and also to the closely-related science of geology: he joined the Linnean Society in 1801 and was one of the founders of the Geological Society in 1807. In March 1801 he reported a botanical field trip with another Quaker to Walthamstow: 'got through classes and orders'. A few weeks later he and two other young Quakers 'had a rich feast of Botany, looking over my specimens. They tell me I have *one* very good thing, – the Juncus acutus.'[69] Another example of this thriving amateur tradition is provided by the prominent lawyer Edward Fry whose hobby was the study of mosses. Although he acknowledged that moss appears a humble subject he recommended 'the study of the Mosses to any, old or young, who really love Nature: I have found in it a great source of pleasure during several years'.[70]

Like Bevan and Collinson, later Quaker botanists often purchased houses with imposing gardens. Fothergill's garden at Upton was stocked with many exotics, and even some bullfrogs, obtained from Quaker collectors in America. Inviting Lettsom to visit his garden Fothergill advised: 'be pleased with its beauties, and be thankful to the Author of Nature for decorating the globe with numberless beauties'.[71] Following his second marriage in 1806 Allen spent much time at his spacious house in affluent Stoke Newington, while later in the century the Listers lived in Upton House close to the house and gardens once owned by Fothergill. Later Victorians moved further afield. Hutchinson acquired 200 acres near Haslemere in 1872 and built his house with a 'very large garden, and well laid out, with a charming old orchard, and two massive ancient Yew Trees just behind the house'. Fry purchased a rambling old house at Failand, overlooking the Bristol Channel. Its garden included a pinetum and many species of tree, but its dominant feature (which he designed) was 'a straight walk tiled with red bricks and with wide borders of grass and of herbaceous plants, leading to a small pond behind which Diana stands robing herself'. Robert Were Fox's garden at Penjerrick near Falmouth has been described as 'one of the loveliest gardens in England'.[72] Men like Hutchinson, Fry and Fox represent the rich, accomplished and cultured Victorians who surrounded themselves with well-stocked gardens and libraries. While such gardens are a statement of social stability, these Quakers also played an active role in botany, thereby combining their social positions, their research interests and their aesthetic and moral appreciation of the natural world. It should come as no surprise to learn that the inventor and manufacturer of the first iron lawnmower was a Quaker![73]

While botany flourished among affluent Quakers, a few of our FRSs held key positions in the British botanical establishment. We have already mentioned Baker's success in organising an exchange club, but in his subsequent career he held the positions of Assistant Keeper and (later) Keeper at the Kew Gardens Herbarium. When he accepted the job of Keeper in 1890 he took over from another of our Quaker FRSs, his friend and neighbour Daniel Oliver who had held that post since 1864, having previously been Assistant Keeper for six years. Thus for some four decades these two key positions at Kew were occupied by Quakers. Oliver also held the Chair of Botany at University College, London from 1861 to 1888. The output of these two botanists was prodigious: over 300 papers prior to 1900. Other Quakers on the list also held teaching positions in botany: William Harvey held the chair of Botany in Dublin from 1856, the Newcastle pharmacist Henry Bowman Brady lectured in Botany at Durham College, while his brother, who was also a physician, held the Chair of Natural History at Newcastle. The Brady brothers were both active in local scientific societies and published extensively, Henry principally on Foraminifera and George mainly on algae.

It would be too limiting to confine discussion to botany, since other branches of natural history were often pursued by the Quaker and ex-Quaker FRSs listed in Appendix 1. A number of them carried out research in meteorology, zoology, geology, astronomy and even anthropology. Like botany these subjects were largely observational and classificatory sciences. The evident commitment of Quakers to these branches of natural history has been a surprising outcome of this research and one that clearly deserves further attention. In part our surprise stems from the work of social historians who usually portray Quakers as practical men and entrepreneurs who spearheaded the Industrial Revolution.[74] Although the pharmacists on our list often made economic use of their botanical and chemical investigations, it is noticeable that the vast majority of the natural history pursued was decidedly non-utilitarian and that entrepreneurial concerns were not nearly as prominent as one might have expected. In this connection it is worth quoting a letter written in 1822 by Luke Howard to Goethe who had asked him why he had not published any papers on chemistry. Howard's reply was short and decided: 'C'est notre *metier* – we have to *live* by the practice of Chemistry as an art, and not by exhibiting it as a science.' Instead, Howard turned to meteorology and published much important work, especially his essay 'On the modifications of clouds' which contains the classification of cloud types still in general use.[75]

Although it is often difficult to disaggregate the various economic, philanthropic, religious and scientific factors affecting Quaker FRSs, their involvement in science is not reducible to economic forces. Instead, the religious appreciation of nature seems to have played a part, often a highly significant part. It should be noted that botany and other branches of natural history were principally experiential sciences. They bring the observer into a direct relation with God's creation and are the source of both aesthetic pleasure and religious enlightenment. This enthusiasm for natural history found incisive expression in a letter from the surgeon Jonathan Hutchinson to his wife. 'Botany', he wrote, 'is really a knowledge of the works of the Deity in plant life: what plants are, and how they have become so; and is full of the beautiful and wonderful.' Likewise, after instructing one of his American correspondents on how to pack specimens, John Fothergill stated that the 'useful, the beautiful, the singular or the fragrant are to us the most material'. But, he added, 'in the midst of all this attention, forget not the one thing needful. In studying nature forget not its author.'[76] Astronomy offered similar attractions and at least four of the FRSs listed in Appendix 1 constructed private observatories at their homes. One of these men, William Allen, recorded that astronomy offered him great pleasure and that at night he often retired to his observatory to witness God's sublime creation. As he emphasised in one of his lectures at Guy's Hospital, the importance of astronomy lay in its demonstration that 'the sustaining hand of God is still necessary, and [that] the present order and harmony which he has enabled us to understand and admire, is wholly dependent upon his will'.[77] This evocation of natural theology possesses a conventional ring, but it clearly demonstrates that Allen was deeply affected by observations of the natural world that led him to a fuller appreciation of God the Creator.

Since the religious sentiments expressed by Hutchinson, Fothergill and Allen were often repeated by the other Quaker (and ex-Quaker) FRSs we have examined, we are clearly dealing with a belief that was shared by the group. Indeed, the moral and theological dimensions of natural history (in its broader sense) appear to have proved particularly attractive to Quakers. As the editor of Allen's diary stated, he possessed a 'taste for philosophical pursuits'.[78] Allen, like many of the other FRSs discussed above, turned this 'taste' into scientific activitity and involvement in the Royal Society of London. Natural theology and the other factors examined in this chapter go a long way towards explaining not only the attraction of science but also why Quakers, as a group, have played such an important role in the Royal Society.

NOTES

1   J. Morrell and A. Thackray, *Gentlemen of Science: Early Years of the British Association for the Advancement of Science*, Oxford, 1981, 19–22. S. T. Coleridge, *On the Constitution of Church and State, According to the Idea of Each*, 2nd edn., London, 1830.

2   As quoted by P. Feyerabend in P. Hoyningen-Huene, 'Two letters of Paul Feyerabend to Thomas S. Kuhn on a draft of *The Structure of Scientific Revolutions*', *Studies in History and Philosophy of Science*, 26 (1995), 353–87, on 363.

3   E. H. Hankin, 'The mental ability of the Quakers', *Science Progress*, 16 (1921–2) 654–64; *Idem., Common Sense and its Cultivation*, London, 1928, 261–7; H. Lyons, *The Royal Society, 1660–1940. A History of its Administration under its Charters*, Cambridge, 1944, 115; S. Mason, 'Religion and the rise of modern science', in *Science and Religion. Proceedings of the Symposium of the XVIIIth International Congress of History of Science* (ed. A. Bäumer and M. Büttner), Bochum, 1989, 2–13, esp. 3–4. Other discussions of Quakers in the Royal Society can be found in Anon., 'Friends and the learned societies', *Journal of the Friends' Historical Society*, 7 (1910), 30–33 and A. R. Fry, *Quaker Ways*, London, 1933, 214–15. This claim was further inflated by A. Raistrick, *Quakers and Science and Industry, being an Account of the Quaker Contributions to Science and Industry during the 17th and 18th Centuries*, Newton Abbot, 1968, 221–2: '. . . in strict proportion to their numbers, Friends have secured something like forty times their due proportion of Fellows of the Royal Society during its long history'.

4   For example, the list published in the *Journal of the Friends' Historical Society* (op. cit. (3)) contains among other erroneous entries the names of two eminent physicians who were not Quakers: Richard Lower (1631–1691, the brother of a Quaker who spent time in prison) and Richard Mead (1673–1754, the son of an independent minister who, by coincidence, shared this surname with some early Quakers). Anthony Lowther, William Penn's brother-in-law, is also sometimes cited, but it is unclear whether this was the same Anthony Lowther elected in 1663. See also criticisms by T. L. Underwood, 'Quakers and the Royal Society of London in the Seventeenth Century', *Notes and Records of the Royal Society of London*, 31 (1976), 133–50.

5   Memoir of M. Barry, *Annual Monitor* (1856), 13–18; *A Memoir of William Pengelly, of Torquay, F.R.S., Geologist, with a Selection from his Correspondence* (ed. H. Pengelly), London, 1897, 49–50. Such convincements were rare; see R. T. Vann and D. Eversley, *Friends in Life and Death. The British and Irish Quakers in the Demographic Transition, 1650–1900*, Cambridge, 1992, 67.

6   E. Isichei, *Victorian Quakers*, Oxford, 1970, 115. Readmissions were rare and apply to none of our Fellows of the Royal Society.

7 The disownments of Birch, Dimsdale, Henry Beaufoy, Dillwyn, Sims, Prichard and Joseph Lister appear to have been directly connected with their marriages to non-Quakers. However, this is doubtless an underestimate since the reasons for disownment are not available in several cases.

8 Entries for Thomas Young and Hudson Gurney in the 'Dictionary of Quaker Biography' deposited in the Library of Friends House, London.

9 'Dictionary of Quaker Biography' entries for Luke and John Eliot Howard; Isichei, op. cit. (6), 45–53.

10 T. W. Reid, *Life of the Rt. Hon. W. E. Forster*, 2 vols., Bath, 1970, i, 266 and ii, 566. An obituary notice even appeared as an appendix to the *Annual Monitor* ((1887), 207–13), a publication normally reserved for those who died while in connection with the Society.

11 During its early years the Royal Society met at Gresham College. Quotation from a letter to J. Aubrey, 13 June 1683, *The Papers of William Penn* (ed. R. S. Dunn and M. M. Dunn), 5 vols., Philadelphia, 1981–7, ii, 394–6.

12 M. Hunter, *The Royal Society and its Fellows 1660–1700. The Morphology of an early Scientific Institution*, Chalfont St Giles, 1982, 184 and 226; H. J. Cadbury, 'Penn, Collinson, and the Royal Society', *Bulletin of the Friends Historical Association*, 36 (1947), 19–24.

13 This evidence is based on Augustus Bozzi Granville's broadside entitled *Science without a Head* which lists the membership in 1830 and shows which Fellows had contributed papers to the Society's *Philosophical Transactions*. Whereas only 16% of the 662 Fellows listed passed Granville's test, four of the ten Quaker and ex-Quakers who were currently Fellows – i.e. 40% – had published in the *Philosophical Transactions*. See [A. B. Granville], *Science without a Head; or, the Royal Society Dissected*, London, 1830. Since Granville only counted publications in the *Philosophical Transactions*, he paid no attention to other forms of scientific productivity; e.g. publication in other journals. The date 1830 is also somewhat arbitrary, but the data omit the highly productive Thomas Young who died the previous year. Lyons, op. cit. (3), 341, gives the proportion of scientific Fellows as 32.3% in 1830 and 52.6% in 1860. Although we have no way of checking his method for defining a 'scientific Fellow', the corresponding percentages for our group are 70% and 75%, if we take the publication of a scientific paper in any journal as our criterion.

14 In the early nineteenth century the admission fee was £10, together with a subscription of £1 per quarter. In a private communication Moti Feingold states that some 24 members were exempted subscription *c.*1700. However, it does not appear that this policy of exemption was applied consistently over the next two centuries. Moreover, it is not clear how patronage affected the election of those who could not afford the subscription.

15 T. L. Ashwood, 'Edward Haistwell, F. R. S.', *Notes and Records of the Royal Society of London*, 25 (1970), 179–87.

16 R. T. Vann, *The Social Development of English Quakerism 1655–1755*, Cambridge, MA, 1969, vii. Dr Thomas Lower (1633–1720), the son-in-law of Margaret Fell, was one of those imprisoned. His brother, Dr Richard Lower,

FRS, together with other Fellows interceded with the King and obtained his release. See *Journal of the Friends' Historical Society*, 5 (1908), 147; M. Webb, *The Fells of Swarthmore Hall and their Friends*, 2nd. edn., Philadelphia, 1896, 262, 279–81, 310–11 and 312–13. On the early history of the Quakers see also W. C. Braithwaite, *The Beginnings of Quakerism*, revised edn., York, 1981; H. Barbour, *The Quakers in Puritan England*, New Haven, 1964.

17   I. Penington, *Some Things relating to Religion, proposed in the consideration of the Royal Society (so termed) to wit, concerning the Right Ground of Certainty therein . . .*, London, 1668, 3.

18   Penn, op. cit. (11), 395. R. M. M. Hunt, *William Penn, Horticulturalist*, Pittsburgh, 1953.

19   E. J. Whittaker, *Thomas Lawson (1630–1691). North Country Botanist, Quaker and Schoolmaster*, York, 1986.

20   Cadbury, op. cit. (12). See also Penn, op. cit. (11), 147 and 155.

21   G. M. Trevelyan, quoted in Vann, op. cit. (16), 207.

22   D. Chapman-Huston and E. C. Cripps, *Through a City Archway. The Story of Allen and Hanburys, 1715–1954*, London, 1954; N. G. Brett-James, *The Life of Peter Collinson*, London, 1926.

23   Chapman-Huston and Cripps, op. cit. (22), 21–22.

24   P. Weindling, 'The British Mineralogical Society: a case study in science and social improvement', in *Metropolis and Province. Science and British Culture 1780–1850* (ed. I. Inkster and J. Morrell), London, 1983, 120–50, on 133; A. W. Slater, 'Autobiographical memoir of Joseph Jewell, 1763–1846', *Camden Miscellany*, 22 (1964), 113–78; Edgar E. Morse, 'Young, Thomas' in *Dictionary of Scientific Biography* (ed. C. C. Gillispie, et al), 14 vols, New York, 1970–80, xiv, 201.

25   J. S. Thompson and H. G. Thompson, *Silvanus Phillips Thompson. His Life and Letters*, London, 1920, 1–5. See also Reid, op. cit. (10), i, 18.

26   H. E. Roscoe, *John Dalton and the Rise of Modern Chemistry*, London, 1901, 201–2. The writer of Dalton's obituary in the *Annual Monitor* ((1845) 40–7) saw much virtue in his relative privation.

27   E. V. Fouldes, *Ackworth School, from its Foundation in 1779 to the Introduction of Co-education in 1946*, London, 1959; F. E. Pollard, et al, *Bootham School 1823–1923*, London, 1926.

28   Joseph Pease entered Parliament on his own affirmation in 1833. See Isichei, op. cit. (6), 195. The six are Henry Beaufoy, Dillwyn, Gurney, Harford, Fletcher and Forster.

29   A. Wood, *Thomas Young. Natural Philosopher, 1773–1829*, Cambridge, 1954, 53–7. It appears that J. C. Prichard spent a year at Cambridge while still a Quaker. See T. Hodgkin, 'Obituary of Dr Prichard', *Journal of the Ethnological Society*, 2 (1848–50), 182–207. Harford also studied at Cambridge but did not take a degree.

30   R. H. Fox, *Dr John Fothergill and his Friends. Chapters in Eighteenth Century Life*, London, 1919.

31   Private communication from Edward Milligan.

32   S. W. F. Holloway, *Royal Pharmaceutical Society of Great Britain 1841–1991: A Political and Social History*, London, 1991, 49.

33 Bevan, Allen, Luke Howard, Richard Phillips, West and Hanbury. H. B. Brady was apprenticed to a leading Quaker pharmaceutical chemist in Leeds, while J. G. Baker attended the Pharmaceutical College in London.

34 D. Hanbury, *Science Papers, Chiefly Pharmacological and Botanical*, London, 1876, 17; Chapman-Huston and Cripps, op. cit. (22), 168.

35 D. H. Pratt, 'English Quakers and the first Industrial Revolution: A Study of the Quaker Community in Four Industrial Counties – Lancashire, York, Warwick, and Gloucester, 1750–1830', PhD dissertation, University of Nebraska, 1975, 95. The success of Quakers in pharmacy and medicine may also bear on their widespread reputation for honesty and trustworthiness at a time when medicines were often adulterated or diluted. See Holloway, op. cit. (31), 8–9; M. Stiles, 'The Quakers in pharmacy', in *The Evolution of Pharmacy in Britain* (ed. F. N. L. Poynter), London, 1965, 113–30; R. Kilpatrick, '"Living in the light": dispensaries, philanthropy and medical reform in late-eighteenth-century London', in *The Medical Enlightenment of the Eighteenth Century* (ed. A. Cunningham and R. French), Cambridge, 1990, 254–80.

36 A. R. Fry, *John Bellers 1654–1725*, London, 1935. J. Bellers, *An Essay towards the Improvement of Physick. In Twelve Proposals* [1714] in *John Bellers. His Life, Times and Writings* (ed. G. Clarke), London, 1987, 177–220, esp. 183 and 189–91. Bellers presented the Royal Society with a copy of his *Essay* in March 1719, soon after he was admitted to the Society and some five years after its publication.

37 J. J. Abraham, *Lettsom. His Life, Times, Friends and Descendants*, London, 1933; Fox, op. cit. (29); *Chain of Friendship. Selected letters of Dr John Fothergill of London, 1735–1780* (ed. B. C. Corner and C. C. Booth), Cambridge, Mass., 1971; Kilpatrick, op. cit. (35).

38 *Life of William Allen, with Selections from his Correspondence*, 3 vols., London, 1846–7, i, 22–62. See also Weindling, op. cit. (24); I. Inkster, 'Science and society in the metropolis: A preliminary examination of the social and institutional context of the Askesian Society of London', *Annals of Science*, 34 (1977), 1–32. The title 'Askesian' was taken from 'ascesis', the practice of self-discipline.

39 R. M. MacLeod, 'Whigs and savants: reflections on the reform movement in the Royal Society, 1830–48', in Inkster and Morrell, op. cit. (24), 55–90; Lyons, op. cit. (3), 228–71.

40 William Miller (FRS 1845) was Professor of Chemistry at King's College London, William Henry Harvey (FRS 1858) was Professor of Botany at Dublin, Joseph Lister (FRS 1860) held the Chairs of Surgery at Glasgow, Edinburgh and KCL, Daniel Oliver (FRS 1863) was Professor of Botany at KCL, Edward Tylor (FRS 1871) was Reader and later Professor of Anthropology at Oxford, H. B. Brady (FRS 1874) lectured in Botany at Durham College, G. S. Brady (FRS 1882) was Professor of Natural History at Newcastle, J. T. Cash (FRS 1887) was Professor of Materia Medica at Aberdeen and S. P. Thompson (FRS 1891) taught at Bristol before becoming Principal of Finsbury Technical College, where he also delivered lectures in Physics. Some earlier Quakers had taught medical students; for example, Allen at Guy's Hospital and West at Leeds.

41 Allen, op. cit. (38), ii, 332.

42 H. Hutchinson, *Jonathan Hutchinson. Life and Letters*, London, 1946, 66 and 116.

43 *Barclay's Apology in Modern English* (ed. D. Freiday), Philadelphia, 1967, 436.

44 [H. Gurney], *Memoir of the Life of Thomas Young, M.D. F.R.S.*, London, 1831, 6.

45 *Memories of Old Friends being Extracts from the Journals and Letters of Caroline Fox of Penjerrick, Cornwall from 1835 to 1871* (ed. H. N. Pym), 3rd edn., 2 vols., London, 1882, i, 52.

46 Allen, op. cit. (38), i, 24–5 and 69.

47 Thompson and Thompson, op. cit. (25), 12. D. Murray-Rust, 'The Manchester Conference and a memoir of Silvanus P. Thompson', *Journal of the Friends' Historical Society*, 57 (1995), 199–207.

48 S. P. Thompson, *The Quest for Truth*, London, 1915, 41–54.

49 S. P. Thompson, 'Religion and science', *Batchelor's Papers*, 2 (1871), 274–82; Thompson and Thompson, op. cit. (25), 319. See also, S. P. Thompson, *A not Impossible Religion*, London and New York, 1918, 118.

50 A. Fry, *A Memoir of the Right Honorable Sir Edward Fry*, Oxford, 1921, 63–4; E. Fry, *Darwinism and Theology*, London, 1872. See also Hutchinson, op. cit. (42), 217 and L. Creighton, *Life and Letters of Thomas Hodgkin*, London, 1917, 341.

51 J. R. Burrow, *Evolution and Society. A Study in Victorian Social Theory*, Cambridge, 1968, 234–59. Tylor's reasons for leaving the Quakers are not known.

52 Certificates of Election, Royal Society Archives. Included in this count is the certificate of the ethnologist Henry Christy who died before his election was scheduled.

53 For example, A. Prior and M. Kirby, 'The Society of Friends and the family firm, 1700–1830', *Business History*, 35 (1993), 66–85: T. A. B. Corley. 'How Quakers coped with business success: Quaker industrialists, 1860–1914', in *Business and Religion in Britain* (ed. D. J. Jeremy), Aldershot, 1988, 164–87.

54 Journal Books of the Royal Society, (7 November 1728), xiii, 254 and (2 November 1727), xiii, 133. See also W. Johnson, 'Benjamin Robins, F.R.S. (1707-1751): New details of his life', *Notes and Records of the Royal Society of London*, 46 (1992), 235–52.

55 The detailed procedures for election changed over time, becoming more stringent in the nineteenth century. See Lyons, op. cit. (3).

56 Certificates of Election, Royal Society Archives.

57 A. E. Gunther, *An Introduction to the Life of the Rev. Thomas Birch D.D., F.R.S. 1705–1766*, Halesworth, 1984, 93.

58 Lists of Fellows, Royal Society Archives.

59 C. R. Weld, *A History of the Royal Society, with Memoirs of its Presidents*, 2 vols., London, 1848, ii, 8. On Franklin's close association with the Quakers see F. B. Tolles, *Meeting House and Counting House; The Quaker Merchants of Colonial Philadelphia 1682–1763*, New York, 1963, 247–50. Tolles (181–7 and 205–29) also provides an excellent discussion of the scientific interests of his Philadelphians.

60 Gunther, op. cit. (57); T. Birch, *The History of the Royal Society of London*, 4 vols., London, 1756–7; Birch's 'The life of the Honorable Robert Boyle' in his *The Works of the Honorable Robert Boyle*, London, 1744.

61 Hutchinson, op. cit. (42), 97–8, 154 and 189.

62 D. E. Allen, *The Botanists. A History of the Botanical Society of the British Isles through a Hundred and Fifty Years*, Winchester, 1986, 69–76.

63 J. H. Collins, *A Catalogue of the Works of W.R. Fox, F.R.S., Chronologically Arranged, with Notes and Extracts, and a Sketch of his Life*, Truro, 1878, 2.

64 See Pym, op. cit. (45); W. Harris, *Caroline Fox*, London, 1944; *Barclay Fox's Journal* (ed. R. L. Brett), London, 1979.

65 Brady's obituary in *Nature*, cited in *Proceedings of the Royal Society*, 50 (1891–2), xii.

66 A. T. Gage and W. T. Stearn, *A History of the Linnean Society of London*, London, 1988; R. Desmond, *Dictionary of British and Irish Botanists and Horticulturalists including Plant Collectors and Botanical Artists*, London, 1977; Allen, op. cit. (38), 44, and private communication.

67 Brett-James, op. cit. (22), 41; Whittaker, op. cit. (19).

68 F. E. Pollard, op. cit. (27). Private communication from Dr Jacqui Stewart.

69 Allen, op. cit. (38), i, 53–4.

70 Fry, op. cit. (50), 93–6; E. Fry, *British Mosses*, London, 1892.

71 J. Fothergill to J. C. Lettsom, 11 August 1770, in Corner and Booth, op. cit. (37), 324.

72 Hutchinson, op. cit. (42), 121; Fry, op. cit. (50), 100; Fox's obituary in *Annual Monitor*, (1878), 82–91.

73 L. Davidoff and C. Hall, *Family Fortunes. Men and Women of the English Middle Class 1780–1850*, London, 1987, 370.

74 Weindling, op. cit. (24); Pratt, op. cit. (35); Raistrick, op. cit. (3).

75 *Luke Howard (1772–1864). His Correspondence with Goethe and his Continental Journal of 1816* (ed. D. F. S. Scott), York, 1976, 4. Initially presented to the Askesian Society this essay was published in L. Howard, *The Climate of London, Deduced from Meteorological Observations, Made at Different Places in the Neighbourhood of the Metropolis*, 2 vols., London 1818–20; H. B. Brady, who was likewise a pharmaceutical chemist, published exclusively on geology and botany.

76 Hutchinson, op. cit. (42), 145; J. Fothergill to W. Bartram, 22 October 1772, in Corner and Booth, op. cit. (37), 391–3.

77 Allen, op. cit. (38), i, 131, 155, 168, 327; ii, 165, 242, 263; iii, 97. Quotation on i, 68.

78 *Ibid.*, i, 2.

APPENDIX 1 QUAKER FRSs

Name	Birth	Death	Quaker?	Date FRS
HAISTWELL, Edward	*c.* 1658	1709	Q	1698
BELLERS, F.	1687	1750	X1711	1711
BELLERS, J.	1654	1725	Q	1719
GRAHAM, George	1675	1751	X	1721
BEVAN, Silvanus	1691	1765	Q	1725
ROBINS, Benjamin	1707	1751	X*c.* 1723	1727
COLLINSON, Peter	1693	1768	Q	1728
BIRCH, Thomas	1705	1766	X*c.* 1727	1735
NICKOLLS, John	*c.* 1710	1745	Q	1744
FOTHERGILL, John	1712	1780	Q	1763
WITCHELL, George	1728	1786	X	1767
DIMSDALE, Thomas	1711	1800	X1741	1769
LETTSOM, John C.	1744	1815	Q	1773
HOWARD, W. A.	1750	1800	?	1778
BEAUFOY, Henry	1750	1795	X1779	1782
BEAUFOY, Mark	1764	1828	X1788	1790
YOUNG, Thomas	1773	1829	X1798	1794
DILLWYN, Lewis W.	1778	1855	X1807	1804
ALLEN, William	1770	1843	Q	1807
WILLAN, Robert	1757	1812	Q	1809
SIMS, John	1749	1831	X1790	1814
BLAND, Michael	1776	1851	X	1816
GURNEY, Hudson	1775	1862	X1803	1818
HOWARD, Luke	1772	1864	X*c.* 1836	1821
DALTON, John	1766	1844	Q	1822
PHILLIPS, Richard	1778	1851	X1811	1822
HARFORD, John S	1785	1866	X1809	1823
PRICHARD, James	1786	1848	X	1827
PHILLIPS, William	1773	1828	Q	1827
LISTER, Joseph J.	1786	1869	Q	1832
BARRY, Martin	1802	1855	C*c.* 1824	1840
MILLER, William A.	1817	1870	X	1845
WEST, William	1792	1851	Q	1846
FOX, Robert Were	1789	1877	Q	1848
MILLER, J. F.	1811	1856	X	1850
MAY, Charles	1801	1860	Q	1854
FLETCHER, Isaac	1827	1879	X	1855
HARVEY, Wm. H.	1811	1866	X*c.* 1846	1858
LISTER, Joseph	1827	1912	X1856	1860

Name	Birth	Death	Quaker?	Date FRS
PENGELLY, William	1812	1894	C*c.* 1850	1863
OLIVER, Daniel	1830	1916	Q	1863
HANBURY, Daniel	1825	1875	Q	1867
TYLOR, Edward B.	1832	1917	X1864	1871
FOX, Wilson	1831	1887	X	1872
BRADY, Henry B.	1835	1891	Q	1874
HOWARD, John E.	1807	1883	X1836	1874
FORSTER, William E.	1818	1886	X1850	1875
BAKER, John G.	1834	1920	Q	1878
HUTCHINSON, Jon.	1828	1913	Q	1882
BRADY, George S.	1832	1921	Q	1882
FRY, Edward	1827	1918	Q	1883
CASH, J. Theodore	1854	1936	X	1887
THOMPSON, S. P.	1851	1916	Q	1891
LISTER, Arthur	1830	1908	Q	1898
HEAD, Henry	1861	1940	X	1899
LISTER, Joseph J.	1857	1927	Q	1900

Abbreviations used in the fourth column:
Q = lifelong Quaker.
X = left/disowned, followed by date.
C = Convert, followed by date of convincement.

10
Improving on Nature?

In what must be one of the most succinct statements of scientific reductionism, the political radical Richard Carlile declared in the late 1820s that 'all known effects are compounds of gases'.[1] Coupled with this chemical creed was an assault on theistic belief. In his sixpenny weekly, the *Lion*, Carlile roared at the defenders of natural theology. 'With the doctrine of intelligent deity', he wrote, 'it is presumption to attempt anything toward human improvement. Without the doctrine, it is not any presumption.'[2] Carlile appears to be suggesting that a natural theology cannot comfortably coexist with any human programme of improving upon nature. It is as if arguments for divine wisdom require this to be the best of all possible worlds, with the corollary that attempts at improvement would be both sacrilegious and ineffective.

As atheistic arguments go, this one from Carlile is rather crude. We saw in chapter 7 how Hugh Miller could envisage collaboration between humanity and God in the improvement of the world. Because Miller shared the same aesthetic sensibilities with his Maker, the two minds could work together in perfecting nature through art. But for all its crudity, Carlile's dig at physico-theology may provide a clue in solving an historical puzzle. In histories of natural theology we often hear of physico-theology, astro-theology, even insect-theology. But how many of us have encountered a chemico-theology? In this chapter we shall find that they have existed but that there have been peculiar and instructive reasons why they have not enjoyed a high profile.

Some reasons may immediately spring to mind. Chemistry, for much of its history, suffered in comparison with celestial mechanics, which revealed the precision of the divine mathematician; and it suffered in comparison with anatomy and physiology, which brought one face to face with final causes. As the science of material change, chemistry was more earthbound. Much of its appeal has surely been sensual rather than cerebral. How many initiates have been drawn to it by vivid colours and vile smells. Even the public loved it when Humphry Davy dished out laughing gas at the Royal Institution. The effect was described by one observer: among much chortling and babbling, some put up their hands, some left the room; but one young man tried to kiss all the women. It was subsequently suggested that the man in question had not partaken of the gas and knew full well what he was about.[3]

Chemistry also satisfied other senses. As the science perhaps most dependent on delicate manipulation and techniques of analysis it could offer tactile pleasures in the pursuit of material refinement. Chemistry was idiosyncratic in other respects. Newton's physics, after all, described how the world is. So, too, did anatomy and physiology. Scientific analysis could terminate in contemplation. But this was less so in chemistry where ambitions to change the world were often rife. Chemistry has been the science of process, *the* science that has sought to improve upon creation. From ancient alchemical dreams of a gold better than the mundane to the industrial chemistry of the twentieth century, when the anti-hero of that cult film *The Graduate* was told that the key to the future lay in the one word 'plastics', chemistry has played a central role in creating what past chemists called an 'artificial philosophy'. Did Carlile, after all, have a point? Did chemistry, with its pretensions to improve the world disqualify itself from systems of natural theology? In his attack on the Paracelsian chemists of the sixteenth century, the Lutheran humanist Andreas Libavius had registered the charge of impiety against their claims to be perfecting nature.[4] The implication that nature had generated imperfect things was unacceptable. Indeed in advising a young pupil to steer clear of it, Libavius had dubbed chemistry the occupation not of philosophers, but of reprobates.

In this chapter we explore the space between chemistry and natural theology because, to our knowledge, it has not been examined before. The idea is to use the history of chemistry to illuminate the broader question of how the applied sciences and technology might affect conceptions of divine Providence. We shall bring out the ingenuity with which chemists did make connections with religious discourse. But we shall also argue that chemistry, perhaps more than any other science, has created problems for natural theology by problematising the natural. By breaking down the barriers between nature and art, chemistry has closed certain doors that other sciences might have left open. But we shall also suggest that it may not have closed the door completely on the kind of process theology typified by Hugh Miller when he spoke of collaboration between man and God.

Alchemical Visions

We might begin with the alchemical dream from which chemistry itself emerged. An ancient Egyptian recipe conjures up the image most of us have of a typical alchemical recipe:

> Take 28 leaves from a pithy laurel tree and some virgin earth and seed of wormwood, wheat meal and the herb calf's snout ... pounded together with ... the liquid of an ibis egg and made into a uniform dough and into a figure of Hermes wearing a mantle, while the moon is ascending ... Let Hermes be holding a herald's staff. And write the spell on hieratic papyrus or on a goose's windpipe ... and insert it into the figure for ... inspiration. [Put the spell] at the feet of Hermes ... and recite as on the altar you burn incense.[5]

Cynics might wonder at the misfortune of those who could find only twenty-seven laurel leaves, or who could not project themselves into the right spiritual state. But at least the ingredients of our problem are here. There is the wish to control nature, whilst success is contingent on a form of piety. Hermes is addressed as 'the prophet of events ... who send[s] forth oracles by day and night'. He is said to 'cure all pains of mortals with ... healing cares'. Finally he is summoned to guarantee the result: 'Hither, O blessed one ... both graciously appear and graciously render the task for me, a pious man'.[6]

Alchemy was to pass through many transmutations before a modern science of chemistry emerged from it. But there was often more to it than making a fast buck. There was the lure of gold, but also of medical cures, of immortality. There was even a theoretical rationale of a kind. If all metals were ultimately composed of the same units of matter, then transmutation was perfectly possible in principle. European alchemists would stress that they were not on a wild goose chase: they were aiming to imitate a process that already occurred in nature. They shared the belief that in subterranean veins, baser metals grew naturally into gold. Alchemists claimed simply to be expediting this natural process, often seeding their concoctions with a little gold by way of encouragement. In Renaissance iconography the alchemist is depicted as following in the footsteps of nature. He is lagging behind but, because he wants to accelerate a natural process, he might be said to be improving on nature – or at least trying to. In fact three images of the alchemist often co-existed: he was the imitator of nature, the improver of nature and, as in Ben Jonson's satirical play, the 'smoky persecutor of nature'.[7] He was, of course, often considered a fraud.

EMBLEMA XLII. *De secretis Naturæ.* 177

In Chymicis versanti Natura, Ratio, Experientia & lectio,
sint Dux, scipio, perspicilia & lampas.

EPIGRAMMA XLII.

DUx Naturatibi, tuque arte pedissequus illi
Esto lubens, erras, ni comes ipsa viæ est.
Det ratio scipionis opem, Experientia firmet
Lumina, quò possit cernere posta procul.
Lectio sit lampas tenebris dilucida, rerum
Verborúmque strues providus ut caveas.   Z   CAS-

Figure 33: The chemist following in the footsteps of Nature, his guide. Reason
is his staff, Experience his spectacles, and Reading his lamp. From Michael
Maier, *Atalanta Fugiens* (1618). Reproduced by courtesy of the Bodleian
Library, University of Oxford. Shelfmark Vet.D2.e.18.

Our question was whether the presumption of the chemist to
improve on nature was inherently sacrilegious. Among the more
dedicated alchemists this would have come as a hard saying. A life of
piety and austerity was often considered a prerequisite of success.

Figure 34: An intimacy between prayer and alchemical practice is suggested by this plate from Heinrich Khunrath's *Amphitheatrum Sapientiae Aeternae* (1598). Reproduced by courtesy of the Bodleian Library, University of Oxford. Shelfmark R.1.9.Med.

Plates from alchemical texts such as Heinrich Khunrath's *Amphitheatrum Sapientiae Aeternae* (1598) show the laboratorium and the oratorium placed side by side. As one recent commentator has observed, 'the alchemists saw their relationship with God as having a distinctive character and frequently included prayers in their works to express this relationship'.[8] A parallel would sometimes be drawn between the creation of the soul by God and the creation of the Philosopher's Stone by the alchemist. The alchemist was a creator, too, working with the matter God had provided. Even at this early stage in the history of chemistry a process theology was the most auspicious kind of theology for the alchemist to embrace. He participated in God's creative activity and for that reason considered his art sacred. As the fourteenth-century alchemist Bernard Trevisan explained: 'It is clear from many irrefutable and uncontestable testimonies that nature by itself procreates and prepares seed-bearing creatures whereas the art [of alchemy] works together with them toward the end which nature creates.'[9]

The art of the alchemist could clearly be presented as sacred, but it could also be seen as suspect. Was it appropriate for sinful man to assume the role of co-creator? One classic alchemical text, the *Summa Perfectionis* attributed to Geber, provided a justification. Here it was argued that the ability to improve on nature was part of human nature. The alchemist's task was no different in kind from the farmer's use of grafting to improve his stock. In such a vision of art outdoing nature we see one of the roots of the Western technological dream.[10] But when alchemists presented their work as a mirror of God's work in creation, how controversial were they being?

It is difficult to generalise about this. Luther, for example, said he liked the science of alchemy 'very well'. This was 'not only for the profits it brings in melting metals, in decocting, preparing, extracting, and distilling herbs' but also 'for the sake of the allegory and secret signification, which', he added, 'is exceedingly fine, touching the resurrection of the dead at the last day'.[11] As the earthly alchemist purified through fire, leaving the dregs in the furnace, so, at the Day of Judgement, the divine alchemist would separate all things through fire, the righteous from the ungodly.

A recent study of Jesuit reactions suggests a greater ambivalence among those who took an interest.[12] As one would expect, however, they were able to make some fine distinctions. Martin Del Rio, who flourished at the end of the sixteenth century, distinguished between natural magic and alchemy and was happy to accept that human art could speed up the natural process of ripening metals. He maintained that alchemical transmutation need not *necessarily* imply the presence of demonic agents. He also distinguished between natural and chemically produced gold. Thus he thought the state was justified in prohibiting the use of artificially-produced gold in commerce and medicine. The artificial gold did not have the same weight as the natural and it contained noxious qualities arising from the mercury used in its production. Del Rio also addressed that crucial question: the spiritual temperament of the adept. There were some who did, but emphatically some who did not, have the right moral attributes of piety and humility. There were clearly limits to his tolerance. He took exception to those who pretended the Bible was an alchemical text to be de-coded and to those who hid their chemical secrets under the cloak of biblical imagery.

For the Jesuit commentators secrecy was out because it might smack of diabolical participation. They made yet more distinctions. Athanasius Kircher had no qualms about the technician's claim to imitate nature. He even wanted alchemical apparatus to imitate the shapes of the caverns, veins and rivers of the underground world.[13] He nevertheless insisted on a difference between metallurgical alchemy and transmutatory alchemy. The latter really was devilish in its allure. Even finer distinctions emerge: Kircher was less censorious of lower types of transmutation, for example the conversion of iron into copper. He also elaborated a distinction between accidental and substantial transmutation as one would expect of a good Aristotelian. At the Jesuit College in Rome, Kircher lived over his pharmaceutical laboratory and explored with relish that category of preternatural effects which would appear supernatural only to those ignorant of the means of their production.[14]

It is difficult to avoid the conclusion that the alchemist's dream was causing problems. When Paracelsus claimed that, given the right recipe, it was possible to create a human being, revulsion was not confined to the Jesuits. At the same time, the imitation of nature, if properly hedged with the right qualifications, could be accommodated. The kind of theology to which alchemy gave rise was, however, a process theology not a simple natural theology. One was working with divine resources to improve the world. It was more a theology of practice than of contemplation.

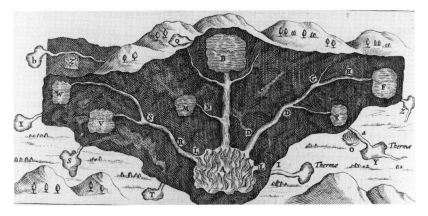

Figure 35: Subterranean chemistry from Athanasius Kircher, *Mundus Subterraneus* (1665), vol. i.

Paracelsus and the Redirection of Chemistry

In histories of chemistry the iconoclastic figure of Paracelsus invariably has a high profile. This is because he gave chemistry a boost by making it the handmaid of medicine. Whereas earlier alchemists could be charged with what appeared to be a selfish quest for gold, Paracelsus redirected chemical techniques towards the relief of human suffering.[15] In so doing he challenged traditional concepts of disease, provoking political controversy wherever he went. Modesty was certainly not his strong suit. 'Let me tell you this,' he railed: 'every little hair on my neck knows more than all your scribes, and my shoe-buckles are more learned than your Galen and Avicenna, and my beard has more experience than all your high colleges.'[16]

Whereas Galen had taught that disease arose from an internal imbalance of the four humours, Paracelsus recognised a greater specificity in the site of disease and its origins. Specific agents invading the body from outside could set up specific diseases in specific organs. The organs in turn were under the aegis of particular planets: Venus for the kidneys, Jupiter for the liver, Mars for the bile. His medical reforms required chemistry to provide the remedies appropriate to each condition. This would involve working with metals and making extracts from herbs.

To some extent this was an extension of folk-medicine and a challenge to the learned physicians. In self-justification Paracelsus complained that the medical experts were too prone to make excuses when they were powerless to help. They were inclined to say that for certain ailments there was no cure. By contrast Paracelsus presented himself as the truly Christian alchemist who would never give up the search. In mercy, God had provided resources to cure all diseases.[17] Through the sweat of our brow we should search them out. Through magic signs God had indicated the therapeutic properties of specific plants. 'Behold the Satyrion root', he urged in a well-known passage:

> Is it not formed like the male privy parts? No one can deny this. Accordingly magic discovered and revealed that it can restore a man's virility and passion. And then we have the thistle; do not its leaves prickle like needles? Thanks to this sign the art of magic discovered that there is no better herb against internal prickling.[18]

Paracelsian therapy, unlike the Galenic, required the treatment of like with like, not neutralisation with an opposite.

In Paracelsus there certainly is a chemico-theology. The redirection of alchemy is justified with reference to a divine precedent: the example of Christ as healer. Only through chemical processes such as distillation, can the good be extracted from the bad, the efficacious from the dross.

There is a sense in which the chemist has a redemptive mission: to redeem nature itself through the hard labour of chemical practice. Alchemy in its Paracelsan formulation, writes one commentator, was the 'perfecting of natural bodies by the separation of their essences'.[19]

Here again we seem to have a blurring of the natural and the artificial in the improvement of nature. But Paracelsus had no difficulty in sanctifying his programme. The Creation of the world had itself been a chemical process. At least Genesis could be read that way, with the divine Chemist separating the elements from a primordial water.[20] Since redemption carried connotations of restoration, there was also a sense in which the improvement of nature would not be sacrilegious. It was all within a providential framework. There were even echoes of the Fall narrative in the chemists' toil and sweat. 'They devote themselves diligently to their labours', Paracelsus affirmed. 'They put their fingers to the coals, the lute, and the dung, not into gold rings.'[21]

Paracelsian chemistry was hugely controversial. Its adversarial character meant that advocates sought the protection of courtly patrons, or, like Paracelsus himself, kept on the move. The chemical cures were themselves contentious. Prescribing mercury to clarify the spleen could induce splenetic reactions. It is also clear that, among the Paracelsians, the rhetoric of redeeming nature could provoke unease. Thus the Calvinist Oswald Croll felt obliged to add some qualifications. In the last analysis God alone could make all things new.[22] It cannot be denied, though, that chemistry was closely integrated with theology within the Paracelsian tradition. The conventional wisdom of Aristotle and Galen would be stigmatised as pagan, as unchristian. Yet the blurring of the natural and the artificial might be thought to preclude a simple natural theology. The image, again, is of the chemist as collaborator in processes requiring time. When Paracelsus spoke of the last stage of the alchemical process, the tincturing of a substance to change its colour, he stated that it 'makes all imperfect things perfect, transmutes them into their noblest essence'.[23]

The 'Indulgent Creator' of Robert Boyle

For our next snapshot of chemical history we turn to Robert Boyle who promoted the science during the second half of the seventeenth century. Observing that it was often demeaned as the preserve of sooty empirics, Boyle gave chemistry intellectual stature as the science that both corroborated a corpuscular theory of matter and exposed the limits of a reduction to pure mechanics.[24] Yet he was not blind to its utility in other respects. He trusted his own chemical remedies more than he trusted his physician. And he had 'much rather, that the physician of any friend of mine, should keep his patient by powerful medicines from dying, than tell me punctually when he shall die, or show me in the opened carcase why it may be supposed he lived no longer'.[25]

According to his contemporary Roger North, when Boyle woke in the morning he would consult his ceiling compass to see from which direction the wind came. He would then open his cupboard of chemical cordials to take the appropriate antidote. So, North continued, if the wind were often to change direction, Mr Boyle was wont to become drunk.[26] As a sober theorist Boyle explored the possibility that chemical properties and chemical reactions might be explained by reference to the architecture of small particles, their shape, texture, arrangement and motion. An acid was conceivably an acid because it was composed of particles with sharp points. That would explain the unpleasant sensation they produced on the tongue. Because chemical reactions might be rationalised in terms of the decomposition and recomposition of corpuscular structures, the scholastic concept of homogeneous substantial forms could be attacked. In this process the distinction between nature and art was blurred through chemical practice.[27]

There was an ulterior sense in which the 'mechanical philosophy' itself assimilated nature to art. One of the mechanists, Henry Power, spoke of nature as full of 'narrow engines' in which there was much 'curious mathematics'. In his own words: 'the architecture of these little fabrics more neatly set forth the wisdom of their maker'. In Power's account of the mechanical philosophy, causes are deduced by reconstructing nature and all things are artificial because 'nature itself is nothing else but the art of God'.[28]

This was the standard argument for design, which Boyle greatly prized.[29] To see nature as the art of God was far from disturbing. But Boyle's chemistry was a challenge to other ways of looking at the relationship between nature and art. For example, could the chemist imitate natural products that according to Aristotle's philosophy possessed a distinctive, homogeneous and inimitable form? If so, this would also dissolve a traditional distinction between nature and art. The artificial production of gems made an excellent test-case. Boyle was drawn to the study of gems partly because of claims for their magic power, but also because of their exquisite beauty.[30] His hypothesis was that they were possibly formed from fluids and consequently contained heterogeneous mineral or metallic traces with which they had been impregnated. A key question was whether the exquisite uniformity 'so admired in gems' might not require a seminal and geometrising principle. At this point we begin to see a tension in Boyle himself. For religious reasons he wanted to celebrate such wondrous workmanship; on the other hand it helped his hypothesis to stress the diversity of configuration rather than any architectonic principle. Hence his rather tortured conclusion:

> though also I willingly allow their shapes to deserve from us a delightful wonder at the curiousness of nature's, or rather her author's, workmanship, yet, upon a more attentive surveying of them, I do not find the uniformity to be near so great as is wont to be imagined; but have rather met with such diversities, as agree well with our hypothesis about their figuration.[31]

Boyle's theorising at this point had a genuinely mechanical aspect: 'In several transparent gems, it seemed manifest enough to me ... that the shape was, in great part, due to the figure of the womb, or mould, wherein the matter, whilst liquid or soft, happened to settle.'[32] In these remarks there is equivocation on at least three points: whether there is evidence of design in gems, whether it is appropriate to speak of the workmanship of *nature*, and whether the mould might still be described in organic terms as a womb.

It is revealing that Boyle's equivocation surfaced in this context of the artificial imitation of nature. Yet he, as with the other chemists we have considered, found ways of making his chemistry theologically respectable. He would almost certainly have believed that the chemists' powers were but a pale imitation of 'nature's, or rather her author's'. It was a long way from the simulation of crystals to the simulation of living organisms. Thus there was no compelling reason to dampen an enthusiasm for chemistry, which in Boyle's case was almost akin to a religious enthusiasm. He had confessed in 1649 that his laboratory had become a 'kind of *Elysium*', so 'transported and bewitched' had he been by Vulcan's power.[33] Chemistry, as with natural philosophy, promised the improvement of the mind and that was itself a theological justification. The gratification of a pious curiosity far outweighed the delusory pleasures of fame, bags, bottles and mistresses.[34]

There was one further consideration that completely over-rode any sense in which the improvement of creation might be thought presumptuous. An anthropocentric conception of Providence allowed Boyle to stress that creation had been designed for human benefit. In seeking to show that even the most despicable of God's creatures might furnish something for the empire of knowledge, Boyle confessed that he had dissected *even* rats and mice. That he was prepared to experiment on fellow men, hiring one to be bitten by a viper, required no apology.[35] And if, as Bacon had said, nature was to be put on the rack, chemistry provided the instruments of torture. Out of the tails of scorpions it could extract an oil that promised relief from kidney stones and, Boyle added, to 'remedy divers other mischiefs, besides those that scorpions can do'.[36] Improving therapy through chemical research would not have struck Boyle as sacrilegious. He simply spoke of 'assisting nature' in the arrest of disease.[37] And that ultimately meant assisting the author of nature.

Once again we have come full circle to the image of a collaborative process. Boyle's theory of matter forged a link between chemistry and a limited process theology. As a contemporary John Beale told him in 1666, 'you will conduct the two rivulets of mechanism and chemistry into the ocean of theology'.[38] The emphasis was, however, rather different from a contemplative natural theology. It required Boyle to seek the Creator's indulgence. To change God's creatures, to improve upon nature, was in Boyle's own words, a 'great honour, that the indulgent Creator vouchsafes to the naturalist'. If only Adam could return to inspect Boyle's laboratory, how he would admire the 'new world' added by human industry.[39]

Boyle's incorporation of chemistry into a providential scheme would be echoed by Isaac Newton, who found chemistry alluring because it offered the means to imitate the work of a subtle spirit responsible for processes of growth in nature. Newton distinguished between two kinds of action in nature: the vegetable and the purely mechanical. Vulgar chemistry, as he called it, was concerned with the imitation of mechanical changes. The art of inducing vegetation, by contrast, was 'a more subtle secret and noble way of working'.[40] The latter was, of course, Newton's way of working. But might it not be considered presumptuous in that one was seeking access to the agency of God? Newton certainly pondered the question. Some notes he made on an alchemical text refer to a paradox in the concurrence of alchemy and theology, the one seeming merely human and the other divine.[41] But the paradox was instantly removed by presenting the Creator as the divine Alchemist. The biblical image of the spirit of God moving on the primordial waters was crucial, the water signifying an 'indigested chaos'. Alchemical processes of extraction, separation and sublimation had all been involved in giving God's creatures the spirit of life.

The claim to be imitating divine alchemy could be seen as either presumptuous or pious, depending on one's point of view. Newton, like Boyle, favoured an indulgent God whose power was enhanced rather than demeaned by the use of creatures in the execution of the divine Will. Newton wrote:

> If any think it possible that God may produce some intellectual creature so perfect that he could, by divine accord, in turn produce creatures of a lower order, this so far from detracting from the divine power enhances it; for that power which can bring forth creatures not only directly but through the mediation of other creatures is exceedingly, not to say infinitely greater.[42]

We presumably count among these creatures so the problem is resolved through our being mediators of divine power. Such reasoning creates the space for God's ongoing activity in the world of matter. The practice of chemistry is a form of collaboration: it is part of the story of God's activity in the natural world just as historical events constitute the story of God's ongoing activity in the moral world.[43]

Process, Progress and Priestley

For our next snapshot we move to the end of the eighteenth century when Joseph Priestley was expanding the number of gases and isolating what Lavoisier would call oxygen. In histories of chemistry Priestley has sometimes had a bad press because he clung to the concept of phlogiston. This was a principle common to all metals and was used to explain their common properties. It was given off when a metal burned in air and was also exhaled in the process of breathing. A mouse would die in a closed container because the air was eventually too phlogisticated to support respiration. The gas that Lavoiser called oxygen Priestley called dephlogisticated air because it supported both respiration and combustion better than ordinary air.

As a polemicist, Priestley resisted Lavoisier's chemistry because it looked like a bid on the part of the French to take over the science by re-naming every compound in accord with the new oxygen theory.[44] But as a polemicist Priestley was most prolific in the sphere of Christian theology. A unitarian critic of established Christianity, he pressed the principles of rational religion as far as they would go. In Priestley's Christianity, as in Newton's, the doctrine of the Trinity has gone. So has the doctrine of original sin, which he considered too severe on those who were not to blame for Adam's sin. Gone, too, was the Calvinist doctrine of election, which he found impossible to reconcile with a God whose love for mankind was supposed to be impartial. The notion that God acted directly on individual minds he dismissed as vulgar superstition. In short, he turned his face against any feature of creation that could be construed as arbitrary.[45]

It was Priestley's happy belief that nature, as a system, had been constructed to promote human happiness. This meant that he had to construct a formal theodicy in which the presence of evil could be rationalised. It is tempting to think that, having jettisoned such doctrines as the Fall and the Atonement, he would be in some difficulty over the improvement of creation. Improvement could no longer be construed in the Paracelsan sense of redemption or in the Baconian sense of restoration. If this is already the best of all possible worlds what role could the sciences have in improving it? But in Priestley's theodicy this was not a problem. Evil was integral to the system because it promoted a greater good. Providence had even allowed the corruption of Christianity because a greater good would be effected through its subsequent purification. One is reminded of Adam Smith's insistence that interference in nature could be perfectly consonant with a beneficent Providence in that agricultural improvement could be construed as redressing an error due to bad stewardship.[46]

Priestley had a keen sense of the dynamics of history in which actions for the worse invariably provoked reactions for the better. Thus the clergy of the established Church were contributing to their own downfall by supporting a war against America which enlarged the national debt. They would contribute to their downfall, too, if they became more grasping in extracting tithes, particularly from dissenters like himself. Consequently, although this is the best of all possible worlds, at any one time there will be scope for improvement. Science has a strategic role to play in this historical process because it can eliminate superstition, promote human welfare and explode the political pretensions of arbitrary power. Consequently Priestley scholars have spoken of his process theology, in which Britain's industrial growth took place at God's behest, not behind His back.[47]

How did chemistry fit the scheme? There would seem to be at least two respects in which it directly supported his theology and two others in which the support was indirect. Directly, chemistry promised progress. And progress implied a beneficent provision. Announcing the properties of his dephlogisticated air, Priestley immediately considered its medical uses. He was concerned lest healthy individuals, by breathing too much of it, might, like a candle, burn themselves out. But he made no secret of his hopes that it might prove a 'fashionable article in luxury'.[48] Every gas was to have its use. Art could improve on nature in the preservation of food. As he wrote excitedly to Alessandro Volta in June 1777: 'Yesterday we ate a pigeon which I had kept in nitrous air near six weeks. It was perfectly sweet and good ... [though] the water in which it had stood was very putrid.'[49]

The second respect in which Priestley's chemistry served his theology had to do with atmospheric restoration. A beneficent system required that there be some mechanism in nature for replenishing the air. Priestley was bent on finding it. In August 1771 he reported that he had 'long been in quest of ... that process in nature by which air, rendered noxious by breathing, is restored to its former salubrious condition'.[50] Experiments with aquatic plants, involving his nitrous air test, showed that purification was the work of vegetation. The results of this research lent themselves to a fine public speech. When Sir John Pringle presented him with the Copley medal in November 1773, he drew the comforting conclusion that 'no vegetable grows in vain'.[51]

Indirectly, chemistry came to the aid of Priestley's theology because it provided examples of economy in nature. There was economy in that a single principle, phlogiston, conferred common properties on all the metals. He even speculated that water might be a common ingredient in all the gases. But there was a more subtle sense, too, in which chemistry found its way into Priestley's polemics. By containing and manipulating his gases he could argue that traditional references to 'spirits' could finally be expunged from a chemical vocabulary. Since he believed that both Christianity and chemistry had been infected by 'spirits', to excise them from the scientific domain set a good precedent for their extermination in theology. Souls and spirits were dispensable for Priestley because he favoured the doctrine of the resurrection of the dead, rather than human immortality. In rationalising the details, chemistry once again intruded: 'Death, with its concomitant putrefaction and dispersion of parts, is only a decomposition; and whatever is decomposed, may be recomposed by the being who first composed it.'[52] By collapsing the distinction between matter and spirit, he reinforced his critique of those established religions in which a dualistic ontology had run riot.

Priestley's chemico-theology was profoundly controversial as were his political sympathies with the French Revolution. His chemical account of a bodily resurrection, for some critics, was going too far. One satirist asked the pointed question: what, in Priestley's view, would happen to a poor fellow who sank in the Thames to be eaten by eels? And suppose the eels were then devoured by a high-living politician:

> Poor Thomas in the Thames was drowned
> And though long sought could not be found ...
> At the last trumpet's solemn sound.
> How mangled will poor Tom be found![53]

An association between chemistry and political radicalism, epitomised by Priestley, drew acerbic comments from Edmund Burke. In his reflections on the French Revolution, Burke accused the republicans of defying the processes of nature like an 'alchymist and empiric'.[54] This is a revealing remark, because it shows how the blurring of nature and art could be read as interfering with or defying nature. It is clear that a purely contemplative natural theology was not possible for Priestley. Indeed his discovery of 'oxygen' symbolised that fact. He was taken aback himself to discover that there was a gas that could support respiration better than normal, natural air. It seemed to symbolise the view that what Providence had provided could be improved. The same symbolism might be seen in his overestimating the restorative effect of shaking noxious airs with water, which he had wanted to believe simulated a natural and beneficent interaction between atmosphere and sea.[55] In one's experiments a presumed imitation of nature could let one down. But this did nothing to undermine his confidence in a theology of process. The chemist, collaborating with the deity, could promise a bright future in which science and rational Christianity would fight side by side against all forms of superstition.

Fighting Against Materialism: The Chemistry of Humphry Davy

In the early years of the nineteenth century it was Davy who made science fashionable in London.[56] In his public lectures at the Royal Institution he, like Priestley, stressed the usefulness of chemistry. 'I am glad to find you agog for chemistry', wrote John Herschel to Charles Babbage in 1813: 'By the Lord, I think we may turn Peterhouse into a Furnace, Trinity into a laboratory ... I should like as a first experiment to make a party for breathing the nitrous oxide.'[57] It was Davy who had dispensed his laughing gas at the Royal Institution, but he had also had the more serious task of persuading the gentry in his audience of the value of chemistry in agricultural reform.[58] In the context of debates about population growth and agricultural output, Davy promoted his chemistry by promising the improvement of infertile land. The chemical analyst was indispensable because only he could expose the hidden constituents of the soil. It was given to the scientific expert to alter and re-constitute nature. And so the question arises again as to how concepts of improvement were incorporated into theological discourse.

The presence of divine purpose in the laws of nature was a conspicuous theme in Davy's lectures. A chemico-theology was not only possible but an integral part of his technique for cultivating his audience. Contrary to Carlile's notion that improving the world was incompatible with religious sentiment, Davy saw in the love of improvement a moral virtue ultimately grounded in reverence towards an intelligent deity. In Davy's opinion, obstruction to the diffusion of knowledge came not from religion but from ignorance or selfishness.[59] The principle of the conservation of matter might be used by the radical press to attack the supernatural; but, for Davy, as for seventeenth-century Platonists, the indestructibility of matter implied the indestructibility of the soul.[60]

One of the defects of Lavoisier's chemistry, as Davy perceived it, was that it had elevated one element, oxygen, at the expense of others. Following Lavoisier, the Swedish chemist Berzelius would say that oxygen was the centre around which the whole of chemistry turned. It was not so for Davy. One of the reasons why he was so pleased when chlorine, fluorine and iodine were proved to be elements was that they were all acid-producers, like Lavoisier's oxygen. They had the effect of destroying the uniqueness of oxygen.[61] Consequently they confirmed Davy's impression that there were what he called 'chains of resemblance' between different elements and compounds. In other words a natural classification of chemical species should prove possible. There were divinely ordained 'chains of being' in chemistry as in plant and animal taxonomy.

Exemplifying a rhetorical strategy that we analysed in chapter 6, Davy constructed chemical arguments against French materialism at a time when it was politically necessary to do so.[62] His main argument was that the properties of compounds can be shown not to depend exclusively on some property-bearing material component. Lavoisier's oxygen theory of acidity was materialistic in the sense that the oxygenic principle conferred the property of acidity on those compounds within which it was bound. The more oxygen they contained the more acidic they should be. Such chemical materialism, in Davy's view, could be defeated by chemistry itself. After all, two very different substances, charcoal and diamond, were made of the same element carbon. This seemed to show that such properties as transparency and hardness did not exclusively depend on a material component. The arrangement of matter by additional powers was an important variable. Compounds containing the same *two* elements could also differ remarkably. To inhale nitrous oxide was a recipe for laughter; to inhale nitrogen dioxide was a recipe for disaster as one choked to death on brown fumes. But the material components were identical. As the lesser chemist but greater poet Samuel Coleridge insisted, a chemical synthesis was a true synthesis – not simply a physical rearrangement of particles.

As for the additional powers, Davy made the forces of electricity his own, turning Volta's battery against the French. Decomposing the alkalis, sodium and potassium hydroxide, he showed that they contained oxygen. He could therefore quip that the principle of acidity of the French chemists could just as easily be termed the principle of alkalinity. But more significantly, Davy's electrochemical researches showed that the reactivity of a chemical agent could be changed simply by giving it a positive or negative charge. There was no way that chemical properties inhered in material particles. In a lecture delivered at the Royal Institution in 1812, the transmutation of chemistry into a chemico-theology was explicit and direct:

> Active powers must be considered as belonging to matter; but it is not necessary to suppose them inherent in it. [Matter] may be regarded ... as inert; and all effects produced upon it as flowing from the same original cause, which, as it is intelligent, must be divine.[63]

From Elements to Compounds: The Natural Theology of William Prout

In the work of William Prout we at last meet a systematic attempt to construct a chemico-theology. It is worth discussing because it reveals in a compelling way the difficulty of the problem, the ingenuity of the solution, and the necessity of a process theology in which the chemist was collaborator with a providential God. Prout was asked to author a *Bridgewater Treatise* that would deal with chemistry and the process of digestion. Writing in the 1830s, he suffered at the hands of a later generation who wished to set science in opposition to religion. In his preface to a posthumous fourth edition, John Tyndall said that he would have thought more highly of Dr Prout had he not read his book. It had clearly been written for the money.[64] But Tyndall, like T. H. Huxley and others of that later generation, had an axe to grind. To criticise a work of natural theology was one way of affirming scientific autonomy.[65]

Tyndall was unduly severe on Prout. The chemistry he popularised was both topical and original in the 1830s. We still remember Prout's hypothesis today. Struck by the fact that so many atomic weights appeared to be whole numbers, he had speculated in an ultimate unity of matter with hydrogen as the primary unit. This belief in an underlying unity of matter he shared with Davy. Prout was also well-versed in the study of digestion, having identified hydrochloric acid in the gastric juice. His treatise reflects the burgeoning science of organic chemistry. Far from lacking depth, his essay in natural theology made an original contribution. He developed a molecular theory of matter, transcending the atomic theory of John Dalton. Prout was one of the few chemists of the first half of the nineteenth century to develop the concept that we associate with Avogadro and Ampère – that the molecules of elementary gases are divisible into two or more identical submolecules.[66] A degree of submolecularity allowed Prout to explain Gay-Lussac's law of gaseous combination, and in particular how two volumes of hydrogen would react with one of oxygen to produce two of water.

Prout began his *Bridgewater Treatise* by considering the objection that chemistry might not help the religious apologist. He knew that William Paley had preferred physical mechanisms and anatomical structures to chemical processes. But there was a reply. Many mechanical devices helped to promote chemical change. In the circulatory system a complicated mechanical apparatus, the lungs, was employed for a simple chemical purpose: to oxygenate the blood. To disqualify chemistry from natural theology would therefore be arbitrary.[67]

Not that the task of constructing a chemico-theology was straightforward. The most direct route to design was through the utility of the chemical elements. The medical uses of iodine showed how a newcomer to the family of elements could be co-opted for altruistic purposes.[68] But there was a problem. What was to be done with the more poisonous elements? Prout's answer was: turn them into compounds! Here, the role of the chemist in improving creation was inscribed in the very text of natural theology. If there were uncomfortable connotations, Prout had a formula to disperse them. It was the properties of compounds, rather than elements, that the deity had envisaged. The secondary properties of the elements themselves had been 'left to be determined as the more general laws of matter might decide'.[69] The objection that the Creator could have chosen to make all the elements innocuous Prout was obliged to accept. The deity *could* have so chosen; but was there not more wisdom displayed in arranging for refractory elements to be processed for higher purposes?[70]

This may sound silly and one may begin to sympathise with Tyndall's reaction. But the argument does bring out that sense of collaboration to which we have referred. The chemist worked to complete or perfect creation. Prout did have other arguments for design. His reference to *laws* of matter is indicative of a trend in nineteenth-century natural theology that we observed in an earlier chapter: scientific advances would be celebrated as disclosures of the Creator's laws. The shift was from divine contrivance to divine legislation. By exposing the laws of matter chemistry, according to Prout, pointed to divine wisdom. And chemistry did now have some laws of its own. Prout could capitalise on Dalton's law of definite proportions, on Gay-Lussac's law of gaseous combination and on the generalisation he claimed as his own: 'all gaseous bodies under the same pressure, and temperature, contain an equal number of self-repulsive molecules'.[71] As 'delegated agencies', such laws pointed to the 'Great First Cause'.[72]

In the new science of organic chemistry, Prout found further, if indirect, support for his natural theology. Crucially, his treatment of living systems was structured by a proposition he had found in Paley. In his discussion of the self-imposed limitation of divine power, Paley had written: 'it is as though one Being should have fixed certain rules; and, if we may so speak, provided certain materials; and afterwards have committed to another being, out of these materials, and in subordination to these rules, the task of drawing forth a creation'. This proposition has attracted attention because it shows how easily natural theology could dig its own grave. When Darwin substituted a personified natural selection for Paley's second being, natural theology graduated into a thoroughgoing naturalism.[73]

Prout could not have foreseen that development and so welcomed Paley's admission of an agency mediating between God and nature. It allowed him to construct a vitalist physiology in which living systems were controlled by powers having a faculty 'little short of intelligence'.[74] As Prout's biographer has pointed out, this vitalism did not obstruct chemical enquiry. One could study the dynamics of disgestion without doubting that metabolic processes were under the control of an agent that was not itself the product of organisation.[75] It was a vitalism that did, however, set limits to what the chemist might achieve in the imitation of nature. The synthesis of an organic compound might be possible, but not a living organism. In fact the efforts of the chemist threw into relief the limitation of his powers. In the very act of imitating nature, the superiority of nature's art was clarified. The point had been made by Coleridge: 'The powers of chemistry are beginning to show us that no force, not even mechanical' power, can make life.[76] Prout was able to embroider the point because, if anything, the artificial synthesis of organic compounds reinforced rather than destroyed his vitalism. The extreme conditions required by the chemist only served to highlight the subtlety and silence of nature's powers. Friedrich Wöhler might have synthesised urea in 1828, but not by a method that truly imitated the process *in vivo*.[77]

This integration of vitalism and scientific research meant that chemistry could give indirect support to natural theology. Prout drew special attention to the refractory nature of carbon, hydrogen, oxygen and nitrogen – the four elements from which living systems had been constructed. Three were invisible gases, one of which – nitrogen – was relatively inert. And as for carbon, it was that unprepossessing stuff encountered as charcoal or soot. Amidst the wonders of creation, Prout exclaimed, 'it is perhaps difficult to say what is most wonderful; but we have often thought, that the Deity has displayed a greater stretch of power, in accommodating to such an extraordinary variety of changes, a material so unpromising and so refractory as charcoal, and in finally uniting it with the human mind; than was requisite for the creation of the human mind itself'.[78] Chemists might improve on nature, but within well defined limits. In the imitation of creative power their very success underscored the limits of the possible.

Not surprisingly, Prout's marriage of vitalism and natural theology was controversial. On the one hand critiques of vitalism could be urged on theological grounds. Did it not detract from divine Sovereignty to celebrate the role of intermediate agents between God and his Creation?[79]

And from the scientific side, there can be irritation when limits are placed on the future scope of science. It is therefore instructive to turn to a critique of chemico-theology that belongs to the next generation when T. H. Huxley argued for the physical basis of life.

Chemistry in the Service of Reductionism

In his defence of Darwinism, Huxley would have no room for a chemico-theology.[80] In fact chemistry became a crucial resource as he argued for the physical basis of life. That catchphrase – the physical basis of life – was the title of one of Huxley's most celebrated 'lay sermons'.[81] He preached it in Edinburgh in 1868 and it helped to make protoplasm a household word. It even found its way into Gilbert and Sullivan's *Mikado*. Against vitalist theories of life and against the kind of chemico-theology we have seen in Prout, Huxley drew on physical principles akin to the conservation of energy to make his case. There could be no vital spark or extra-mechanical agent beyond the conversion of protoplasm into work. Even the mental activity of a lecturer, Huxley ruefully observed, depended on the loss of bodily substance.[82] But it was chemistry that furnished a crucial argument for Huxley's reductionist philosophy. His argument was that the physical basis of life lay in the protoplasm of the cell. His ace card was that all forms of protoplasm so far analysed contained the same four chemical elements: carbon, hydrogen, oxygen and nitrogen.[83] All forms of protoplasm appeared to behave similarly when subjected to chemical reagents, electric shock or heat. Crucially, in all living things, there was an underlying unity of composition. For Huxley, chemistry had penetrated the mystery of life. Unity of composition implied common ancestry in a single evolutionary process. The argument was a cruder version of what we often hear today – that there is much in common between the DNA of chimpanzees and humans.

The critical question again was whether the chemist might imitate nature, so breaking down the barriers between nature and artifice. By the time Huxley was preaching, the metaphor of the chemical laboratory was commonly used to refer to living organisms. Huxley broke the barriers down by describing plants as 'fine chemists'.[84] As with earlier inroads into the nature/art dichotomy the case was highly controversial. Huxley's critics bounced back by driving a wedge between what the chemist could do and what occurred *in vivo*. His fiercest critic, Lionel Smith Beale, objected that Huxley's line on the chemical nature of protoplasm was flawed because, *after analysis*, one could not call protoplasm the living substance. There was something of Wordsworth's 'we murder to dissect' in his position. In fact Beale advised Huxley that he should really call nerve, muscle and bone the physical basis of death. Against Huxley's reductionism he protested that the really significant fact was the multiplicity of differences of structure and property associated with similarity of composition. That, for Beale, implied a vital power which lay beyond the bounds of the chemist.

One of the things that makes historical research so rewarding is that controversies of this kind often conceal other issues that, once recovered, add spice to the whole debate. In this case Huxley had been a candidate for the Chair at King's College London that Beale had won. But their differences were rooted more deeply. Beale set himself up as custodian of a conventional morality that had been threatened by Darwinism. He is usually described as a broad churchman who treated the differences between humans and animals as absolute.[85] He later laced his scientific works with attacks on atheism, materialism, agnosticism and monism – all those '-isms' with which the Darwinians were apt to flirt. In short, what may seem a small matter of chemical analysis could be at the heart of an immensely complex debate concerning the limitations of scientific analysis. Huxley certainly did not have it all his own way. When he was elected Rector of Aberdeen in the 1870s he was lampooned in a volume entitled *Protoplasm, Powheads, Porwiggles; and the Evolution of the Horse from the Rhinoceros: illustrating Professor Huxley's scientific mode of getting up the Creation and Upsetting Moses: a Guide for Electors in choosing Lord Rectors.*[86]

In the debate between Beale and Huxley the question whether chemists could reconstruct vital processes was clearly central. Beale, for example, took special exception to a remark of W. R. Grove who had spoken of the electric battery and its effects as 'the nearest approach to a man-made organism'. Beale pounced on what he took to be an extraordinary show of ignorance: 'everything that lives – every so-called living machine – grows of itself, builds itself up, and multiplies, while every non-living machine is made, does not grow, and does not produce machines like itself'.[87] Beale inevitably sounds like a reactionary, but his attacks on the notion of an intercellular substance gives him a significant place in revisions of cell theory, whilst his claim that Huxley was using the word 'protoplasm' indiscriminately was very much to the point.

Meanwhile in France, chemistry was pressed into the service of both reductionism and positivism by the scientific guru of the Third Republic, Marcellin Berthelot. His goal was to perfect methods of organic synthesis that showed, once and for all, that the chemist could match natural processes. His new synthetic methods allowed him to produce in the laboratory acetylene, ethyl alcohol, formic acid and many complex derivatives. He was arguably the first to accomplish the direct synthesis of organic compounds from their elements. When he synthesised formic acid (which came from ants) in November 1855, he did so directly from carbon monoxide and steam – compounds that were themselves immediate products of their elements. Berthelot's science of organic chemistry based on synthesis carried an unmistakable message: 'in reality and without reservation', the chemical forces that govern organic matter are the same as those governing inorganic matter.[88] He could pride himself on having removed the space for vital forces and any chemico-theology based upon them. His case was, however, over-stated; for, as Louis Pasteur observed, the chemist could not yet control the centres of asymmetry in a complex organic molecule.[89]

The Chemical Interventionism of Eleanor Ormerod

For our last historical example we return to England and to a context in which there were economic incentives to apply chemical knowledge. The issue concerns the early use of pesticides and their advocacy by a Victorian spinster, Eleanor Ormerod. As a technological scientist Ormerod makes a revealing case-study because here was a woman penetrating a male domain.[90]

Ormerod was a member of the gentry who, in May 1882, became Honorary Consulting Entomologist to the Royal Agricultural Society. Her interventionist approach to insect control stands in sharp contrast to principles derived from a conservative natural theology. The earlier entomologist William Kirby held providentialist views on the balance of nature which dissuaded him from chemical controls.[91] For similar reasons, the Quaker Edward Newman had wished to rely only on insect predators – a form of biological control. 'You see', he explained, 'Providence has foreseen that the earth might at any time be desolated, or totally unpeopled, by the natural increase of many kinds of animals, and He has provided against it.'[92] There were clergymen who had no doubt that insects should be killed when they make a nuisance of themselves. Ormerod's campaign is striking because of the seemingly masculine way in which she wished to dominate nature with her chemicals. A pioneeer in the use of 'Paris green' she has been described as having 'implored farmers to drench Nature in a slurry of poison'.[93] There was poignancy in her career in that she created a niche of expertise that she herself could not fully occupy precisely because she was a woman. In 1889 the University of Edinburgh decided to establish a chair in economic entomology. Ormerod's response is revealing:

> Who ever is to take the position of lecturer? I am complimented by the expression of a wish from the authorities who have the election in hand that I should take it; but then Lady Professors are not admitted in Scotland ... I think I could do all that is wanted, but then, oh! Shades of John Knox![94]

To some observers, Ormerod transgressed both the etiquette of natural theology and of womanhood. Appalled by her unfeminine crusade against God's creatures one clergyman reminded her, 'how far nobler is the crusade against sin and fashion, which are the real and awful causes of misery, suffering and poverty .... I would to God that you, madam, would turn your great talents in the truest interests of the poor.' She was put in her place with the request that she should not 'steel' her 'compassionate, womanly heart' with her scientific studies.[95] This could certainly be described as male chauvinism at its worst, but we need to know that what had incited the Revd J. E. Walker's reproach was Miss Ormerod's campaign to annihilate house sparrows, which she believed were a menace.

The use of pesticides was clearly controversial for many reasons. At the end of the nineteenth century there was, however, a rhetoric to justify this aspect of chemical industry. Agricultural practices were themselves artificial in that they interfered with nature. The concentration of crops in one area was not nature's method. The price was the concentration of insect pests that would otherwise be denied so convenient a livelihood. The argument therefore was that the use of pesticides was helping to restore the natural balance, which had been upset by the simple expediency of growing food. We are back again with the blurring of the natural and the artificial in more ways than one. Ormerod herself maintained that the unwelcome hordes of house sparrows had resulted from the destruction of their natural enemies. She wanted a counterbalance – a 'legal and economic, rather than a natural, balance'.[96]

Conclusion

One reason for offering these chemical snapshots is that they expose some of the difficulties that arose in integrating an interventionist science with a contemplative natural theology, but also how the difficulties were overcome. In contexts where the meaning and scope of 'nature' became progressively blurred, so the scope of a natural theology would become increasingly problematic. But what we have also seen is that one kind of theology might survive – the kind that sees in the alleged improvement of nature a collaboration between human beings and their Maker. It is nevertheless striking how heavily this argument hinged on the subservience of chemistry to medicine. In the Scottish universities of the eighteenth century chemistry was both institutionalised within and eventually emancipated from medicine, becoming an academic discipline in its own right,[97] as also happened in France where Lavoisier famously used physical principles in his analysis of chemical composition. In gaining its independence, it perhaps became less propitious as a resource for religious reflection. Throughout the nineteenth century it continued to promise improvements to the world, especially in the domain of agriculture. And it would be wrong to say that it completely lost touch with religious discourse. The great German chemist Justus von Liebig would argue that to ignore the natural laws that governed fertility was to sin against God and humanity. It was the abuse of the land, milking it for excessive profit, the *refusal* to use chemical fertilisers, that represented an 'interference in the divine world order'.[98] As we have just seen, those who favoured pesticides would appeal to a similar logic.

What might a future historian make of *our fin de siècle* techniques? The chemist is still around, claiming, through biotechnology, to improve upon nature. Looking back on the 1990s one would recognise new techniques, including the freezing of embryos, that allowed women the freedom to have their children when they wanted, even when past the menopause. A future historian would also note that the gene for the ageing process was about to be isolated, with the prospect of a pill that would add fifty years to life expectancy. She or he might wryly observe that the alchemists' dream lived on. There would surely be comment, too, on experiments in genetic engineering that had led to the patenting of pigs and mice. In the production of such transgenic animals, our future historian might well see a near-final collapse of all distinction between nature and art. In the 1990s it was, after all, a requirement for the award of a patent that the animal be deemed an invention, a novelty, something that nature alone could not produce. Our future historian might even chance upon a copy of *GenEthics News* for October 1995, where the patenting of animals was indeed seen as a qualitative change in the human enclosure of nature. 'Now', wrote one concerned observer, 'we are not merely dominating nature, but claiming intellectual origination'.[99] The historian would find the same observer adding that 'from the point of view of anyone who believes in God(s) [the claim to have invented an animal] is simply claiming to be God'.

An historian familiar with the text of this chapter might pause to consider whether such a view was correct. Did it not overlook the model of collaboration that had been the precarious concomitant of chemico-theologies? But the qualitative change would be perceived as real enough and of great concern to the public. In the 1990s the instincts of those who practised transgenic experiments were telling them that there would be a revulsion threshold beyond which the public would be intolerant. The unlimited replacement of genetic material in pigs with human DNA would surely become offensive. But in 1995 there was very little philosophy helping to define the limits.

All this would be clear to our future historian who would no doubt be intrigued by the rhetoric of today's scientists. In the context of patent law it was the artifice that had to be stressed. In the pursuit of invention there seemed to be nothing to check the scientist from doing all that it was practically possible to do. But, in the context of public relations, there was the check of audience concern, however inarticulately expressed. And when the name of the game was re-assuring the public, a quite different rhetoric surfaced – not then the rhetoric of invention but the rhetoric of a secularised natural theology. It exhibited a form similar to that seen in earlier chemico-theologies.

Genetic engineers, for example, were saying in the 1990s that they were not doing anything essentially different from earlier breeders who had dedicated themselves to the improvement of plant and animal stocks. They were collaborating with nature, not violating her. In justifying experiments on surplus human eggs, it was some-times suggested that nature in its prodigality legitimated the practice because so many eggs are rejected in normal reproductive processes. Locating a dialogue on this very issue, our future historian would find one contributor rejecting the argument but still affirming that 'if we consider ourselves as part of nature, it might be reasonable to consider research as treating the eggs with respect, and to view selec-tions made by us as part of the natural selection process'.[100] This naturalising of what we do had evoked a sympathetic response from the theologian Gordon Dunstan:

> I believe that scientific intervention at this point is precisely to increase
> selectivity in an evolutionary process in which what to us is waste is in fact
> a selection for biological, evolutionary ends. We are, in a way, aligned with
> a selective force against what appears to be an otherwise wasteful use of
> material.[101]

What will our future historian make of such references to alignment with a force beyond ourselves? Were there still reputable scholars in the late twentieth century who would interpret that alignment as alignment with the purposes of God? Or was the rhetoric of a secu-larised natural theology totally and invariably secular? Our future historian would find that theological essays on the subject had not dried up. Books with titles such as *Cosmos as Creation* were still appearing in university libraries, containing essays entitled 'The evol-ution of the created co-creator'.[102] In these one would encounter the argument that guiding principles are necessary for interventionist technologies – principles that recommend the maximising of oppor-tunities for greater love and greater freedom. Whether such high ideals actually meshed with the complexities of decision making would be a moot point. Freezing embryos might give women greater freedom, but the question was being asked whether the choice of motherhood late in life would be the most loving in relation to the child? Transgenic animals might enrich medical resources, in tracking diseases, in facilitating organ transplants and in replacing dysfunctional genes. But how were the benefits to be weighed against the threat both to animal welfare and to existing eco-systems?[103]

To future observers, the idealism of the theologian might also seem strangely out of tune with economic and political realities that in 1995 appeared to be riding roughshod over those concerned with defining limits. There would be evidence from the USA of resistance to moratoria on transgenic experiments – a resistance based on the fear that US biotechnology might lose its leadership in the field.[104] But there would still be evidence of countervailing trends. Perhaps the most visible trans*cultural* animal of the 1990s would be the ethics committee, so many of which had sprouted in response to biotechnology.[105] Looking back on this phenomenon, the historian might reflect that by the 1990s moral theologians had come to occupy a smaller niche than they once did, but that there was still a space in which they could collaborate with moral philosophers and scientists themselves.[106] That future historian might finally discern the most radical agenda yet for the reconstruction of nature – the changing of human nature itself through genetic manipulation. But, by then, what would that historian's *own* nature have become?

NOTES

1 R. Carlile, *Lion*, 3 (1829), 281–2.
2 *Ibid.*, 2 (1828), 488–9. Carlile's critique of natural theology is discussed by J. R. Topham, ' "An infinite variety of arguments": The *Bridgewater Treatises* and British natural theology in the 1830s' PhD dissertation, Lancaster University, 1993, 210–17.
3 We take this anecdote from J. Read, *Humour and Humanism in Chemistry*, London, 1947.
4 O. Hannaway, *The Chemists and the Word: The Didactic Origins of Modern Chemistry*, Baltimore, 1975, 76–9.
5 Cited by B. P. Copenhaver in his Introduction to *Hermetica*, Cambridge, 1992, xxxv.
6 *Ibid.*, xxxvi.
7 Ben Jonson, *The Alchemist* (ed. D. Brown), London, 1966, 31.
8 W. Theisen, 'John Dastin: the alchemist as co-creator', *Ambix*, 38 (1991), 73–8, on 74.
9 *Ibid.*

10   W. H. Brock, *The Fontana History of Chemistry*, London, 1992, 21–2.

11   Cited by S. J. Linden, 'Alchemy and eschatology in seventeenth century poetry', *Ambix*, 31 (1984), 102–24, on 102.

12   M. Baldwin, 'Alchemy and the Society of Jesus in the seventeenth century', *Ambix*, 40 (1993), 41–64.

13   *Ibid.*, 49.

14   M. J. Gorman, '*Deus ex machinis*: bounding natural knowledge in the Collegio Romano', paper presented at the 3rd British–North American History of Science Meeting, Edinburgh, 23–26 July, 1996.

15   W. Pagel, *Paracelsus: An Introduction to Philosophical Medicine in the Era of the Renaissance*, Basel, 1958; A. G. Debus, *The Chemical Philosophy: Paracelsian Science and Medicine in the Sixteenth and Seventeenth Centuries*, 2 vols., New York, 1977.

16   Cited by J. R. R. Christie, 'The Paracelsan body', in *Paracelsus. The Man and his Reputation, his Ideas and their Transfomation* (ed. O. Grell), Dordrecht, in press.

17   Hannaway, op. cit. (4), 38–47.

18   *Paracelsus: Selected Writings* (ed. J. Jacobi), London, 1951, 196–7.

19   Christie, op. cit. (16).

20   A. G. Debus, *Chemistry, Alchemy and the New Philosophy, 1550–1700*, Aldershot, 1987, 126.

21   Christie, op. cit. (16).

22   Hannaway, op. cit. (4), 52.

23   Christie, op. cit. (16).

24   A. Clericuzio, 'A redefinition of Boyle's chemistry and corpuscular philosophy', *Annals of Science*, 47 (1990), 561–89; *idem.*, 'From Van Helmont to Boyle: a study of the transmission of Helmontian chemical and medical theories in seventeenth-century England', *British Journal for the History of Science*, 26 (1993), 303–34; S. Schaffer, 'Godly men and mechanical philosophers: souls and spirits in Restoration natural philosophy', *Science in Context*, 1 (1987), 55–85.

25   Cited by H. J. Cook, 'The new philosophy and medicine in seventeenth-century England', in *Reappraisals of the Scientific Revolution* (ed. D. C. Lindberg and R. S. Westman), Cambridge, 1990, 397–436, on 417.

26   M. Boas [Hall], *Robert Boyle and Seventeenth-Century Chemistry*, Cambridge, 1958, 18–19.

27   R. Hooykaas, 'The discrimination between "natural" and "artificial" substances and the development of corpuscular theory', *Archives Internationales d'Histoire des Sciences*, 1 (1948), 640–51; *idem.*, *Religion and the Rise of Modern Science*, Edinburgh, 1972, 54–74.

28   H. Power, *Experimental Philosophy, in Three Books containing New Experiments Microscopical, Mercurial, Magnetical*, London, 1664. The relevant citations are from M. B. Hall, *Nature and Nature's Laws*, London, 1970, 122–5 and 128–30.

29   T. Shanahan, 'Teleological reasoning in Boyle's *Disquisition about Final Causes*', in *Robert Boyle Reconsidered* (ed. M. Hunter), Cambridge, 1994, 177–92.

30 Robert Boyle, *Works* (ed. T. Birch), 6 vols., London, 1772; reprint edition, Hildesheim, 1966, iii, 528.

31 *Ibid.*, 533.

32 *Ibid.*, 533–4.

33 C. Webster, *The Great Instauration: Science, Medicine and Reform, 1626–1660*, London, 1975, 388.

34 Boyle, op. cit. (30), ii, 5, 9 and 60.

35 *Ibid.*, ii, 14 and 86.

36 *Ibid.*, ii, 28.

37 *Ibid.*, ii, 89.

38 S. Shapin and S. Schaffer, *Leviathan and the Air Pump: Hobbes, Boyle, and the Experimental Life*, Princeton, 1985, 322.

39 Boyle, op. cit. (30), ii, 14–15.

40 J. Golinski, 'The secret life of an alchemist', in *Let Newton Be!* (ed. J. Fauvel, R. Flood, M. Shortland and R. Wilson), Oxford, 1988, 147–67, on 151.

41 I. Newton, Keynes MS 33, microfilm 661, Cambridge University Library, 3–4.

42 I. Newton, Portsmouth Collection MS Add. 4003, Cambridge University Library; B. J. T. Dobbs, *The Janus Faces of Genius*, Cambridge, 1991, 36.

43 Dobbs, *ibid.*, 84.

44 For two contrasting approaches to the study of Priestley's stand against Lavoisier, see J. G. McEvoy, 'Causes and Laws, Powers and Principles: the metaphysical foundations of Priestley's concept of phlogiston', in *Science, Medicine and Dissent: Joseph Priestley, 1733–1804* (ed. R. Anderson and C. Lawrence), London, 1987, 55–71; and J. Golinski, *Science as Public Culture: Chemistry and Enlightenment in Britain, 1760–1820*, Cambridge, 1992, 50–152.

45 For this and the following account of Priestley we draw heavily on J. H. Brooke, '"A sower went forth": Joseph Priestley and the ministry of reform', in *Motion Toward Perfection: The Achievement of Joseph Priestley* (ed. A. T. Schwartz and J. G. McEvoy), Boston, 1990, 21–56.

46 For a fuller discussion see J. Dunn, 'From applied theology to social analysis: the break between John Locke and the Scottish Enlightenment', in *Wealth and Virtue* (ed. I. Hont and M. Ignatieff), Cambridge, 1983, 119–35.

47 A. D. Orange, 'Oxygen and one God', *History Today*, 24 (1974), 773–81.

48 H. Hartley, *Studies in the History of Chemistry*, Oxford, 1971, 12.

49 J. Priestley to A. Volta, 5 August 1779, in *A Scientific Autobiography of Joseph Priestley (1733–1804); Selected Scientific Correspondence* (ed. R. Schofield), Cambridge, Mass., 1966, 174.

50 J. Priestley to T. Lindsey, August 1771, in *ibid.*, 133.

51 F. W. Gibbs, *Joseph Priestley: Adventurer in Science and Champion of Truth*, London, 1965, 81.

52 J. Priestley, *Disquisitions Relating to Matter and Spirit*, London, 1777; reprint edn., New York, 1975, 161.

53 A. Bicknell, *The Putrid Soul. A Poetical Epistle to Joseph Priestley on his Disquisitions Relating to Matter and Spirit*, London, 1780, 17–18.

54   M. Crosland, 'The image of science as a threat: Burke versus Priestley and the "Philosophic Revolution"', *British Journal for the History of Science*, 20 (1987), 277–307, on 284.

55   J. G. McEvoy, 'Joseph Priestley, "Aerial Philosopher": metaphysics and methodology in Priestley's chemical thought, 1772 to 1781', part 2, *Ambix*, 25 (1978), 93–111, especially 100–101. Compare also S. Schaffer, 'Priestley's questions', *History of Science*, 22 (1984), 151–83.

56   D. M. Knight, *Humphry Davy: Science and Power*, Oxford, 1992; now reprinted by Cambridge University Press.

57   Cited by T. H. Levere, *Poetry Realized in Nature: Samuel Taylor Coleridge and Early-nineteenth Century Science*, Cambridge, 1981, 172.

58   Golinski, op. cit. (44), 188–203; M. Berman, *Social Change and Scientific Organization: The Royal Institution, 1799–1844*, Ithaca, 1978.

59   R. Siegfried, 'Davy's "Intellectual Delight" and his Lectures at the Royal Institution', in *Science and the Sons of Genius: Studies on Humphry Davy* (ed. S. Forgan), London, 1980, 177–99, especially 180.

60   D. M. Knight, *The Transcendental Part of Chemistry*, Folkestone, 1978, 74.

61   J. H. Brooke, *Thinking About Matter: Studies in the History of Chemical Philosophy*, Aldershot, 1995, ch. 3.

62   Knight, op. cit. (60), 61–90.

63   *Ibid.*, 68.

64   W. H. Brock, 'Prout's Chemical *Bridgewater Treatise*', *Journal of Chemical Education*, 40 (1963), 652–55, especially 653.

65   F. M. Turner, 'The Victorian conflict between science and religion: a professional dimension', *Isis*, 69 (1978), 356–76.

66   Brock, op. cit. (64), 653–4; Brooke, op. cit. (61), ch. 9; N. W. Fisher, 'Avogadro, the chemists, and historians of chemistry', *History of Science*, 20 (1982), 77–102; 212–31.

67   W. Prout, *Chemistry, Meteorology, and the Function of Digestion Considered with Reference to Natural Theology*, 2nd edn., London, 1834, 22.

68   W. H. Brock, *From Protyle to Proton: William Prout and the Nature of Matter 1785–1985*, Bristol and Boston, 1985, 67.

69   Prout, op. cit. (67), 183.

70   *Ibid.*, 185.

71   *Ibid.*, 25, 144–5, 149, 157 and 164.

72   *Ibid.*, 556–7.

73   J. R. Durant, 'The meaning of evolution: post-Darwinian debates on the significance for man of the theory of evolution, 1858–1908', PhD dissertation, Cambridge University, 1977, 57; J. H. Brooke, 'The relations between Darwin's science and his religion', in *Darwinism and Divinity* (ed. J. R. Durant), Oxford, 1985, 40–75, especially 55–7.

74   Prout, op. cit. (67), 25 and 440; Brock, op. cit. (68), 71.

75   Brock, op. cit. (68), 71–2; Prout, op. cit. (67), 436–42.

76   Levere, op. cit. (57), 51.

77   Brooke, op. cit. (61), ch. 5.

78   Prout, op. cit. (67), 446.

79   Divergent responses to this question have been discussed in Brooke, op.

cit. (61), ch. 4. For an attempt to correlate vitalist and materialist positions with political preferences, see L. S. Jacyna, 'Immanence or transcendence: theories of life and organization in Britain, 1790–1835', *Isis*, 74 (1983), 311–29.

80 On Huxley's role as Darwin's 'bulldog', see A. Desmond, *Archetypes and Ancestors*, London, 1982; *idem.*, *Huxley: The Devil's Disciple*, London, 1994.

81 T. H. Huxley, 'On the physical basis of life', in *Lay Sermons, Addresses, and Reviews*, London, 1870, 132–61.

82 *Ibid.*, 145–6.

83 *Ibid.*, 148–51.

84 G. L. Geison, 'The protoplasmic theory of life and the vitalist-mechanist debate', *Isis*, 60 (1969), 273–92, on 281.

85 G. L. Geison, 'Lionel Smith Beale', *Dictionary of Scientific Biography* (ed. C. C. Gillispie), 18 vols., New York, 1970, i, 539–40.

86 Geison, op. cit. (84), 284.

87 *Ibid.*, 287.

88 M. Berthelot, *Leçons sur les Méthodes Générales de Synthèse en Chimie Organique*, Paris, 1864, 17.

89 Brooke, op. cit. (61), ch. 8.

90 J. F. M. Clark, 'Eleanor Ormerod (1828–1901) as an economic entomologist: "pioneer of purity even more than of Paris Green"', *British Journal for the History of Science*, 25 (1992), 431–52.

91 J. F. M. Clark, 'Science, secularization and social change: the metamorphosis of entomology in nineteenth-century England', PhD dissertation, Oxford University, 1994, 208.

92 *Ibid.*

93 *Ibid.*, 228.

94 *Ibid.*, 220.

95 Clark, op. cit. (90), 450.

96 Clark, op. cit. (91), 236.

97 A. Donovan, *Philosophical Chemistry in the Scottish Enlightenment*, Edinburgh, 1975. The key figure of William Cullen is also discussed by Golinski, op. cit. (44), 11–49.

98 O. Sonntag, 'Religion and science in the thought of Liebig', *Ambix*, 24 (1977), 159–69, especially 161–5.

99 D. King, 'Ethics and the oncomouse', *GenEthics News*, no. 8, Sept./Oct. 1995, 7.

100 B. Modell, in *Human Embryo Research. Yes or No?*, The Ciba Foundation, London and New York, 1986, 19.

101 *Ibid.*

102 P. Hefner, 'The evolution of the created co-creator', in *Cosmos as Creation* (ed. T. Peters), Nashville, 1989, 211–32.

103 See Hastings Center Report, January/February 1994, published as Special Supplement in vol. 24 no. 1, January/February 1994.

104 M. Fox, 'Transgenic animals: ethical and animal welfare concerns', in *The BioRevolution: Cornucopia or Pandora's Box* (ed. P. Wheale and R. McNally), London, 1990, 31–45.

105   For general historical perspectives on the rise of biotechnology, see R. Bud, *The Uses of Life: A History of Biotechnology*, Cambridge, 1993.

106   For example, the study group that met at the Ciba Foundation in November 1985, and which subsequently published in op.cit. (100), included among its members John Bowker, Gordon Dunstan and Arthur Peacocke. See also the contribution of Andrew Linzey to Wheale and McNally, op. cit. (104). The difficulties faced by the theologian who, on medical ethics committees, may not wish to collude with secular moral philosophy are sensitively discussed by J. M. Soskice, 'Creation and relation', in *Medicine and Moral Reasoning* (ed. K. W. M. Fulford, G. Gillett and J. M. Soskice), Cambridge, 1994, 19–28.

Index of Names

Abraham, 55
Abraham, J. J., 309n
Acland, Henry, 31
Acquaviva, Claudio (Father General of the Jesuit Order), 136n
Adams, John 196, 206n
Airy, G. B., 168n
Allen, D. E., 311n
Allen, William, 292–3, 294, 295, 298–9, 301, 303, 305, 309n, 310n, 311n, 312
Ampère, André Marie, 332
Anderson of Newburgh, Dr, 147
Anderson, R., 343n
Anscombe, E., 239n
Anselm, 144
Appleyard, Bryan, 76, 77, 81, 82, 102n
Aquinas, Thomas, 192
Arago, Dominique, 295
Aristotle, 20, 33, 84, 86, 124, 136n, 183, 322, 323
Arnold, Matthew, 286
Ashburton, Anne Louisa (wife of Baron Ashburton), 156
Ashburton, Baron (Tory diplomat), 156
Ashwood, T. L., 307n
Atkins, Peter, 233–5, 243n
Aubrey, John, 307n
Augustine of Hippo, 114
Avicenna (Abū ʿAlī al-Ḥusayn ibn ʿAbd Allāh ibn Sīnā), 321
Avogadro, Amedeo, 332

Babbage, Charles, 329
Bach, Johann Sebastian, 167
Bacon, Francis, 16, 26, 325
Baker, G. P., 103n
Baker, John Gilbert, 301, 302, 304, 309n, 313
Baldwin, M., 342n
Banner, M. C., 11n
Banton, M., 172n
Barberini, Maffeo (Pope Urban VIII), 109–10, 112–13, 117, 119–20, 121–2, 123, 129, 130, 131–2

Barbour, H., 308n
Barbour, Ian G., x, 98, 104n, 241n, 275–6, 281n
Barclay, O. R., 72n
Barclay, Robert, 294
Barlow, N., 11n, 174n
Barnes, B., 41n
Barrett, P. H., 40n
Barrow, John D., 177, 203n, 204n, 242n
Barry, Martin, 285, 299, 306n, 312
Barth, Karl, 231, 242n
Barton, R., 278n
Bartram, W., 311n
Bäumer, A., 306n
Beale, John, 325
Beale, Lionel Smith, 335–6
Beaufoy, Henry, 307n, 308n, 312
Beaufoy, Mark, 312
Bebbington, D. W., 280n
Beer, A., 237n
Beer, G., 202n
Bell, Charles, 156, 158, 205n
Bellarmine, Robert (Cardinal), 24, 39n, 69, 109, 111, 112, 114–15, 118–19
Bellers, F., 312
Bellers, John, 292, 299, 300, 309n, 312
Bellini, Vincenzo, 231
Benjamin, A. E., 206n
Bennett, J. A., 238n
Bentley, Richard, 8, 22, 194, 205n, 223, 239n
Berman, Morris, 81, 102n, 344n
Berthelot, Marcellin, 21–2, 336–7, 345n
Berzelius, Jöns Jacob, 330
Bevan, Silvanus, 289–90, 298, 299, 300, 303, 309n, 312
Biagioli, Mario, 110, 128–30, 134n, 136n, 138n
Bichat, Marie François Xavier, 54
Bicknell, A., 343n
Birch, Thomas, 299–300, 311n, 312, 343n

Blackwell, R. J., 135n, 136n
Blair, A., 236n, 241n
Blair, Hugh, 183
Bland, Michael, 312
Bloom, W., 81–2, 102n
Blumenbach, Johann Friedrich, 95
Bohm, D., 104n
Bohr, Niels, 80, 96–7, 227, 229
Bois-Reymond, Emil du, 96
Bonaparte, Napoleon, 52, 79, 101
Bondi, Herman, 227
Booth, C. C., 309n, 311
Borgia (Cardinal) (adversary of
     Urban VIII), 119
Boulton, J. T., 204n
Bouratinos, Emilios, 85, 86, 103n
Bowker, John, 233, 242n, 346n
Bowler, Peter J., 162, 169n, 173n
Boyle, Robert, 16, 17, 26, 33, 88,
     144–5, 149, 177, 212, 216, 219,
     238n, 242n, 300, 322–6, 343n
Bradlaugh, Charles, 150
Brady, George S., 293, 298, 304, 309n,
     313
Brady, Henry Bowman, 293, 301, 302,
     304, 309n, 311n, 313
Brahe, Tycho, 111, 137n, 212–13, 229
Braithwaite, W. C., 308n
Brecht, Bertolt, 106, 126–7
Brett, R. L., 311n
Brett-James, N. G., 308n, 311n
Brewster, David, 60, 141, 147, 168n,
     253, 277n
Bright, John, 295–6
Brock, W. H., 241n, 278n, 342n, 344n
Brocklesby, Richard, Dr, 290
Brooke, J. H., xi, xiin, 10n, 11n, 38n,
     39n, 40n, 72n, 133n, 136n, 168n,
     169n, 170n, 170–1n, 171n, 172n,
     173n, 174n, 203n, 237n, 238n,
     240n, 242n, 343n, 344n, 345n
Brougham, Henry, 156, 182, 198,
     203n, 206n, 269
Brown, A. W., 277n, 280n
Brown, D., 341n
Browne, Janet, 248, 277n
Browning, D., 242n
Brunner, Emil, 242n
Bruno, Giordano, 108, 118, 151, 213
Brush, Stephen G., 94, 104n
Buchwald, Jed Z., 83, 102n

Buckland, William, 61, 155–6, 157,
     159, 160, 171n, 184–5, 185illus,
     186, 187, 188, 189illus, 190,
     204n, 205n
Buckley, Michael J., 150–2, 170n, 198,
     205n, 206n
Bud, R., 346n
Budd, S., 70n
Buffon, George-Louis Leclerc, Comte
     de, 255, 278n
Bunsen, Robert Wilhelm von, 252
Burckhardt, R. W., 38n
Burke, Edmund, 187, 204n, 329
Burnet, Thomas, 185
Burrow, J. R., 310n
Butler, Joseph, 147, 169n, 190
Butler, Samuel, 132
Büttner, M., 306n

Caccini, Tommaso, 108, 118, 136n
Cadbury, H. J., 307n, 308n
Cairns, D., 37n, 205n, 241n
Calvin, John, 136n
Campanella, Tommaso, 109, 113,
     133n
Campbell, C., 71n
Campbell, D. M., 241n
Campbell, George, 181, 183–4, 190,
     192, 203n, 204n, 205n
Cannon, W. F., 169n, 175n
Cano, Melchior, 118
Cantor, Barbara, xi
Cantor, G. N., 41n, 102n, 206n, 241n
Capek, Milic, 82, 102n
Capra, Fritjof, 77–81, 82, 83–90,
     90–4, 97–101, 102n, 103n, 104n,
     105n
Carlile, Richard, 314, 315, 330, 341n
Carlisle, Anthony, 158
Carlyle, Thomas, 251–2, 274
Carnap, R., 69n
Carpenter, J. Estlin, 263illus, 279n
Carpenter, Lant, Rev Dr, 264, 279n
Carpenter, Mary, 264
Carpenter, R. L., 279n
Carpenter, William Benjamin, 262–8,
     263illus, 274, 275, 279n, 280n
Cartwright, N., 236n
Carus, W., 280n
Cash, John Theodore, 293, 309n, 313
Caspar, M., 38n, 237n

Castelli, Benedetto, 113, 131
Caverni, Raffaello (Galileo's biographer), 126
Cesi, Prince Federico, 108
Chadwick, Owen, 173n
Chalmers, Thomas, 15, 17, 26, 152, 156, 157, 170n, 171n, 192, 195, 205n, 231
Chambers, Robert, 148, 156, 159, 160, 205n, 270, 275
Chandrasekhar, S., 40n, 240n, 241n, 243n
Chang, Hasok, 97, 104n
Chapman-Houston, D., 308n, 309n
Charles II (King of England), 283
Charleton, Walter, 103n, 213, 216, 219, 236n, 239n
Chilton, William, 159
Christie, J. R. R., 206n, 342n
Christina, Grand Duchess, 39n
Christy, Henry, 310n
Ciampoli, Giovanni, 108, 121
Cicero, 183
Cioli, Lord Bali, 134n
Clark, J. F. M., 345n
Clark, J. W., 40n, 172n, 280n, 281n
Clarke, G., 309n
Clarke, Samuel, 150, 151, 154, 197, 206n
Clavius, Christopher, 121
Clayton, J., 168n, 169n, 170n
Clayton, P., 11n
Cleanthes (character in Hume's *Dialogues*), 150
Clericuzio, A., 342n
Close, Frank, 227–8, 241n
Cohen, H. F., 39n
Cohen, I. B., 41n, 205n, 239n
Coleman, W., 38n
Coleridge, Samuel Taylor, 95, 282, 306, 331, 334
Collier, K. B., 70–1n
Collins, Anthony, 151
Collins, H. M., 41n
Collins, J. H., 311n
Collinson, Peter, 289–90, 298, 299, 300, 301, 302, 303, 312
Colloms, B., 174n
Colombe, Lodovico delle, 113–14
Combe, George, 147
Comte, Auguste, x, 8, 45, 47–57, 66, 70n

Congreve, Richard, 55–6, 70n
Conti, Carlo (Cardinal), 111, 134n
Cook, H. J., 342n
Coope, Jonathan, 104n
Cooter, R., 169n
Copenhaver, B. P., 341n
Copernicus, Nicolas, 19, 213, 214–15, 221, 237n
Corley, T. A. B., 310n
Cornell, Ezra, 18
Corner, B. C., 309n, 311n
Corsi, P., 38n, 174n
Cosimo II, Grand Duke, 129
Cosslett, A. T., 278n
Cotes, Roger, 194
Coyne, G. V., 168n, 242n
Creasey, C. H., 277n, 278n
Creighton, L., 310n
Crick, Francis H. C., 6, 11n
Cripps, E. C., 308n, 309n
Croll, Oswald, 322
Crombie, Alexander, 187, 197, 204n, 205n, 206n
Crosland, Maurice P., 82, 102n, 105n, 344n
Cunningham, A., 104n, 309n
Cushing, J. T., 104n
Cuvier, Léopold Chrétien Frédéric Dagobert, Georges, 18, 190

Dalton, John, 224, 241n, 283, 290, 295, 308n, 312, 332, 333
Darwin, Annie, 31
Darwin, Charles Robert, ix, 7, 17, 18, 19, 29–30, 31, 32, 40n, 148, 155, 160, 161–7, 173n, 174n, 177, 224, 225–6, 230, 231–2, 248, 249, 253, 254–5, 257, 258–9, 267, 273, 274, 275, 297–8, 333
Darwin, F., 40n, 173n, 174n, 240n, 279n
Darwin, Robert Waring, 31
Davidoff, L., 311n
Davies, Graeme, xi
Davies, Paul, 75–7, 82, 102n
Davy, Humphry, 30–1, 95, 224, 314, 329–31, 332
Dawkins, Richard, 7, 16, 17, 38n, 46, 66, 167, 169n, 177–8, 203n, 232, 242n
de Beer, G., 173n, 174n
De Vaux, Clotilde, 52

Dear, P., 39n, 40n
Debus, A. G., 342n
Del Rio, Martin, 319–20
Demea (character in Hume's
    Dialogues), 150
Democritus, 196, 197
Dennett, Daniel, 44, 69n, 167, 175n,
    232
Derham, William, 149, 169n, 179,
    184, 185–6, 189, 190, 192, 193,
    197, 204n, 205n, 206n
Desaguliers, John Theophilus, 197
Descartes, René, 2, 4illus, 5, 6, 78,
    85–7, 88–91, 93, 103n, 132, 144,
    213, 216, 219–20, 239n
Desmond, Adrian, 40n, 67–8, 69,
    72n, 157, 172n, 173n, 174n,
    204n, 240n, 248, 277n, 280n,
    281n, 345n
Desmond, R., 311n
Dessain, C. S., 279n
Dick, Stephen J., 133n, 222illus, 236n,
    239n
Dick, Thomas, 187, 203n, 204n
Diderot, Denis, 150, 195, 197
Digges, Thomas, 215, 237n
Dillenberger, J., 136n, 169n
Dillwyn, Lewis W., 299, 307n, 308n,
    312
Dimsdale, Thomas, 292, 307n, 312
Diodati, Elia, 136n
Dobbs, Betty Jo T., 10n, 89, 103n,
    343n
Dobrzycki, J., 133n
Donovan, A., 345n
Drake, S., 10n, 40n, 103n, 133n,
    134n, 136n, 237n
Draper, John W., 126, 137n
Drees, W., 243n
Dreyfus, Alfred, 261
Drummond, Henry, 161, 164
Duhem, Pierre, 47
Dunn, J., 343n
Dunn, M. M., 307n, 308n
Dunn, R. S., 307n, 308n
Dunstan, Gordon, 340, 346n
Dupree, A. H., 173n
Durant, J. R., 38n, 173n, 174n, 175n,
    240n, 242n, 344n
Dürer, Albrecht, 215
Durkheim, Emile, 63

Dyster, Frederick, 72n

Eddington, Arthur Stanley, 98, 283
Edgerton, S. Y., 10n, 236n
Einstein, Albert, 79, 80, 97, 98, 104n,
    126, 227, 229, 230, 234, 240n
Eliot, George, 55
Ellegard, A., 173n
Emerson, Ralph Waldo, 251
Emerton, N. E., 239n
Epicurus, 195, 196, 197
Erikson, E. H., 277n
Eve, A. S., 277n, 278n
Eversley, D., 306n
Ewen, F., 137n

Faber, John, 57
Fairholme, George, 57, 58–62, 64,
    71n
Fantoli, A., 40n, 121, 134n, 135n,
    136n, 137n, 138n
Faraday, Michael, 33–4, 67, 79, 229,
    230, 252, 296
Fauvel, J., 10n, 169n, 239n, 343n
Feingold, Moti, xi, 307n
Feldhay, Rivka, 11n, 113, 133n, 134n,
    135n, 136n, 137n
Fell, Margaret, 307n
Ferguson, James, 223–4
Ferguson, M., 84, 102–3n
Feuer, L. S., 236n
Feyerabend, Paul, 127–8, 132, 137n,
    138n, 306n
Fichte, Johann Gottlieb, 95, 251
Field, J. V., 168n, 237n
Finocchiaro, Maurice, 39n, 117,
    132n, 134n, 135n, 136n, 137n,
    138n
Fisch, H., 168n
Fisch, M., 168n, 170n, 203n
Fisher, N. W., 344n
Fitzgerald, George Francis, 97
Fletcher, Isaac, 308n, 312
Flood, R., 10n, 169n, 239n, 343n
Fontenelle, Bernard le Bovyer de,
    217, 220, 222–3, 222illus, 238n,
    239n
Force, J. E., 170n
Forgan, S., 344n
Forster, William Edward, Rt Hon,
    286, 287, 307n, 308n, 313

Foscarini, Paolo, 39n, 114, 115, 118
Foster, Michael, 19–20, 39n, 302
Fothergill, John, 291, 292, 302, 303, 305, 311n, 312
Fouldes, E. V., 308n
Fownes, George, 201, 206n
Fox, Barclay, 311n
Fox, Caroline, 295, 310n
Fox, George, 283, 287, 288, 293, 302
Fox, M., 345n
Fox, R. H., 308n, 309n
Fox, Robert Were, 290, 295, 301–2, 303
Fox, Wilson, 313
Franklin, Benjamin, 300, 310n
Freiday, D., 310n
French, A. P., 241n
French, R., 309n
Fry, A. R., 306n, 309n, 310n, 311n
Fry, Edward, 287, 293, 297, 303, 310n, 311n, 313
Fulford, K. W. M., 346n
Funkenstein, A., 11n

Gage, A. T., 311n
Galen (Claudius Galenus), 321, 322
Galileo, 2, 3illus, 6, 8–9, 10n, 23–4, 28, 36, 39n, 55, 69, 78, 84, 87–8, 103n, 106–32, 212, 213, 237n, 248
Gall, Franz Joseph, 55
Gassendi, Pierre, 85, 116illus, 216, 237n
Gautrey, P. J., 40n
Geach, P. T., 239n
Geber, 319
Geertz, Clifford, 158, 172n
Geison, G. L., 345n
Genuth, S. S., 240n
Ghazali, Al-, 143–4, 168n
Gibbon, C., 169n
Gibbs, F. W., 343n
Gifford, Adam, Lord, ix–x, 176, 177
Gilbert, W. S., 335
Gilbert, William, 89
Gillespie, N. C., 173n, 174n, 203n, 205n
Gillett, G., 346n
Gilley, S., 11n
Gillispie, Charles C., 57, 58, 61, 63, 70n, 105n, 171n, 308n, 345n

Gilson, E., 103n
Gingerich, O., 134n, 237n
Glacken, Clarence J., 175n, 178, 203n
Glanvill, Joseph, 216, 238n
Goethe, Johann Wolfgang von, 95, 240n, 251, 304
Golinski, J. V., 40n, 41n, 202n, 343n, 344n, 345n
Gooding, D. C., 105n
Goodman, D. C., 240n
Gordon, E. O., 171n, 172n
Gore, Charles, 165, 174n
Gorman, M. J., 342n
Gouk, P., 239n
Gould, Stephen Jay, 44, 75
Gow, H., 280n
Graham, George, 300, 312
Granville, Augustus Bozzi, 307n
Grassi, Horatio, 108–9, 110, 111, 120, 129, 131, 132
Gray, Asa, 162, 173n, 234
Gregory, F., 173n
Grell, O., 342n
Grendler, P. F., 136n
Grew, Nehemiah, 219
Gribbin, J., 242n
Griffiths, Richard, 106, 132n
Grove, William R., 265, 336
Gruber, J. W., 278n
Gruner, R., 39n
Guiducci, Mario (Galileo's friend), 131
Gunther, A. E., 310n, 311n
Gurney, Hudson, 286, 294–5, 299, 307n, 308n, 310n, 312
Gustavus Adolphus of Sweden, 119

Habgood, John (former Archbishop of York), 7
Hacking, I., 105n
Hahn, H., 69n
Hahn, R., 41n, 105n
Haistwell, Edward, 287, 289, 312
Hakfoort, C., 69n
Hall, A. R., 239–40n, 240n
Hall, C., 311n
Hall, M. B., 237n, 342n
Hall, T. S., 103n
Halley, Edmond, 1, 10n
Hallyn, Fernand, 38n, 215, 237n
Hanbury, Daniel, 292, 299, 309n, 313

Hankin, E. H., 306n
Hannaway, O., 243n, 341n, 342n
Hanson, N. R., 236n
Hardenberg, Friedrich von (Novalis), 95–6, 104n
Hardy, Thomas, 55, 222
Harford, John S., 308n, 312
Harries, Richard, 209–10, 236n
Harrington, John, 223
Harris, W., 311n
Harrison, John, 300
Hartley, H., 343n
Harvey, William, 89, 142, 293
Harvey, William Henry, 304, 309n, 312
Harwood, J. T., 10n, 238n
Haught, J. F., 281n
Head, Henry, 300, 313
Hefner, P., 340, 345n
Heisenberg, Werner Karl, 26, 80, 82, 98, 102n, 228, 229
Helmholtz, Hermann von, 96
Helmstadter, R. J., 72n, 204n, 279–80n
Henry, J., 238n
Herbert, S., 40n
Herder, Johann Gottfried, 240n
Herschel, John, 27, 280n, 329
Heyck, T. W., 41n
Hick, John 11n,, 235, 243n
Hiebert, E. N., 104n
Higgins, J. C., 241n
Hilton, Boyd, 38n, 204n, 270, 280n
Hilton, T., 40n
Hirst, Thomas Archer, 253
Hodge, Charles, 161, 173n
Hodgkin, T., 308n
Hoeniger, F. D., 237n
Holbach, Paul Heinrich Dietrich, Baron d' (Jean-Baptiste de Mirabaud), 195, 198–9, 206n
Holland, Alan, 166, 175n
Holloway, S. W. F., 308n, 309n
Hont, I., 343n
Hooke, Robert, 2illus, 6, 145, 146illus, 169n, 216, 217–19, 218illus, 238n, 239n
Hooker, Joseph Dalton, 36, 259, 279n, 298
Hooykaas, Reijer, x, 20, 38n, 39n, 67, 72n, 342n

Hopkins, H. E., 280n
Horace, 214
Horne, George, 154, 170n
Horton, Robin, 64–5, 72n
Horwich, P., 237n
Houghton, John, 286
Houston, R. A., 38n
Howard, John, 292
Howard, John Eliot, 286, 307n, 313
Howard, Luke, 286, 290, 299, 304–5, 307n, 309n, 311n, 312
Howard, W. A., 312
Howell, K. J., 237n
Hoyningen-Huene, P., 306n
Hughes, T. M., 40n, 172n, 280n, 281n
Hull, D. L., 280n, 281n
Humboldt, Friedrich Heinrich Alexander, Baron von, 61, 95
Hume, David, 147, 148, 150, 157, 170n, 178, 181, 195, 231
Humphreys, C., 69n
Hunt, R. M., 308n
Hunter, L., xi, 203n
Hunter, M., 10n, 38n, 168n, 238n, 307n, 342n
Hutchinson, H., 310n, 311n
Hutchinson, Jonathan, 294, 301, 303, 305, 313
Hutchinson, K., 238n
Hutton, James, 154–5
Huxley, L., 279n
Huxley, Thomas Henry, 7, 30, 35illus, 36, 40n, 55, 67–8, 69, 70n, 72n, 164, 174n, 231–2, 242n, 253, 254, 255, 257, 259, 262, 276, 279n, 298, 331, 334–6, 345n

Ignatieff, M., 343n
Inkster, I., 308n, 309n
Isaiah, 55
Isichei, E., 306n, 307n, 308n

Jacob, M. C., 170n
Jacobi, J., 342n
Jacyna, L. S., 345n
Jaki, Stanley L., x, xiin
James, F. A. J. L., 11n, 168n
James, William, 63, 71n
Jardine, Nicholas, 104n, 134n, 137n, 138n, 210–12, 236n, 237n, 240n, 241n

Jenner, Edward, 293
Jensen, J. V., 11n
Jeremy, D. J., 310n
Jesus Christ, 55, 248, 322
John Paul II (Pope), 107, 123
Johnson, N., 204n
Johnson, W., 310n
Jonson, Ben, 316, 341n
Jordanova, L. J., 171n, 203n, 206n
Josephus, Flavius, 58, 61

Kaiser, C., 39n, 277n
Kant, Immanuel, 37, 157, 168n, 178
Kargon, R. H., 103n
Keble, John, 210
Kelvin, William Thomson, Lord, 248, 253, 296
Kemp, M., 237n
Kenny, Chris, xi, 197, 206n
Kepler, Johannes, 19, 26, 89–90, 122, 177, 209, 212, 214, 215–16, 220, 229, 236n
Khunrath, Heinrich, 318
Kilpatrick, R., 309n
King, D., 345n
King, Martin Luther, 248–9
Kingsley, Charles, 162–3, 173–4n
Kingsley, F. E., 174n
Kinns, Samuel, 62, 71n
Kirby, M., 310n
Kirby, William, 156, 186, 191, 196, 205n, 206n, 337
Kircher, Athanasius, 320
Kirwan, Richard, 154–5
Klaaren, E. M., 38n
Knapp, S., 11n
Knight, D. M., 40n, 224, 240n, 344n
Knox, Robert, 158
Koestler, Arthur, 129, 135n, 236n
Kohn, D., 40n, 41n, 175n, 240n
Koyré, Alexandre, 103n, 247–8, 277n
Kuhn, Thomas S., 83, 96, 102n, 103n, 104n, 133n

La Mettrie, Julien Offray de, 153
Lafrance, J., 277n
Lamarck, Jean Baptiste Pierre Antoine de Monet, Chevalier de, 18, 195, 196, 275
Lang, P., 242n

Lansbergen, Philip, 213
Laplace, Pierre Simon, Marquis de, 37, 79, 92–3, 101, 104n, 180, 195, 196, 197, 198, 275
Larmor, Joseph, 97
Laszlo, P., 241n
Latour, B., 41n
Lattis, J. M., 134n, 136n
Lavoisier, Antoine Laurent, 55, 224, 326, 330, 338
Lawrence, C., 343n
Lawson, Thomas, 288
Leibniz, Gottfried Wilhelm, 22
Lenard, Philipp, 126
Lenoble, Robert, 39n
Lenoir, T., 103n
Lenzer, G., 70n
Leo XIII (Pope), 262
Leslie, J., 242n
Lettsom, John C., 292, 303, 311n, 312
Levere, T. H., 344n
Lewes, George Henry, 55
Lewis, D. L., 277n
Libavius, Andreas, 243n, 315
Liddon, Henry, 253
Liebig, Justus von, 104n, 339
Lightman, B., 72n, 204n, 279–80n
Lindberg, D. C., 41n, 71n, 104n, 173n, 203n, 237n, 342n
Linden, S. J., 342n
Lindsey, T., 343n
Linnaeus, Carl, 224, 240n
Linzey, Andrew, 346n
Lister, Arthur, 313
Lister J. J., 291, 313
Lister, Joseph Jackson, 312
Lister, Joseph, Lord, 283, 293, 300, 303, 307n, 309n, 312
Livingston, James C., 174n
Livingstone, David N., 25, 39n, 40n, 173n, 278n
Lloyd, J. T., 278n
Lonsdale, Kathleen, 283
Lorentz, Hendrik Antoon, 97
Lorini, Niccolo, 108
Louis XIII (King of France), 119
Lovejoy, A. O., 133n, 240n
Lovelace, Ada, Countess, 159
Lovelock, James, 95
Lower, Richard, 306n, 307–8n
Lower, Thomas, 307n

Lowther, Anthony, 306n
Lucas, J. R., 11n
Lucretius, 178, 179, 195, 196
Lummer, Otto Richard, 97
Luther, Martin, 133n, 136n, 248, 319
Lyell, Charles, 59, 70n, 71n, 162, 253, 267, 273
Lyons, H., 306n, 307n, 309n, 310n

Mach, Ernst, 97, 282–3
MacKenzie, J. M., 38n
Macleod, D., 169n
MacLeod, R. M., 309n
Maculano, Vincenzo, 113
Maier, Michael, 317illus
Maignan, Emmanuel, 237n
Mandelbrote, S., 239n
Mantell, Gideon, 3illus, 10n
Manuel, F. E., 10n, 41n, 277n
Martin, F. D., 241n
Martin, John, 2, 3illus, 6
Martin, R. N. D., 69n
Martineau, Harriet, 55
Martineau, James, 264, 266
Marx, Karl, 46, 292
Mason, S., 306n
Massin, Caroline (wife of Auguste Comte), 52
Mathias, P., 168n
Maxwell, James Clerk, 79, 97
May, Charles, 312
McAllister, J. W., 242n
McClendon, James W., Jr, 249, 277n
McCosh, James, 25, 161
McEvoy, J. G., 172n, 343n, 344n
McGuire, J. E., 103n, 170n, 239n
McMillan, N. D., 278n
McMullin, Ernan, 70n, 103n, 135n, 237n, 241n, 242–3n
McNally, R., 345n, 346n
Mead, Richard, 306n
Medcalf, S., 238n
Mersenne, Marin, 20, 22
Merton, Robert K., 9, 11n, 236n
Michelangelo, 123
Mill, John Stuart, 55
Miller, Hugh, 38n, 147–8, 161, 169n, 173n, 212, 224–6, 225illus, 314, 315
Miller, William, A., 293, 300, 309n, 312
Millhauser, M., 70n

Milligan, Edward W., xi, 308n
Milton, J. R., 39n
Milton, John, 194, 205n
Mivart, F. St George, 278n
Mivart, St George Jackson, 68, 123, 255–62, 260illus, 266, 274–5, 276–7, 278n, 279n
Modell, B., 345n
Mohammed, 55, 248
Moigno, François, 253
Mollan, R. C., 278n
Monk, S. H., 204n
Monod, J., 242n
Moore, Aubrey, 165, 174n
Moore, James R., xiin, 38n, 40n, 71n, 72n, 172n, 173n, 174n, 206n, 240n, 248, 277n, 281n
More, Henry, 88
Moriarty, M., 205–6n
Morland, G., 167n
Morrell, J., 306n, 308n, 309n
Morris, K. J., 103n
Morse, Edgar E., 308n
Moses, 52
Moss, J. D., 133n, 135n, 136n
Mozart, Wolfgang Amadeus, 231
Mozley, J. B., 253, 278n
Mulkay, M., 41n
Murchison, Roderick, 268
Murdoch, D., 104n
Murphy, N., 11n, 39n, 168, 170n
Murray-Rust, D., 310n

Needham, Joseph, 19, 39n, 216, 238n
Neurath, O., 69n
Newman, Edward, 337
Newman, John Henry (Cardinal), 257, 259, 262, 270, 275, 279n
Newton, Isaac, 1–2, 5, 6–7, 10n, 17, 22, 26, 34, 37, 48, 55, 60, 67, 70n, 78–9, 88–9, 91, 147, 149, 150, 151, 154, 169–70n, 170n, 176, 177, 194, 203n, 205n, 220, 223, 229, 234, 239n, 239–40n, 240n, 248, 249–50, 265, 289, 314, 325, 326, 343n
Niccolini, Francesco, 121, 134n, 137n, 138n
Nicero, Jean-François, 237n
Nickolls, John, 312

Nieuwentijt, Bernard, 178, 188, 195, 197, 203n, 204n, 205n, 206n
Nightingale, Florence, 156
Norlind, W., 133n
North, Roger, 323
Novalis (Friedrich von Hardenberg), 95–6, 104n
Numbers, Ronald L., 41n, 71n, 104n, 173n, 203n
Nye, M. J., 240n

Oakley, Francis, 20, 39n, 247, 277n
O'Brien, James, 159
O'Connor, D., 277n
Oersted, Hans Christian, 95
O'Hear, Anthony, 210, 236n
Oken, Lorenz, 95
Olby, R. C., 11n
Oliver, Daniel, 293, 299, 302, 304, 309n, 313
O'Malley, C. D., 133n, 134n
O'Neill, J., 236n
Orange, A. D., 343n
Ormerod, Eleanor, 337–8
Osiander, Andreas, 108
Ospovat, D., 240n
Ostwald, Wilhelm, 46
Owen, Richard, 160–1, 160illus, 255, 256
Owen, Robert, 252

Pagel, W., 342n
Pais, A., 104n, 227, 240n, 241n
Paley, William, 160, 163, 177, 178, 179, 183, 184, 187, 190, 191, 193, 203–4n, 204n, 205n, 234, 270, 332, 333
Palma, R. J., 242n
Paracelsus (Philippus Aureolus Theophrastus Bombastus von Hohenheim), 320, 321–2, 342n
Pascal, Blaise, 149
Paschen, Louis Carl Heinrich Friedrich, 97
Passmore, John, 69n
Pasteur, Louis, 337
Patrides, C. A., 103n
Paul, H. W., 39n
Peacocke, Arthur R., 39n, 168n, 170n, 174n, 233, 241n, 242n, 346n
Pease, Joseph, 308n

Pedersen, O., 135n
Peirce, C. S., 240n
Pengelly, H., 306n
Pengelly, William, 285, 313
Penington, Isaac, 288, 308n
Penn, Granville, 57
Penn, William, 286, 287, 288, 302, 306n, 307n
Perry, M., 102n
Peters, T., 345n
Phillips, Richard, 290, 309n, 312
Phillips, William, 290, 312
Piccolomini, Ascanio (Archbishop of Siena), 137n
Pickering, M., 69n, 70n
Pius IX (Pope), 257
Planck, Max, 96, 97, 227
Plato, 20
Playfair, John, 155, 171n
Pliny (Gaius Plinius Secundus) the Elder, 61
Polanyi, Michael, 212, 221, 232, 233, 236n, 237n, 239n, 240n, 241n, 242n
Polkinghorne, John C., 39n, 177, 203n, 229, 241n, 242n
Pollard, F. E., 308n, 311n
Pond, M. M., 277n
Popper, Karl, 44–5, 69n
Porter, R. S., 171n, 203n
Poupard, Cardinal, 133n
Powell, Baden, 125illus
Power, Henry, 323, 342n
Poynter, F. N. L., 309n
Pratt, D. H., 309n, 311n
Prichard, James C., 299, 307n, 308n, 312
Priestley, Joseph, 67, 158, 264, 265, 326–9, 343n
Pringle, John, Sir, 328
Pringsheim, Ernst, 97
Prior, A., 310n
Prout, William, 156, 186, 191, 204n, 205n, 253, 331–4, 344n
Ptolemy (Claudius Ptolemaeus), 214
Pugin, Augustus, 255, 256illus
Pym, H. N., 310n, 311n
Pythagoras, 220

Quinn, M., 70n
Quintilian, 183

Radner, D., 103n
Raistrick, A., 306n, 311n
Ramsay, Andrew Michael, 154
Rattansi, P. M., 168n, 169n, 237n, 239n
Raven, D., 39n
Ray, John, 145, 177, 179, 183, 190, 203n, 204n, 221–2, 239n, 288
Rayleigh, Robert John Strutt, 4th Baron, 97
Read, J., 341n
Redondi, Pietro, 103n, 130–2, 136n, 138n
Redwood, J., 169n
Rehbock, P. F., 172n
Reid, T. W., 307n, 308n
Reid, Thomas, 183
Rendu, Louis, 253
Renieri, Giovanni Battista, 125
Reston, James, 123, 133n, 134n, 136n, 137n, 138n
Reynolds, E. E., xi
Rhodes, F. H. T., 241n
Richards, J. L., 240n
Richardson, R. C., 103n
Richardson, W. M., 11n, 175n
Ritter, Johann Wilhelm, 95
Robbins, K., 11n
Roberts, J. H., 173n
Roberts, William W., 257, 279n
Robins, Benjamin, 298, 302, 312
Robison, John, 38n
Robson, J. M., 204n, 205n
Roe, S. A., 103n
Roger, J., 103n
Roget, Peter Mark, 156, 205n
Rolston, H., 167, 175n
Romanes, George John, 29, 162, 173n
Rorty, Richard, 249, 277n
Roscoe, H. E., 308n
Rossi, P., 133n
Roszak, Theodore, 99, 104n
Rudwick, Martin J. S., 10n, 57–8, 71n, 280n
Rumford, Count, 293
Rupke, N. A., 58, 71n, 171n, 172n, 173n
Ruskin, John, 31–2, 223
Russell, Bertrand, 82, 102n
Russell, C. A., 39n, 41n, 175n, 241n
Russell, R. J., 39n, 168n, 170n, 242n
Rutty, John, 294

Saint-Simon, Comte de, 47
Salviati (chief protagonist in Galileo's *Dialogue*), 134n
Santillana, G. de, 136n
Sarjeant, W., 71n
Sarpi, Paolo, 119, 136n
Schaffer, S., 10n, 40n, 168n, 170n, 202n, 203n, 238n, 342n, 343n, 344n
Scheiner, Christopher, 113, 120
Schelling, Friedrich Wilhelm Joseph von, 95
Scheuchzer, Johann, 57
Schlotheim, Ernst Friedrich, Baron von, 61
Schoenl, W. J., 279n
Schofield, R., 343n
Schrödinger, Erwin, 98, 100
Schwartz, A. T., 172n, 343n
Schwarzschild, Karl, 234
Scott, D. F. S., 311n
Scott, J. F., 239–40n, 240n
Sebba, A., 277n
Secord, J. A., 169n, 171n, 205n, 280n, 281n
Sedgwick, Adam, 27, 62, 71n, 156, 157, 171n, 268–74, 271illus, 275, 280n, 281n
Segre, M., 137n
Settele, Guiseppe, 123
Seubert, Adolf Friedrich, 172n
Shaftesbury, Anthony Ashley Cooper, 7th Earl of, 62
Shanahan, T., 168n, 342n
Shapin, S., 40n, 41n, 103n, 343n
Sharpe, Eric J., 71n, 72n, 241n
Sharratt, M., 134n, 135n, 136n, 137n, 138n
Shea, W. R., 135n
Sheldrake, Rupert, 81, 102n
Sherry, Patrick, 209, 236n
Shirley, J. W., 237n
Shortland, M., 10n, 40n, 169n, 239n, 240n, 277n, 343n
Siegfried, R., 344n
Simeon, Charles, 270
Simplicio (defender of Aristotelianism in Galileo's *Dialogue*), 110, 132, 134n
Sims, John, 307n, 312
Sina, Ibn, 144

Slater, A. W., 308n
Sloane, Hans, 289
Smart, Ninian, 174n
Smith, Adam, x, 68, 72n, 159, 327
Smith, Crosbie, 37n, 38n, 205n, 248, 277n
Smith, S., 40n
Smuts, Jan Christian, 101, 105n
Snow, C. P., x, xiin
Söderqvist, Thomas, 277, 281n
Sonntag, O., 345n
Soskice, J. M., 346n
Southgate, B. C., 238n
Spinoza, Benedict de, 195, 197, 238–9n
Spurway, Neil, ix–x, xi, xiin, 203n
Stanley, Arthur, 253
Stearn, W. T., 311n
Steffens, Henrik, 95
Steiner, George, 207, 235n, 236n
Stephens, W., 170n
Stevin, Simon, 89
Stewart, Charles Edward, The Young Pretender, 154
Stewart, Jacqui, xi, 311n
Stewart, L., 170n
Stewart, M. A., 238n, 242n
Stiles, M., 309n
Stoeger, William R., 39n, 168n, 242n
Stokes, George, 15
Strand, K., 237n
Stuewer, R. H., 240n
Sullivan, Sir Arthur, 335
Swift, Jonathan, 153–4, 170n
Swinburne, Richard, 232, 234, 242n

Tait, Peter Guthrie, 253
Temple, Frederick (Archbishop of Canterbury), 36, 41n, 164, 174n, 234
Templeton, John M., 69n
Tennant, F. R., 165–6, 174n
Teresa, Mother, 249
Thackray, A., 306n
Thayer, H. S., 10n, 11n, 239n
Theisen, W., 341n
Thérèsa of Lisieux, Saint, 249
Thomas, Keith, 175n, 221, 239n
Thompson, H. G., 308n, 310n
Thompson, J. S., 308n, 310n
Thompson, Ross, 81, 102n

Thompson, Silvanus P., 290, 293, 295–6, 297, 309n, 310n, 313
Thomson, James, 15
Thomson, William, Lord Kelvin, 15–16, 17
Tibawi, A. L., 168n
Tilling, L., 239–40n, 240n
Tipler, F. J., 203n, 242n
Todhunter, I., 167n, 168n
Todorov, T., 203n
Toland, John, 151
Tolles, F. B., 310n
Tolosani, Giovanni, 121
Topham, Jonathan R., xi, 40n, 171n, 172n, 203n, 204n, 278n, 341n
Torrance, T. F., 242n
Torricelli, Evangelista, 125
Trevelyan, G. M., 308n
Trevisan, Bernard, 319
Tristram, Henry Baker, 36
Turnbull, H. W., 239–40n, 240n
Turner, Frank M., 41n, 253, 278n, 344n
Tylor, Edward, 293, 297, 298, 309n, 310n, 313
Tyndall, John, 25, 95, 250–5, 250illus, 262, 274, 275, 277n, 278n, 331–3
Tyrrell, George, 163–4, 174n

Underwood, T. L., 306n
Urban VIII (Maffeo Barberini) (Pope), 24, 109–10, 112–13, 117, 119–20, 121–2, 123, 129, 130, 131–2
Ure, Andrew, 57, 62, 71n, 281n
Ussher, James (Archbishop of Armagh), 59

Van Helden, A., 10n
Vanheste, Thomas, xi, 102n
Vann, R. T., 306n, 307n, 308n
Vickers, B., 243n
Victoria (Queen), 62
Viviani, Vincenzio (Galileo's biographer), 123–5
Vogt, Carl, 172n
Volta, Alessandro, 328, 331, 343n
Voltaire, 145, 147, 169n
Vyvyan, Richard, Sir, 159

Wagner, Richard, 231

Wakley, Thomas, 158
Walker, Revd. J. E., 338
Wallace, Alfred Russel, 162
Warfield, Benjamin, 25
Watson, James D., 6, 11n
Watts, Robert, 25
Weaver, M. J., 279n
Webb, M., 308n
Webb, R. K., 264, 279–80n
Webster, C., 38n, 343n
Weindling, P., 308n, 309n, 311n
Weld, G. R., 310n
Werner, Abraham, 273
West, William, 309n
Westfall, Richard S., 10n, 45, 70n,
    138n, 169–70n, 203n, 248, 277n
Westman, Robert S., 103n, 133n, 134n,
    136n, 170n, 214, 237n, 342n
Whately, Richard, 183, 192, 205n
Wheale, P., 345n, 346n
Wheaton, B., 104n
Whewell, William, x, 27, 40n, 141–2,
    152–3, 156, 157, 160, 167n,
    168n, 170n, 172n, 182–3, 186,
    190, 192, 193, 198, 203n, 204n,
    205n, 206n, 234
Whiston, William, 22, 150, 151, 170n
White, Andrew Dickson, 17–18, 38n
White, Thomas, 217
Whitehead, Alfred North, 19, 38n
Whitrow, G. J., 241n
Whittaker, E. J., 308n, 311n
Whytt, Robert, 91–2, 103n
Wigner, Eugene P., 227, 241n
Wilber, Ken, 98, 102n, 104n

Wilberforce, Samuel (Bishop of
    Oxford), 7, 35illus, 36, 68, 69,
    279n
Wildman, W. J., 11n, 175n
Wilkins, John, 145, 169n
Willan, Robert, 299, 312
Wilson, R., 10n, 169n, 239n, 343n
Winkler, M. G., 10n
Wise, M. Norton, 37n, 38n, 248,
    277n
Wiseman, Nicholas, 255
Witchell, George, 312
Wittgenstein, Ludwig, 179, 210
Wöhler, Friedrich, 334
Wollheim, R., 170n
Wood, A., 308n
Woodward, H. H., 280n
Woolf, H., 105n
Woolgar, S., 41n
Woolman, John, 292
Wright, T. R., 70n
Wrightsman, B., 133n
Wybrow, C., 39n

Yates, F., 136n, 170n
Yeo, R., 40n, 168n, 277n
Young, R. M., 40n, 242n
Young, Thomas, 283, 286, 290,
    294–5, 299, 300, 307n, 312

Zajonc, Arthur, 81, 102n
Zilsel, Edgar, 19, 39n
Zohar, Danah, 86, 102n, 103n
Zukav, Gary, 81, 83, 102n, 104n
Zuñiga, Diego de, 134n

Index of Subjects

Académie Royale des Sciences, 144
acids, neutralisation by bases, 141–2
Ackworth School, 290, 303
Actonian Prize, 206n
aesthetic appraisal, types, 210–12
aesthetic appreciation
  basis of Mivart's Catholicism and
    scientific interests, 255, 256–7
  and mechanism, 216–20
  and natural theology, 314
  and religious sensibilities, 224,
    226–8, 231–2
  and science, 207–35, 236n
  and scientists, 223–8
aesthetics
  and the design argument, 185–7
  and religious experience, 209–10
African cosmology, nature, 64–5
agnosticism, Tyndall's attitude to,
  250–5
agricultural reform, Davy's support,
  329
alchemy, 316–22, 317illus, 318illus,
  320illus
Allen and Hanbury, 292
Alpha Centauri, parallax, 137n
analogy and the design argument,
  190–2
anamorphic images, uses, 237n
Andersonian Institution (Glasgow),
  71n
animal suffering, and Darwinism,
  166–7
anthropic principle, 177
anthropocentrism, 221–3, 224, 239n
anti-slavery campaign, Quakers and,
  292
antithesis, use in the design
  argument, 193–5
apartheid, 101
Apology for the True Christian Divinity
  (Robert Barclay), and social
  behaviour, 294
apothecaries, Quakers as FRSs,
  291–3, 309n
Apothecaries' Gardens (Chelsea), 290

Aquarius, Age of, 81–2
architecture and Catholicism, 255
Aristotelianism
  and Christian theology, 7–8
  Galileo's criticism, 111
  and Islam, 143–4
artificial selection, and breeding of
  pigeons, 29illus, 30
the artist as prodigy in Renaissance
  biography, 124
astronomy
  and the design argument, 187
  Quaker interest in, 305
  reconstructions, 19
atheism, 194–200
  development, 150–1
atheists, as Satanic, 194, 197
atomic theory, Dalton's view, 241n
atomism, 131, 194
  and Cartesian dualism, 85–6
authority, 114, 118

Bampton Lectures, 253
Beacon controversy (1836), 286
beauty in natural theological
  narratives, 185–7
Belfast, and reception of Darwinism,
  25
Bible (*see also* scripture)
  authority, 33
  criticism
    and natural science, 167
    and scientific practice, 16
    and reconstruction of nature, 20
    Roman Catholic Church's attitude
      to interpretation, 261
biographies, function in presentation
  of religion and science, 31–2
biography
  historical styles, 123–7
  and science–religion relationships,
    247–50, 274–7
biology, development, 142
birthright Quakers, 284–5
black holes and origins of the
  universe, 232

Bootham School (York), 290, 302–3
botany, Quaker interest in, 302–5
Boyle Lectures, 194, 223
    blamed for growth of atheism,
        150–1
Brahe's system of the world, 111–12,
    112illus, 117, 137n
Brewster–Whewell debate, 141
Bridgewater Treatises, 152, 182, 186,
    200
    attitudes to, 253, 331–2
    and the design argument, 177
    and French science, 195, 196
    publication, 156–7
    Tyndall's attitude to, 253
    use of illustrations, 184–5, 185illus,
        188, 189illus
Bristol Philosophical and Literary
        Institution, 264
British Association for the
        Advancement of Science, 7, 25,
        27
    Adam Sedgwick addresses 1833
        meeting, 171n
    Adam Sedgwick addresses miners
        at Newcastle-upon-Tyne (1838),
        27, 157, 269, 280n
    early membership, 282
    John Tyndall addresses Belfast
        meeting (1874), 252–3
    meeting between Huxley and
        Wilberforce (1860), 7, 36, 279n
    William Buckland addresses
        Oxford meeting (1832), 155

calendar, Comte's re-ordering, 52–5
Calvinism and Darwinism, 25
Cambridge, cholera epidemics, 152–3
Cambridge University, 268, 269, 272,
    274, 291, 302
Cartesianism, 78, 80, 100
    and aesthetic appreciation, 219–20
    and atomism, 85–6
    Newton's criticisms, 88–9
    Whytt's criticisms, 91–2
cartoons and implications of
        Darwinism, 161
Catholic–Protestant relations, effects
        on the Galileo affair, 118–19
Catholicism
    and evolution, 255, 257, 259, 260–1

Mivart's attitude to, 255, 256–7,
    259–62
Tyndall's reactions to, 251, 252–3
chance, 199
chaos, and the design argument,
    193–5, 199
chaos theory, 142
chemico-theology, 314, 315, 339–41
    Boyle's views, 324
    Davy's views, 330–1
    Newton's views, 325–6
    Paracelsus's views, 321–2
    Priestley's views, 326–9
    Prout's views, 331–4
chemistry
    and aesthetic appreciation, 224,
        243n
    historical development, 316–38
    and mechanism, 191
    and natural theology, 10
    standing, 314–15, 338–9
Chinese science, nature, 19
cholera epidemics, 152–3
Christian theology and Aristotelian
        philosophy, 7–8
Christianity, reputation, 144–5
Claridges (Mivart's Hotel), 255
clergy, social standing, 36
Commissary of the Holy Office, 123
Committee for the Public
        Understanding of Science, 200
conservation, 16
Copenhagen Interpretation, 94, 97
Copernican system
    Brahe's objections to, 229
    Church's difficulties with, 107–8,
        111–18, 120–1
    Galileo's support of, 28, 122, 129
    and Ptolemaic system, 214–16, 221
    suggested pretext for Galileo's trial,
        131–2
    weakness, 128
Cornell University, charter, 17–18
corpuscularianism, 87
cosmographies, 106, 107–9, 111–18
cosmological argument, 143–4
cosmology
    effects, 119
    and theism, 232–3
Cosmos as Creation (Peters), 340
creation, Christian doctrine, 19–20

Creationism, 57, 59
critical realism, 21
crystallography, 141

Daniel, prophecies, 151
Darwinism (*see also* evolution)
    and animal suffering, 166–7
    Carpenter's attitude to, 267–8, 275
    Mivart's attitude to, 257–9, 262,
        275, 276
    and natural theology, 161–6
    Quaker attitudes to, 297–8
    reactions to, 275
    reception influenced by local
        circumstances, 25
deism, 151, 154, 196, 198
the deluge, 59–60, 61
    geological confirmation, 155, 156
Dentdale, industrialisation, 268, 273
Descent of Man (Darwin), 258
design argument (*see also* God), 9, 27,
        202, 323
    as defence against atheism,
        196–200
    historical context, 142
    Hooke's support for, 145
    as inductive argument, 180–95
    and promotion of science, 154–7
    Prout's views, 332–4
    and religious apologetics, 148–52
    rhetorical presentation, 176–80,
        184–95
    Tyndall's attitude to, 253
    variations, 160–1
    Whewell's support for, 141–2
devil's chaplain, 165, 174n
dialectical materialism, 46
disownment, 285–6, 307n
Disruption, 147
DNA, double helix model, 5, 6
Dominicans and Jesuits, 113, 121
Dublin University, 304
Durham College, 304

earth, distance from sun, 188
earth sciences and aesthetic
        appreciation, 224–7, 225illus
Eastern religious philosophies, 81
Ecumenical Movement, 282
Edinburgh University, 337
education, Quakers and, 290, 291

elements, 224
    identification, 330, 335
    Prout's view of use, 332–3
embryology, views about, 92
energy, God and conservation, 15–16
engagement, meaning, 7–8
England, nationalist views of
        Scotland, 17
Epicureanism, 196
Ersatzreligion, 46, 48–9
essentialism, 275–7
eternal damnation, doctrine, 261
ethics committees, 341, 346n
evolution (*see also* Darwinism)
    and aesthetic appreciation, 224
    and Catholicism, 255, 257, 259,
        260–1
    Sedgwick's attitude to, 273–4, 275
    and theism, 233–4
    theory, 7, 18
    Tyndall's attitude to, 254, 275
ex-Quakers, 286
experimental philosophy, 33
experiments, notions, 84
extra-terrestrial intelligence, 213, 219
eyes, Nieuwentijt's discussion of
        structure and function, 178–9

Faraday Award, 200
Fellows of the Royal Society
    election, 298–9
    Quakers as, 283–306, 307n
    scientific interests, 302
final cause, Whewell's support for,
        142, 168n
fish scales, beauty when magnified,
        217, 218illus
fleas, magnification, 2illus, 6, 219
flies, eyes, 145, 146illus
Frame of Government for Pennsylvania
        (Penn), 288
French Revolution, attitudes to, 195–7
FRS *see* Fellows of the Royal Society
functional analysis and the
        relationship between religion
        and science, 26–7

Galileo affair, 106–32
    Mivart's attitude to, 260–1, 276
gardens, Quaker interest in, 290,
        303–4

Gay-Lussac's law of gaseous
    combination, 332, 333
gems, Boyle's study, 323–4
gender roles, importance for Comte,
    49, 50–2
General Dispensary, 292
Genesis, theology, 167
GenEthics News, 339
genetic engineering, 340–1
genre, 179
Geological Society, 269, 273, 301, 303
geology
    irreligion, 153–4
    pictorial representations, 185n
    and religious faith, 147–8
    Ruskin's faith affected by, 31–2
    and scripture, 8, 45, 57–62, 63, 66
    Sedgwick's interest in, 269, 272–3
giant sloths, as examples for design
    argument, 155
Gifford Lectures, ix–x
Glasgow Philosophical Society, 282
God (*see also* design argument)
    competition with science, 17
    as creator, 6
    Darwinism and conceptions about,
        162–6, 226–7
    and energy conservation, 15–16
    existence, 9
    role and Carpenter's view of,
        265–6, 267–8
    understanding about, ix
The Graduate, 315
gravity
    Newton's explanation, 70n, 149, 151
    theory, 22
Great Being, Comte's understanding,
    50
Great Devonian Controversy, 57
Gresham College, 307n
Grove House School (Tottenham),
    290
Gulliver's Travels (Swift), 153–4

heavens, Decartes's depiction, 2,
    4illus, 5
heresy, Bellarmine's reactions to,
    118–19
Hiroshima, 127
historians, understanding of religion
    and science, 66–9

historical analysis and appreciation of
    science, 212–20
historical contexts
    effects, 23–6
    importance for understanding
        theistic proofs, 142–8
    nature of, 22–3
    and understanding of natural
        theology, 35–7
historical enquiry, value, 107–9, 113
history
    Capra's use, 83–94, 97–101
    nature, 132
    and science, 75–101, 127–9
    subservience to partisan interests,
        17–19
holism, 85–7, 101
house sparrows, 338
Humanity
    Comte's understanding, 50–7
    decentring, 213, 216–23, 239n
Hunterian Society, 301

imagination, role, 184–95
Index Librorum Prohibitorum, 261
the individual, Comte's
    understanding of social role, 49
inductive arguments, use in natural
    theology, 181–95
inference, inductive forms, 181
Inquirer, 265, 266
Institute of Physics, 282
institutions
    social history, 282–3
    social norms, 293
instrumentalism, 21
intermarriage, and membership of
    Society of Friends, 284–6
Islam and Aristotelianism, 143–4

Jesuits
    and alchemy, 319–20
    conflicts with Dominicans, 113
    relations with Galileo, 120–1,
        136n
    views on cosmography, 111
Joint Appeal from Religion and
    Science, 167
Jupiter, moons, 106

kangaroos, development, 142

Kendal Natural History and Scientific Society, 269
kenosis, 165–6
Kew Gardens, 290, 304

Lamarckism, 173n
language, function in presentation of religion and science, 28, 30–1
laughing gas, Davy's use, 314–15, 329
lawn mowers, 304
Leeds Mechanics' Institute, 269
legal terminology, use in the design argument, 192
liberal theology, 76
life sciences, explanation, 91illus
light, theories, 83
Linnean Society, 301, 302, 303
living systems, purpose, 142
local history and relationship between science and religion, 24–5
logical positivism, 47
London Botanical Society, 301, 302
London Positivist Society, 56
London season, conversational gambits, 156
London University, 263, 264, 304
Lux Mundi, 165

Maddona and child, Comte's conception, 51illus
magnetism, 89–90
  Descartes's explanation, 91illus
Manchester Conference (1895), 296
Marburg University, Tyndall attends, 252
marriage, Comte's understanding, 50–2
master-narratives, xi, 8, 17–22, 66, 69, 76–7, 80, 82, 101
materialism
  Sedgwick's attitude to, 273–4
  Tyndall's views, 252
mathematics and physical sciences, 227–8
matter, theories, 86, 130–2
mechanism, 87–8, 191
  and aesthetic appreciation, 216–20, 238n
  and quantum physics, 97–8
  and vitalism, 91–2

medical profession, Quakers and, 290, 291, 292, 309n
Medical Society of London, 292, 301
medicine, historical development, 321–3, 325
megatheria, 188, 189illus
men, Comte's understanding of their role, 51
metaphors
  Darwin's use, 30
  and the design argument, 192
Metaphysical Society, 277n
microscopes, development, 145, 146illus
microscopy, 217–18
Mikado (Gilbert and Sullivan), 335
mind, concepts about, 86
Mivart's Hotel (Claridges), 255
modelling, 207
moon, Galileo's perception, 2, 3illus, 6
moral law and natural law, 164
morality, Comte's understanding, 49
Mosaic flood, 155
Munich Brief, 257

narrative-methods, 127
natural law and moral law, 164
natural philosophy, 1
natural religion, 145, 147
natural science
  and natural religion, 147
  and natural theology, 9, 142
  and philosophy, 1
natural selection, metaphors for, 30
natural theology
  attitude to atheism, 194–200
  Carlile's criticisms, 314, 315, 330
  and chemistry, 10, 315
  and Darwinism, 161–6
  functions, 26–7
  historical context, 35–7
  meaning, ix–x
  and natural science, 9, 142
  and politics, 157–60
  and religion, 148–52
  renewal of interest in, 200, 201–2
  and revealed theology, 176
  and rhetoric, 180–200
  and science, 153–7
  social functions, 177–80

nature
  mechanisation, 16
  Newton's view, 89
  reconstruction, 2–7, 20
Naturphilosophie, 95–6, 104n
nebular hypothesis, 180, 182, 198,
  266, 275
needles, viewed under microscopes,
  146illus
Neptunian theory, 273
Neurological Society, 301
New Age movement, 80–2, 94–6, 99
  conception of paradigms, 83–4
  historiography, 216, 220
  prophets, 8
New Dictionary of National Biography,
  247
Newcastle University, 304
Newcastle-upon-Tyne, miners,
  addressed by Sedgwick, 27, 157,
  269, 280n
Newtonian mechanics, 78–9
Non-Intrusion and the Disruption,
  147
Norwich Cathedral, Sedgwick
  becomes prebendary of, 269–70
novelty and the design argument,
  187–90

On the Genesis of Species (Mivart),
  attack on Darwinism, 258–9
ontological argument, 144
Opthalmological Society, 301
Ordnance Survey, 251
organic chemistry, historical
  development, 333–7
Origin of Species (Darwin)
  Carpenter's review, 267
  publication, ix
  Quaker reactions to, 297
  response to, 249, 257
  Sedgwick's criticisms, 273–4
Oscott College, Birmingham, 255
Oxford University, 291
oxygen, 326, 329, 330, 331

paradigms, 83–4, 102–3n
Paris green, 337
Parliament, Quakers as MPs, 291
partisan interests, interpretations of
  history, 17–19

Pathological Society, 301
patronage system, 128–30
penicillin crystals, 207, 208illus
Pennsylvania, 288, 289
pesticides, early use, 337–9
Peterborough Cathedral, Sedgwick
  offered deanery, 269
Philosophical Magazine, Tyndall edits,
  252
philosophy and natural science, 1
phlogiston, 326, 328
physical science and aesthetic
  appreciation, 227–8
physical world, wonders as support
  for design argument, 188–90
physico-theology (*see also* natural
  theology), 148–9
physics
  development, 83–91
  and spirituality, 98
physiology, views about, 91–2
pigeons, breeding and artificial
  selection, 29illus, 30
Pisa, Leaning Tower, 124, 125illus
planetary motion, Kepler's third law,
  19
planets
  orbits, Newton's perception, 5illus,
  6
  retrograde motion, 210–11,
  211illus
Plough Court Pharmacy, 289, 291–2
politics and natural theology, 157–60
popular education and natural
  theology, 156–7
positivism, 47–57
prayer, Comte's understanding, 50
Princeton, and reception of
  Darwinism, 25
probability, 93–4
professions, openness to Quakers,
  290–1
Protestant–Catholic relations, effects
  on the Galileo affair, 118–19
protoplasm, 335
Providentissimus Deus, 261
Ptolemaic system and Copernican
  system, 214–16, 221
public opinion, influence on
  scientific developments, 339–40
purgatory, doctrine, 238n

Quaker Faith and Practice, 293
Quakers (*see also* Society of Friends)
    attitude to science, 294–7, 307n
    as Fellows of the Royal Society,
        283–306
    identification, 284–6
    scientific interests, 10, 302–5
    and social reform, 292–3
    social standing, 289–93, 299–300,
        303
quantum mechanics, 79–82
quantum physics, development,
    96–100
quantum theory, interpretation, 44
Quarterly Review, 258, 259
Queenwood College, Tyndall teaches
    at, 252

racism, 101
reductionism, 86, 230, 314
    and Huxley, 334–5
religion (*see also* theology)
    Carpenter's view of, 265–8
    function of language in
        presentation, 28, 30–1
    historical context, 35–7
    interpretations, 44–5
    and natural theology, 148–52
    nature
        and historical study, 62–3, 64–9
        and practice, 32–4
    presentation through biography,
        31–2
    and science, 234–5
        perceived conflicts in the Galileo
            affair, 107–18
        relationships between, 17–25
        research funding, 43–4, 45
Religion of Humanity, 8, 48–57, 64, 66
religion–science, social history of
    institutions, 282–3
religion–science relationships, and
    biography, 247–50, 274–7
religious apologetics and design
    arguments, 148–52
religious beliefs
    interrelation with scientific beliefs,
        161
    and scientific investigation, 1, 6–10
religious communities, attitudes to
    science, 9–10

religious doctrines, not compromised
    by natural theology, 156
religious experience and aesthetic
    experience, 209–10
religious faith and geology, 147–8
religious sensibilities and aesthetic
    appreciation, 224, 226–8, 231–2
resurrection, doctrine, 251
revealed theology and natural
    theology, 176
rhetoric
    as genre, 176–80
    status, 183–4
    use, 28, 30, 180–200, 214
Roman Catholic Church
    attitude to science, 122–3
    and Galileo, 8–9, 23–4, 107–32
Romanticism
    and science, 94–6, 104n
    and Tyndall, 252, 254, 274
Royal Agricultural Society, 337
Royal College of Physicians, 291
Royal College of Surgeons, 158, 301
Royal Humane Society, 292
Royal Institution, 206n
    and Tyndall, 252
Royal Medical and Chirurgical
    Society, 301
Royal Physical Society, 147
Royal Society, 144, 145, 263
    election of Fellows, 298–9
    and the Society of Friends,
        283–306
    women elected as Fellows, 283,
        287

sacraments, Comte's use, 50
saltationism, 258, 279n
Salvation Army, 282
Sandemanians, 34
schools, Quakers' interest in, 290
science
    and aesthetic appreciation, 207–35,
        236n
    attraction for Quakers, 294–7, 307n
    Carpenter's view of, 265–8
    competition with God, 17
    decline in popularity, 200–2
    education in, 291
    function of language in
        presentation, 28, 30–1

science – *continued*
  function within theology, 26–7
  and geology, 57–62
  historical context, x–xi, 23–5, 35–7,
    127–9
  historical views, 75–101
  idealist philosophy, 141–2
  interpretations, 44–5
  Mivart's attitude to, 262
  and natural theology, 153–7
  nature
    and historical study, 62–9
    and practice, 32–4
  presentation through biography,
    31–2
  profile of scientific interests held
    by FRSs, 302
  and religion, 234–5
    perceived conflicts in the Galileo
      affair, 107–18
    relationships between, 17–25
    research funding, 43–4, 45
  Roman Catholic Church's attitude
    to, 122–3, 257, 260–1
  and Romanticism, 94–6, 104n
  Sedgwick's attitude to, 272–4
  and theology, 15–17
  Unitarians' attitude to, 264–5
science–religion, social history of
  institutions, 282–3
science–religion relationships, x–xi,
  xiin
  and biography, 247–50, 274–7
scientific beliefs, interrelation with
  religious beliefs, 161
scientific clerisy, 282
scientific investigation and religious
  belief, 1, 6–10
scientific practice and biblical
  exegesis, 16
scientific societies and Quakers, 301
scientific theories, epistemological
  status, 21
scientism, 45–6, 57, 66
scientist, coinage of word, 141
scientists
  and aesthetic appreciation, 223–8
  biographies, 9
  moral responsibility, 127
Scotland, nationalist views of
  England, 17

Scots, Whewell accused of disliking,
  141
scripture (*see also* Bible)
  authority, 108, 113–15
  Galileo's attitude to, 113–14, 118, 119
  and geology, 8, 45, 57–62, 63, 66
  and tradition, 118
sermons, 30–1
shells, architecture, 225illus
simplicity, criteria, 209, 228, 241n
skeletal types, 160illus
smallpox, inoculation against, 292, 293
social norms and Quakers, 293–6
social reform and Quakers, 292
social standing
  and Quakers, 289–93, 299–300, 303
  support for scientific proof, 33
society, secularisation, 18–19
Society of Apothecaries, 289
Society for Bettering the Condition of
  the Poor, 293
Society of Friends (*see also* Quakers)
  membership and intermarriage,
    284–6
  and Royal Society, 283–306
  social norms, 293–4
  social structures, 298
Society for Inoculating the Poor, 292
solar system, instability, 37
soul, Comte's understanding, 50
South Place Ethical Society, 233
spirituality and physics, 98–100
St Chad's, Birmingham, 255, 256illus
St Mary's Hospital Medical School
  (London), 255
St Thomas's Hospital (London), 291
stellar parallax, 137n
Strand Gallery (London), 205n
Strasbourg, great clock as model of
  the heavens, 5, 6
sublimity and the design argument,
  187
Summa Perfectionis, 319
sun, distance from earth, 188
Supreme Being, Comte's
  understanding, 50
symmetry, role in crystallography, 141

Tablet, 282
taxonomy, 224
teleology, 86, 160–1

Templeton Foundation, funding for studies of science and religion, 43–4, 45, 66
Test Acts, repeal (1871), 291
theism
  and cosmology, 232–3
  and evolution, 233–4
theistic proofs, historical context, 142–8
theology (*see also* religion)
  Comte's understanding, 48
  function within science, 26–7
  and science, 15–17
  Sedgwick's attitudes to, 269–73
theories, falsification of and aesthetic appreciation, 229
theory construction, 134n
Thirsk Natural History Society, 301
thunder and lightning, illustrative of design argument, 186
tidal movements, 110, 117, 132
Toleration Act (1689), 289
Tractarians, 270, 274–5
tradition and scripture, 118
transformationism, 275
transubstantiation, 131, 251
Trent, Council, 115
trilobites, eyes, 186

ugliness and aesthetic appreciation, 227
Unitarianism, 326–7
  and science, 264–5, 266

universe, religious ambiguity, 9, 235

vegetables, metaphor and the design argument, 193
Venus, phases, 106, 115, 116illus
Vestiges of the Natural History of Creation (Chambers)
  anonymity, 148, 156, 159, 172n
  Carpenter's view of, 266
  reactions to, 275
  Sedgwick's criticisms, 270–1, 273
Vienna Circle, 47
vitalism, 333–4
  and mechanism, 91–2
vivacity in natural–theological narratives, 184–5
voluntarist theology, 15, 20, 247

Wernerian theory, 273
Whewell–Brewster debate, 141
Wigton school (Cumbria), 290
The Witness (Free Church newspaper), 147
women
  and chemistry, 337–8
  Comte's understanding of their role, 49, 50–2
  election as Fellows of the Royal Society, 283, 287
world, transitoriness and energy dissipation, 15–16
worship, 50, 56